mini MOVES for EVERY WRITER

---- 50 ----

Transferable Techniques for Writing Across the Content Areas

SAM FUTRELL

REBEKAH O'DELL

Copyright © 2025 by Solution Tree Press

Materials appearing here are copyrighted. With one exception, all rights are reserved. Readers may reproduce only those pages marked "Reproducible." Otherwise, no part of this book may be reproduced or transmitted in any form or by any means (electronic, photocopying, recording, or otherwise) without prior written permission of the publisher. This book, in whole or in part, may not be included in a large language model, used to train AI, or uploaded into any AI system.

AI outputs featured in the text generated with the assistance of OpenAI and Gemini.

555 North Morton Street
Bloomington, IN 47404
800.733.6786 (toll free) / 812.336.7700
FAX: 812.336.7790

email: info@SolutionTree.com
SolutionTree.com

Visit **go.SolutionTree.com/literacy/MMEW** to download the free reproducibles in this book. To access the exclusive reproducibles in this book, enter the unique access code found on the inside front cover. Readers with ebooks, please email orders@solutiontree.com to receive access.

Printed in the United States of America

Library of Congress Cataloging-in-Publication Data

Names: Futrell, Sam (Samantha), author. | O'Dell, Rebekah, author.
Title: Mini moves for every writer : fifty transferable techniques for
    writing across the content areas / Sam Futrell, Rebekah O'Dell.
Description: Bloomington, IN : Solution Tree Press, [2025] | Includes
    bibliographical references and index.
Identifiers: LCCN 2024053944 (print) | LCCN 2024053945 (ebook) | ISBN
    9781960574701 (paperback) | ISBN 9781960574718 (ebook)
Subjects: LCSH: Language arts--Correlation with content subjects. | English
    language--Composition and exercises--Study and teaching (Secondary) |
    Composition (Language arts)--Study and teaching (Secondary)
Classification: LCC LB1631 .F87 2025 (print) | LCC LB1631 (ebook) | DDC
    428.0071/2--dc23/eng/20250121
LC record available at https://lccn.loc.gov/2024053944
LC ebook record available at https://lccn.loc.gov/2024053945

Solution Tree
Jeffrey C. Jones, CEO
Edmund M. Ackerman, President

Solution Tree Press
Publisher: Kendra Slayton
Associate Publisher: Todd Brakke
Acquisitions Director: Hilary Goff
Editorial Director: Laurel Hecker
Art Director: Rian Anderson
Managing Editor: Sarah Ludwig
Copy Chief: Jessi Finn
Senior Production Editor: Tonya Maddox Cupp
Proofreader: Elijah Oates
Text and Cover Designer: Laura Cox
Content Development Specialist: Amy Rubenstein
Associate Editor: Elijah Oates
Editorial Assistant: Madison Chartier

For the Dragons with a K.
—*Sam and Rebekah*

Acknowledgments

Ultimately, every book is an experiment: An experiment to scale a teaching idea to a book-size concept. An experiment to attempt to translate concepts and practice into coherent words another teacher can use. An experiment of collaboration and vision aligning. An experiment in pushing the limits of friends' and family's patience. An experiment in maintaining one's sanity.

We are tremendously grateful to everyone we've dragged through this experiment alongside us.

- » Our families, who also survived the writing of this book and cheered us on every step of the way
- » Our students, who inspire us to keep learning and growing and becoming better teachers
- » The teachers with whom we have collaborated, who have trusted us to experiment in their classrooms and through their students, especially Stacy Knoechel, Katie Bills-Tenney, Rebecca Huff, and Stacey Goldblatt
- » The Kragons, the best people we have ever known and the best reason for coming to work every day
- » Hilary Goff, our acquisitions editor, who first gave us the vision for this book
- » And everyone else who has served as a constant variable in our lives over the past two years

SAM

Thanks to my parents for being my first teachers and for teaching me to love books and to learn and ask questions (even if they did make me raise my hand at the dinner table despite being an only child—I was very chatty). Thank you to Stephen and all our emotional support animals (Bender, Squish, and Archie) for serving me tea and cuddles while I annoyingly typed on the couch for hours each evening. And to Finn, who wrote part of this book with me; we'll remember you forever.

Thank you also to my dear friend, whom I fully love, Rebekah O'Dell. Almost everything I've learned about teaching writing, I have learned from you. Thank you for being my teaching partner, best friend, therapist, and constant companion for these past seven years. I can't believe we wrote a freaking book.

REBEKAH

Thanks, Mom and Dad, for saying, "Let us know what you need help with so you can finish writing." Thank you, Georgia and Will, who have constantly been told, "I can't; I have to write," over the last few months. Thank you for understanding, for encouraging me, and for being proud of Mom's work-outside-of-work. And thank you, Evan, the person who has always said, "Yeah, you should do it!" and believed that I will be able to.

Most of all, thank you, Sam, whom I fully love, for pressuring me to write this book. You're the smartest, fiercest teacher I have ever known, and I will always be honored to have my name mentioned in the same breath as yours. I'm glad I don't have a sister because whoever she would be, she could never hold a candle to you.

Solution Tree Press would like to thank the following reviewers:

Lindsey Bingley
Literacy and Numeracy Strategist
Foothills Academy Society
Calgary, Alberta, Canada

John D. Ewald
Educator, Consultant, Speaker, Teacher
Frederick, Maryland

Teresa Kinley
Humanities Teacher
Calgary, Alberta, Canada

Erin Kruckenberg
Fifth-Grade Teacher
Jefferson Elementary School
Harvard, Illinois

Jolie Morgan
Instructional Coach
Dallas Center-Grimes High School
Grimes, Iowa

Visit **go.SolutionTree.com/literacy/MMEW** to download
the free reproducibles in this book.

To access the exclusive reproducibles in this book,
enter the unique access code found on the inside front cover.
Readers with ebooks, please email orders@solutiontree.com to receive access.

Table of Contents

Reproducibles are in italics.

About the Authors xi

PART 1 | An Introduction to Mini Moves 1

CHAPTER 1
The Case for Mini Moves 3
- The Power of Intentional Writing Instruction in Every Class 5
- Mentors Teaching Writing 7
- The Benefits of Mentor Texts 7
- What Mini Moves Are 9
- What Mini Moves Bring to Your Classroom, Your Department, or Your School Community 10

CHAPTER 2
Mini Moves in Your Classroom 13
- The Mini-Move Lesson: Step by Step 14
- Three Different Ways to Use Mini Moves in Your Classroom 16
- Mini Moves in Review 21

PART 2 | Moves for Every Writer 23

CHAPTER 3
Moves That Introduce 27
- Just-the-Facts (Level 1) 28
- Make the Case (Level 2) 31
- What They Said (Level 3) 33
- Scene-Drop (Level 4) 36
- Then-and-Now (Level 5) 41
- Student Samples 45
- *Writing Application Practice: Moves That Introduce* 46

CHAPTER 4
Moves That Make a Claim 49
- The Big Idea (Level 1) 50
- Outline It (Level 2) 52
- This-and-That (Level 3) 55
- Not-This-But-That (Level 4) 57
- Synthesize It (Level 5) 60
- Student Samples. 62
- *Writing Application Practice: Moves That Make a Claim* 64

CHAPTER 5
Moves That Define 67
- It Is What It Is (Level 1) 68
- Say My Name (Level 2) 70
- Keep It Appositive (Level 3) 72
- Gimme an Example (Level 4). 74
- Engage With Etymology (Level 5) 76
- Student Samples. 80
- *Writing Application Practice: Moves That Define* .81

CHAPTER 6
Moves That Describe 83
- Describing Lists (Level 1). 84
- Say It Again, But Make It Specific (Level 2) 86
- Dash That Describes (Level 3) 89
- Let's Imagine . . . (Level 4) 91
- Figurative Language Comparison (Level 5) 93
- Student Samples. 97
- *Writing Application Practice: Moves That Describe* 98

CHAPTER 7
Moves That Provide Evidence 101
- Hyperlink Layers (Level 1) 102
- Reference a Visual (Level 2) 105
- The Fold In (Level 3) 110
- Paraphrase It (Level 4) 112
- End With Analysis (Level 5) 116
- Student Samples. 119
- *Writing Application Practice: Moves That Provide Evidence* 121

CHAPTER 8
Moves That Summarize 123

- Define and Detail (Level 1) 123
- Pivot Synopsis (Level 2) 127
- The Devil in the Details (Level 3) 129
- Cause and Effect Sandwich (Level 4) 132
- Quote It to Me (Level 5) 136
- Student Samples 139
- *Writing Application Practice: Moves That Summarize* 141

CHAPTER 9
Moves That Contextualize 143

- Let's Compare (Level 1) 143
- Double Date (Level 2) 146
- Show Me the Data (Level 3) 148
- Educated Inference (Level 4) 151
- Past and Present Connection (Level 5) 154
- Student Samples 157
- *Writing Application Practice: Moves That Contextualize* 158

CHAPTER 10
Moves That Add Voice 161

- Say It Slang (Level 1) 162
- Ask a Question (Level 2) 164
- Put It in Parentheses (Level 3) 166
- Connect Personally (Level 4) 169
- Make It Metaphorical (Level 5) 172
- Student Samples 174
- *Writing Application Practice: Moves That Add Voice* 175

CHAPTER 11
Moves That Conclude 177

- What We Don't Know and What We Do (Level 1) 178
- What's Next? (Level 2) 181
- Share the Last Word (Level 3) 183
- The Bottom Line (Level 4) 186
- Solve the Problem (Level 5) 188
- Student Samples 191
- *Writing Application Practice: Moves That Conclude* 193

CHAPTER 12
Moves That Organize 195
    Topic Sentence Transition (Level 1) 196
    Hinge Transition (Level 2) 198
    List It (Level 3) 200
    Add Subheadings (Level 4) 203
    Visual Anchoring (Level 5) 205
    Writing Application Practice: Moves That Organize 209

Epilogue 211

Appendix A: Mini-Move Lesson Plan Templates 213
    Progression of Chapters 215
    Mini-Move Lesson Plan Template: Direct Instruction 216
    Mini-Move Lesson Plan Template: Student-Driven Inquiry 218
    Student Organizer for Mini-Mentor Text Stations 220
    Mini-Move Lesson Plan Template: Independent Student Work 221

Appendix B: All Moves by Content Area 223
    All Pop Culture Moves 224
    All English Moves 234
    All Mathematics Moves 244
    All Science Moves 254
    All Social Studies Moves 264

Appendix C: Writing Application Practice 275
    English Writing Application Practice 276
    Mathematics Writing Application Practice 277
    Science Writing Application Practice 278
    Social Studies Writing Application Practice 279

Appendix D: Moves Remix 281
    Moves Remix Lists 282

Appendix E: Standards and Mini Moves Connected 283
    English Language Arts Standards 285
    Grades 6–12 Literacy in History/Social Studies, Science, and Technical Subjects . . 287
    Standards for Mathematical Practice 290

References and Resources 291

Index 313

About the Authors

Samantha (Sam) Futrell teaches middle school social studies at St. Michael's Episcopal School in Richmond, Virginia. With a master's degree in history and over a decade of experience as a social studies educator, Sam has made significant contributions to the field through curriculum development and professional development for educators.

Sam also serves as the president of the Virginia Council for the Social Studies, the Virginia affiliate of the National Council for the Social Studies, where she and her team curate high-quality professional development opportunities for Virginia's social studies educators. She has won several awards for her leadership in the Virginia educational community and her dedication to civil rights advocacy.

Rebekah O'Dell teaches seventh- and eighth-grade English language arts in Richmond, Virginia. Before moving to middle school, Rebekah taught high schoolers for over a decade in classes ranging from inclusion to International Baccalaureate.

Alongside Allison Marchetti, Rebekah is a cofounder of *Moving Writers* (https://movingwriters.org), a popular blog for grades 6–12 writing teachers, as well as the host of the Moving Writers Community. She is the coauthor of three other books on writing instruction: *Writing With Mentors: How to Reach Every Writer in the Room Using Current, Engaging Mentor Texts* (2015); *Beyond Literary Analysis: Teaching Students to Write With Passion and Authority About Any Text* (2018); and *A Teacher's Guide to Mentor Texts, 6–12* (2021). She's a frequent speaker and workshop leader across the United States.

Rebekah has a bachelor's degree in English and a master of teaching in secondary English education from the University of Virginia.

To book Sam Futrell or Rebekah O'Dell for professional development, contact pd@SolutionTree.com.

PART 1

An Introduction to Mini Moves

Today at school, our students will go to classes, raise their hands, doze in the back row, listen to their earbuds, whisper with their friends, and scream and giggle in the hallway. They will have heartbreaks and victories and nerves and excitement. They will likely live many lives in just one day of middle or high school.

But whatever else our students do in their seven-hour school day, they will write—in ways large and small, in single words and phrases and paragraphs. They will write to learn and write to show what they have learned. In some way and in every class, our students will write all day long.

And this is why we're here.

We are excited to share an approach to writing instruction that has helped our students learn, transfer, and master ubiquitous writing tasks across the curriculum while building writerly identity, preserving student choice and agency, and valuing authentic student voice.

That's a tall order, isn't it?

We are where you are. In our English and social studies classrooms, we long to help students craft stronger and more authentic writing: the kind of writing that they can parlay into the real-world writing they will need to do as adults—in college, in the workforce, in their personal lives, and in futures we cannot even fully imagine yet.

What we've found—and what we hope you are about to find—is that getting small and teaching concrete writing moves that accomplish a wide range of common writing tasks across the curriculum is just what students need to become skillful and confident writers.

Part 1 of this book lays the foundation for just that. In chapter 1, we'll first think about our role as writing teachers (even if we're *not* technically writing teachers). Then, we'll introduce you to mentor texts and convince you that they are the most logical, most beneficial way to teach writing in any classroom. Finally, we'll envision what mini-move instruction might bring to you, to your classroom, and to your school community. In chapter 2, we'll get into your classroom and explore what this type of teaching looks like and how it can fit into what you already teach.

In part 2 of this book, we focus on ten skills all writers use, regardless of discipline, topic, or genre.

1. Introducing a piece of writing
2. Making a claim
3. Defining
4. Describing
5. Providing evidence
6. Summarizing
7. Contextualizing
8. Adding voice
9. Concluding
10. Organizing

For each of these skills, we share five moves writers use to achieve it. For every move, you'll find an annotated mini-mentor text from pop culture, along with additional mini-mentor texts from English, mathematics, science, and social studies. Within each chapter, moves are arranged from least challenging to most challenging so you can locate the strategies that best fit your students.

And let's not forget the appendices. (To be honest, these are where all the *best* treats are tucked away.) In appendix A, you'll find a progression of the chapters to help you locate moves with the right level of rigor for the writers in your classroom. We also provide lesson plan templates to help you implement the instruction described in chapter 2. In appendix B, you'll find all the moves organized by content area (just like in the online "*Mini Moves for Every Writer* Student Workbook") so you don't need to flip through each chapter to find the move and mentor text you want to teach. We think these will be the pages that you dog-ear. Appendix C puts all the writing application practice from each part 2 chapter in one place so you can easily find it. Appendix D, our favorite appendix, pulls together groups of moves across chapters to help you see common skills; this way, you can help your students build connections in their learning about the writing moves across the curriculum. Appendix E shows you how the mini moves in this book fit in with the standards we are asked to teach; it will also help you match moves to standards.

Welcome—we're so glad you're here. Let's get started.

CHAPTER 1

The Case for Mini Moves

In *Guns, Germs, and Steel: The Fates of Human Societies*, scientist and historian Jared Diamond (1999) makes a startling claim in regard to the development of civilizations: "Writing marched together with weapons, microbes, and centralized political organization as a modern agent of conquest" (pp. 215–216). Diamond (1999) goes on to argue that writing is not just a vessel for the transmission of knowledge or information, which can be used to exert power; writing is power unto itself.

In our global social media state, that claim rings truer than ever before. Writing is power, and regardless of what you teach, the students sitting in your classroom are writers. They are poets and science reporters. They are investigative journalists and mathematicians. They are novelists and historians and literary critics and diarists and influencers and editorialists.

While *writer* may not be an identity your students advertise (or even recognize), they create, generate, and curate content through writing both inside and outside the classroom every day. Think about the writing students do in just *your* class. There's a good chance students are writing even more than you realize. Across the school day, students are composing the following.

- » Class notes
- » Short-answer responses
- » Summaries
- » Hypotheses
- » Problem sets
- » Answers to word problems
- » Presentations
- » Explanations
- » Warm-ups
- » Exit tickets
- » Lab reports
- » Essays
- » Reflections

On any given school day, students text, analyze, explain, post, summarize, email, synthesize, report, discuss, and reflect in writing.

They write all the time, and this volume matters. To become skilled writers, students need to write more than we can ever possibly grade (National Council of Teachers of English, 2018). But students also become skilled writers by learning, practicing, and mastering discrete, transferable writing skills.

Writing well—clearly, concisely, with the appropriate level of detail, and for myriad audiences and purposes—is a life skill that transcends far beyond a student's academic experience. Communication, including the ability to "communicate in a clear and organized manner so that others can effectively understand," is a key competency of a career-ready workforce (National Association of Colleges and Employers, 2024, p. 3). Researcher Rachael Gabriel (2023) states:

> Ensuring that students learn specific ways to communicate about new content and ideas provides greater access and independence to learn, read, and write beyond the context of the class. Access to the language of the discipline, the ways of talking, reading, and writing that are associated with the ideas and actions, allows students to participate or engage with them independently, even outside of the classroom. (p. 20)

No matter where they go or what they do after their secondary education, we can bet writing will be involved.

Take, for example, Will, the HVAC repair person who recently serviced Rebekah's air-conditioning unit. Before leaving her house, he handed her a page-long, multi-paragraph report detailing what he observed, tested, and found broken in the system. The final sentences of the report explained how he fixed the unit—and thank God he did; her house was turning into a fully carpeted sauna, and the pets were not impressed. Chances are Will didn't think about writing pages of service reports every day when he chose HVAC repair as a career. And yet, it's a critical part of his job.

Think about the sheer number of emails you write in a day (and the number of poorly written emails you receive), the cover letters you have created for various jobs, or the simple art of sending a text message. Each medium has its own rules, styles, and patterns that, when violated, can have negative consequences that range from simple misunderstandings to missed employment opportunities to your crush never texting you back because your messages were giving "desperate" and you didn't even know it.

Without question, our students will write every single day of their adult lives in our increasingly digital, increasingly written world. It's not just an English teacher bias that says the ability to write confidently and skillfully is one of the most important skills we can give them.

In this chapter, we discuss why writing instruction is a vital part of every content-area class and introduce the concept of teaching writing through mentor texts. We share the benefits of using mentor texts for you, your department, and your students and show you a special kind of mentor text that supercharges student writing.

The Power of Intentional Writing Instruction in Every Class

So, we have to teach students to become skillful writers.

We *all* have to teach them.

Students write in your class because "writing promotes learning" (Writing Across the Curriculum Clearinghouse, n.d.). Just as your students are already writers, you are already a writing teacher.

There is immense power not just in writing itself but in *teaching* writing. Writing instruction is a vessel for so much goodness, especially when it is partnered with content instruction. Teaching writing specific to your discipline "is not one more thing to teach; it is a way of teaching for engagement, empowerment, and full participation" (Gabriel, 2023, p. 11). Writing instruction in content classes builds on the "integrative relationship between writing and knowing" to help students learn more about both the writing process itself and the discipline they are learning (Carter, 2007, p. 386).

Partnering writing instruction with content instruction helps *teachers* do the following (International Literacy Association, 2017).

- » Increase the speed of content instruction.
- » Teach content and skills all at once.
- » Home in on topics that interest students.
- » Curate interdisciplinary learning.

Partnering writing instruction with content instruction helps *students* do the following (International Literacy Association, 2017).

- » Retain concepts and information.
- » Build organizational skills.
- » Explore content that interests them in more depth.

Here's just one example of how Sam, a social studies teacher, joins content instruction with writing instruction. At the beginning of a school year, Sam was studying the Civil War with her seventh-grade history class when she realized that her students were having a really hard time summarizing events. It seemed to her that this inability to summarize events in the war correlated with and was caused by a lack of comprehension regarding cause and effect. Rather than halting content instruction to practice summarizing, they continued forward by studying the next topics in the unit through the lens of summary.

Students learned about the Battle of Antietam and the Richmond Bread Riot by studying summaries historians wrote about the events. Then, as writers, they noticed that when historians write summaries, they often do the following.

- » Begin with an observation about the event.
- » List the central causes.
- » Include details about what happened during the event, including dates, names of people involved, locations, and so on.
- » End by explaining the effects of the event.
- » Situate the event within a larger historical narrative.

Then, students reinforced their understanding of the Battle of Gettysburg by writing their own summaries of the event using the techniques that they had gathered from the historians' summaries. This allowed them to move forward with content (at an even more rapid pace), learn new writing techniques, and develop historical skills such as chronology, analysis, and citation of evidence.

OK. We know. You probably weren't trained to be a writing teacher. (In fact, sadly, most English teachers weren't trained to be writing teachers!) And if you've encountered a "writing across the curriculum" initiative sometime in your career, chances are you received the message that you needed to create writing opportunities in your classroom, but that message didn't make you feel any more empowered or equipped to teach students to write well. In fact, it might have made you more overwhelmed. It might have even made you resentful at the idea of being asked to do one more thing in your classroom without any practical guidance or instruction.

That is exactly why we wrote this book—to support educators who are being asked for too much and given too little. We wrote this book for you.

Maybe you are an English teacher, and teaching writing is an important component of your daily curriculum. But you feel a bit unmoored—what are the most essential writing skills to teach when absolutely everything feels important? How should you be prioritizing? Or perhaps you're struggling with transfer; every year, it seems like your students have never written a sentence before in their lives, and you're starting from scratch. You want to teach writing in a way that is authentic and meaningful—in a way that will actually stick.

This book is for you, too.

So, what exactly is writing instruction? And how can there be one type of writing instruction that works in every core discipline?

We're so glad you asked. Let us show you.

Mentors Teaching Writing

Since the dawn of time (this isn't scientific, but it's a strong hunch), people have learned their craft by looking to mentors—those who are a bit more seasoned or skilled. By watching them practice their craft, younger or more novice workers picked up the kinds of skills and knowledge that couldn't be conveyed through anything but experience (Wallis, 2019). This apprenticeship system has worked for blacksmiths, wheelwrights, chefs, auto mechanics, and teachers, and it works for writers, too.

It's also a simple, elegant teaching solution. Want students to write well? Let them learn from mentors who write well.

Writing mentors create mentor texts—pieces of professional writing that can guide and inspire writers (Marchetti & O'Dell, 2015). That is, mentor texts give students a vision for the kind of writing that is possible in the world beyond school, and they teach students specific writing skills they can use in their own writing.

Say your students are writing opinion pieces; show them an op-ed from your local paper. Perhaps your students are making storytelling podcast episodes; share an episode of the famous storytelling podcast *The Moth*. Maybe your students are writing lab reports in which they have to describe their scientific process; find a description of the scientific process in a journal article to share. There's magic in this: "Good writing makes writers want to write" (Kittle, 2008, p. 74).

Let us define our terms.

- » **Mentor text:** A relevant, engaging piece of professional writing that guides and inspires student writing
- » **Mini-mentor text:** A super-short mentor text, typically an excerpt, that is one sentence to a couple of paragraphs long
- » **Mini move:** A single writing technique lifted from a mini-mentor text and highlighted for instruction

The Benefits of Mentor Texts

There are oodles of benefits to using mentor texts to teach students how to write well.

- » **Mentor texts help students practice authentic patterns of learning that will help them face future writing challenges:** We can't possibly prepare every student for every type of writing they will need to do in the future. Some of those types of writing haven't even been invented yet! But we can help students build an intentional practice of looking for mentor texts to help them approach any future writing task. Learning from mentors isn't just a writing skill—it's a life skill. And when we show students how to use the work of mentors to help them accomplish more in their own work, we are giving them a transferable skill they will use for a lifetime (Marchetti & O'Dell, 2021).

» **Mentor texts build students' writing identity:** When we connect students to professional writing and say, "See how this professional writer makes this move? You can make this move, too!" we are implicitly telling students over and over again that they, in fact, *are* writers. They are empowered to make writing choices. They are capable of doing the same kind of writing as professional writers. Each time we present students with a mentor text, we are boosting their writerly identity and helping them see themselves as writers (Marchetti & O'Dell, 2021).

» **Mentor texts help student writers create authentic pieces of writing:** Students have incredibly sensitive trash detectors, and they instantly know when an assignment is made-up, silly, fake, or just for school and when an assignment has real relevance in the world. When students use the writing of professional writers as their teacher, they are engaged in authentic writing . . . and they know it (MacArthur & Graham, 2016; Marchetti & O'Dell, 2021)! This helps us as teachers as well. We no longer have to rack our brains (or search online), hunting for ideas for writing assignments. We can simply ask, "What kinds of writing do professionals do in our field?" Then, we find examples (those are the mentor texts), share them with students, and use them to spur on student writing.

» **Mentor texts diversify the teaching voices in the classroom:** We are two cisgender white women, so our perspectives are extremely limited. But when we bring in mentor texts written by writers with different identities and intersectionalities, we include their voices in our classrooms as guest teachers who can enrich the perspectives to which our students have access (Marchetti & O'Dell, 2021; Muhammad, 2015).

» **Mentor texts strengthen content-area literacy:** When you use mentor texts in your subject area, you are also strengthening the disciplinary literacy within your class by providing your students with many more opportunities to read discipline-specific texts. And the more practice they get, the better their comprehension will be. This does not even mention the fact that studying mentor texts requires careful, close, analytical reading. While this isn't one of the main reasons we use mentor texts in our classes, it's a fantastic bonus (International Literacy Association, 2017; Marchetti & O'Dell, 2021).

> » **Mentor texts make writing instruction possible for every teacher:** Mentor texts show writers how to write, and they show teachers what to teach. When mentor texts form the backbone of your writing instruction, you don't have to wonder how to magically explain good writing to students. All you have to do is find a writer who has already done the kind of writing you want your students to do, show it to them, talk about what you notice together, and let students give it a go. (Much more on this in the next chapter!) In her book *Study Driven: A Framework for Planning Units of Study in the Writing Workshop*, teacher educator Katie Wood Ray (2006) encourages us that "recognizing that you don't have the content expertise you'd like to have in writing doesn't have to limit your teaching or your students' learning. You can have *instructional* expertise instead" (p. 29). That kind of instructional expertise in teaching writing is what we aim to share with you in this book.

What Mini Moves Are

A mini move is the smallest, simplest form of mentor text–based writing instruction—a single, transferable writing technique lifted from a mentor text and highlighted for instruction.

Here's how this might work in class: Rebekah wanted her students to work on analyzing themes and understanding nuance. While reading a book review by Tahneer Oksman (2023a) for *NPR* titled "Mostly Through Images, a Daughter Grieves Her Mother in 'Ephemera,'" she discovered this mentor text:

> The daughter cannot access a ghostly presence that is nearly always at a distance. Her longing—for connection, for touch—is nonetheless apparent in every plant leaf she strokes, every seedling she concentrates on, waiting, first as a child, later as an adult, to see if she can apprehend its growth.

She could potentially teach a number of moves using just those two sentences—writing about a theme, using lists as a way of adding evidence to writing, and following many comma rules. But here's the mini move she wanted her students to try: using em dashes as interrupters to add nuance to an idea.

Do you see them there? Those em dashes pop up in the middle of the sentence to make "longing" more specific and nuanced, to show that "longing" can mean many different things to many different people in many different time periods, but here's what it means to this character at this time.

Rebekah shared this mini move with students, named it Nuance Interrupter, and let them try it in their own writing. And since mini moves are transferable, they could practice this move again and again throughout the week.

» Students could use this move in Rebekah's English class to write about a theme in a whole-class text in a reading response.

» They could use this move again in Sam's history class as they write about the effects of World War II on geopolitics.

» They could practice it in Georgia's mathematics class in an end-of-class exit ticket as they reflect on what they just learned about Thales' theorem.

» They could practice it one more time in Bruce's science class to describe how the results of their crayfish dissection lab compare to their pre-lab hypothesis.

By the time they have tried this same move on handfuls of occasions and across disciplines, they've probably gotten pretty good at it. By the end of the year, they may have even mastered it—and now it's just part of their regular writing repertoire that they can access and use when needed.

If you're eager to see how one move looks in different disciplines, don't worry. For every move in this book, you will see examples of how professional writers use the move in pop culture, English, mathematics, science, and social studies. And, in the next chapter, we dig deeper into the many ways you can use mini moves in your instruction and what that can look like in your daily classroom routines.

What Mini Moves Bring to Your Classroom, Your Department, or Your School Community

It's hard to write the "why you should keep reading" section of a pedagogy book and not feel like announcers on an infomercial—but we're going to try our best to keep QVC out of it.

Here goes: Each of you has come to this book for a different reason. You might be trying to improve writing instruction within the four walls of your own classroom or be seeking continuity within your department. Or, maybe you're working as a whole school to streamline writing instruction so you can see students make measurable gains. The beauty of these writing techniques is that they can be applied on a micro or macro level.

Mini Moves at Your Fingertips

This book is chockful of videos ready to teach your students how to use each and every move. Visit **go.SolutionTree.com/literacy/MMEW** to access them. Additionally, we have even more moves at our YouTube channel, Mini Moves for Writers, where there are dozens of classroom-produced mini-move lessons you can watch and share with your students anytime!

Whether you're trying to serve the student sitting at the desk in front of you or you're mapping out a new writing instruction strategy within your school district, this book can help.

Mini moves can help us do the following.

» **Essentialize what we focus on in writing instruction:** The moves we share in this book are certainly not exhaustive; they couldn't be! There is no limit to what we can learn about great writing. (And, in fact, once you begin this work with your students, you will be discovering new moves on your own all the time!) But focusing on a collection of mini moves that accomplish some of the most common writing tasks (describing, defining, incorporating evidence, explaining evidence, and making claims, for instance) helps us essentialize and focus our instruction. These moves become the foundation from which writers can grow. Moreover, you'll see that the moves mirror your state's learning standards. Not only do they align with English writing standards, but they also align with writing standards for college and career readiness and writing standards in history, science, and technical subjects. By using mini moves to teach students to write more clearly and confidently in your class, you aren't adding to what's already on your instructional plate; you're meeting your standards more efficiently.

» **Provide common language for writing between classes:** Humanities departments are notoriously riddled with friendly debate. In those we have taught in, teachers could never agree on what to call a thesis statement. (Is it a claim? An opinion? A main idea?) Consequently, when students arrived in their new English or social studies classes each year, teachers started from scratch as they built up new vocabulary around familiar concepts. It was needlessly complicated and time-consuming, but that's what they did because each teacher wanted to use their own term. When common language is used in a department or school, common expectations are set, connection points are clear, and an accessible shorthand is established; that makes it easier for students to understand what they need to do and easier for teachers to assess that work (Hannah & Saidy, 2014). Additionally, using a common language for writing moves begins to establish a sense of writing community within your school. Think about the students in our Nuance Interrupter example (page 9). As they move from class to class and teachers ask them to use the Nuance Interrupter move in different contexts, the expectations are clear. Students know what that is. They know what it looks like and sounds like. They know how to do it.

> » **Provide multiple opportunities and strategies to practice a writing skill:** We know that true mastery in learning is accomplished over time; students need lots of opportunities to practice a new skill before they can claim it as their own. We also know that learning strategies are not one-size-fits-all. The strategy that unlocks a skill for one student may not work for the next. One of the beautiful things about mini-move instruction is that we can offer students multiple ways to achieve the same skill so that students can find one that meets their needs, wherever they are in their writing practice now. When students have lots of ways to be successful and lots of opportunities to practice, mastery happens.
>
> » **Empower every teacher to teach writing:** Bite size. Concrete. Practical. Mini moves enable and empower any teacher to help students become better writers within their discipline by giving them the tools they need to articulate what strong writing looks like.

Mini moves can change your classroom as much or as little as you'd like. These moves can triage writing needs in your classroom from time to time, they can form the backbone of your curriculum, and they can even be adopted by an entire school or district for a truly comprehensive across-the-curriculum approach to writing.

No matter the scope or frequency of use, any application of these techniques will instantly elevate students' writing and offer them power. Writing is still, as Diamond (1999) argued years ago, an agent of conquest. But the landscape of conquest has changed. Our students do not wish to conquer civilizations (we hope), but rather their own goals and the problems of modern society. Teaching them to write and to write well is a democratizing process because it empowers them to use their voice and share their ideas as agents of change, progress, and our future.

CHAPTER 2

Mini Moves in Your Classroom

Teaching with mini moves follows a predictable pattern, regardless of whether we use them to teach a whole class, a small group, or an individual student. This is the same basic structure we also use in our video lessons. You can find all of them at this QR code.

The structure is predictable for a reason. When students are engaged in a predictable pattern of learning, they:

- » Don't spend mental energy wondering what's about to happen next or what they will be asked to do
- » Are able to anticipate next steps
- » Approach their work with more focus (Clayton, 2021)
- » Have more brain space for creative and complex thinking tasks—specifically, writing (Berne, 2009)

But a predictable lesson structure does so much for us teachers as well. When teachers utilize a predictable pattern of instruction, we:

- » Make more productive use of our planning periods (Berne, 2009)
- » Lower the pressure to create elaborate pedagogical song-and-dance numbers (complete with jazz hands) to get students' attention
- » Have more mental energy to truly teach and authentically respond to students' needs—the very reason you took this job in the first place

In this chapter, we share a step-by-step method for teaching a mini-move lesson in your classroom to elevate students' writing. Using a gradual release model, we also show three different ways to employ mini moves in your instruction. You'll see how, as students become familiar with this kind of work, they can start to use mentor texts to answer their own inquiry questions about writing and utilize mini moves independently.

The Mini-Move Lesson: Step by Step

A mini-move lesson teaches a single writing technique. We do this for the sake of clarity and in the interest of mastery—it is far easier for students to manage the cognitive load of understanding and practicing one writing technique at a time. It also keeps our lessons simple and efficient; each lesson will take fifteen to thirty minutes, including student practice.

To keep these writing lessons brief, concise, and helpful, each lesson follows the same steps.

1. Highlight a writing need this lesson will address.
2. Name the move you will be teaching.
3. Share a mini-mentor text that uses the move.
4. Discuss how the move is used and its effect.
5. Set students free to try the move in their own writing.

Let's dig into each step of this instructional process.

Step 1: Highlight a Writing Need This Lesson Will Address

We begin these writing lessons by presenting a problem or task that writers face. Each chapter of this book focuses on a specific writing task. In our classes, and in the videos at **go.SolutionTree.com/literacy/MMEW**, we front-load the need, or the problem, writers face to engage students from the very start of the lesson in order to do the following.

» Humanize the writing process. (Writers—they're just like us!)

» Identify when students will need this particular writing skill.

Step 2: Name the Move You Will Be Teaching

Next, we give the writing move a name so that writers can remember it, recall it, and use it later. It gives us a shorthand for talking about writing and makes communication between student and teacher far easier. This also aids in transfer between classes and content areas.

These names don't come from a list of literary terms in a textbook glossary. There are a few different reasons for this. First, an official term for a particular writing move often doesn't exist. We won't find "This-and-That claim" in a writing textbook or a list of Advanced Placement (AP) terms, for instance. If we limit our teaching to the terms in our textbook, we run the risk of not teaching many moves at all.

Second, we want the name of the move to be simple and clear and tell the writer what the move does. This way, writers can remember it and actually use it.

This language can also be cocreated with students.

Step 3: Share a Mini-Mentor Text That Uses the Move

Next, we share an example of a professional writer using this move. We want our students to see that this move is, in fact, a real solution that real writers use to meet their writing goals. We also want students to see this move in context. Separate from context, it's difficult for writers to understand when and how this move is used and what it sounds like in real writing.

Step 4: Discuss How the Move Is Used and Its Effect

We explicitly point to the move in the writing, name it again for the students, and talk about what it's doing: how it's helping the writer communicate, how it's helping the reader comprehend the writer's idea. This involves close, critical reading. Students may need this modeled for them the first few times you break down a move in class. Not to worry—for every move in the book, we have annotated our noticings of the mini-mentor text, which you can use as a cheat sheet for modeling or checking this work with students.

Step 5: Set Students Free to Try the Move in Their Own Writing

Finally—and this is the most important part—students try this move in their own writing.

Up to this point, the lesson has primarily focused on close, critical reading. (And what a nice bonus boost to your literacy instruction!) But now, we turn sharply toward the writing itself. Can the student writer not just understand the move but use it?

We like to ignite students' writing by asking them guiding questions. These are questions that directly connect what they noticed in the mentor text with their own work. In the "*Mini Moves for Every Writer* Student Workbook," we identify at least two guiding questions or tasks for each move. Visit **go.SolutionTree.com/literacy/MMEW** to access the workbook.

When students try the move themselves (in a piece of current writing, writing from earlier in the year, or off-the-cuff writing generated in the moment), it ensures students have instant application of the writing lesson, provides them with an opportunity to ask questions, and gives the teacher a chance to informally assess students' understanding.

Three Different Ways to Use Mini Moves in Your Classroom

Mini moves are flexible teaching tools, and we can use them in lots of different ways in our classrooms. *I go*, *we go*, *you go*—the gradual release of responsibility (Fisher & Frey, 2021)—is a powerful scaffold to gradually release ownership of learning to students. You'll see that mirrored here in the following ways.

1. Direct instruction (*I go*)
2. Student inquiry (*we go*)
3. Independent writing work (*you go*)

Ultimately, we're aiming for a balance of these three kinds of instruction inside our classrooms. There will always be times when it makes the most sense to deliver the lesson directly, while at other times, we will want to get students working together to figure out what makes a writing move tick. And, certainly by the time they leave us, we want students to be able to do this work on their own: noticing the moves real writers make, understanding how they affect a piece of writing, and then using them to enhance their own writing. Let's look at how you can use mini moves in direct instruction, in student-driven inquiry, and in independent writing work.

Using Mini Moves in Direct Instruction

Mini moves in direct instruction are best for the following.

- » Providing whole-class instruction
- » Providing one-to-one student instruction
- » Addressing students new to mentor text instruction
- » Dealing with limited time

Direct instruction is the fastest, simplest way to teach a new writing move. In direct instruction, the teacher is the transmitter of the new content. In a fifteen- to thirty-minute minilesson, you can share a move with students, tell them when they might use it, and let them try it on for size. These lessons can be delivered live, via one of our videos, or in a video lesson you create!

Whole-class instruction is an obvious choice for most teachers when it comes to writing instruction. However, mini-move lessons can also work for more targeted differentiation in small groups or individually.

- » Pull together a small group of students who need extra practice with a skill for a mini-move lesson.
- » Identify students who are ready for a next step beyond the whole-class instruction. Pull these students into a small group for a mini-move lesson that can help take their writing to the next level.

» Quickly and effectively remediate students who have missed skills in previous classes or grades.

» Share a recorded mini-move lesson with individual students to address the needs you see in their writing.

Using Mini Moves for Student-Driven Inquiry

Mini moves that employ student-driven inquiry are best for the following.

» Getting students up and learning together

» Providing small-group instruction

» Incorporating multiple mentor text examples

» Addressing students who have had practice with mentor text instruction

In direct instruction, the teacher is in the driver's seat of the learning. The teacher decides what move is taught to which students and at what time. And this is where all teaching with mini moves should begin. But as students become more familiar with mini-move instruction, we can begin to move some of the heavy lifting of learning to students themselves.

Why would we want to do this when direct instruction is so simple? Inquiry leads to deeper and more flexible learning:

> Using inquiry in the classroom poses an opportunity for the teacher to structure lessons that embrace disciplinary expertise and modern literacies in tandem. Students learn content through questioning and investigating, and, as they grow in maturity and experience, students are able to take on more freedom in the inquiry process. (Stern, Ferraro, Duncan, & Aleo, 2021, p. 180)

In a mini-move inquiry lesson, the teacher still begins by stating a need that writers face and follows it with a question. Then, the teacher chooses a move from this book that addresses the need. Then, the teacher can give students the name for this move—Question Theme. Then, the teacher grabs the corresponding mini-mentor text for that move, puts it in front of students, and asks them to study it and determine what choice the writer made to address that need.

What does this look and sound like? It might look and sound something like the following.

Tips for Making Your Own Mini-Move Videos

We suggest the following for making mini-move videos.

- Focus on content: While your students might be impressed by fancy videos, they won't learn better just because you have some nice editing. Don't be intimidated by trying to make perfect videos. Just press record and clearly communicate your lesson.

- Be one-and-done: Few of us enjoy watching ourselves back on video, and too much rewatching can often lead to the kind of scrutiny that causes you to film again and again and again until you've spent an entire planning period making a four-minute video. Before you begin, commit to trying to be one-and-done. Give it your best shot and accept the results.

- Start with screencasting: The simplest way to record yourself is by using a screencasting app. Our favorite is Screencastify (www.screencastify.com). This allows you to share your screen and record your voice and face.

> "Sometimes, when we're trying to write about the theme of a book, or movie, or album, or TV show, we realize that we can't really summarize the theme in one nice, neat statement. There are a lot of different ideas that are swirling around. What's one way we could articulate the theme of a text when the theme isn't just one thing?"

The teacher separates students into small groups and directs them to mini-mentor texts posted around the room.

> "Take a walk around the room, and stop at each mini-mentor text. Study the mentor text and, as a group, discuss: What is the writer doing to state the theme? What do you notice? What do these three mentor texts have in common?"

Here are the three mentor texts:

> In that regard, the novel is asking an important question: What if, instead of disorder, conflict might instead lead to harmony? —David L. Ulin (2020), "Review: Once Upon a Time in . . . South Brooklyn," *Los Angeles Times*

> The first two acts of *jeen-yuhs*, the excellent decades-in-the-making Netflix documentary about Kanye West's rise to fame, revolve mostly around one big question: Why won't anyone take him seriously as a rapper? —Justin Sayles (2022), "No One Knows What 'Donda 2' Means for Music, but It's Provocative," *The Ringer*

> The movie seems to ask, why bother saving humanity at all? —Aisling Walsh (2022), "Of *Terminator* and Motherhood: Why My Mom's Franchise Fandom Finally Makes Sense" *Literary Hub*

Then the teacher directs students to gather to share their findings.

> "All right. When you've had a chance to think about all three mentor texts, take your seat, and let's share what we noticed."

In this scenario, students will notice that each writer is wrapping up the text ideas in a big, overarching question. They will also probably note the colon that introduces the question in the first two mentor texts.

Finally, the teacher asks students to pull out their own writing and try this move themselves. Maybe they wrote about a theme earlier in the year, and now they can revise their theme statement using the Question Theme move. Or the teacher asks them to try this move as they consider the theme in a current whole-class or independent reading text.

As students become more confident with inquiry work, they can start developing the inquiry questions themselves and begin pursuing their own interests and needs in writing.

Teaching Students to Use Mini Moves Independently

Providing students opportunities to use mini moves independently not only gives them practice with this important skill but also can be helpful in a few other scenarios.

- » Preparing substitute teacher plans
- » Providing flipped classroom instruction
- » Addressing students who have had lots of practice using mentor texts in their own writing

We hope that all the noticing and analyzing and talking and practicing will form a habit of mind in students where they begin to naturally notice writing moves around them all the time. While this is a goal for every student, this may not be something that every student can immediately achieve. And that's OK! (That's another reason why a whole-department or whole-school approach to writing instruction is so critical.) This is rigorous, abstract thinking that takes practice and brain development. You will have some students who can move toward independence early in the year and others who may not be ready even when the school year is over.

Here are some ways you might have students independently use mini moves in your class.

- » Create a curated choice board of mini moves for students to select from (figure 2.1, page 20). Not only does this give students agency to make choices and practice moves on their own, but it also gives you extra time to confer with writers!
- » Send students to the Mini Moves for Writers YouTube channel or pull videos from the online resources for them to choose a mini move they think will improve their piece of writing. (This is also a great way to flip your writing classroom!)
- » Ask students to look for what interests them in a piece of writing and to find and try their own mini move. This could come from an article, mentor text, or whole-class read that everyone in the class is using. You could also direct students to a particular publication to use ("Find a move in the science section of *The New York Times* today") or ask them to find a move in their independent reading.

You'll notice the options have differing levels of teacher support and student autonomy over what writing moves are learned. Even within independent practice, there is a spectrum of release (table 2.1, page 20); we can provide support while students are continuously nudged to do more and more on their own.

Long Story Short Helps you move quickly through a stretch of time without giving too much detail	**Personal Parentheses** Adds voice—and humor!—to your writing	**Single-Sentence Transition** Helps you move from one idea to the next in a dynamic, interesting way
Magic Three List Builds rhythm and readerly satisfaction into your writing	**Scene-Drop Intro** Helps you draw in your reader from the very first sentence	**Opening With Context** Gives you a smooth way to provide a little extra context or background information

Figure 2.1: Mini-move choice board for an "I'm really into . . ." essay.

Table 2.1: A Spectrum of Student Independent Practice

	Guided Independent Practice	Independent Inquiry Practice	Fully Independent Practice
Teacher Role	1. Identify the writing move you want students to learn, and select mini-move videos (ones from this book, ones from our YouTube channel, or ones you make) for students.	1. Identify the writing move from this book you want students to learn, and choose the mini-mentor texts that demonstrate that move. 2. Articulate a writing need, and share the mini-mentor texts with students.	1. Support student writers through individual writing conferences as needed.
Student Role	1. Watch the video and try the move.	1. Study the mini-mentor texts to see how writers address that particular writing need. 2. Try the move.	1. Identify a need in your own writing. 2. Find a mini-mentor text where a writer has addressed that need using a writing move. 3. Name the move. 4. Try the move.

Students will show you that they are ready for these steps when they are consistently noticing, understanding, and effectively applying writing moves in their own work. We also know a student is ready for greater autonomy when we see them transferring writing moves from one piece of writing, one unit of study, and one class to another.

But truly, what's the worst that can happen? Say a student who is not quite ready yet selects a mini move from a teacher-curated choice board, has only a partial understanding of the mini move, and isn't successful in applying it. That's OK! That's a teachable moment, too. We simply pull that student into a writing conference, compliment their attempt and approximation, and then show them how they can use that move a little more effectively. And then they try again next time. It's hard to go wrong when we are putting high-quality writing in front of students, giving them a chance to engage with it, and talking to them about their work.

Mini Moves in Review

The mini-move lesson pattern that we detail in this chapter—a process used to learn new writing moves via direct instruction, student inquiry, and independent practice—is utilized when teaching a new writing move for the first time.

But if we are giving students intentional opportunities to practice these skills again and again in different settings, on different topics, and in different classes, we won't always be teaching the writing moves for the first time. We will also find ourselves in situations where we simply need to remind students of the move they have already practiced, quickly review it, and send them on their way to write.

When we learn writing moves for the first time, we isolate them—learning them and practicing them one at a time. But the power of mini moves is that their bite-size nature gives us the chance to practice them with students many times over as they add the moves to their individual writing toolboxes.

When reviewing moves with students, you might do the following.

- » Keep a running chart of writing moves visible in your classroom so that students have quick access to the techniques they have already learned.

- » Give students a choice of moves for a specific writing task. For instance, allow students to choose from any of the moves that define what they have learned so far to share a definition for a key concept in your class.

- » Quickly show a mini-mentor text using a familiar move in your subject area, and then encourage students to try the familiar move in this new, unfamiliar writing situation.

- » Use the writing application practice to give students a chance to practice those writing moves in your particular discipline.

PART 2

Moves for Every Writer

Each of the next ten chapters contains five moves that home in on a particular aspect of writing, from introductions to organization to voice. That means, over the next 186 pages, you will find fifty moves that will elevate students' writing in any core class (English, mathematics, science, and social studies).

For each move, we selected mini-mentor texts from professional writers about pop culture, English, mathematics, science, and social studies. This, we hope, emphasizes that each of the techniques highlighted in this book transcends not only academic disciplines but various types of writing projects as well.

TEN CHAPTERS

Five moves in each chapter

Five mini-mentor texts for each move

Moves scaled 1-5 (from easier to more challenging)

Pop culture (fully annotated)
English
Mathematics
Science
Social studies

Keep the following in mind as you venture into part 2.

» **Chapter order doesn't matter:** While you could follow the order of moves in the chapters to meet the needs of a full year's writing curriculum, you do not have to go chapter by chapter. Cover chapters in any order based on how they align with your curriculum and with students' writing needs.

» **Choose the move that works for you and your students:** The same goes for the moves within each chapter. Choose the move your class or individual students study based on their needs, their ability levels, their interests, or the writing product you want students to create.

Most moves begin with a pop culture example. This serves a dual purpose: to hook students and to show the ubiquity of the move. It's not just a "school thing"—this is a move that is really used by real writers writing about topics that interest our students. In our classes, we often introduce mini moves with these pop culture examples before moving into examples specific to our content areas.

That being said, some moves fit better in certain writing contexts than others. It would be unlikely, for example, for anyone to use the Scene-Drop move (page 36) in an on-demand writing piece, like a response to a document-based question or free-response question on an AP exam. Writing on demand capitalizes on expedient argumentation and an evidence-forward introduction, whereas the Scene-Drop move slowly draws the reader into the piece and focuses on craft, rather than information.

» **Formulas break down the moves into components:** For most moves, we have provided (to the best of our ability) a formula. These formulas are not an exact science but an attempt to label and compartmentalize mini moves' components to help students get started. Once students have had practice with a move over time, they will naturally begin to innovate on the formula, increasingly making it their own. Writing is not prescriptive, but we do think these formulas will help young writers visualize the strategies experts use to make their writing outstanding. If a student asks to try a variation on a formula as they experiment with the mini move, we encourage them! We want our students to make their writing their own.

You will also notice that as we move from level 1 moves to level 5 moves in each chapter, the formulas become looser and harder to pin down. This makes sense—as writing itself becomes more sophisticated, it becomes less rigidly formulaic.

In short, if the formulas help you and your students move forward, great! You know your students best, though, so you should use your best judgment on when to introduce the formulas and when to skip them.

» **Use the student workbook pages:** The book you're reading now is teacher facing and can stand completely on its own. But one of our goals is to make classroom application of mini moves as easy as possible. We have read many professional texts that offer an amazing new instructional paradigm but fail to fully connect that paradigm to student work. That's why we developed an online student workbook, which you can use in conjunction with this teacher text. The workbook pages directly align with each chapter and move in this book and offer physical space for students to practice mini moves. If used together, the workbook and this teacher text offer fifty comprehensive writing lessons, which can apply to any core class. Visit **go.SolutionTree .com/literacy/MMEW** to access the "*Mini Moves for Every Writer* Student Workbooks."

» **Embrace the videos:** Each of the mini moves in this book has a corresponding video lesson at the previously mentioned URL if you cannot access via the QR codes given in appendix B (page 223). These videos are student facing and follow the mini-move lesson pattern outlined on pages 14–15; you access them via the code on the inside front cover of this book. Consider these an additional, free resource for how to successfully implement mini moves in every classroom. We use these videos in our own classrooms all the time for the following.

* Substitute teacher plans
* Flipped classroom instruction
* Student choice boards
* That sick day we *should* take, but instead try to slog through

Our hope is that what follows is your one-stop shop for skill-based writing instruction that transcends every content area and can be applied in every classroom today.

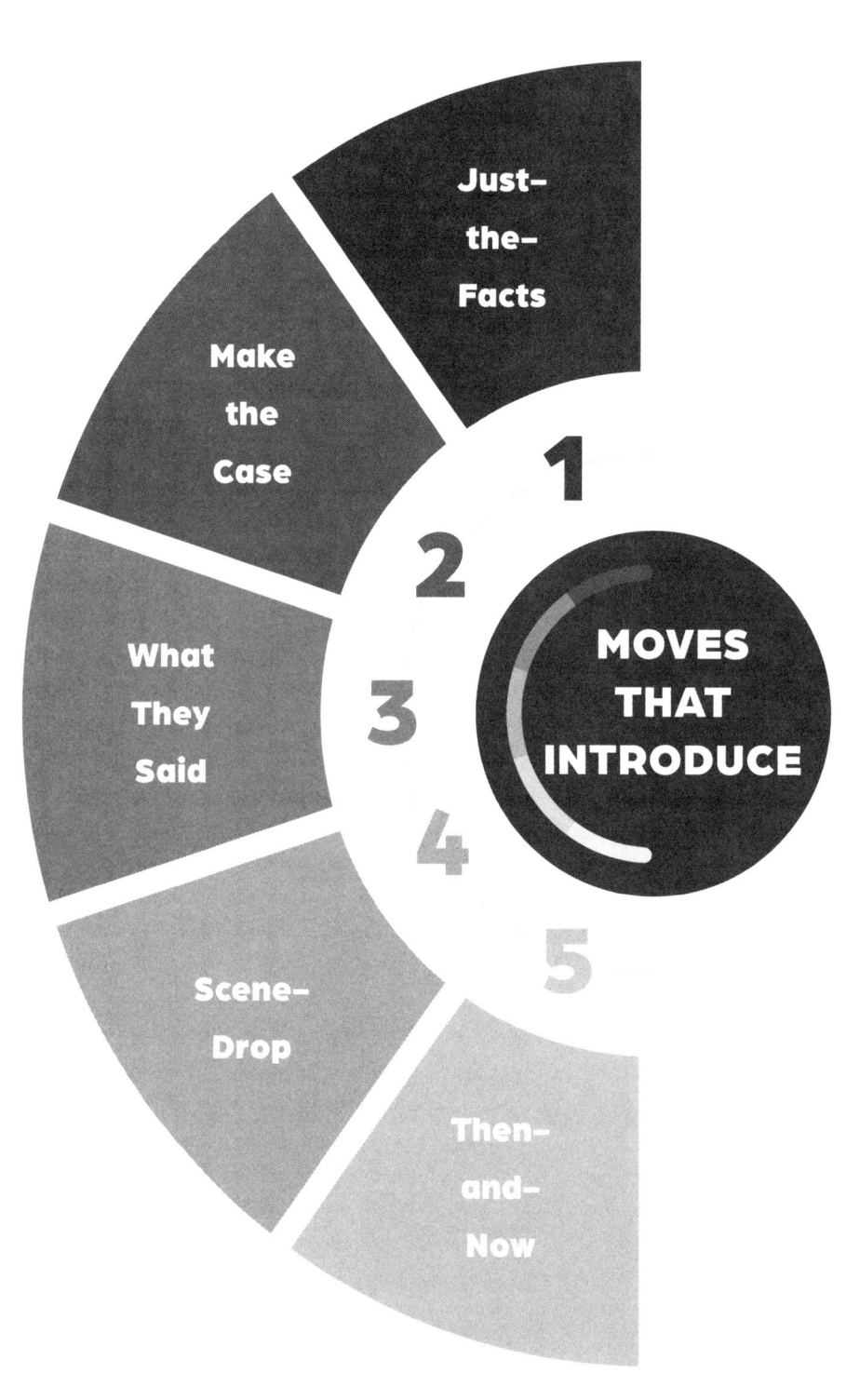

CHAPTER 3

Moves That Introduce

The way we open our writing sets a tone for the entire piece. As we write this very opening statement for you, we, as the writers, are questioning the metaphysical state of our relationship with you as the reader.

> "How can we impart the importance of those initial words that crack open a window between the author's mind and the readers'? How can we ensure that the subsequent breeze is both ardent and emphatic? How do we say something less stupid than what we just wrote?"

The opening to any piece of writing is not just a way to begin; it is a way to envelop the reader in the writing itself. With the right opening, the reader becomes part of the writing—ingrained and invested in its success from the very start.

Since you're reading this book, you know what many writing teachers might not know—there is no one way to open a piece. For example, everyone knows the student whose fourth-grade teacher taught them to begin their writing with a rhetorical question.

Sam was that student. She's pretty sure her answer to an AP United States History document-based question began this way: "Have you ever been at the supermarket and thought, 'I wonder how the Civil War started'?" She could have benefited from a teacher pulling her aside and asking, "Sam, how often are you really thinking about the Battle of Gettysburg next to the kumquats?"

It's not that a rhetorical question is always a bad way to open a piece of writing—sometimes, it's the perfect move to make. It's just that, in many instances like that one, the question feels disingenuous, far-fetched, and tonally mismatched. The takeaway here is this: The opening to a piece of writing must be authentic and curated in both style and substance to fit the writing itself. See table 3.1 (page 28) for recommendations on when best to use particular introductory moves. When you go to teach these moves, remember to use the instructional model conveyed in chapter 2 (page 13).

Table 3.1: Writing Needs and Moves That Introduce

When Writers Need...	Start Here...
To write a simple, no-frills introduction	Just-the-Facts (page 28)
To center the argument in their introduction	Make the Case (page 31)
	Then-and-Now (page 41)
To add voice and creativity to their introduction	What They Said (page 33)
	Scene-Drop (page 36)
	Then-and-Now (page 41)
To play with time in their introduction	Scene-Drop (page 36)
	Then-and-Now (page 41)
To write an evidence-centered introduction	Just-the-Facts (page 28)
	What They Said (page 33)
	Then-and-Now (page 41)

Just-the-Facts (Level 1)

According to the National Center for Education Statistics (2012), only 25 percent of U.S. students are proficient writers by the time they leave high school. (The next national assessment for writing is slated for 2032; National Assessment of Educational Progress, 2024a.) So, let's begin our opening moves with one that is perfect for both burgeoning writers and those who might need more support.

A Just-the-Facts intro asks writers to begin their piece with information that they learned while researching. It is an excellent way to incorporate objective evidence, like data, into the initial paragraphs of any piece. It is also, perhaps, the most natural way to begin any piece of writing.

We love using the Just-the-Facts intro for expository or argumentative writing because it answers some of what are commonly known as the *reporter's questions*: Who? What? When? Where? Why? Opening with these specific details about a larger topic offers the reader just enough background information to be engaged with the rest of the piece and establishes the writer as a reliable narrator.

This is the basic formula: Objective Observation + Reporter's Answers.

POP CULTURE

Consider this method in the context of the annotated mentor text in figure 3.1.

When we talk to students about a Just-the-Facts intro, we cover the following.

» We start by noticing how much information—how many facts—is presented in just the first sentence of this piece.

» The first sentence gives the *who* (Gwyneth Paltrow and Terry Sanderson), the *what* (a not-liable decision in favor of Paltrow), and the *when* (Thursday). From the very beginning, the reader knows exactly what the essay will be about.

» Students might notice that the author uses last names to elevate formality.

» When naming Terry Sanderson, the author gives a brief descriptor of who this person is ("retired optometrist"). The author assumes, rightly so, that the reader knows who Gwyneth Paltrow is.

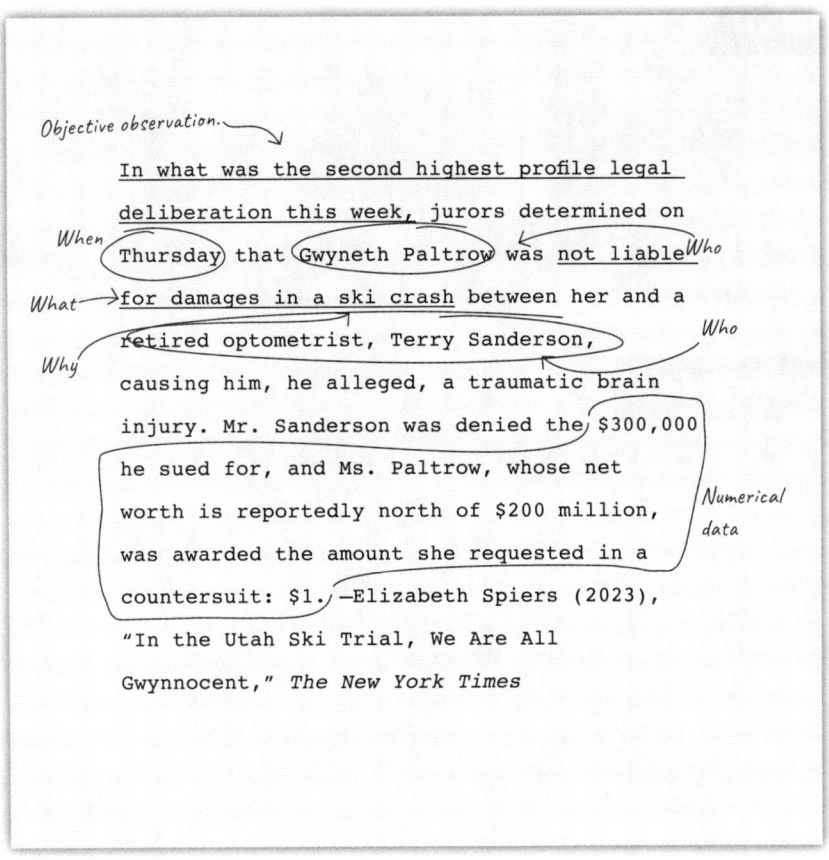

Figure 3.1: Just-the-Facts, annotated mentor text.

» It makes sense that the author uses past tense in a Just-the-Facts intro because it relies on established information to set up what's to come.

» Numerical data (dollar amounts, in this example) appear throughout the introduction. While numerical data are not a necessity in the Just-the-Facts intro, those data can offer excellent context for the reader.

» Students might notice that the question "Where?" is not answered here. That's OK! Writers do not have to answer every question in a Just-the-Facts intro, just those that are essential for the reader to have answered at the beginning of the piece. Here, the author leaves the *where* unanswered in the intro so they can elaborate on these two questions in the body of the piece. You can apply this same thinking when using this move in the other content areas detailed in this section.

ENGLISH

Climate activist Greta Thunberg who, at age 15, led school strikes every Friday in her home country of Sweden—a practice that caught on globally—has now, at 20, managed to bring together more than 100 scientists, environmental activists, journalists and writers to lay out exactly how and why it's clear that the climate crisis is happening. —Barbara J. King (2023), "Greta Thunberg's 'The Climate Book' Urges World to Keep Climate Justice Out Front," *NPR*

MATHEMATICS

In the 1950s, four decades before he won a Nobel Prize for his contributions to game theory and his story inspired the book and film "A Beautiful Mind," the mathematician John Nash proved one of the most remarkable results in all of geometry. Among other features, it implied that you could crumple a sphere down to a ball of any size without ever creasing it. He made this possible by inventing a new type of geometric object called an "embedding," which situates a shape inside a larger space—not unlike fitting a two-dimensional poster into a three-dimensional tube. —Mordechai Rorvig (2021), "Mathematicians Identify Threshold at Which Shapes Give Way," *Quanta Magazine*

SCIENCE

On Feb. 3 a train carrying hazardous materials derailed in East Palestine, Ohio. Some of the contents immediately caught fire. Three days later authorities released and burned off additional material from five tankers. These fires caused elevated levels of harmful chemicals in the local air, although the Environmental Protection Agency says that the pollution wasn't severe enough to cause long-term health damage. —Paul Krugman (2023), "Conspiracy Theorizing Goes off the Rails," *The New York Times*

SOCIAL STUDIES

A nearly 60-foot replica of a 4,000-year-old boat—complete with a sail made from goat hair—recently launched off the coast of Abu Dhabi, the capital of the United Arab Emirates.

According to a statement from Zayed University, the vessel passed numerous trials over two days at sea. It journeyed 50 nautical miles in the Arabian Gulf, reaching speeds of up to 5.6 knots (6.4 miles per hour). —Julia Binswanger (2024), "This Bronze Age Ship Replica, Made From Reeds and Goat Hair, Just Sailed 50 Nautical Miles," *Smithsonian Magazine*

Make the Case (Level 2)

Sometimes, beginning with the piece's central claim is the best opening move to make. It's direct, it orients the reader to the writing's key argument, and it is especially useful for writers who need a guiding light to return to throughout their piece.

The Make the Case intro is slightly more complex than the Just-the-Facts intro because it asks for a bold, up-front take followed by a paragraph of contextual evidence.

This is the basic formula: Claim + Evidence.

POP CULTURE

Consider this method in the context of the annotated mentor text in figure 3.2.

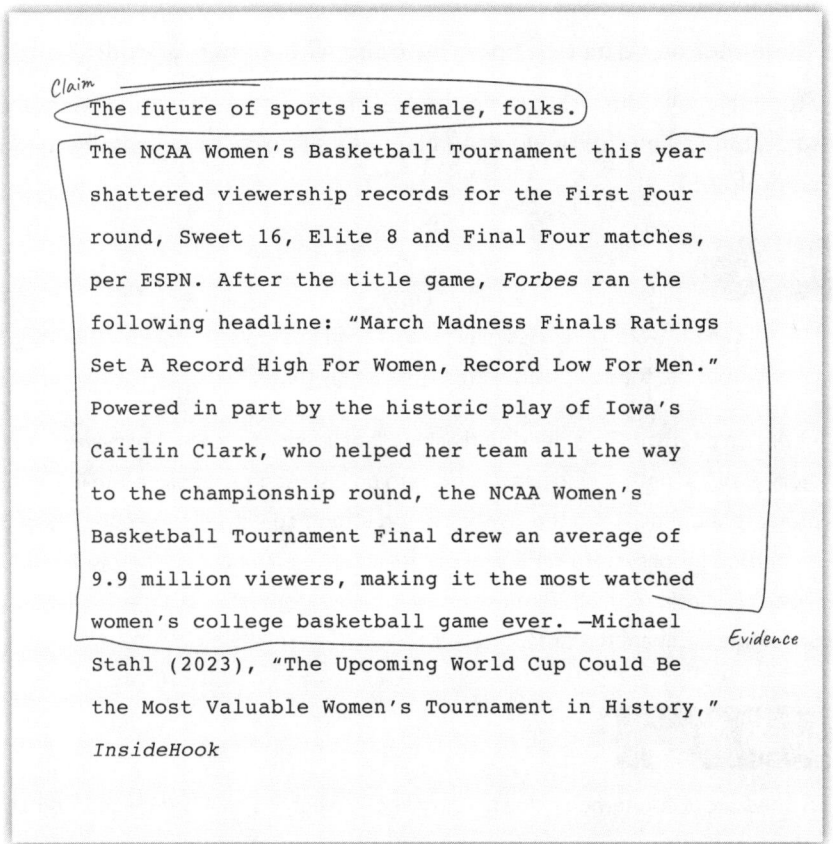

Figure 3.2: Make the Case, annotated mentor text.

Here is what we would discuss with our students about the Make the Case intro.

» Students will notice the claim stands alone in its own paragraph not just here but in all the mentor texts. This allows the reader to visually position the argument up front in their mind.

» Students might point out the use of the term "folks." The words writers choose—especially those in the first sentence—determine the tone of the piece. By speaking directly to the reader here, the author establishes a congenial tone.

» The evidence paragraph answers many of those reporter's questions (Who? What? When? Where? Why?) that we saw in the Just-the-Facts intro. But the evidence paragraph also answers other questions, like, "How many viewers were there?"

» The author uses data to support the claim with numerical evidence.

» Students may notice that the claim is simple—it uses a helping verb and totals only a handful of words. A claim doesn't have to be lengthy to be profound.

ENGLISH

Dennis Lehane's *Small Mercies* may take place in Boston's Southie neighborhood in 1974—but the topics it deals with are incredibly timely.

At once a crime novel, a deep, unflinching look at racism, and a heart-wrenching story about a mother who has lost everything, this narrative delves into life in the projects at a time when the city of Boston struggled with the desegregation of its public school system—and a lot [of] residents were showing their worst side.
—Gabino Iglesias (2023), "Dennis Lehane's 'Small Mercies' Is a Crime Thriller That Spotlights Rampant Racism," *NPR*

MATHEMATICS

In a new proof, a long-neglected mathematical object has finally gotten its moment in the spotlight.

At first glance, modular forms—functions whose abundant symmetries have intrigued mathematicians for centuries—seem to have garnered more than enough attention. They crop up in all sorts of problems: They were a key ingredient in Andrew Wiles' 1994 proof of Fermat's Last Theorem, which resolved one of the biggest open questions in number theory. They play a central role in the Langlands program, an ongoing effort to develop "a grand unified theory of mathematics." They've even been used to study models in string theory and quantum physics. —Jordana Cepelewicz (2023b), "New Proof Distinguishes Mysterious and Powerful 'Modular Forms,'" *Quanta Magazine*

SCIENCE

Speaking two languages provides the enviable ability to make friends in unusual places. A new study suggests that bilingualism may also come with another benefit: improved memory in later life.

Studying hundreds of older patients, researchers in Germany found that those who reported using two languages daily from a young age scored higher on tests of learning, memory, language and self-control than patients who spoke only one language. The findings, published in the April issue of the journal *Neurobiology of Aging*, add to two decades of work suggesting that bilingualism protects against dementia and cognitive decline in older people. —Jaya Padmanabhan (2023), "Bilingualism May Stave Off Dementia, Study Suggests," *The New York Times*

SOCIAL STUDIES

President Biden's most significant failure during his first two years in office is the lack of progress on the truly domestic portion of his domestic agenda.

Earlier in the pandemic, the federal government did more to help parents than it ever did before. Washington temporarily mandated paid leave for many workers, it gave billions of dollars in aid to child care businesses, and for several glorious months in 2021, it even expanded the child tax credit to provide assistance to most families with children. —Binyamin Appelbaum (2023), "And Child Care for All," *The New York Times*

What They Said (Level 3)

A Teacher's Guide to Mentor Texts tells us that "all writing is a reflection of decision making" and "when we read like writers, we notice the decisions they have made" (Marchetti & O'Dell, 2021, p. 7). Understanding the patterns of a writing move also asks us to read like writers.

Writers often open their pieces with quotes. Doing so immediately adds another voice to the conversation. This lends authority and nuance to the piece from the get-go.

Consider this move the older sibling to the Just-the-Facts intro. While operating on the same basic structure, a What They Said intro requires research to find the right

quotes, as well as a more sophisticated understanding of grammar and text-evidence explication.

This is the basic formula: Quoted + Source + Quote + Commentary.

POP CULTURE

Observe the mentor text annotations in figure 3.3.

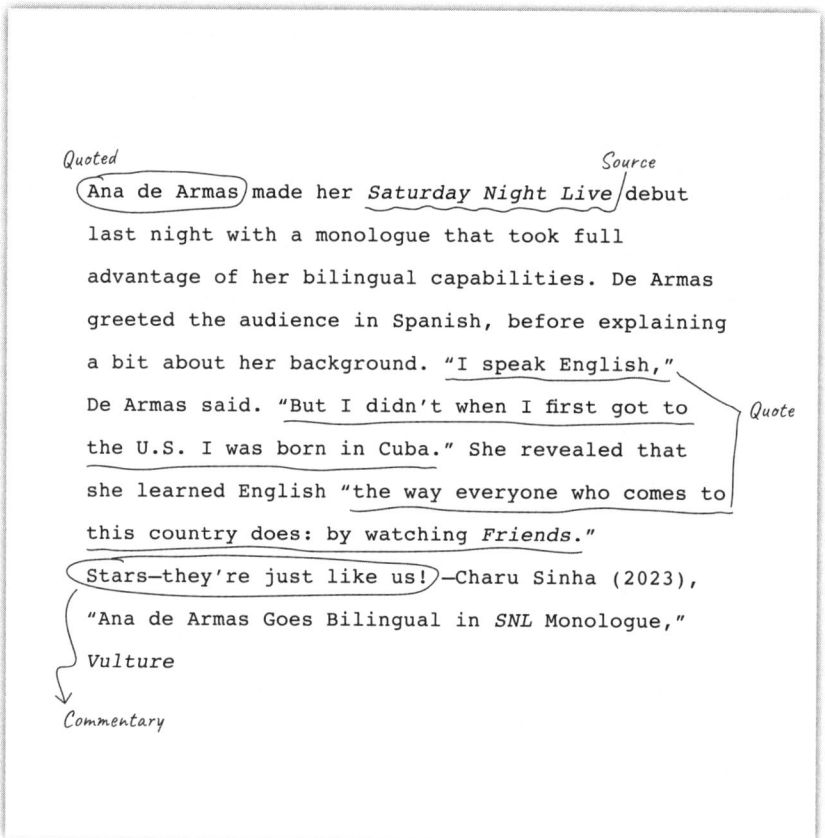

Figure 3.3: What They Said, annotated mentor text.

Here's how we might break down this mentor text with our students.

» The quoted person is named right away in this mentor text. Students should feel free to use this strategy—it helps the reader immediately know whose voice the writer is bringing into the conversation. But we would point out that's not the case in all the content-area examples. Students should feel free to order the components of this mentor text as they see fit.

» The author indirectly cites the source of this quote as *Saturday Night Live*. If this structure feels odd or difficult for students, the mathematics and social studies (page 36) mentor texts contain examples of more direct citations.

» Students who are looking for grammatical observations in this mentor text will note that the first quote is broken up with a comma (which is inside the quotation mark) and a phrase of attribution ("De Armas said"). When the author picks the quote back up, they begin with a capital letter and end the quote with a period inside the quotation mark.

» The second quote does not need a comma, as it is incorporated into the author's sentence.

» The commentary provides a simple explanation of why the quote feels significant to the author.

ENGLISH

Parable of the Sower was first published in October 1993. It tells the story of 15-year-old Lauren Olamina, a young Black woman living through a time of severe societal collapse. She creates (through observation and deduction) a new religion, Earthseed, which she expounds between her diary entries in simple verses that are both axiomatic and richly open-ended: "The Self must create / Its own reason for being. / To shape God, / Shape Self." —Roz Dineen (2024), "On the Simple Prophecy of Octavia Butler's *Parable of the Sower*," *Literary Hub*

MATHEMATICS

"For me, mathematics exists in the space between us," Emmy Murphy wrote in accepting the 2020 New Horizons in Mathematics Prize.

That space, for her, is a realm of art, perhaps even more than science. And like an artist, she is most fulfilled when exploring the fertile ground where constraint meets creation. The objects she studies are "beautiful to me in the same way that architecture or fashion or expensive furniture is beautiful—the way they are both highly constrained by their geometry and also highly flexible," she told *Quanta*. —Erica Klarreich (2023a), "Emmy Murphy Is a Mathematician Who Finds Beauty in Flexibility," *Quanta Magazine*

SCIENCE

"As I imagine it," Carl Sagan once said, "there will be a multilayered message. First there is a beacon, an announcement signal, something that says, *Pay attention. This is not some natural astronomical phenomenon. This is a signal from intelligent beings* . . . Then, the next layer is one that says, *This message is directed specifically to you guys on Earth. It isn't directed to anybody else.* And the third part of the message is the real content, which is a very complex set of data in a new language, which is also explained."

He was describing his novel, *Contact*, a 370-or-so-page answer, literally or in spirit, to every question we can ask about how finding alien intelligence might go. Yes, there's conflict and strife—acts of terrorism, government obstruction, frustration and loss and death—but at its core the story promises an inviting cosmos. A door opening to a galactic community. We're not only not alone but also welcomed. This hope is central to the idealistic origins of the search for extraterrestrial intelligence (SETI), to Sagan's motivations as a scientist and communicator. It also makes it especially weird that the novel ends with its heroine finding proof that God is real, but we'll get to that. —Jaime Green (2023), "Why Does *Contact* Say So Much About God?," *The Atlantic*

SOCIAL STUDIES

"Millennials are many things, but above all, they are murderers," *Mashable* noted in 2017, introducing a list of 70 items and institutions that Millennials were purported to have "killed," including napkins, breakfast cereal, department stores, the 9-to-5 workday, and marriage. The list was tongue-in-cheek—the cereal aisle persists—but it captured something essential about a generation that has reshaped old habits of American life.

Even amid this slaughter of tradition, Millennials are best known for another characteristic: how broke they are. Millennials, it's often said, are the first American generation that will do worse than its parents financially. —Jean M. Twenge (2023), "The Myth of the Broke Millennial," *The Atlantic*

Scene–Drop (Level 4)

It's a balmy September morning in the third week of school. The air-conditioning is broken in Sam's classroom—again—and she and her students can feel the humidity closing in on them. Yet, in spite of the moisture accumulating on the whiteboard, which makes her purple dry-erase marker about as effective as a paintbrush in an aquarium, her class is beginning their first venture into writing on demand.

Sam describes introductory paragraphs and tells the students that they need to include context in their introductions. Otherwise, she says, "I feel like Bear Grylls being dropped into the middle of the Amazonian rainforest with only a backpack full of peanuts—disoriented, disheartened, and possibly anaphylactic, since I'm allergic to peanuts."

She waits for laughter. It doesn't come.

"Are you really allergic to peanuts?" Linnea asks.

"No. It was a joke," Sam says.

"My cousin is allergic to peanuts," Emerson says.

"Well, a lot of people are," Sam responds.

"He has to carry an EpiPen!" Emerson shouts. "I get to stab him with it, if he accidentally eats one."

She realizes she's losing control of the room.

"OK. OK," she says, holding her hands up as Emerson begins to speak again. "I am glad you're prepared to stab your cousin, Emerson. But the point is—you need background information in your introductions. Otherwise, the reader will be lost right from the start."

"Yeah . . ." Linnea has re-entered the chat. "But what if the context is coming later? Like, what if I'm building up to it?"

Sam considers this and begins to nod her head in agreement. "Yeah," she says. "That's interesting! Let's see if we can find a mentor text for that."

We've all read great pieces of writing that do not front-load the opening paragraph with context. These pieces often take a microscopic lens to the opening sentences to set a particular scene before zooming out to consider the larger context. Such a beginning adds an element of personality and investment to the piece. We want to keep reading to figure out how this scene we've been dropped into connects to the larger topic of the writing as a whole. Adding narrative elements to non-narrative writing is also just plain fun.

This is the basic formula: Sensory Imagery(Setting + Characters).

POP CULTURE

Consider the annotated mentor text in figure 3.4 to understand this method.

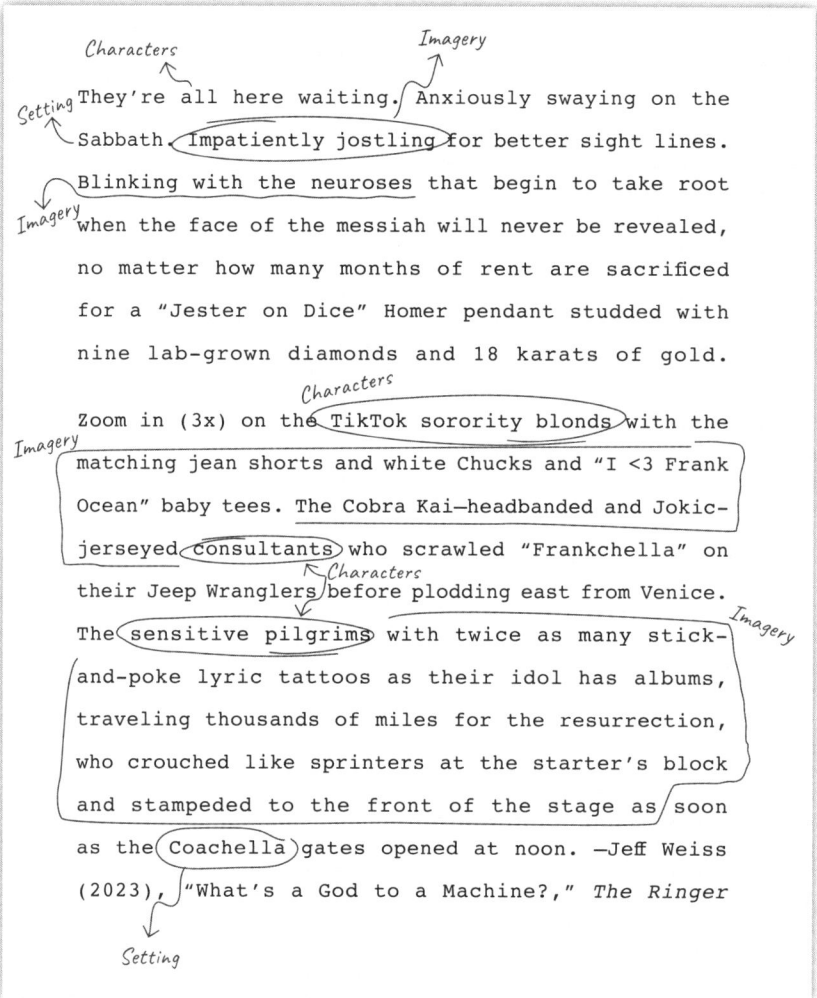

Figure 3.4: Scene-Drop, annotated mentor text.

Like most mini moves that require more writerly choice and direction, the Scene-Drop intro does not have an exact formula. But here's what we would notice with our students.

- » If asked to explain how the author brings the reader into the scene, students might notice that the author begins by using present tense. This makes the reader *feel* as if the scene is happening right now.
- » We would ask our students to identify the imagery that the author uses in this Scene-Drop intro and what sensory experiences they connect to. Though answers will vary, students might note the following.
  - * Phrases like "anxiously swaying" and "impatiently jostling" tell the reader about the characters' movements and what the author feels in the scene.
  - * "Zoom in (3x) on the TikTok sorority blonds" tells the reader what the author sees in the scene.
  - * Words like "plodding" and "stampeded" give more descriptions of movement, but also describe what the author hears in the scene.
- » Though the author is describing a real-life experience, the people in the Scene-Drop intro are described so vividly that they seem like characters in a novel.
- » Students might notice that the central topic of the piece is not revealed until the end of the Scene-Drop intro. By prioritizing imagery and tone over context, the author elevates suspense.
- » This mentor text includes a hyperspecific compound, contrasting description: "the Cobra Kai–headbanded and Jokic-jerseyed consultants." While not a necessity of the Scene-Drop intro, this is an excellent imagery technique for students who want a challenge to try in their writing.
- » Carefully chosen diction is key to a Scene-Drop intro. Here, diction is a through line for analysis. The author uses "Sabbath," "messiah," and "sacrifice" to establish their argument that Coachella, for some, is a religious experience.
- » Finally, students might notice in this mentor text, and some of the content-area mentor texts, that the central topic of the piece is not revealed until the second paragraph. "Burying the lede" like this can elevate the tension of the scene.

ENGLISH

The small, sickly African girl who arrived in Boston on a seafaring vessel in 1761 had already been stripped of her family and her home. She missed her father, who suffered after having his young child "snatched," she would later lament in writing. She longed for her mother, whose morning libations to the sun had imprinted on her an enduring memory. She was naked beneath her only physical covering, a "dirty carpet." She owned nothing, not even herself.

A little over a decade later, this same girl, named Phillis Wheatley after the slave ship that had transported her (the Phillis) and the enslavers who had purchased her (Susanna and John Wheatley), was an author. Her widely read 1773 book of verse, *Poems on Various Subjects, Religious and Moral*, was striking in its creativity and spoke up for Black humanity. In his erudite, enlightening new biography, *The Odyssey of Phillis Wheatley*, the historian David Waldstreicher points out that the remarkable and unlikely story of this Revolutionary-era Black celebrity, who was both highlighted and castigated for her race, turns on such reversals and contradictions. Wheatley emerges in these pages as a literary marvel. Waldstreicher's comprehensive account is a monument to her prowess. —Tiya Miles (2023), "The Great American Poet Who Was Named After a Slave Ship," *The Atlantic*

MATHEMATICS

A few minutes into a 2018 talk at the University of Michigan, Ian Tobasco picked up a large piece of paper and crumpled it into a seemingly disordered ball of chaos. He held it up for the audience to see, squeezed it for good measure, then spread it out again.

"I get a wild mass of folds that emerge, and that's the puzzle," he said. "What selects this pattern from another, more orderly pattern?"

He then held up a second large piece of paper—this one pre-folded into a famous origami pattern of parallelograms known as the Miura-ori—and pressed it flat. The force he used on each sheet of paper was about the same, he said, but the outcomes couldn't have been more different. The Miura-ori was divided neatly into geometric regions; the crumpled ball was a mess of jagged lines. —Stephen Ornes (2022), "The New Math of Wrinkling," *Quanta Magazine*

SCIENCE

The giant new spaceship was all fueled up and ready to go. Its stainless-steel exterior gleamed in the South Texas sun. Everyone gathered at the launch site was elated to witness the first uncrewed test flight of Starship, the futuristic spacecraft that Elon Musk wants to someday use to take people to Mars. The crowd erupted in cheers as the 33-engine rocket booster below the spacecraft ignited its engines and rose from the launchpad, generating twice the thrust of the Saturn V rocket that propelled Apollo astronauts to the moon more than 50 years ago.

But as Starship climbed higher, toward the edge of space and the next move in the sequence, something went wrong. The spaceship and the rocket booster failed to separate as intended, and started tumbling. Four minutes after a beautiful liftoff, Starship exploded over the Gulf of Mexico. —Marina Koren (2023), "Elon Musk's Explosive Day," *The Atlantic*

SOCIAL STUDIES

The sky above the Mississippi River stretched out like a song. The river was still in the windless afternoon, its water a yellowish-brown from the sediment it carried across thousands of miles of farmland, cities, and suburbs on its way south. At dusk, the lights of the Crescent City Connection, a pair of steel cantilever bridges that cross the river and connect the east and west banks of New Orleans, flickered on. Luminous bulbs ornamented the bridges' steel beams like a congregation of fireflies settling onto the backs of two massive, unbothered creatures. A tugboat made its way downriver, pulling an enormous ship in its wake. The sounds of the French Quarter, just behind me, pulsed through the brick sidewalk underfoot. . . .

After the transatlantic slave trade was outlawed in 1808, about a million people were transported from the upper South to the lower South. More than one hundred thousand of them were brought down the Mississippi River and sold in New Orleans. —Clint Smith (2021), *How the Word Is Passed: A Reckoning With the History of Slavery Across America*, p. 3

Then-and-Now (Level 5)

When we began our YouTube channel, Mini Moves for Writers (www.youtube.com/@minimovesforwriters4503), in 2021, we wanted to offer free writing resources for students—especially those who might have "fallen behind" during the COVID-19 pandemic.

Now, this book builds off that mission, offering even more resources to supplement those videos and even more videos to support writing instruction.

One way that writers of all kinds begin a piece of writing is by identifying a contrast or comparison between what has happened in the past and what is happening now. When writers do this, they aren't always trying to write about history. The passage of time offers writers a natural stage for comparison, which creates context for the ideas they are about to reveal. This little history-corner moment provides a dynamic beginning in any content area—from art to economics to ecology.

This is the basic formula: How Something Used to Be + How It Has Evolved.

POP CULTURE

Consider the annotated mentor text for this method in figure 3.5.

How something used to be

If you thought Taylor Swift was going to shake off the moody melancholy of "Folklore" and "Evermore"— the double dose of alluring alt-folkiness that she gave us in 2020—think again.

"Midnights"—the pop superstar's much-anticipated new album that, after arriving at the stroke of midnight on Friday, will be keeping Swifties up all night—is designed for the quiet of the dark. Indeed, Swift's 10th album—which comes almost exactly 10 years after she began to make her play for pop dominance with 2012's "Red"—is a far grayer shade of the 32-year-old singer-songwriter. —Chuck Arnold (2022), "Taylor Swift Goes Dark on New Album 'Midnights,'" *New York Post*

How it has evolved

Figure 3.5: Then-and-Now, annotated mentor text.

As with all the advanced mini moves, the formula for the Then-and-Now intro is not an exact science. And that's why we love it! Students have more choice and agency in these advanced moves, and they can choose what to take away from the mentor text. Here's what we might notice about this Then-and-Now move when we introduce it to our classes.

» The topic of the piece is named right away, and the first paragraph explains and evaluates the past iterations of the topic. Here, that topic is Taylor Swift's musical career.

» Students might notice that the author provides a date in the first paragraph to help the reader understand that these albums came out several years prior.

» The first paragraph is used to either compare or contrast with the second.

» If comparing, the author uses parallel imagery or diction in the first and second paragraphs to highlight similarities (specifically, they use the Dash That Describes move, page 89).

» If contrasting, the author uses binary vocabulary within each paragraph to emphasize differences.

» We would point out to students that analysis makes up the majority of this intro. That *Folklore* and *Evermore* are "alt-folk" and *Midnights* is made for "the quiet of the dark" are the author's own evaluations. In this way, the Then-and-Now intro is the more complex version of the Make the Case intro.

» Even if the author is identifying a comparison between then and now, the author will still explain how something has evolved.

ENGLISH

Back in 1995, Russia's two major art museums, in St. Petersburg and Moscow, mounted exhibitions a month apart that attracted considerable attention. Not so much because of the art, although much of it was spectacular, but because Russia openly identified it as art looted from Nazi Germany at the end of World War II. . . .

. . . Last month, those "twice saved" treasures came to mind with the news that a German government delegation had traveled to Nigeria to return 20 precious artifacts, a tiny portion of the vast trove of what are known as Benin Bronzes, plundered by British colonial soldiers from what was the West African kingdom of Benin. (The kingdom is now part of Nigeria; modern Benin is a separate, neighboring state.) —Serge Schmemann (2023), "'She Comes Back to Where She Belongs,'" *The New York Times*

MATHEMATICS

In the fourth century, the Greek mathematician Pappus of Alexandria praised bees for their "geometrical forethought." The hexagonal structure of their honeycomb seemed like the optimal way to partition two-dimensional space into cells of equal area and minimal perimeter—allowing the insects to cut down on how much wax they needed to produce, and to spend less time and energy building their hive.

Or so Pappus and others hypothesized. For millennia, nobody could prove that hexagons were optimal—until finally, in 1999, the mathematician Thomas Hales showed that no other shape could do better. Today, mathematicians still don't know which shapes can tile three or more dimensions with the smallest possible surface area. —Jordana Cepelewicz (2023a), "Mathematicians Complete Quest to Build 'Spherical Cubes,'" *Quanta Magazine*

SCIENCE

Alex Wiltschko began collecting perfumes as a teenager. His first bottle was Azzaro Pour Homme, a timeless cologne he spotted on the shelf at a T.J. Maxx department store. He recognized the name from *Perfumes: The Guide*, a book whose poetic descriptions of aroma had kick-started his obsession. Enchanted, he saved up his allowance to add to his collection. "I ended up going absolutely down the rabbit hole," he said.

More recently, as an olfactory neuroscientist for Google Research's Brain Team, Wiltschko used machine learning to dissect our most ancient and least understood sense. Sometimes he looked almost longingly at his colleagues studying the other senses. "They have these beautiful intellectual structures, these cathedrals of knowledge," he said, that explain the visual and auditory world, shaming what we know about olfaction. —Allison Parshall (2022), "Machine Learning Highlights a Hidden Order in Scents," *Quanta Magazine*

SOCIAL STUDIES

When up to 190,000 Russian soldiers invaded Ukraine last February, even its most ardent foreign supporters expected the nation's far more limited defenses would collapse within days.

But one year later, Russia has lost a reported 200,000 men, including many high-ranking military officials, and President Vladimir Putin has been embarrassed by the Ukrainian Army's successes and the resilience of Ukraine's many citizen militias. —Christina Pazzanese (2023), "One Year Later: How Does Ukraine War End?," *The Harvard Gazette*

Use the reproducible "Writing Application Practice: Moves That Introduce" (page 46) to introduce.

Student Samples

The following student samples include moves that introduce.

This sample uses Just-the-Facts (level 1):

> Chromium is an element discovered by Louis Nicolas Vauquelin in 1797 in Paris, France. He discovered it by experimenting with different particles and created the element we now use for many different purposes like material for our pots and pans, the silver parts of our tires, and even our kitchen sinks. —Presley, Ninth Grade

This sample uses What They Said (level 3):

> "You would be a pro if you did this a million times." That was Mr. Hayward's response to a student's peril in math today. We are working on quadratic equations and just got to the point where we are factoring unfactorable expressions. I know, sounds so easy. After he explained the topic, we tried it on our own with limited success. People who didn't understand (which was the majority) paraded around the room with questions. Unfortunately, the math was still not mathing. —Saniya, Eighth Grade

This sample uses Then-and-Now (level 5):

> Over time scientists have kept getting closer and closer to what an atom really looks like. For example in 440 BC in Greece Democritus thought an atom was something that could continuously be split apart and cut in half that will go on forever. But he had no clue what an atom really looked like. The next person to study atoms and make a discovery was John Dalton, who said that every substance is made of atoms and that atoms can create compounds. J.J. Thompson took both of these theories and combined them and figured out that there were more particles in the middle of an atom. Much trial and error has gotten us to where we know a lot about atoms. Atoms have been studied for 2000+ years and after all that we are finally understanding what they really are. —Bryce, Ninth Grade

Writing Application Practice: Moves That Introduce

After teaching your students one of these moves—or all of these moves—you'll be looking for an opportunity for them to practice these skills immediately.

For each writing task, we have provided a prompt you could use to get your students writing. They can use this prompt to practice a single move for that writing task or to begin combining, mixing, and matching moves. You can find all writing application practice from the whole book in one place in appendix C (page 275).

Content Area	Writing Application Practice
English	Choose one of the moves that introduce, and use it to introduce a book you've recently read to someone who has not yet read it.
Mathematics	What did you learn or practice today in class? Use a move that introduces to introduce the topic to a parent or friend.
Science	Pretend you are rewriting a chapter from your science textbook. Write a brief introduction to your current unit using one of the moves that introduce.
Social Studies	Who is the most significant figure in the unit you are now studying in class? Introduce this person by using one of the moves that introduce.

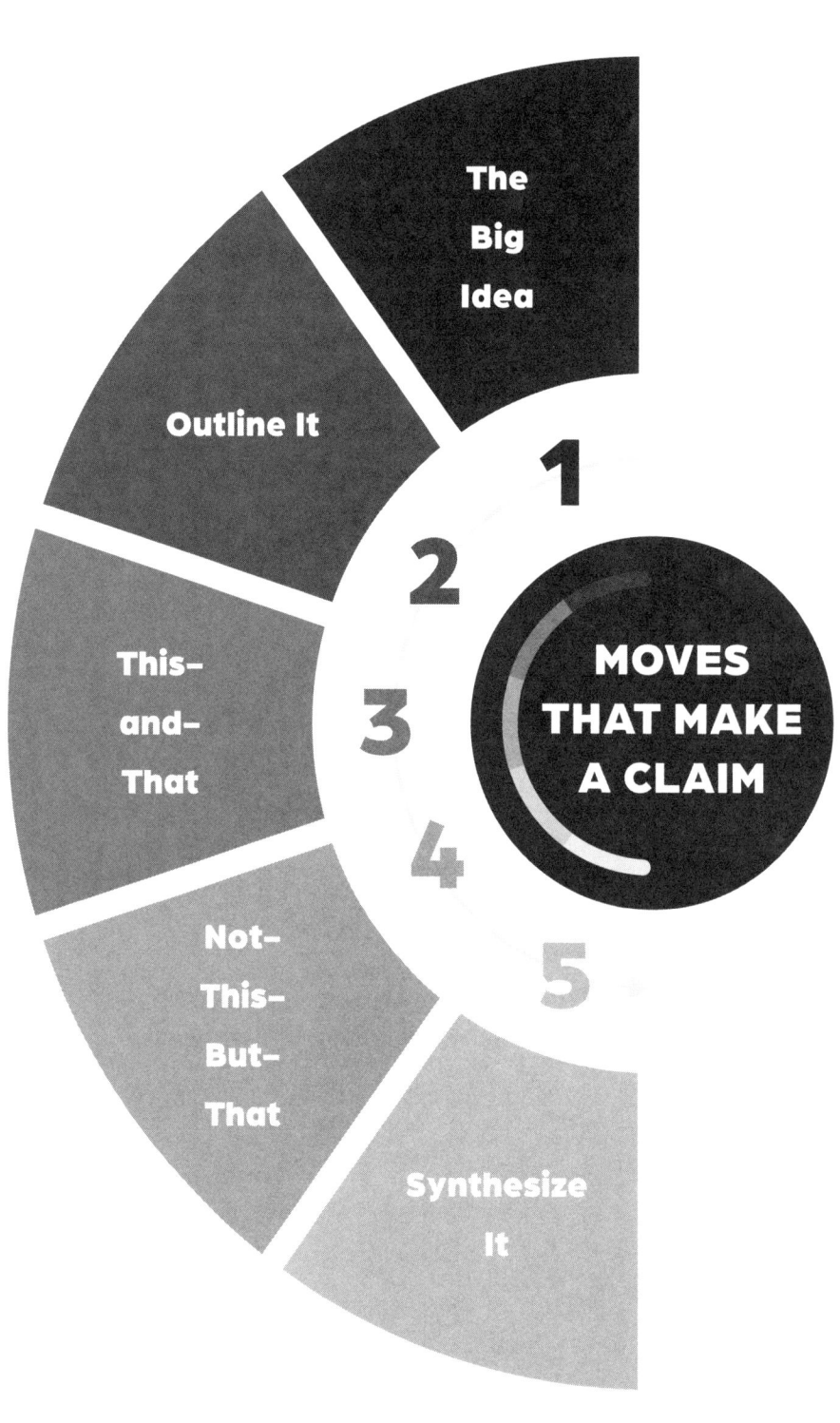

CHAPTER 4

Moves That Make a Claim

Argumentative and analytical writing are central pillars of academia, and writers cannot construct arguments without making a claim. So, if arguments are the pillars of academia, claims are the cornerstones. They are the very foundation for any argumentative writing. Sorry—we're trying to see how many construction metaphors we can fit into this opening paragraph. Perhaps that's enough. We can always *build* in more from here. (We're so sorry.)

Before we move on, let's define a claim: *Claim* (noun)—the central thesis or argument in a piece of writing.

Throughout this chapter, we use the words *claim* and *thesis* interchangeably. Maybe, at some point, you were taught that they were different. For us, they're the same. A claim and a thesis both state the central argument within your writing.

Claims are often taught in terms of formulas—in terms of what they say, the order in which they say it, and where they appear in the piece of writing (almost always the last sentence of the last paragraph, right?). But professional mentors show us that there is a world of creativity and variety awaiting writers of claims. While all claims must state the central argument of the writing, the type of claim chosen will have different effects. A claim, just like every other move in this book, is a tool. Writers can use claims to outline ideas, isolate a paradox, confront an inaccurate assumption, or synthesize concepts.

The type of claim used and where and when it's employed in a piece of writing can affect how the reader engages with the argument—and whether they agree. See table 4.1 (page 50) for when best to use a particular claim method.

Table 4.1: Writing Needs and Moves That Make a Claim

When Writers Need...	Start Here...
To structure a simple claim that highlights the central ideas (perfect for younger or less experienced writers)	The Big Idea (page 50)
	Outline It (page 52)
To make an interesting, unique, or descriptive claim	This-and-That (page 55)
	Not-This-But-That (page 57)
To analyze complicated topics	This-and-That (page 55)
	Synthesize It (page 60)
To subvert the reader's expectations about a topic	This-and-That (page 55)
	Not-This-But-That (page 57)
To compare two or more ideas	This-and-That (page 55)
	Synthesize It (page 60)
To contrast two or more ideas	Not-This-But-That (page 57)
	Synthesize It (page 60)
To contextualize two or more ideas	Synthesize It (page 60)

The Big Idea (Level 1)

As students get into upper-level writing classes, there is a push to make claim statements as complex and interesting as possible. This isn't necessarily a bad thing—we love reading writing that is complex, and we definitely love reading writing that is interesting. However, a claim statement does not *have* to be either of these things.

The beauty of argumentative writing is that nuance, electricity, and the general art of persuasion can be woven into any aspect of the piece. For students who are burgeoning as writers or struggling with a particular piece, the complexity of their claim statement is not nearly as important as its clarity.

Writing a strong claim is about controlling the direction of the argument. And sometimes, the simplest and strongest way to do this is to prune the edges of a thesis down to the big, central idea that a writer wants to convey. So, in the spirit of being as clear and straightforward as possible, let's call this the Big Idea claim.

This is the basic formula: Topic + Being Verb + Big Idea.

POP CULTURE

See figure 4.1 for an annotated mentor text that explores this method.

Here are some things we might dissect about the Big Idea claim with our students.

» The first thing students might notice about this claim is its length. It's just one sentence! This should provide a sense of comfort to our emerging writers or any student who is struggling—all they need to do to develop a strong claim statement is to write one sentence. Every student is absolutely capable of that!

» We might cover up the opening phrase, "in both its incarnations," allowing students to notice the mini move's basic formula.

» Students who want more of a challenge might complicate the Big Idea claim with the use of more advanced diction, prepositional phrases, and conjunctions (see the science mentor text, page 52, for reference).

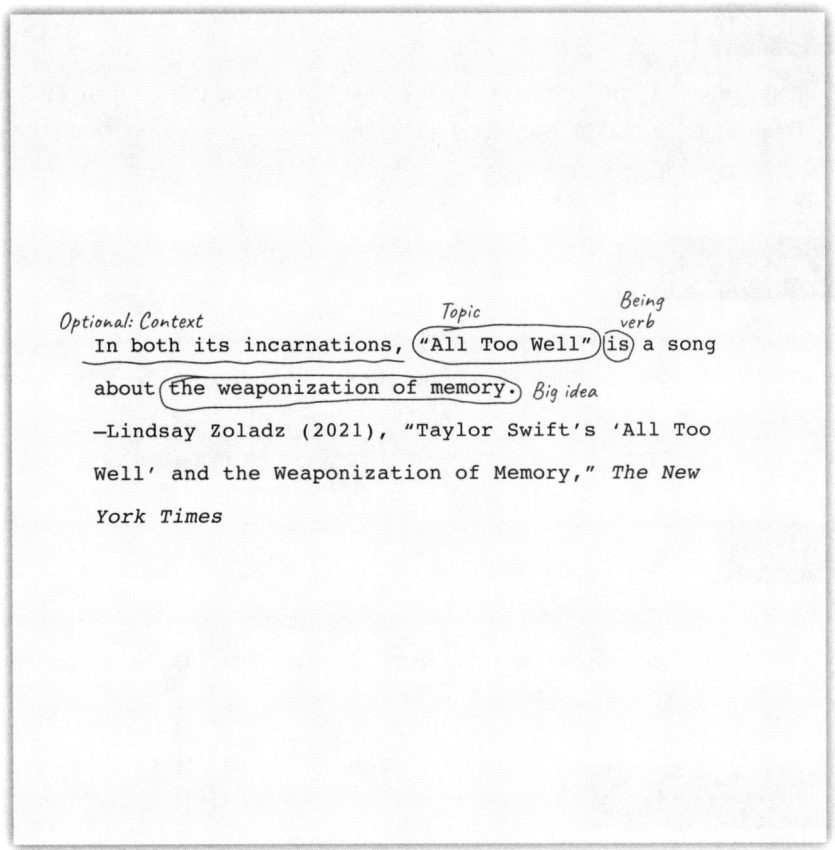

Figure 4.1: The Big Idea, annotated mentor text.

» We may eventually ask students to assess why the author includes "in both its incarnations" at the beginning of the claim. Encourage students to note that even in a Big Idea claim, if an important piece of contextual information is needed to understand what topic the author is referring to, it should be woven into the claim. A way to identify if any contextual information is needed in a Big Idea claim is to write the claim in the simple formula: Topic + Being Verb + Big Idea. Then, students can ask themselves if any key questions about the topic need to be answered so the reader understands the central premise of their argument before moving forward. In this case, Taylor Swift has two versions of "All Too Well"—the original and the much more famous ten-minute version. To avoid the question of "Wait—which version of 'All Too Well' are they talking about?," the author has helpfully included the phrase "in both its incarnations."

For more tips and five mini moves relating to contextualization, see chapter 9 (page 143)!

ENGLISH

Dennis Lehane's *Small Mercies* is a crime thriller that spotlights rampant racism. —Gabino Iglesias (2023), "Dennis Lehane's 'Small Mercies' Is a Crime Thriller That Spotlights Rampant Racism," *NPR*

MATHEMATICS

In a 912-page paper posted online on May 30, Szeftel, Elena Giorgi of Columbia University and Sergiu Klainerman of Princeton University have proved that slowly rotating Kerr black holes are indeed stable. —Steve Nadis (2022a), "At Long Last, Mathematical Proof That Black Holes Are Stable," *Quanta Magazine*

SCIENCE

Though we can't see them, X-rays are widespread in outer space. —Carlyn Kranking (2024), "See 25 Stunning Images of the Cosmos From the Chandra X-Ray Observatory as It Celebrates 25 Years in Space," *Smithsonian Magazine*

SOCIAL STUDIES

Washington's message was this mandate: We must guard our inheritance. —Alexis Coe (2023), "How George Washington Wrote His Farewell Address," *Smithsonian Magazine*

Outline It (Level 2)

Though Outline It is on our scale as a level 2 move, it is one of the most frequently taught ways to write a thesis statement. Outline It is classic because it organizes the author's ideas, provides the reader with a road map of the upcoming argument, and is highly scalable.

When Sam began teaching, before she met Rebekah, she thought that the only way to teach her middle schoolers how to write a thesis statement was through an Outline It claim. In her history classes, this move just seemed to make the most sense. If students were writing about a topic and wanted to prove multiple points, why not list them all for the reader? It helped students organize their thoughts and gave the reader a heads-up of what to expect in the piece. She even gave her students a plug-and-play formula to use for writing on demand: [Restate the prompt] + [list your main ideas].

While it's effective, Sam now knows that this is not the *only* way to write a thesis statement—it's not even the only way to write an Outline It claim! Outline It claims can certainly use the formula we've provided, but they can also be modified to provide a more complex assertion of the central argument.

This is the basic formula: Restated Prompt + Main Ideas.

POP CULTURE

See figure 4.2 for an annotated mentor text that invites this method.

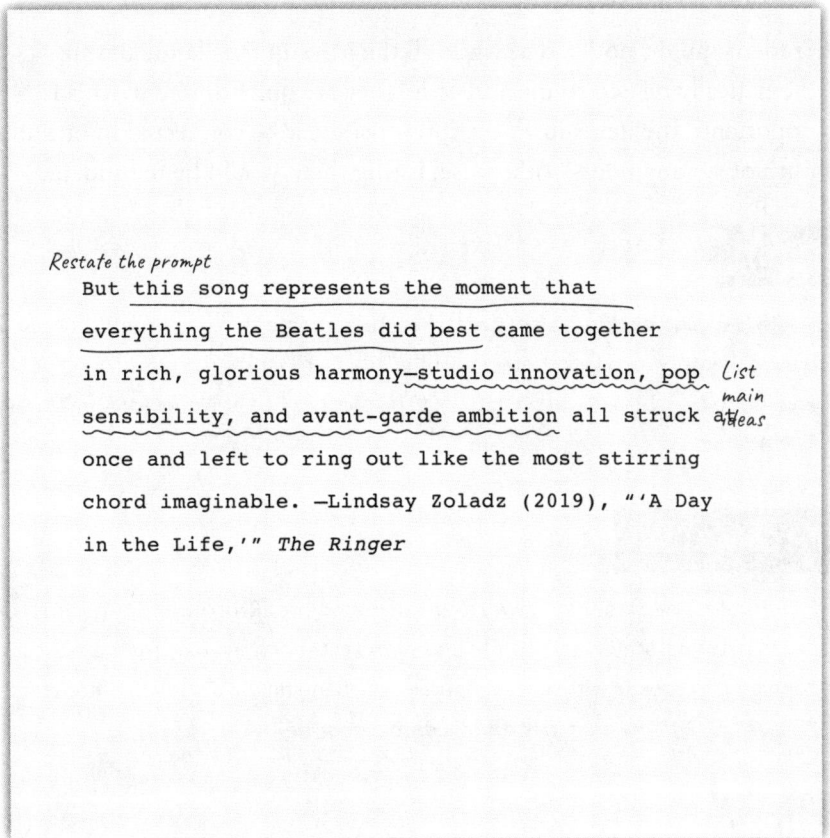

Figure 4.2: Outline It, annotated mentor text.

Here are some things we might notice with our students about the Outline It claim.

» Although this is a level 2 move, this particular mini-mentor text is a more advanced example of the move. To show the class how this claim might be simplified, we would ask students how the argument changes when the claim is read as "this song represents the moment that everything the Beatles did best came together—studio innovation, pop sensibility, and avant-garde ambition." The answer should be, "It doesn't change the argument at all."

» Students who are still honing their writing and critical thinking skills might consider writing their initial Outline It claim using the simplified version of the mentor text (shared in the first bullet point) as inspiration.

» Almost any mentor text claim can be reverse-engineered to discover what prompt or inquiry question the author is trying to answer. In this mentor text, we can assume the central question this author is trying to answer is, "What does this Beatles song represent to the band's discography?" As a writing strategy, students can reverse-engineer their own prompt (if they don't have one already).

» Students might notice that while all the ideas in the claim's list are thematically related to musical style, they are quite different. This is important: The items in a descriptive list must be connected to one another but not synonymous—otherwise, listing them would be redundant.

ENGLISH

While *Fledgling* explores a host of far-reaching themes—racial anxiety, codependency, memory (or a lack thereof)—Butler seems most keen on examining power and intimacy. —Lovia Gyarkye (2022), "The Octavia Butler Novel for Our Times," *The Atlantic*

MATHEMATICS

Four Fields Medals were awarded for major breakthroughs in geometry, combinatorics, statistical physics and number theory, even as mathematicians continued to wrestle with how computers are changing the discipline. —Konstantin Kakaes (2022), "The Year in Math," *Quanta Magazine*

SCIENCE

And once the real MOMA gets to Mars, approximately in 2030, Brinckerhoff and his colleagues will use the prototype—as well as a pristine copy kept in a Mars-like environment at NASA—to test tweaks to experimental protocols, troubleshoot issues that come up during the mission and facilitate interpretation of Mars data. —Carmen Drahl (2023), "The Mission That Could Transform Our Understanding of Mars," *Smithsonian Magazine*

SOCIAL STUDIES

The history of American barbecue is as diverse as the variations themselves, charting the path of a Caribbean cooking style brought north by Spanish conquistadors, moved westward by settlers, and seasoned with the flavors of European cultures. —Natasha Geiling (2023), "The Evolution of American Barbecue," *Smithsonian Magazine*

This-and-That (Level 3)

This is a fun one. In this move, writers can create a claim statement that is both cheekily cute and highly sophisticated. In a This-and-That claim, students will assert their central argument through a paradox.

By arguing that the topic of their writing is two contradictory things at once, students can create a nuanced claim that could be featured in the pages of *Vulture* or submitted as part of their AP English Literature or English Language exam.

This is the basic formula: Topic(Descriptor One + Descriptor Two).

POP CULTURE

See figure 4.3 for an annotated mentor text demonstrating this method.

> The vivid bloodletting "Traitor" was alternately coffeehouse quiet and arena bombastic, and equally persuasive in both modes. —Jon Caramanica (2022), "Olivia Rodrigo's Punky Heartbreak Revue," *The New York Times*

Figure 4.3: This-and-That, annotated mentor text.

Some of the noticings we might make with our students while looking at this mentor text follow.

> » We would ask students to first notice the length of this thesis. Similar to what some of our advice says, it's short! But this short sentence is a total powerhouse. Not a single word is wasted.

> » Students might notice the first phrase, "the vivid bloodletting." And, if they have not watched *Game of Thrones* recently, they may even ask what bloodletting is. We would share with our students that *bloodletting* refers to the medieval medicinal act of releasing a patient's blood to balance their

humors and cure their disease. Then, we'd ask, "Why does the author use 'bloodletting' to describe 'Traitor'?" Though answers may vary, students might say the following.

- Students should eventually come to the conclusion that the author is equating Rodrigo's heartbreak with a disease.
- By pairing "bloodletting" with the adjective "vivid," the author is able to convey a sentiment along the lines of "Isn't it clear that Olivia Rodrigo wrote this song to heal her heartbreak?"

» Our more grammar-astute students might point out that since "Traitor" is a song on a larger body of work, *Sour*, it is framed by quotation marks.

» Here, the noun-adjective pairs in this claim are the "this" and "that" in the This-and-That claim.

» The first pair sets up the paradox by providing an initial opinion on the topic that will ultimately contradict with the second noun-adjective pair.

- Students might notice that in this mentor text, the noun is a place and the adjective describes the noise level of that place. This is a nice touch, as it adds a sensory element to the claim. However, this is not required.
- It is not even required that the "this" and the "that" always be noun-adjective pairs; they simply must be descriptors that offer a seemingly paradoxical comparison.

» The conjunction "and" joins the paradoxical phrases. This indicates to the reader that though these descriptors seemingly contradict, in this instance, they work in harmony to provide a more complete description of the topic.

ENGLISH

By her presence, Moreno teaches us how to approach this movie, as both an affectionate tribute and a gentle corrective. —Justin Chang (2021), "Steven Spielberg's 'West Side Story' Will Make You Believe in Movies Again," *NPR*

MATHEMATICS

But it turns out that shapes with nonnegative Ricci curvature are more flexible and less well behaved than mathematicians had expected—complicating their understanding of the relationship between local geometric properties and global topological ones. —Jordana Cepelewicz (2024b), "Strangely Curved Shapes Break 50-Year-Old Geometry Conjecture," *Quanta Magazine*

SCIENCE

The measurements of mutation rates could be critically useful in calibrating the gene-based molecular clocks that biologists use to determine when species diverged, and they offer useful tests of several theories about how evolution works. —Yasemin Saplakoglu (2023), "Animal Mutation Rates Reveal Traits That Speed Evolution," *Quanta Magazine*

SOCIAL STUDIES

This spindly labyrinth of a swamp holds both the costs of slavery and the prices paid to resist it. —Lex Pryor (2022), "The Hidden and Eternal Spirit of the Great Dismal Swamp," *The Ringer*

Not-This-But-That (Level 4)

This move will make students feel like sassy geniuses. In a Not-This-But-That claim, the author counters expectations or assumptions that the reader might have about the topic at hand. For some reason, our students love this move. We think it's the natural teenage impulse to be like, "You don't get me," because that's essentially what this claim is saying: "You think one thing about this topic, but that's not true (or at least not the whole truth). This is."

For this claim, students will have to be intimately acquainted with their topic—enough to evaluate hidden truths about it and to understand the general consensus on the topic within the community they are writing about.

This is the basic formula: Topic + Is Not (This) But (That).

POP CULTURE

See figure 4.4 (page 58) for an annotated mentor text demonstrating this method.

Here's how we might break this mentor text down with our classes.

» We would begin by asking students to identify the topic of this claim. Students should identify *two* topics here: (1) the song "We Don't Talk About Bruno" and (2) the movie *Encanto*. If asked, the students might identify that the author includes both these topics in the claim because the messages in the song and the movie are intertwined. While this is definitely a technique students could adopt in their own Not-This-But-That claim, it is not necessary.

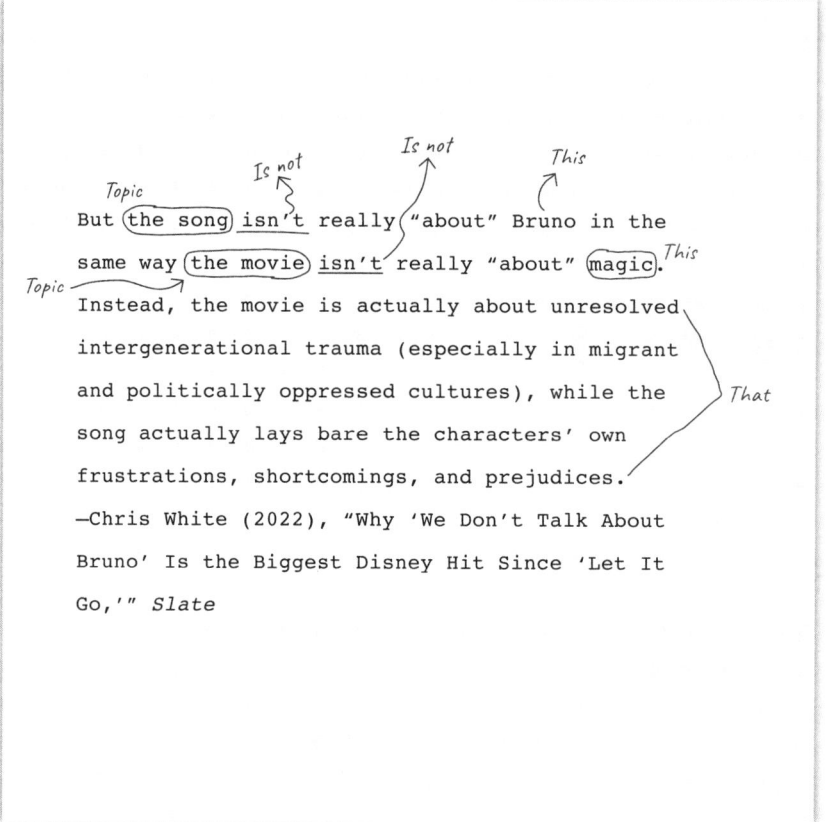

Figure 4.4: Not-This-But-That, annotated mentor text.

» Hopefully, by now, your students are noticing a pattern in claim statements—the topic is almost always mentioned at the beginning of the claim to anchor the reader before diving into the argument or analysis.

» At some point in a Not-This-But-That claim, the author must explain to the reader what the topic is not actually about. The order of the "not this" and the "but that" is irrelevant. Some writers put the "not this" first, and other writers affirm what the thing is first and then follow it with what it's not. Both ways work.

» When making a claim as to what something is *not* about, the author must identify something that would be a popular point of consent among their audience.

* For example, here, the author tells the reader that the movie is not really about "magic." Anyone who has seen *Encanto* might bristle at this. Of course, the movie is about magic—it's all about magic and the absence of magic, right?

- ∗ But the author reveals a deeper meaning to what might be our initial read on the topic. Yes, magic is part of *Encanto*, but magic is actually a storytelling element.
- » Check out the innovation in the social studies mentor text. While it doesn't use the exact Not-This-But-That formula, the sense of it is still present. It's the same thing, just slightly subtler.
- » Students might notice that the author uses parentheses to help the reader understand what they mean by "unresolved intergenerational trauma." This is an excellent example of Put It in Parentheses (page 166).

ENGLISH

[Clarence Thomas's] efforts at reconciliation ultimately illustrate the extent to which "originalism" is merely a process of exploiting history to justify conservative policy preferences, and not a neutral philosophical framework. —Adam Serwer (2023), "The Most Baffling Argument a Supreme Court Justice Has Ever Made," *The Atlantic*

MATHEMATICS

General relativity has transformed our understanding of gravity, depicting it not as an attractive force between massive objects, as had long been held, but rather as a consequence of the way space and time curve in the presence of mass and energy. —Steve Nadis (2022b), "Mass and Angular Momentum, Left Ambiguous by Einstein, Get Defined," *Quanta Magazine*

SCIENCE

Biodiversity might hinge on what species have in common, not their particular niches. —Veronique Greenwood (2023b), "A New Explanation for One of Ecology's Most Debated Ideas," *The Atlantic*

SOCIAL STUDIES

What should have been a moment of political danger for Trump instead has become another stage for him to demonstrate his dominance within the party. —Ronald Brownstein (2023), "Why Trump Might Just Roll to the Presidential Nomination," *The Atlantic*

Synthesize It (Level 5)

Synthesis is the art of bringing two or more ideas together in your writing. To accomplish this in a thesis is difficult but totally doable. And it will set young writers up to do some serious analysis within the larger body of their writing.

To make a synthesis claim, students must compare, contrast, or contextualize two or more topics with one another. These topics might span geographic regions, time periods, political ideas, or cultures. And to complete the synthesis claim, the author must evaluate the connection between the topics.

This is the basic formula: Topic One + Topic Two + Comparison/Contrast/Connection + Significance.

POP CULTURE

This kind of claim is unmistakably challenging—just take a look at these mentor texts, starting with figure 4.5!

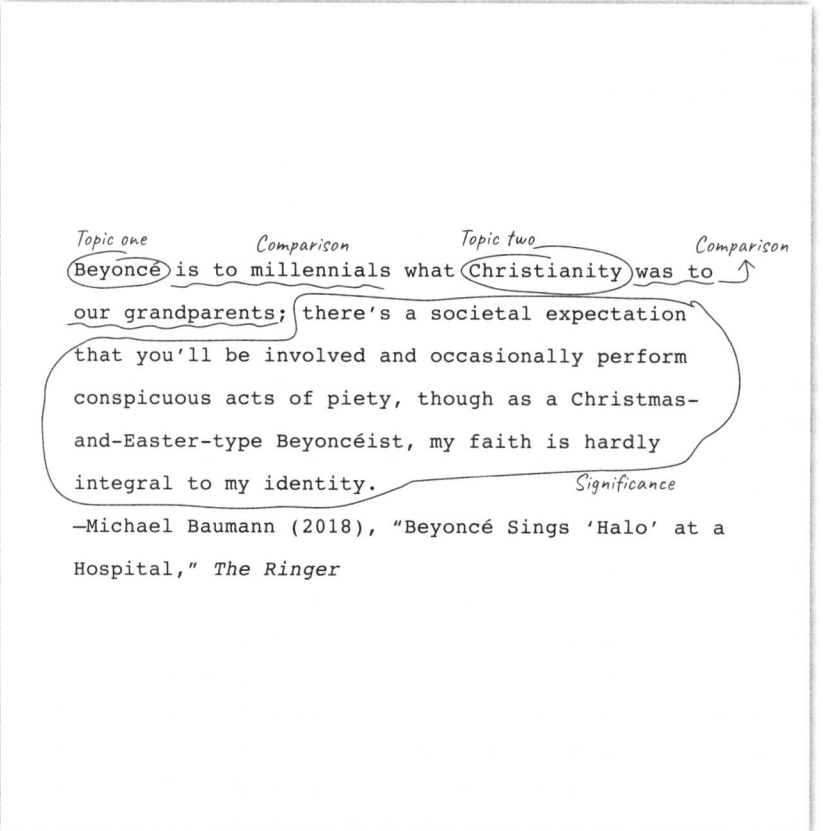

Figure 4.5: Synthesize It, annotated mentor text.

Let's go over some noticings we would talk about with our students.

» This kind of claim is beautifully complicated and would benefit from a wee bit of diagramming with students. We would begin by asking students to identify the topics being compared, contrasted, or contextualized in this claim.

  * Students should notice that the two topics are "Beyoncé" and "Christianity."
  * The two topics in a synthesis claim are often identified early on in the claim.
  * We would then write, "<u>Beyoncé</u> is to <u>millennials</u> what <u>Christianity</u> was to our <u>grandparents</u>," on the board and ask students to identify this comparison method. Some students (especially those who have had SAT or ACT prep) will be able to identify this as an analogy.

» An analogy can be an effective way to set up a comparative synthesis claim, though it certainly is not required.

  * At this point in the synthesis claim, what is important to note is that the author has *told* us something about each of the topics they plan to compare, contrast, or contextualize.

» Students may notice that this author explains the significance of the comparison they are making between Beyoncé and Christianity.

  * We would share with our students that unlike some of the simpler moves that make a claim, the Synthesize It claim cannot simply establish a comparison, contrast, or contextualization between two or more topics. It must explain the significance of the synthesis—there is a religiosity to fans' devotion to Beyoncé, and similarly, there is a fandom to Christianity.

» Students who want to add another element to their synthesis claim might consider including a piece of personal evidence that bolsters their argument as the author of the pop culture mentor text does.

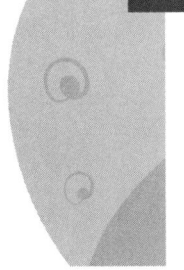

ENGLISH

Freedom Song, Amit Chaudhuri's third novel, is set in Calcutta in 1993. The book is pointillist in form, capturing both the inner and outer voices of its many characters. If Dylan Thomas, with his uncanny ear for unspoken thoughts, had written *Under Milk Wood* set not in a Welsh village but in an Indian city, this might be it. —Wendy Doniger (2024), "A Quiet Roar: Wendy Doniger on Amit Chaudhuri's *Freedom Song*," Literary Hub

MATHEMATICS

What we do know is that the mathematical technique now known as the Chinese remainder theorem was devised sometime between the third and fifth centuries CE by the Chinese mathematician Sun Tzu (not to be confused with Sun Tzu who wrote *The Art of War* almost 1,000 years earlier). . . .

. . . Sun Tzu never proved this formally, but later the Indian mathematician and astronomer Aryabhata developed a process for solving any given instance of the theorem. —Lakshmi Chandrasekaran (2021), "How Ancient War Trickery Is Alive in Math Today," *Quanta Magazine*

SCIENCE

COVID-19 has disrupted everyday life worldwide. It is the first disease event since the 1918–20 H1N1 Spanish influenza (flu) pandemic to demand an urgent global healthcare response, propagated by the speed and likelihood of potential transmission. —Grace E. Patterson, K. Marie McIntyre, Helen E. Clough, and Jonathan Rushton (2021), "Societal Impacts of Pandemics: Comparing COVID-19 With History to Focus Our Response," *Frontiers in Public Health*

SOCIAL STUDIES

Instead of following the Soviet model of development, which leaned heavily towards industry alone, China would "walk on two legs": the peasant masses were mobilized to transform both agriculture and industry at the same time, converting a backward economy into a modern communist society of plenty for all. —Frank Dikötter (2011), *Mao's Great Famine: The History of China's Most Devastating Catastrophe, 1958–1962*, p. xi

Use the reproducible "Writing Application Practice: Moves That Make a Claim" (page 64) to make a claim.

Student Samples

The following student samples include moves that make a claim.

This sample uses The Big Idea (level 1):

> Joni Mitchell was an observer; one who brought people together while remaining on the fringe. —Natalia, Eighth Grade

This sample uses This-and-That (level 3):

> In Freewater, Amina Luqman-Dawson depicts slavery as violent and dehumanizing. —Elizabeth, Eighth Grade

This sample uses Synthesize It (level 5):

> In Freewater, Amina Luqman-Dawson depicts slavery and, particularly, enslavers as barbaric, as most texts about slavery do. However, Amina Luqman-Dawson also shows how enslaved people fought against tyranny. This includes literally fighting back and separating themselves from authority, much like the Americans did during the Revolution. —Alex, Eighth Grade

Writing Application Practice: Moves That Make a Claim

After teaching your students one of these moves—or all of these moves—you'll be looking for an opportunity for them to practice these skills immediately.

For each writing task, we have provided a prompt you could use to get your students writing. They can use this prompt to practice a single move for that writing task or to begin combining, mixing, and matching moves. You can find all writing application practice from the whole book in one place in appendix C (page 275).

Content Area	Writing Application Practice
English	Choose one of the moves that make a claim, and write a claim statement about the current book you're reading.
Mathematics	Consider your current unit in mathematics class. What is the most important mathematical concept to understand in order to be successful in this unit? Write a claim making that argument.
Science	What is the most important issue facing scientists today? Write a claim that makes that argument.
Social Studies	What event did you last study in your social studies class? Write a claim statement that explains the significance of this event within your current unit of study.

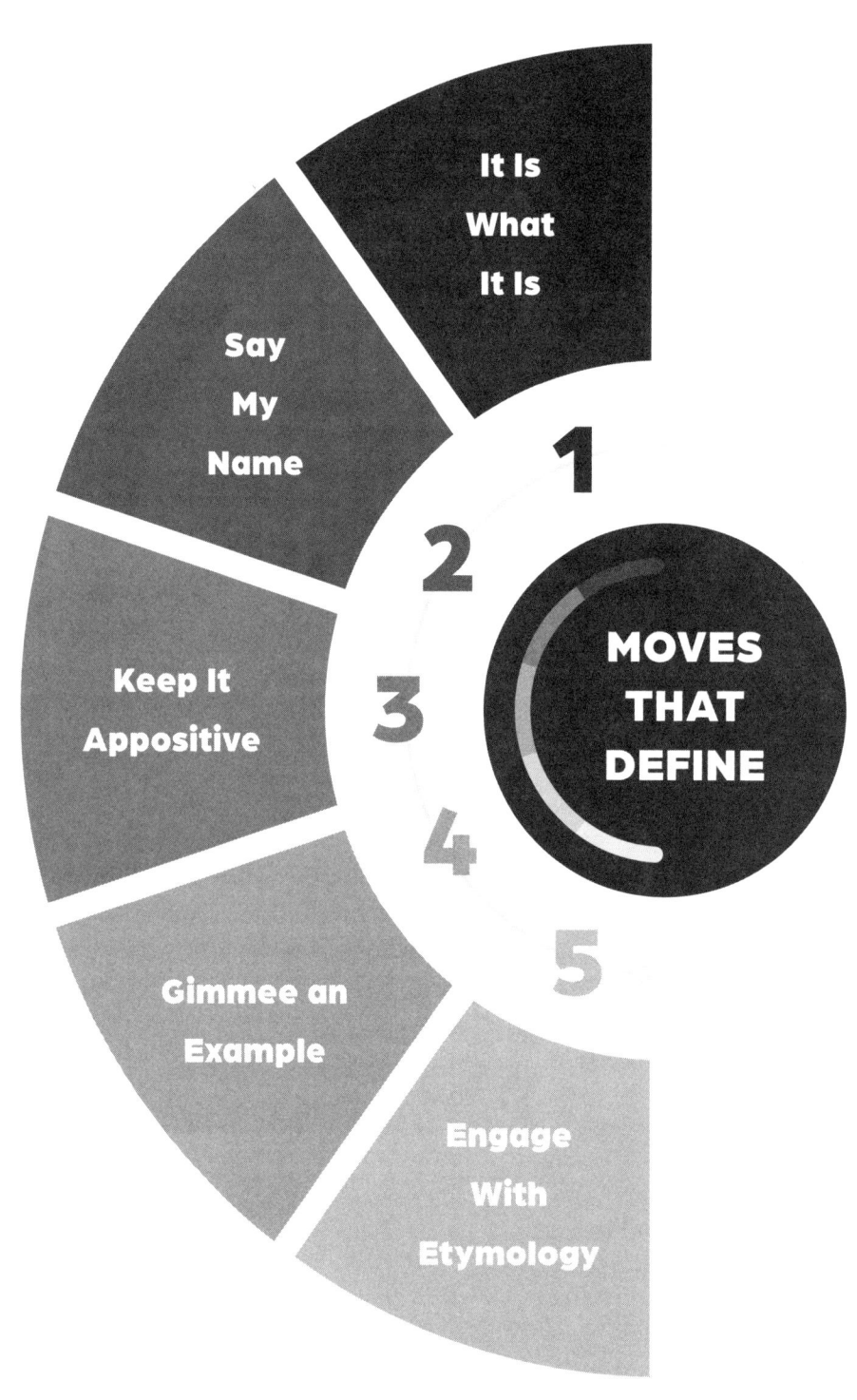

CHAPTER 5

Moves That Define

Let's be honest; writing definitions isn't high profile. It doesn't smack of creativity or style. It's rarely groundbreaking. In fact, before we set out to write this book, Rebekah never explicitly taught her writers different strategies for defining in their writing. Turns out defining is everywhere. And it *is* very important.

Here's why: Defining is a reader service—it's all about the writer considering how to make comprehension easier for the reader. Defining key terms and ideas is an accessible way for young writers to clarify their thoughts and bring the reader into their writing. Writing teacher and author Roy Peter Clark (2023) observes, "[Writers] face dangers and temptations. . . . We know too much and forget what readers do not yet know" (p. 17). Young writers often fall prey to this temptation and don't share all they know with readers, which leads to "one, two, skip a few" thinking and confusing prose. (Defining and describing are parts of the contextualization family. But they are such critical writing skills that we thought they needed their own chapters! See chapters 6, page 83, and 9, page 143, for ten more mini moves writers can use to contextualize their writing.)

When writers define, they share the exact meaning of a word so that their reader can understand what is being discussed. In this way, the definition itself is for the reader. But the moves writers make when they define adapt to fit their own needs. As you'll see in the following moves, sometimes, the definition is loud and bold—a full stop in the flow of ideas meant to emphasize it and give it importance. Other times, writers slide in a definition quickly and deftly—a covert handoff of information that allows the reader to seamlessly understand how the word fits into a larger point in the piece. See table 5.1 (page 68) for recommendations on what moves writers can use when they need to define.

Table 5.1: Writing Needs and Moves That Define

When Writers Need...	Start Here...
To create a significant pause in the flow of the writing to define an important term	It Is What It Is (page 68)
	Engage With Etymology (page 76)
To subtly slip in a definition of an important term	Say My Name (page 70)
	Keep It Appositive (page 72)
To give an alternate or more nuanced definition	Gimme an Example (page 74)
	Engage With Etymology (page 76)

It Is What It Is (Level 1)

We love a simple starting point, and nothing could be simpler than the It Is What It Is definition. Writers often use this move when they think the reader might be unfamiliar with the term. The sheer simplicity of this move focuses the reader on the definition and prevents any potential misunderstandings. Writers also use this defining move when they want to slow the pace with lucid language that provides a crystal-clear definition of the term in question. Rather than folding in the definition, this move pauses the flow of the writing action. It's a stop sign for the reader; they have to understand this definition before continuing forward.

This is the basic formula: Term Being Defined + *is* + Definition.

POP CULTURE

See figure 5.1 for a mentor text using this method.

```
          Term being defined           Definition
    Ballet is an otherworldly art, more than a few cool
    moves strung together by a trendy choreographer.
    —Gia Kourlas (2024), "What Is Ballet in the 21st
    Century? It's All Over the Place," The New York
    Times
```

Figure 5.1: It Is What It Is, annotated mentor text.

Here are some other features you and your students might consider together.

» Lots of writing teachers ban *to be* verbs. But on occasion, they are exactly what you need. In this move, writers often use the simple verb *is*. It's clear. It's straightforward. It just works.

» However, *is* can be replaced by a different verb. Check out the following science example. The writer uses "identifies . . . as" in place of *is*. The exact words you use aren't as important as how clear and direct you are in providing the definition.

» Students might notice that the definition is the opening phrase of the sentence. Writers typically use this move at the beginning or end of a sentence (or as a stand-alone sentence) to create that pausing effect we referenced in the introduction.

» Let's think about word choice. Just because this type of defining work is direct, that doesn't mean it has to be boring or without style. A writer's word choice always matters, and when writing clear definitions, word choice is particularly potent! In the ballet example, the choice of "otherworldly" feels intentional and interesting as it describes ballet as an art form. Contrast it with the casual (almost snarky!) choices of "cool moves," "strung together," and "trendy choreographer" that follow it, demonstrating what ballet is *not*.

» This move works to provide definitions for many different things. In just the following examples, we see this move being used to define concepts, people, and items.

ENGLISH

Of course, it is Breyer's patience for sifting through the most finicky details that made him such a scrupulous jurist. He is dedicated, precise and deliberate. —Jennifer Szalai (2024), "The Retired Justice Who Doesn't Understand the Supreme Court," *The New York Times*

MATHEMATICS

To formalize how close to a square a rectangle is, mathematicians use a number called the aspect ratio. It is simply the length divided by the width. —Kevin Hartnett (2024a), "Mathematicians Identify the Best Versions of Iconic Shapes," *Quanta Magazine*

SCIENCE

Cosmologists' reigning model of the universe identifies dark energy as the energy of space itself and pegs it at 70% of the universe's contents. —Liz Kruesi (2024), "Fresh X-Rays Reveal a Universe as Clumpy as Cosmology Predicts," *Quanta Magazine*

SOCIAL STUDIES

The Great Chain of Being is, perhaps, the most ancient metaphorical device for organizing nature and society. God and the angels sit on top with matter in all its forms scaled downward: humans in order of their ranks and occupations; followed by birds, fish, and beasts; then trees and other plants; and finally rocks and earthen things. —Steven Stoll (2008), "Pattern Recognition," *Lapham's Quarterly*

Say My Name (Level 2)

A Say My Name definition is almost an It Is What It Is definition in reverse. Instead of beginning with the term and following it with the definition, a Say My Name definition begins with a definition and then gives the term that is used for that definition.

What?

Let us show you.

Remember the ballet example—"Ballet is an otherworldly art"? That's an It Is What It Is definition. Now, let's flip it: "More than a collection of cool moves strung together by a trendy choreographer, this is an otherworldly art called ballet."

Now, why would a writer want to use this move? Isn't it simpler to use It Is What It Is? Once again, we have to put ourselves in the position of the reader. Sometimes, a reader is familiar with a concept but doesn't know the correct term for that idea. That's when a writer can help them by using Say My Name to tell the reader what that thing is called. It's about giving an accessible concept a more specific or technical name that will empower the reader's understanding throughout the rest of the piece.

This is the basic formula: Basic Definition + *called* + Term.

POP CULTURE

See figure 5.2 for a mentor text that uses this method.

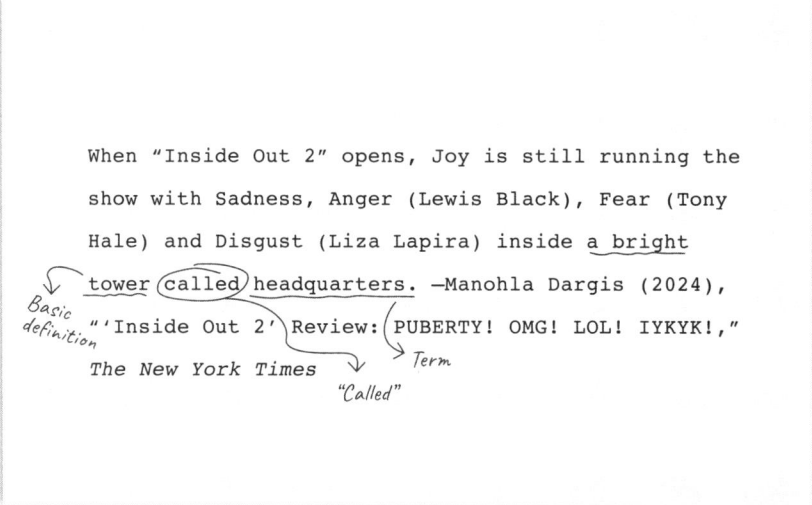

Figure 5.2: Say My Name, annotated mentor text.

When you look at this move with your students, here are some ideas that might come up.

» Notice that we aren't looking for dictionary definitions for this move. That would be awkward. These are incredibly basic, simple definitions. In our pop culture example, the definition of headquarters is "a bright tower." In the English example, rook cranes are defined as "gigantic birds." In the science example, mitochondria are defined as "powerhouse organelles."

» This move slips in a definition more smoothly by using it as part of the writer's language. Unlike the It Is What It Is move, the reader doesn't take a time-out to process the definition. This happens more fluidly within the context of the writer's ideas.

» While this move isn't complex, it does require a bit more of the writer to blend their own ideas with the definition and the technical term. It might take a writer a try or two to get the syntax just right, and that's OK.

ENGLISH

Here, hurricanes and tides have made building collapse a constant danger, the freeway is visible only on low-tide days, food is government rations, the wealthy have fled "upriver to scattered little freshwater townships," and gigantic birds called rook cranes are everywhere. —Jessamine Chan (2024), "In Téa Obreht's Latest, a Refugee Seeks Home in a Ruined World," *The New York Times*

MATHEMATICS

This process (seen below), called the unfolding of the billiard path, allows the ball to continue in a straight-line trajectory. —David S. Richeson (2024), "Unfolding the Mysteries of Polygonal Billiards," *Quanta Magazine*

SCIENCE

The powerhouse organelles called mitochondria are dutifully churning out energy. —Veronique Greenwood (2024a), "Cellular Self-Destruction May Be Ancient. But Why?," *Quanta Magazine*

SOCIAL STUDIES

Until the early 20th century, it was standard practice to assemble all-female juries, called "juries of matrons," to determine whether a woman was pregnant and could therefore avoid hanging for capital offenses. —Alice Neikirk (2024b), "How All-Female 'Juries of Matrons' Shaped Legal History," *The Conversation*

Keep It Appositive (Level 3)

Keep It Appositive is a classic move that adds sophistication to any writer's composition because it is just so smooth. An appositive is a phrase that defines the noun that comes before it. It's not essential. It's whipped cream—a definition you don't absolutely need to have, but one that offers a bit of tasty clarity all the same.

It has the added benefit of gently tucking a definition into a sentence without causing a stir. The reader barely notices. So, a writer might want to try this move when they feel confident most readers will know the definition, but a few may need a brief reminder.

This is the basic formula: Noun, + Definition, + Continuation of the Sentence, or Noun, + Definition.

POP CULTURE

See figure 5.3 for an annotated mentor text demonstrating this method.

```
Comma  It was that same friend, she said, who coaxed her
        into trying what's known as aggressive or in-line
        street skating, a style heavy on tricks and stunts
  Noun  like grinding curbs, skidding on railings and    Definition
        spinning along half-pipes. —Max Berlinger (2023),
        "At More Skate Parks, an 'Aggressive' Takeover,"
        The New York Times
```

Figure 5.3: Keep It Appositive, annotated mentor text.

Here are some extra tidbits to consider as you share this move with students.

» In the pop culture example, the sentence ends after the definition. But in some of the following examples, the sentence continues! In these cases, the writers need another comma (or dash) after the definition before jumping back into the main flow of the sentence.

» Students who look at the content-area mentor texts in addition to the pop culture mentor text will notice that the order of this move's components is irrelevant. What differentiates Keep It Appositive from other moves is the way the appositive is tucked into the sentence, and a comma (or dash) separates the term and definition.

» Writers can use a dash instead of a comma to separate the term and definition in an appositive phrase. As you see in the English and mathematics examples, a dash creates a larger, more dramatic pause in the sentence. It's just a style choice. Have students experiment with using commas and dashes and then reading them aloud to see how the choice of punctuation changes the effect of this move.

ENGLISH

The Talk explores the question of how people—in this case, a precocious, geeky, and artistic young man, the child of a white mother and Black father—know what they know. —Tahneer Oksman (2023b), "'The Talk' Is an Epic Portrait of an Artist Making His Way Through Hardships," *NPR*

MATHEMATICS

Alongside this came the work of Christopher Clavius—a German Jesuit astronomer who helped Pope Gregory XIII to introduce the Gregorian calendar—and other mathematicians on fractions. —Madeleine S. Killacky (2023), "Shakespeare by Numbers: How Mathematical Breakthroughs Influenced the Bard's Plays," *The Conversation*

SCIENCE

All of the characteristics of the odd ants—the wings, the social behaviors and the reproductive traits—were caused by what geneticists call a supergene, a collection of genes that are inherited as a unit and are highly resistant to being broken up. —Viviane Callier (2023), "A Mutation Turned Ants Into a Parasite in One Generation," *Quanta Magazine*

SOCIAL STUDIES

The great French historian and resistance martyr, Marc Bloch, is supposed to have said that history was like a knife: You can cut bread with it, but you could also kill. —Fritz Stern (2008), "Imperial Hubris," *Lapham's Quarterly*

Gimme an Example (Level 4)

Definitions have their limitations. Have you ever found a definition in the dictionary only to become more confused than when you started? Sometimes, a traditional definition alone isn't the best way to clearly explain a concept. Sometimes, including a well-chosen example or two is even better.

In a Gimme an Example definition, the writer makes a statement and then follows it with one to three brief, simple examples that, without further explanation, will define what the writer means. The examples are meant to be easily understood so that they act like a shorthand for the reader and writer to better understand each other.

This is the basic formula: Term + Definition With One to Three Examples.

POP CULTURE

See figure 5.4 for an annotated mentor text demonstrating this method.

> *Term*
> (Cringe:) the ultimate insult of our era. It   *Definition with 1–3 examples*
> implies a kind of pathetic attachment to hope,
> to sincerity, to possibility. Cringe is not
> exclusively female; the musical "Hamilton," written
> by a man, Lin-Manuel Miranda, is definitely cringe.
> —Lydia Polgreen (2023), "Why Is Everyone Suddenly
> Listening to a Staple of My Angsty Adolescence?,"
> *The New York Times*

Figure 5.4: Gimme an Example, annotated mentor text.

As you teach this move to your students, here are some things to consider.

» This is a level 4 move because when you first study it with your students, these examples may not instantly feel like definitions in the same way that levels 1–3 moves do. One way to talk to students about this is to explain that a definition answers the question, "What is it?" or "What does it mean?"

   * For example, "What is ballet?" Definition answer: It's an "otherworldly art."

   * In this case, a reader might ask, "Well, what is cringe?" The answer is having a "pathetic attachment to hope, to sincerity, to possibility."

» Students might notice that the space between the term and the definition in this move is filled with the writer's claim. This also makes the move more advanced—there's room for variation as to when the writer chooses to include their definition with examples.

» The pop culture and science mentor texts include a completely separate sentence to give the examples. In the English, mathematics, and social studies examples, the writers slip in the examples using commas or dashes, similar to appositives. Both ways work! Have students try them both and see what sounds best to them.

ENGLISH

And so it starts with being an altar boy for those Masses in Enniscorthy, the stained glass, the light, the Cathedral, the choir, the amazing choir singing Mozart . . . all of that mattered enormously, as did later at St. Peter's, which was half a seminary and half a Diocesan school where a lot of the real influences on, certainly on me, were priests. —Caoilinn Hughes (2024), "Colm Tóibín on James Baldwin's Enduring, International Influence," *Literary Hub*

MATHEMATICS

In general, a set is a group if it comes with some operation that, like addition, combines two elements into a third element in a way that satisfies some basic requirements. —Leila Sloman (2023), "Probability and Number Theory Collide—in a Moment," *Quanta Magazine*

SCIENCE

Venus has more than volcanic outbursts; the planet also sinks in places, like the chest of a recumbent giant exhaling. This process is called subduction, a phenomenon that also occurs on Earth, albeit by a different mechanism. —Shi En Kim (2024), "The Six Most Amazing Discoveries We've Made by Exploring Venus," *Smithsonian Magazine*

SOCIAL STUDIES

A large number were public figures—influential lawyers, journalists, playwrights or physicians, some of whom were the only women in their fields—and often had their names in the papers for the work they were performing. —Laura Kiniry (2024), "The All-Woman Secret Society That Paved the Way for Modern Feminism," *Smithsonian Magazine*

Engage With Etymology (Level 5)

Writers define words to help their readers more fully understand their meaning. On occasion, the definition itself is so juicy and interesting that it deserves a deep dive to unpack the layers of meaning.

Etymology is the study of a word's origin and how that meaning has evolved over time. Writers engage with etymology when they want to take readers on a bit of a historical word journey to reveal a word's depth of meaning. By stopping to discuss a word's history, the writer reveals many different ways of understanding that particular word. And this excavation of meaning yields the deepest understanding.

This is the basic formula: Term + Meanings From Etymology + "So what?" Connection.

POP CULTURE

See figure 5.5 for a demonstration of this method in a mentor text.

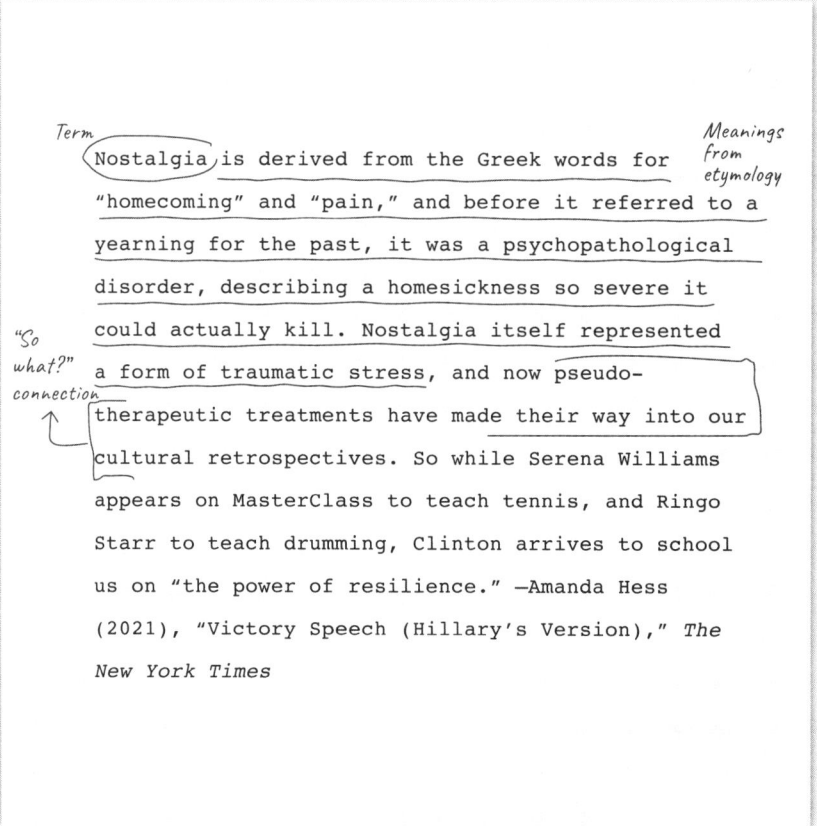

Figure 5.5: Engage With Etymology, annotated mentor text.

Here are some ideas you might discuss as you study this move with your students.

- » A writer has to do a lot to use this move. First, they have to research the term. Here are some guiding questions we would share with our students.
    * What is the definition of the word as it is used now?
    * Where and how did the word originate? What did it mean in its original context?
    * Has it changed or evolved?
    * Do these layers of meaning add anything to the ideas you are communicating in your piece of writing?
- » Students may note that while there are a lot of words in the mentor text, only one's etymology is explicated. This is a good takeaway: Only some words in a piece of writing are so significant and complex that their etymology bears discussion.
- » While many dictionaries contain interesting etymological information, we love etymonline.com as a one-stop shop for etymological research for you and your students!
- » Sometimes, writers include an evolution of a word's meaning over time, like in the pop culture, English (page 78), and mathematics (page 79) mentor texts. But this isn't always the case. Students who need more support might examine the science and social studies mentor texts (page 79), which analyze the word's meaning in a specific time period. This can be a more approachable way to try Engage With Etymology.
- » After the writer uncovers etymological information that actually benefits the ideas in their writing, they have to clearly share that information and draw a connection that tells the reader why it matters in the context of what they have been reading. In other words, so what?
- » Students may notice that this move is much longer than the other moves in this chapter. Because so much writing is required to analyze a word's etymology, this move will naturally lead to a substantial pause in the flow of the piece. Students should consider whether this feels appropriate for their writing and adjust accordingly.

Figure 5.6 (page 78) will help you and your students see the circular path a writer takes to incorporate this move.

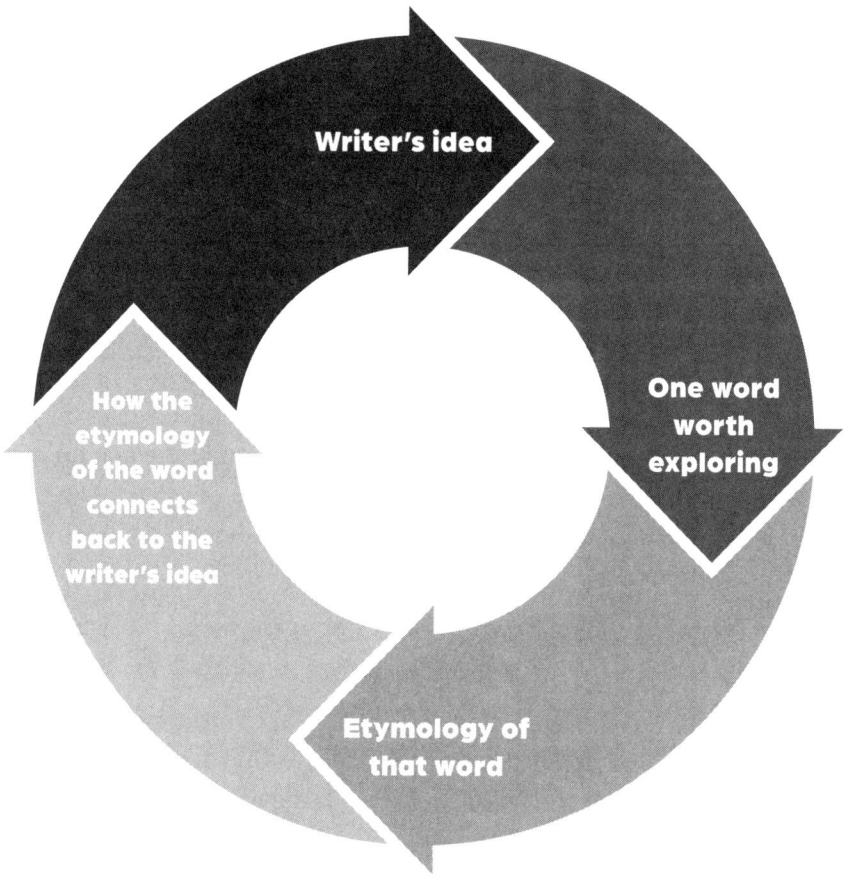

Figure 5.6: Circular movement of Engage With Etymology.

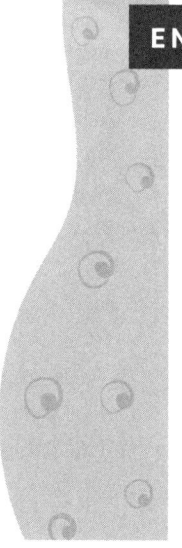

ENGLISH

Loneliness is a compound or multidimensional emotion: It contains elements of sadness and anxiety, fear and heartache. The experience of it is inherently, intensely subjective, as any chronically lonely person can tell you. A clerk at a crowded grocery store can be wildly lonely, just as a wizened hermit living in a cave can weather solitude in perfect bliss. (If you want to infuriate an expert in loneliness, try confusing the word "isolation" with "loneliness.") For convenience's sake, most researchers still use the definition coined nearly three decades ago, in the early 1980s, by the social psychologists Daniel Perlman and Letitia Anne Peplau, who described loneliness as "a discrepancy between one's desired and achieved levels of social relations." Unfortunately, that definition is pretty subjective, too. —Matthew Shaer (2024), "Why Is the Loneliness Epidemic So Hard to Cure?," *The New York Times*

MATHEMATICS

The term *tally* comes from the French verb *tailler*, "to cut," like the English word *tailor*; the root is seen in the Latin *taliare*, meaning "to cut." It is also interesting to note that the English word *write* can be traced to the Anglo-Saxon *writan*, "to scratch," or "to notch."

. . . Counts were maintained by making scratches on stones, by cutting notches in wooden sticks or pieces of bone, or by tying knots in strings of different colors or lengths. —David M. Burton (2011), *The History of Mathematics: An Introduction*, p. 2

SCIENCE

The word "apocalypse" is derived from the Latin for "revelation," and our current predicament draws out the irony of that double meaning, as we mistake obsessing about the "end of the world" for acting on it. —Amanda Hess (2022), "Apocalypse When? Global Warming's Endless Scroll," *The New York Times*

SOCIAL STUDIES

As the industrial historian S. Martin Gaskell [1980] writes in an article titled "Gardens for the Working Class: Victorian Practical Pleasure," the word "garden" denoted:

> On the one hand, something that was the personal and private preserve of the upper classes, whether in immediate proximity to the great house or in locked London square, or, on the other, a place of gratification and amusement, frequently associated with a drinking establishment, nearly always a scene of dissipation, and more than usually of ill-repute.

These competing interpretations—one gesturing toward the hidden and secretive, one toward a general debauchery—made gardens a suitable locale for crime and detective fiction, genres that, aside from providing suspense and intrigue, have long been concerned with exploring the darker sides of industrialization, urbanization, and modernization—and indeed humanity itself. —Tim Brinkhof (2024), "What Do Gardens and Murder Have in Common?," *JSTOR Daily*

Use the reproducible "Writing Application Practice: Moves That Define" (page 81) to define.

Student Samples

The following student samples include moves that define.

This sample uses It Is What It Is (level 1):

> America is a democratic republic, which means that America is governed by the people. —Grace, Eighth Grade

This sample uses Keep It Appositive (level 3):

> The U.S. government is often referred to as a representative democracy, a government that has elected officials as well as elements of a direct democracy in smaller matters. —Will, Eighth Grade

This sample uses Engage With Etymology (level 5):

> Civic virtue is derived from several Latin phrases and was originally used to describe a man with excellence and worth pertaining to citizenship. Civic virtue has transformed into a more specific meaning, stated as the qualities that make a good participant in a government system. This implies that to be an excellent politician, you must also have the attributes that define a good citizen. —Bridgette, Eighth Grade

Writing Application Practice: Moves That Define

After teaching your students one of these moves—or all of these moves—you'll be looking for an opportunity for them to practice these skills immediately.

For each writing task, we have provided a prompt you could use to get your students writing. They can use this prompt to practice a single move for that writing task or to begin combining, mixing, and matching moves. You can find all writing application practice from the whole book in one place in appendix C (page 275).

Content Area	Writing Application Practice
English	Think of a topic you know everything about—a topic you could discuss for an hour without getting bored. Now, what's a term within that topic that most people wouldn't know? Write a few sentences telling a friend about your topic. Include that term you've identified, and choose one of the definition moves to include a definition.
Mathematics	Think of a new and significant term in your current mathematics unit. Explain what you have been learning using that term, and be sure to include a definition using one of the moves that define.
Science	Choose one word from science class today that you believe is the most important word for understanding today's class. Write a few sentences explaining what you learned today. Be sure to include that most important word and its definition using one of the moves that define.
Social Studies	Take sixty seconds to write down as many vocabulary terms as you can that are connected to your current unit. Then, write a paragraph describing your unit in which you define at least one of the key terms using one of the moves that define.

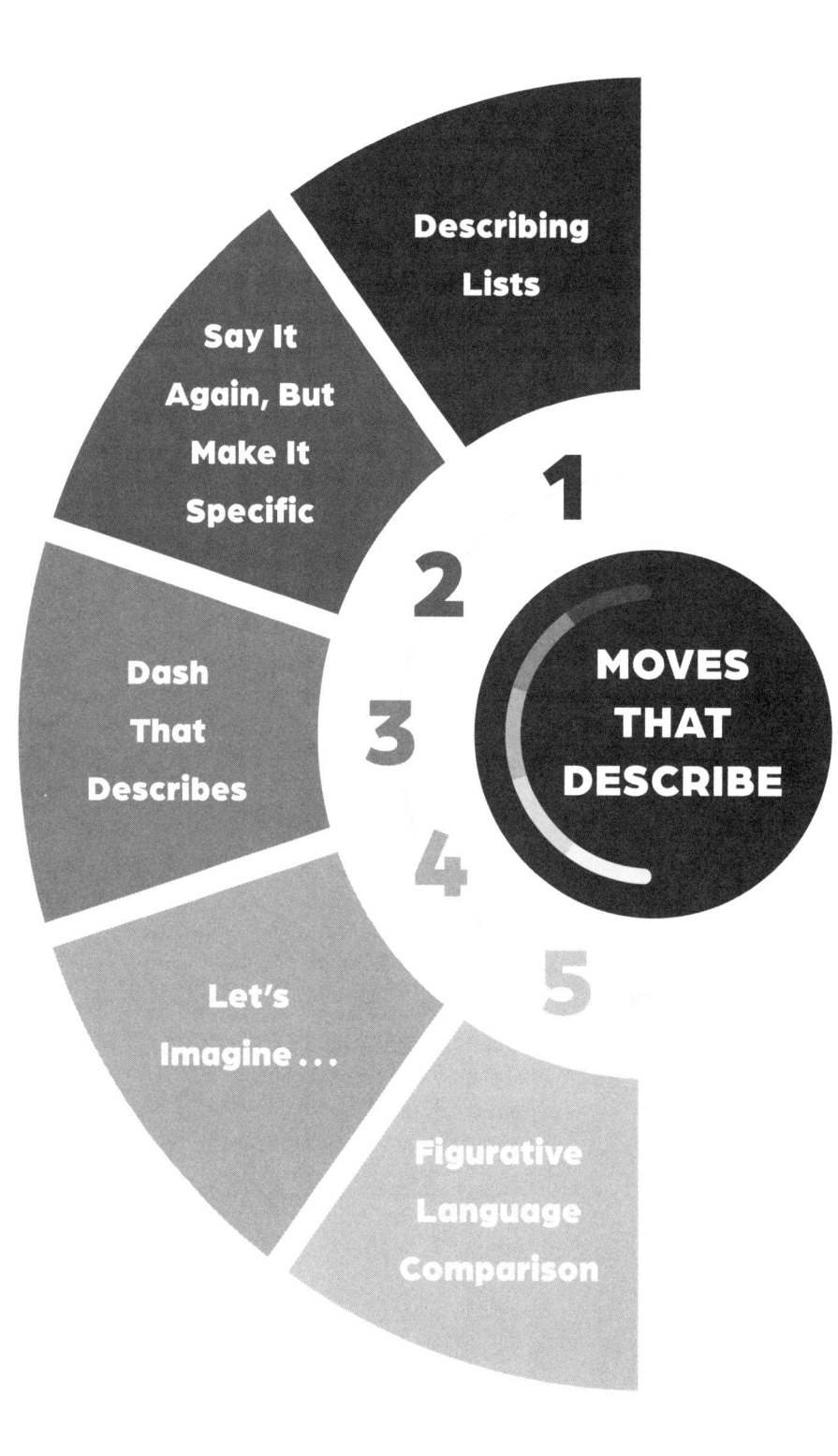

CHAPTER 6

Moves That Describe

Of all the writing tasks shared in this book, describing might be the most important because description is what takes information and brings it to life for the reader. Description helps a reader see, imagine, and experience.

We all have read a description that has changed us. As we work on this book, we are preparing to take our students on a field trip to the Great Dismal Swamp—a field trip that was sparked by Lex Pryor's (2022) emotional and mystical descriptions of the swamp as a refuge for runaway enslaved people prior to the Civil War. Here's an excerpt of the piece he wrote for *The Ringer*, "The Hidden and Eternal Spirit of the Great Dismal Swamp":

> From the vacant entrance, I followed the raised wooden pathway with sideburns of verdant moss growing on its edges. I walked through towering black gum groves with limbs 60 feet high. I trekked past so much green that it started to blur—too much green to even see the leaves—until I hit the Underground Railroad pavilion, nestled in the mire. It's a small, wall-less structure, made of metal and painted dark green.
>
> It appeared abandoned. Not decrepit—its floorboards were relatively fresh. On the eastern-facing side, a film of dust had bloomed beneath a mounted informational display titled "Maroons and Resistance in the Great Dismal Swamp." Some dirt lined the top.
>
> There was no litter on the premises, no footprints whatsoever. The ferns, from the forest, were ready to creep over the floor. Someone had built this monument in the web of vegetation. And there were hardly any traces that it had been visited.
>
> I stepped out from underneath the roof. The structure looked rejected in the gleam of the morning light. The pathway out to the road seemed to shrink from this vantage point. After 10 feet of boardwalk, the swamp appeared to engulf its sides. The land would take it, if we will not have it. I pictured [a runaway] moving in the brush, swaying with the leaves.

I turned back to the trail. It was there and then it wasn't. The path seemed hidden. The tangle surrounded me.

A mockingbird called out from the pines. (Pryor, 2022)

When we read this, we hadn't been to the Great Dismal Swamp. And yet, we had. Pryor took us there. Descriptions have the power to transport us, move us, and give us a sensory experience. Descriptions also give us details that add richness to the text but are not necessary for understanding. We see this in Pryor's (2022) use of the Dash That Describes move (page 89): "I trekked past so much green that it started to blur—too much green to even see the leaves—until I hit the Underground Railroad pavilion, nestled in the mire." The reader could still understand that the forest was green without the use of the detail within the dashes, but the inclusion of "too much green to even see the leaves" gives the swamp texture and dimension.

Descriptions are the lifeblood of writing. So, it comes as no surprise that one of the most common pieces of feedback students find in the margins of their writing is, "Add detail!" or "Say more!" or "Elaborate!" When students receive this kind of feedback, what their teacher is really asking for is more (and better) description. The five moves in this chapter will help students weave dynamic description into any kind of writing. See table 6.1 for some needs that might arise with your student writers paired with the moves that can help.

Table 6.1: Writing Needs and Moves That Describe

When Writers Need . . .	Start Here . . .
To use a simple descriptive structure (perfect for younger or less experienced writers)	Describing Lists (page 84) Say It Again, But Make It Specific (page 86)
To describe the highlights (without getting lost in the nitty-gritty)	Describing Lists (page 84) Dash That Describes (page 89)
To describe complicated or multistep topics	Say It Again, But Make It Specific (page 86) Let's Imagine . . . (page 91) Figurative Language Comparison (page 93)
To use data to describe a topic	Say It Again, But Make It Specific (page 86) Dash That Describes (page 89) Let's Imagine . . . (page 91)
To paint a picture for the reader	Dash That Describes (page 89) Figurative Language Comparison (page 93)
To describe something that seems to defy description	Let's Imagine . . . (page 91) Figurative Language Comparison (page 93)

Describing Lists (Level 1)

As you've probably already noticed while reading this book, listing is a common move in all types of writing. A describing list is a relatively simple move—name the topic and follow it with a list of descriptors, with each descriptor creating an increasingly vivid and specific image in the reader's mind. That list can take the typical form of items in a series joined by commas, or it can be separated into multiple sentences (like in our pop culture mentor text). The way writers choose to configure their describing list will inform the pace and tone of the description.

This is the basic formula: Name the Topic + Verb + Descriptor One + Descriptor Two + Descriptor Three.

POP CULTURE

See figure 6.1 for a mentor text that prompts this method.

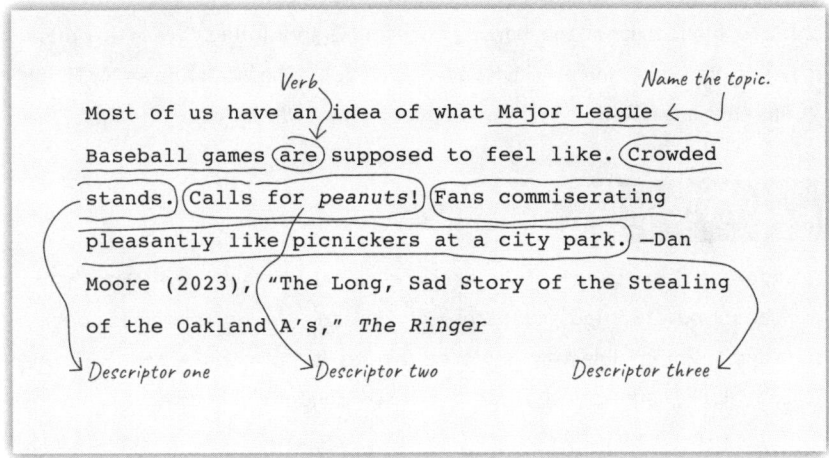

Figure 6.1: Describing Lists, annotated mentor text.

Here are some other features you and your students might consider together.

» Lists don't have to be boring! We love the way this example adds loads of voice with those intentional sentence fragments, the way the writer invokes the sound of the vendor shouting, "Peanuts!" and plays with an alliterative *p* ("pleasantly," "picnickers," "park").

» Students might point out that each item in the list is one thing that the author sees, hears, or feels. This is such an approachable structure for students to try to replicate.

» This particular list has a great rhythm because the items in the list follow a short, medium, long pattern. Of course, this isn't necessary for items in a list, but it does give this list a particular feeling of craftedness.

» Students will notice that there are three items in this list, which is classic. Looking at the following content-area examples, most describing lists do have three items; it's a natural rhythm. However, the social studies example (page 86) has five items in its list. No need to be formulaic—your list should have as many items as it needs to have to adequately describe the topic.

» In the mathematics example (page 86), you see another artful way to craft a list—using the repetition of a phrase ("it is impossible") at the beginning of each item in the list.

ENGLISH

I wanted to find what she discovers in our borderlands, to see if it's as dearly held as my memory of a childhood bedroom window opening southward to a daily breeze of blended language, barking dogs and Grandmother's whistled greetings to her neighbors. —Marcela Davison Avilés (2023), "'The Wind Knows My Name' Is a Reference and a Refrain in the Search for Home," *NPR*

MATHEMATICS

Wantzel used his results to resolve other classical problems by proving that they can't be solved—it is impossible to trisect some angles, it is impossible to double the cube and it is impossible to construct certain regular polygons. —David S. Richeson (2023b), "How Math Achieved Transcendence," *Quanta Magazine*

SCIENCE

More than four decades ago, field ecologists set out to quantify the diversity of trees on a forested plot on Barro Colorado Island in Panama, one of the most intensively studied tracts of forest on the planet. They began counting every tree with a trunk wider than a centimeter. They identified the species, measured the trunks and calculated the biomass of each individual. They put ladders up the trees, examined saplings and recorded it all in sprawling spreadsheets. —Veronique Greenwood (2023a), "The Key to Species Diversity May Be in Their Similarities," *Quanta Magazine*

SOCIAL STUDIES

The parade included parents who had served prison terms for noncompliance, a cart filled with unvaccinated children, an open hearse bearing a child's coffin inscribed ANOTHER VICTIM OF VACCINATION, doctors riding backward on cows, and an effigy of vaccine pioneer Edward Jenner that was eventually hanged and decapitated. —Nadja Durbach (2023), "Our Medical Liberties," *Lapham's Quarterly*

Say It Again, But Make It Specific (Level 2)

Sometimes, a writer makes a statement and then thinks, "You know, I probably need to say a little more about that." Teachers often see students approach this writing quandary by just repeating the exact same thing a second time, perhaps with slightly different wording.

Say It Again, But Make It Specific is the perfect move for this situation—ensuring that the student is able to double down on the idea they are communicating in a way that is fresh and meaningful for the reader.

This is the basic formula: Topic + Observation or Claim About the Topic + Claim Restated Using More Specific, Descriptive Words.

POP CULTURE

See figure 6.2 for an annotated mentor text demonstrating this method.

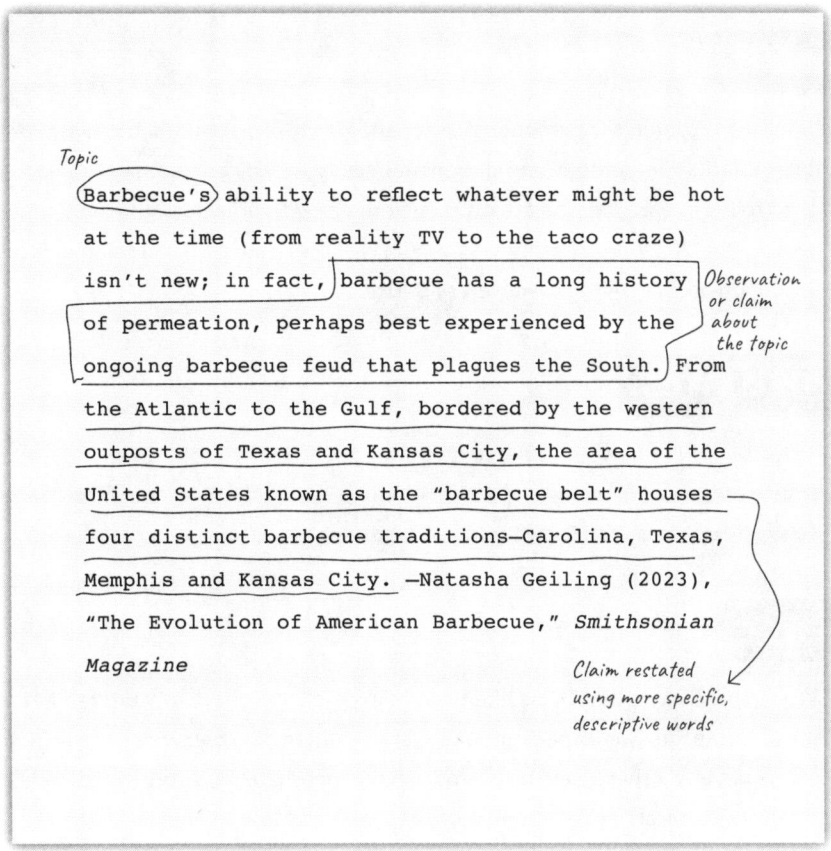

Figure 6.2: Say It Again, But Make It Specific, annotated mentor text.

Consider this when sharing this move with your students.

» We can't help but notice the parenthetical phrase in the first sentence that gives two specific examples of "whatever might be hot at the time." This isn't a necessary characteristic of the Say It Again, But Make It Specific move, but it is a nice addition. It gives voice and specificity to the piece.

» In this pop culture example about barbeque, the writer states the idea again using more specific geographic terms. However, the specific language student writers will use might not be geographic. Looking at the other examples will help students see a range of possibilities for making language more specific.

» The following mathematics example uses the introductory phrase *in other words* at the beginning of the second sentence. What a great transition! This is one your students can try on and borrow, too!

» This move can be combined with our previous move, the describing list! Both the English and science examples use a describing list in the second sentence as a way to be more specific.

ENGLISH

Britell deftly captures the emotional dissonance at the heart of the show. His score's dual capacity for harmony and dissonant chords underlines the nuanced nature of so many interactions, as affection is clouded by trauma, jealousy, and anger. —Ali Royals (2023), "Hereditary Venom: On Nicholas Britell's 'Succession: Season 4' Soundtrack," *Los Angeles Review of Books*

MATHEMATICS

Let's call $g(x)$ the new quadratic function we get when we replace x with $x + 4$. In other words, let $g(x) = f(x + 4)$. —Patrick Honner (2023c), "The Symmetry That Makes Solving Math Equations Easy," *Quanta Magazine*

SCIENCE

Research indicates that these chemicals can be dangerous. Exposure to PFAS is linked to cancers, weakened immune systems among children, weight gain, and a wide range of other health problems. —Benji Jones (2023b), "You Probably Have 'Forever Chemicals' in Your Body. Here's What That Means," *Vox*

SOCIAL STUDIES

The old representative democracy is starting to crack up. In its place there is a digital or direct democracy. By email or tweet, small bands of vigilantes can track down our representatives and cling, Fury-like, until they vote the right way. —Thomas Geoghegan (2020), "In the People's House There Are Many Mansions," *Lapham's Quarterly*

Dash That Describes (Level 3)

To use the Dash That Describes move, all the writer has to do is write a complete sentence, choose a noun that could use additional description, add a dash after it, and then describe that noun. A Dash That Describes is a smooth, flexible tool. It can go at the end of a sentence (take a look at some of the following examples) or smack-dab in the middle. It can incorporate a little bit of description or a lot. But no matter what, the Dash That Describes brings a little bit of drama and attention to the description being added because the dash does such a good job of grabbing the reader's attention and, briefly, halting their reading. The dash says, "Wait. Let me tell you something interesting."

Here, we might remind our students that the difference between description and contextualization is the nature of the detail the writer chooses to include. A descriptive detail is not necessary to the reader's understanding, but it adds something diverting to the text. The grammatical use of the dash indicates this to the reader in this move by segregating the detail from the heart of the sentence as if it is a bonus piece of information.

This is the basic formula: Idea— + Description of Idea— + Continuation of the Sentence. Or, Idea— + Description of Idea.

POP CULTURE

See figure 6.3 for an annotated mentor text demonstrating this method.

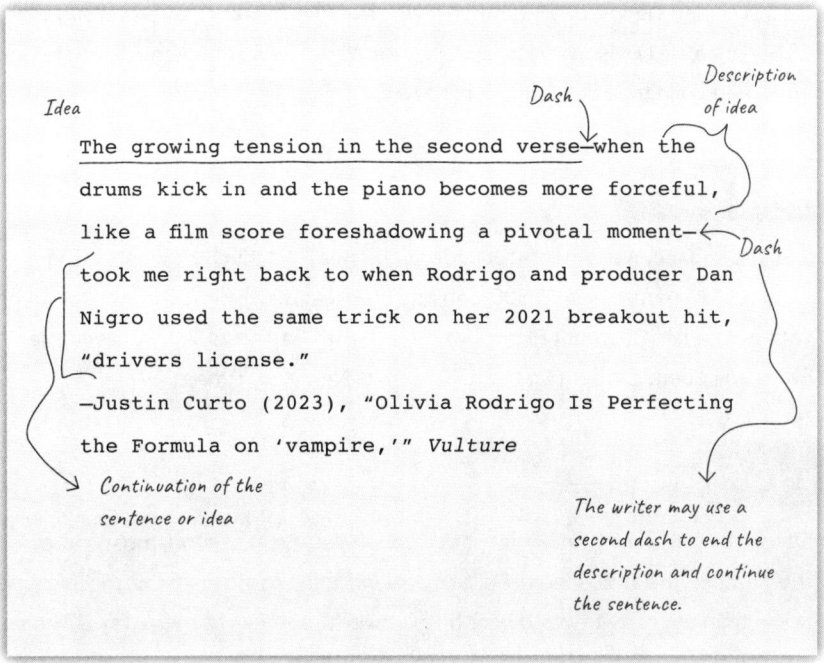

Figure 6.3: Dash That Describes, annotated mentor text.

Here are some extra tidbits to consider as you share this move with students.

» In this particular description, the writer uses a simile ("like a film score foreshadowing a pivotal moment") to flesh out the description even more deeply. This isn't necessary, but it is cool and adds a layer of nuance.

» Like other moves that describe, the Dash That Describes answers a question. Here, the question is usually a reiteration of the idea. For example, we might ask the author, "How do you feel the tension growing in the second verse?" They would respond, "The drums kick in and the piano becomes more forceful, like a film score foreshadowing a pivotal moment."

» A dash changes the way the reader processes information—it creates a big, dramatic pause. Students enjoy thinking about how their punctuation choices influence a reader's brain.

» Point out that the description that follows the dash is nonessential, meaning we don't need it to make sense of the sentence. It's extra. Bonus. So, to check if you've used the dash correctly, read your sentence and ignore the dash and description. Ask yourself, "Is this still a complete sentence? Does this sentence still make sense without the dash and description?" If so, you've used it correctly!

ENGLISH

The Wind Knows My Name is a tale of two child immigrants—a boy who escapes Nazi occupied Vienna in 1938 and a girl who escapes military gangs in El Salvador in 2019. —Marcela Davison Avilés (2023), "'The Wind Knows My Name' Is a Reference and a Refrain in the Search for Home," *NPR*

MATHEMATICS

Still, the impact on payments for undergraduates is relatively modest—an addition of about $2 a month on a $5,500 loan (the first-year maximum borrowing amount), with a standard 10-year repayment term. —Ann Carrns (2023), "Expect Interest Rates on Federal Student Loans to Rise," *The New York Times*

SCIENCE

Of the 100 trillion neutrinos that pass through you every second, most come from the sun or Earth's atmosphere. But a smattering of the particles—those moving much faster than the rest—traveled here from powerful sources farther away. —Thomas Lewton (2023), "A New Map of the Universe, Painted With Cosmic Neutrinos," *Quanta Magazine*

SOCIAL STUDIES

After the first day of battle, Meade replaced Abner Doubleday, commander of I Corps and a staunch Republican, with a more junior Democratic officer—a move that prompted criticism from within his own ranks. —Nicholas Liu (2023), "After Winning the Battle of Gettysburg, George Meade Fought With—and Lost to—the Press," *Smithsonian Magazine*

Let's Imagine . . . (Level 4)

When writers tackle topics with which their readers may not be familiar, it becomes more difficult to find an apt description. Perhaps they are writing about a breathtaking place the reader has never been. Or about a shocking play in a baseball game you had to see to believe. Or about a highly anticipated song with a fresh, innovative sound.

To do this, writers can appeal to the reader's imagination and ask them to call forth other sounds, emotions, images, or situations that might more precisely describe the topic for the reader. The following mentor text offers an elixir of pop culture allusions and everyday references. Managing all of this takes a deft hand. But it's also a fun, creative way to add description to a topic. The Let's Imagine . . . move comes alongside the reader like a co-conspirator, beckoning them to become not just a passive consumer but an active participant in uncovering the topic.

This is the basic formula: Topic + Claim + *imagine* + Specific Imaginative Scenario. Or, *imagine* + Specific Imaginative Scenario + Topic + Claim.

POP CULTURE

See figure 6.4 (page 92) for a mentor text that demonstrates this method.

As you teach this move to your students, here are some things to consider.

- » The writer has to be careful to paint an imaginative picture that will actually help the reader rather than confuse the reader.
    - * The imaginative comparison needs to be fairly brief and relatively simple.
    - * The imaginative journeys in these mentor texts are evocative yet simple and clear.
    - * The reader has to be able to easily hold the imaginative side trip in their head alongside the topic the writer is describing.
- » All of the following content-specific examples are evoking commonplace, easily accessible images that most readers should be able to relate to.
- » In our pop culture example, the writer presents the specific imaginative scenario first and then connects it to their topic and claim. It also works in the opposite order, with the topic and claim coming first! Students can play around with the order here to see what works best for them.

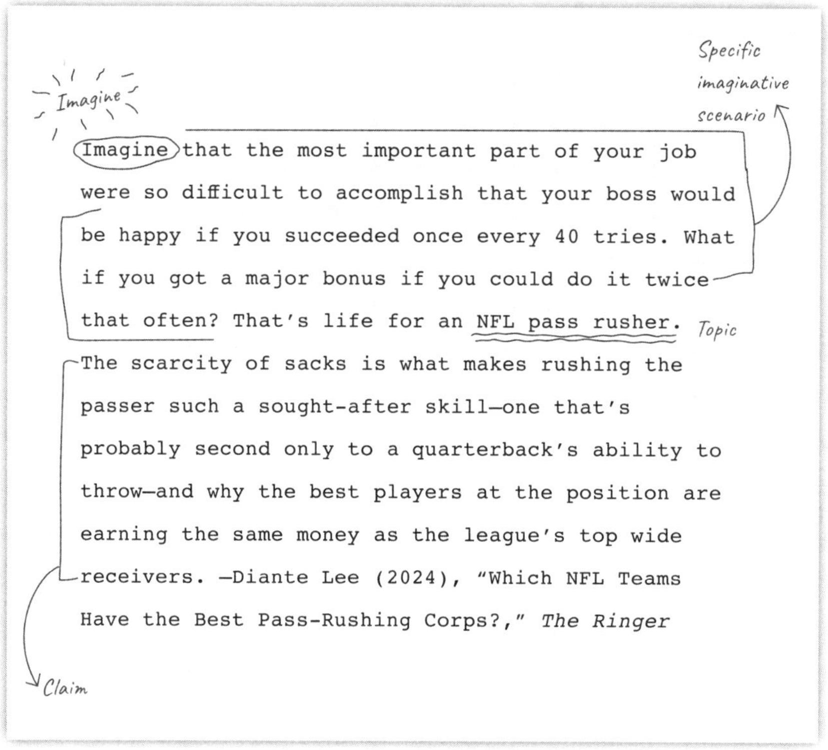

> *Imagine*
>
> (Imagine) that the most important part of your job were so difficult to accomplish that your boss would be happy if you succeeded once every 40 tries. What if you got a major bonus if you could do it twice that often? That's life for an NFL pass rusher. The scarcity of sacks is what makes rushing the passer such a sought-after skill—one that's probably second only to a quarterback's ability to throw—and why the best players at the position are earning the same money as the league's top wide receivers. —Diante Lee (2024), "Which NFL Teams Have the Best Pass-Rushing Corps?," *The Ringer*

Specific imaginative scenario · *Topic* · *Claim*

Figure 6.4: Let's Imagine . . . , annotated mentor text.

ENGLISH

Few delights bring as much comfort as good food, so imagine how cheering a good cup of coffee and a fresh donut would have been to soldiers on the front lines in World War II. But also imagine how women recruited to serve food to soldiers might view the value of their contribution when they see the life-and-death sacrifices those men had to make. That's one of the animating conflicts in the heartfelt novel *Good Night, Irene* from Pulitzer Prize finalist Luis Alberto Urrea. —Michael Magras (2023), "*Good Night, Irene* by Luis Alberto Urrea," *BookPage*

MATHEMATICS

Let's imagine our line-filling tiles to be letters that stick together to form sequences. If the tiles and the rules we adopt for placing them allow us to create a string of letters that goes on infinitely in both directions, we can "tile the line." For example, let's say we have two tiles, A and B, and two rules for putting them together:

1. Next to an A, on either side you can only place a B.
2. Next to a B, on either side you can only place an A.

Can we tile the line with these tiles and these rules? Absolutely. Suppose we put an A down first. —Patrick Honner (2023a), "Math Patterns That Go On Forever but Never Repeat," *Quanta Magazine*

SCIENCE

Bjånes likens the setup of their brain-machine interface to a football game. Imagine that your brain is the football stadium, and each of the neurons is a person in that stadium. The electrodes are the microphones you lower into the stadium to listen in. "We hope that we place those near the coach, or maybe an announcer, or near some person in the audience that really knows what's going on," he explains. "And then we're trying to understand what's happening on the field. When we hear a roar of the crowd, is that a touchdown? Was that a pass play? Was that the quarterback getting sacked? We're trying to understand the rules of the game, and the more information we can get, the better our device will be." —Marla Broadfoot (2023), "The Brain-Computer Interfaces That Could Give Locked-In Patients a Voice," *Smithsonian Magazine*

SOCIAL STUDIES

Imagine a heated prehistoric game of basketball where the two teams, the Skins and the Furs, use an inflated mammoth bladder for the ball. One player jams his finger and notes that it is pointing sideways. Instinctively, he yanks on it and successfully realigns the dislocation. Next week a teammate incurs the same injury, and the experienced one performs the same restorative maneuver. Over time he continues to learn from experience and achieves local acclaim as the go-to bonesetter. These skills are then passed down to his children. These bonesetters, along with shamans, midwives, and herbalists, developed in many cultures, including ancient Egypt and early Hawaii. —Roy A. Meals (2020), "A Brief History of Surgeons," *Lapham's Quarterly*

Figurative Language Comparison (Level 5)

When we ask students to use the Let's Imagine . . . move, we ask them to think about their topic and call forth what they hear, see, think, smell, and feel. Figurative Language Comparison demands a much more direct, creative, and abstract parallel between what is and what isn't. Figurative Language Comparison pulls the reader into the writer's psyche by drawing a descriptive likeness between the writer's topic and something unexpected.

In the Figurative Language Comparison move, writers elicit figurative language techniques, like metaphor, simile, personification, hyperbole, onomatopoeia, and more. What follows is an examination of a mini-mentor text from Laura Snapes's (2023) review of Olivia Rodrigo's single "vampire." Snapes wants to describe the song's sound, particularly the way it builds as the song progresses. But how does she describe that sound—that feeling the sound infuses into the listener—without playing the song? She anthropomorphizes the instruments, she personifies the pre-chorus, and she uses metaphor and simile to compare the song's crescendo to concepts that the reader associates with urgency.

The power here is the fact that writers use interesting and occasionally unusual pieces of figurative language. These aren't clichés. They make the reader pause for a moment, conjuring a feeling, an image, or an experience they can use to build a connection.

This is the basic formula: (Topic + Comparative Figurative Language)Ad Infinitum.

POP CULTURE

See figure 6.5 for an annotated mentor text that uses this method.

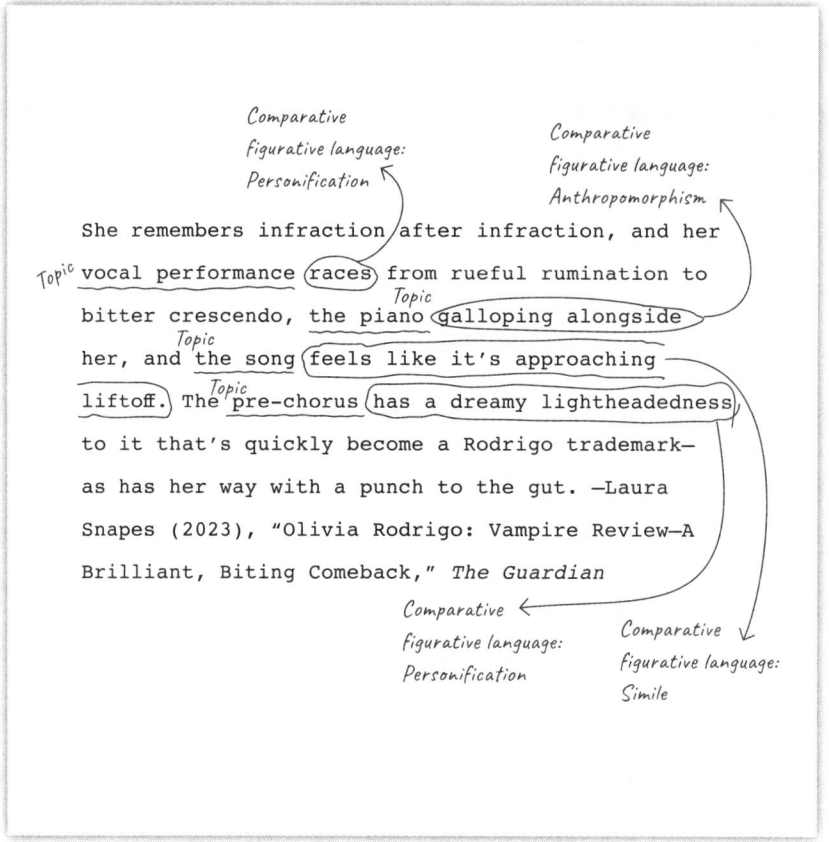

Figure 6.5: Figurative Language Comparison, annotated mentor text.

As you teach this move to your students, here are some things to consider.

- » Notice that Snapes uses multiple pieces of figurative language here—two examples of personification, a metaphor, and a simile all in two sentences! It's not necessary to stack pieces of figurative language in this way, but it does pack a punch!
- » While the writer doesn't want to craft figurative language that is so strange it throws the reader completely offtrack, the writer does want to make the figurative language highly specific. This is for two reasons.
  * First, clichéd figurative language—the kinds of similes and metaphors that you've heard a million times before—doesn't actually add description that helps the reader.
  * Second, when the writer begins dealing in clichés, the reader's eyes glaze over, and the writer loses the opportunity to make the reader see the topic in a new way. The more specific the figurative language, the clearer the reader's understanding.
- » In some ways, the writer is drawing out a reader's own experiences when crafting this figurative language. You might ask students to share what the figurative language in this particular example causes them to think about or understand differently. (Perhaps they could sketch it or turn and talk with a peer.)
  * For example, when we read Snapes's description of Rodrigo's song, we can almost physically feel the increasing pace and building tension because she tells us the song "races," is "galloping," and is "approaching liftoff."
  * As we think about the song, we see horses running. And that simile—"like it's approaching liftoff"—makes us think of movies with astronauts strapped into their seats in a rocket, filled with adrenaline and anticipation and total fear as the ship rumbles deafeningly beneath them.
  * Without hearing the song, the reader becomes physically engaged through the use of figurative language not typically associated with music.

ENGLISH

Seemingly overnight, Bridget was to digital correspondence what Chandler Bing was to comic timing: a fresh metronome for the last gasp of the 20th century. —Elisabeth Egan (2023), "Bridget Jones Deserved Better. We All Did," *The New York Times*

MATHEMATICS

These classical problems could go down in infamy as sirens whose songs lured mathematicians to crash on the rocky shores of impossibility. But I see them as muses who inspired generations of creative thinkers. —David S. Richeson (2020), "When Math Gets Impossibly Hard," *Quanta Magazine*

SCIENCE

We make an analogy to an orchestra. The musicians need to play in synchrony for the music to work. When you lose the cellos and the woodwinds, the remaining musicians can't deliver the piece as effectively as when all players are present. Similarly, when brain tumors hijack the areas surrounding it, the brain is less able to effectively function. —Saritha Krishna and Shawn Hervey-Jumper (2023), "Brain Tumors Are Cognitive Parasites—How Brain Cancer Hijacks Neural Circuits and Causes Cognitive Decline," *The Conversation*

SOCIAL STUDIES

Celebrity culture is religion in disguise. It pretends to be junk while giving us the sustenance that we need. Celebrities live like gods; they act like gods. They dwell in the dark recesses of our souls where we crave the images of gods. In the aisles of the supermarkets they stare down at us like the saints and gargoyles that once crowded the cornices of medieval cathedrals with the iconography of suffering, or like sculptures in Hindu temples that celebrate birth, sex, death, rebirth. —Stephen Marche (2011), "Consumer Products," *Lapham's Quarterly*

Use the reproducible "Writing Application Practice: Moves That Describe" (page 98) to describe.

Student Samples

The following student samples include moves that describe.

This sample uses Describing Lists (level 1):

> Just like every other day I came home from school, but something was missing. The feeling of a full house, the sound of paws thumping down the stairs to find me, and the feeling of fur brushing up against my legs. She was gone. Hope was gone. —Milania, Eleventh Grade

This sample uses Let's Imagine . . . (level 4):

> Volunteering is a rush. Imagine you've just helped your friend study for a test and they end up getting a really good grade. That tingling of dopamine and selflessness floods your body. You feel as if you're glowing with generosity. —Aly, Eleventh Grade

This sample uses Figurative Language Comparison (level 5):

> Hard work is a whetstone. It sharpens your senses, your ethics, your personality, and even your relationships. —Beck, Eleventh Grade

Writing Application Practice: Moves That Describe

After teaching your students one of these moves—or all of these moves—you'll be looking for an opportunity for them to practice these skills immediately.

For each writing task, we have provided a prompt you could use to get your students writing. They can use this prompt to practice a single move for that writing task or to begin combining, mixing, and matching moves. You can find all writing application practice from the whole book in one place in appendix C (page 275).

Content Area	Writing Application Practice
English	Describe a moment from your life—just a few minutes—that has left a powerful imprint on your memory. Which moves that describe can help you bring this moment to life for a reader?
Mathematics	Describe how you solved the hardest problem in last night's mathematics homework. Find a move (or moves) that describes to help you.
Science	Describe the process you used to conduct an experiment or lab. How might the moves that describe help you make your process clear and vivid to a reader?
Social Studies	Use the Library of Congress or another database to locate a primary source that relates to a current topic you have studied in social studies. Use a move or multiple moves that describe to help your reader see that source.

Mini Moves for Every Writer © 2025 Solution Tree Press • SolutionTree.com

Visit **go.SolutionTree.com/literacy/MMEW** to download this free reproducible.

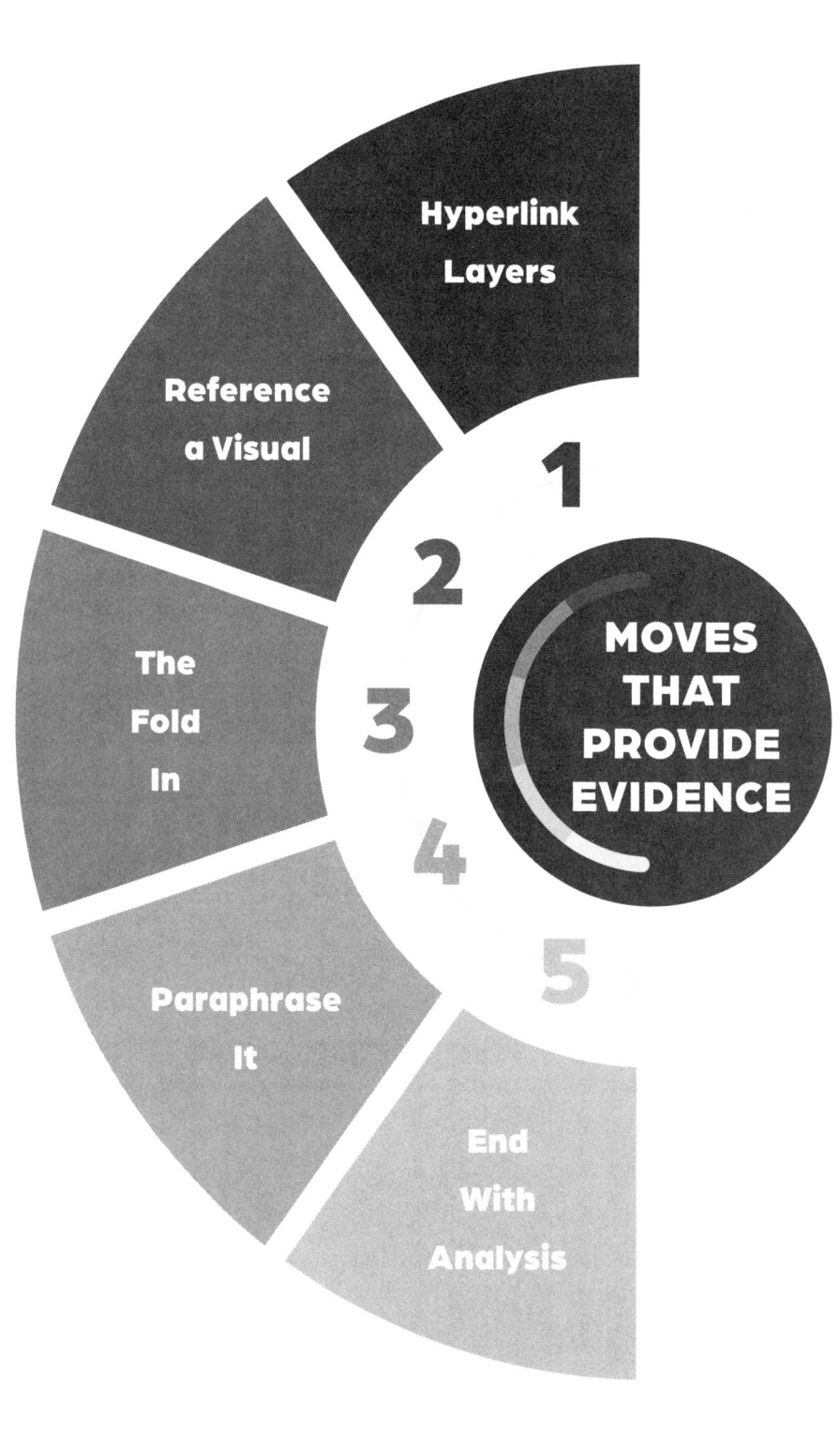

CHAPTER 7

Moves That Provide Evidence

Evidence—the stuff writers use to help prove their claims—is a cornerstone of non-fiction writing. Like writing claims, incorporating evidence can be fraught with rigid rules and expectations. For instance, colleges and universities across the United States have some pretty concrete ideas about how writers should provide evidence in their writing.

According to the University of Michigan's Gayle Morris Sweetland Center for Writing (n.d.), there are three ways to incorporate evidence into academic writing:

- Quotation, which is anything from a word to several sentences taken word-for-word from the original source and enclosed in quotation marks
- Paraphrase, which is a rephrasing in your own voice and sentence structure of one portion of the original source and is about the same length as the original sentence or sentences you are paraphrasing
- Summary, which is shorter than the original source and gives the text's central idea in your own words

Writing Tutorial Services (n.d.) at Indiana University Bloomington tells us this:

In order to use evidence effectively, you need to integrate it smoothly into your essay by following this pattern:
1. State your claim.
2. Give your evidence, remembering to relate it to the claim.
3. Comment on the evidence to show how it supports the claim.

Providing yet another different perspective, the Harvard College Writing Program's (n.d.) *Guide to Using Sources* says that "scholars in the humanities tend to summarize, paraphrase, and quote texts; social scientists and natural scientists rely primarily on summary and paraphrase."

However, despite these institutions' claims that there are strict rules for providing evidence, their inability to agree on one method proves that there are, in fact, many different ways writers can incorporate evidence into their work.

We believe there are many different ways to provide evidence, and like the University of North Carolina at Chapel Hill's Writing Center (n.d.), we believe evidence can come in many different forms—hyperlinks, text references, and visuals, just to name a few. In this chapter, we'll explore five moves that will help students incorporate evidence into their writing. See table 7.1 for recommended strategies to employ in certain circumstances.

Table 7.1: Writing Needs and Moves That Provide Evidence

When Writers Need...	Start Here...
To refer the reader directly to their sources	Hyperlink Layers (page 102)
To use a visual as evidence	Reference a Visual (page 105)
	End With Analysis (page 116)
To quote a text directly	The Fold In (page 110)
	End With Analysis (page 116)
To paraphrase a text	Paraphrase It (page 112)
To use a snippet of someone else's ideas to support their own	The Fold In (page 110)
	Paraphrase It (page 112)

Hyperlink Layers (Level 1)

Sometimes, the easiest way to cite a source and incorporate evidence is to direct the reader to the source itself. In this move, students will provide evidence to support their ideas by directly hyperlinking to sources via keywords in their writing. We love this move because it is so practical for 21st century students and nonacademic writers. This is a great way to reference a text, fold additional ideas into a piece of writing, and provide evidence without having to break up the writer's train of thought.

Now, because this is a book in print, we can't literally hyperlink. (Oh, that we could!) Instead, we've shared the hyperlinks' destinations in annotations in the pop culture mentor text and as numbered lists beneath each content-specific mentor text.

This is the basic formula: (Name the Topic + Ideas + Keywords With Hyperlink) Ad Infinitum.

POP CULTURE

See figure 7.1 for an annotated mentor text that incorporates hyperlinks.

Here are some other features you and your students might consider together.

» We always have to remind our students how to hyperlink keywords—you might, too! It's Ctrl+K on a PC and Command+K on a Mac.

» The central topics of the piece (in this case, Beyoncé and *Cowboy Carter*) are named quickly here (and in the other mentor texts listed) to help orient the reader.

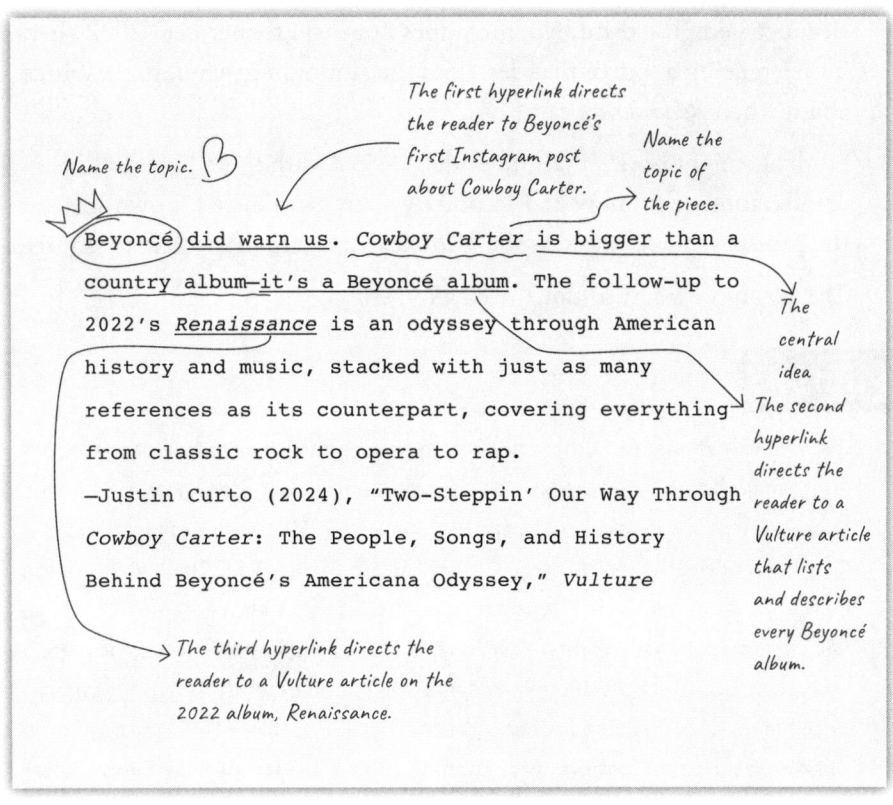

Figure 7.1: Hyperlink Layers, annotated mentor text.

» The first hyperlink comes before the central idea. This is completely optional—students can have fun playing with the order of the components of the Hyperlink Layers move.

» The number of keywords that are used for hyperlinks is less important than the words themselves. In the pop culture mentor text, the keywords of the first hyperlink create a fragment, the keywords of the second hyperlink could stand alone as a sentence, and only one keyword is used for the third hyperlink. The writer's goal is to choose the fewest number of words that directly allude to the source and topic they are referencing. Less is more here, but there are no hard-and-fast rules.

» A hyperlink is essentially akin to a reference or even an allusion, so it's important to select the keywords that best describe that allusion. For example, the first hyperlink does not include Beyoncé's name because what the author is referencing is not really about Beyoncé but about something

Beyoncé said. The third hyperlink does not include the year "2022" because it's referencing a source that describes the album in general, not a source about when *Renaissance* came out.

» Students might notice that the evidence cited with these hyperlinks is a combination of primary and secondary sources—Beyoncé's own Instagram is the primary source, whereas the *Vulture* articles are the secondary sources.

» The author's own ideas don't need a hyperlink.

ENGLISH

It's a minor-league mind that chooses to make sport of sports. Not that there aren't major-league authors who do so, among them George Orwell[1] ("Serious sport is war minus the shooting") and H. L. Mencken[2] ("It is impossible to imagine Goethe[3] or Beethoven being good at billiards or golf"). Their thinking hurts the ball club. As a nation, it is through the prism of sports that we frame our ethical values, remember our history, envision our future, and find the figures of speech that create our common culture and define our national identity. Walt Whitman[4] once whimsically described American democracy as "athletic"; history has borne out his observation in more ways than he could have foreseen. —Simon Apter (2010), "Wordplay," *Lapham's Quarterly*

```
1. A brief Lapham's Quarterly biography of George Orwell
2. A brief Lapham's Quarterly biography of H. L. Mencken
3. A brief Lapham's Quarterly biography of Johann Wolfgang von Goethe
4. "Playing Ball and Base," an essay wishing American men were able to
   spend more time outdoors in athletic recreational pursuits by Walt
   Whitman
```

MATHEMATICS

After the start of the pandemic, Yang-Hui He[1], a researcher at the London Institute for Mathematical Sciences, decided to take on some new challenges. He had been a physics major in college, and had gotten his doctorate from the Massachusetts Institute of Technology in mathematical physics. But he was increasingly interested in number theory, and given the increasing capabilities of artificial intelligence, he thought he'd try his hand at using AI as a tool for finding unexpected patterns in numbers. (He had already been using machine learning[2] to classify Calabi-Yau manifolds[3], mathematical structures that are widely used in string theory.) —Lyndie Chiou (2024a), "Elliptic Curve 'Murmurations' Found With AI Take Flight," *Quanta Magazine*

```
1. A brief biography of Yang-Hui He at the London Institute
2. An academic article about machine learning by Yang-Hui He
3. A Quanta Magazine article about the mathematician Eugenio Calabi and
   his work
```

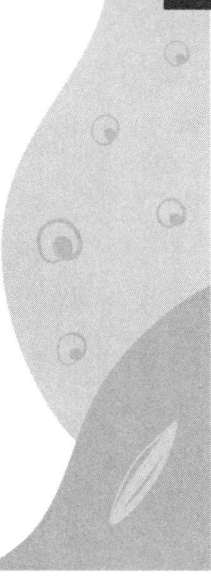

SCIENCE

The age of dinosaurs was probably longer than you think. *T. rex* lived at the end of the Cretaceous period, just before the dinosaur-killing asteroid strike[1] 66 million years ago. *Stegosaurus*[2], and other popular Jurassic dinosaurs such as *Diplodocus*[3], lived around 150 million years ago. —Abi Crane (2024), "Five Things You Probably Have Wrong About the *T. rex*," *JSTOR Daily*

```
1. An academic article from Biological Sciences affirming that an
   asteroid, not a volcano, caused dinosaur extinction
2. A profile of a Stegosaurus from the Natural History Museum, London
3. A profile of a Diplodocus from the Natural History Museum, London
```

SOCIAL STUDIES

When it comes to war, American leaders have a long history of deceiving the public. In light of the Congressional introduction of the Executive Accountability Act in 2009[1], scholar Louis Fisher examines a record of misleading statements by US presidents used to justify conflicts[2], including the Mexican-American[3], Spanish-American[4], Vietnam[5], and Iraq[6] wars. —Matthew Wills (2024), "Using False Claims to Justify War," *JSTOR Daily*

```
1. A GovInfo profile of the Executive Accountability Act (2009)
2. A scholarly article from Presidential Studies Quarterly about
   misleading statements by presidents
3. A JSTOR article about the Treaty of Guadalupe Hidalgo
4. A JSTOR article about the annexation of Cuba
5. A JSTOR article about the confluence of opposition to the Vietnam War
   and men coming out as gay
6. A JSTOR article about how American soldier Jessica Lynch became a
   symbol of women in the U.S. military
```

Reference a Visual (Level 2)

Sometimes, when teaching writing to our students, we can easily get pinned into teaching evidence as something that comes from a text. However, evidence can come in many forms. In the case of this move, it comes in the form of a visual.

Pull up the home page of any major news outlet, magazine, or journal, and we guarantee you'll find a visual in almost every piece of writing. Writers use visuals—photographs, videos, screenshots of email exchanges, graphs, drawings, and so on—to provide the reader with evidence that they can see.

When using a visual as evidence, writers will not only name the subject and describe what they see but also provide commentary on the image. This could come in the form of an observation, context, or analysis, depending on the writer's needs.

For this move, we've added an annotated mentor text from only a pop culture example to a social studies one with a visual. "Why?" you may ask. The answer: copyright laws!

You'll also notice that the other mentor texts do not include images. "Why?" you may ask again. The answer, once again, is copyright laws. Instead, we've let ChatGPT describe these images for you. We think ChatGPT did a pretty great job, but we highly encourage you to visit the original articles to look at the images with your students.

This is the basic formula: Visual + Citation + Name the Subjects + Describe + Commentary.

SOCIAL STUDIES

See figure 7.2 for a mentor text that references visuals.

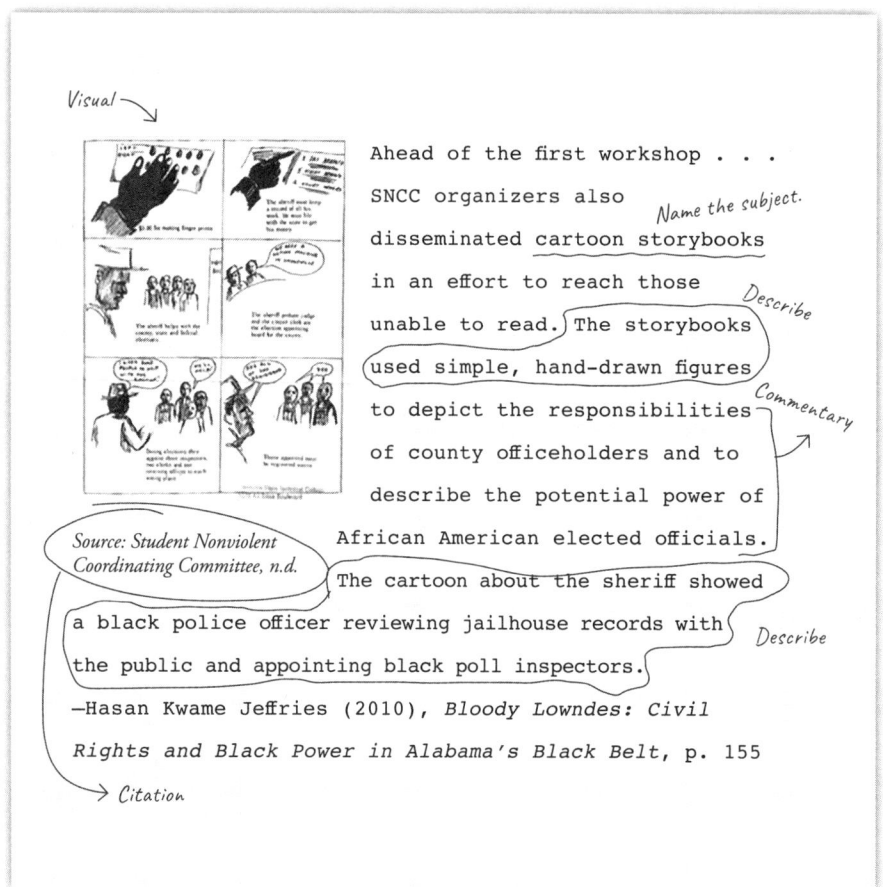

Source for description: Developed collaboratively with Gemini. (2025, March 23). Gemini [Large language model]. Accessed at https://gemini.google.com/app/3397db10768b8898 on March 23, 2025.

Figure 7.2: Reference a Visual, annotated mentor text example one.

Here are some extra tidbits to consider as you share this move with students.

» Students will probably notice that the citation for this visual is included directly below the image. While the citation style (APA, MLA, Chicago, and so on) might differ from publication to publication, a citation is usually provided directly beneath the visual. Here, historian Hasan Kwame Jeffries cites the creator of the freedom primer: the Student Nonviolent Coordinating Committee (SNCC).

» The subject of the visual is named at the beginning of the first sentence. If there are no people featured in the image to name, the author might just share the type of source they're referencing, like Jeffries does here.

» To describe a visual, the author answers the question, "What do you see?" Here, if Jeffries were asked, "What do you see in this cartoon storybook?" his answer could be the following.

  * "Simple, hand-drawn figures"
  * "A Black police officer reviewing jailhouse records with the public"
  * "The sheriff . . . appointing Black poll inspectors"

» Students might notice that the description leads the author directly into their analysis. In this example, Jeffries's analysis of the storybooks evaluates their purpose and significance in the Lowndes County Black Power movement.

POP CULTURE

See figure 7.3 for another mentor text that references a visual.

Name the subject.

Describe the visual.

(Michelle Yeoh) looks like a classic movie star at the Balenciaga Couture show in this floor-length leather trench and oversize sunnies. I want to channel this energy every time I leave the house. —Brooke LaMantia (2024), "What Michelle Yeoh, Tyler, the Creator, and Paris Hilton Wore This Week," *The Cut*

Commentary

[The image that would be provided alongside the writing in this figure shows Michelle Yeoh wearing a long black leather coat with a belt at the waist. She is also wearing large, dark sunglasses. The scene appears to be outside, likely at an event or a gathering, as there are photographers and people around her taking pictures. Her hair is short and dark. She is confident, while a crowd of onlookers and security personnel surround her. The overall atmosphere suggests a high-profile event.]

Source for description: Developed collaboratively with Gemini. (2025, April 23). Gemini [Large language model]. Accessed at https://gemini.google.com/app/3397db10768b8898 on March 23, 2025.

Figure 7.3: Reference a Visual, annotated mentor text example two.

ENGLISH

Behold the hulking Arctic explorer Peter Freuchen and his chic wife, Dagmar, in an unforgettable picture from 1947. . . .

. . . For one thing, look at the proportions! He is so *large*, swaddled in a colossal polar-bear coat, and she is so *tiny*, in her pert black suit and pearls, her one extravagance (a hat with a bow and netting, the millinery trend in those days) dwarfed by his opulent pelage. And then there are their expressions. His: leathered and intimidating, as if he were staring down a predator he intends to harpoon.

[*The image is a black-and-white photograph featuring two individuals, a man and a woman, who are both dressed in distinctive attire.*

- *Man on the left: He is standing and wearing an oversized, heavy fur coat that almost engulfs him, making him appear larger and more imposing. The fur coat is thick and covers him from his shoulders down to his ankles. The man's facial expression is serious, with a full beard, adding to his rugged appearance.*
- *Woman on the right: She is seated on what appears to be a draped fabric or cushion. She is dressed elegantly in a dark, formal outfit with a knee-length dress and heels. She is also wearing a stylish hat with a decorative element, which adds to the sophisticated look. Her pose is composed, with one leg crossed over the other and her hands resting on her lap.*

The photograph likely has a historical or artistic context, with the contrasting appearances of the two subjects creating a striking visual effect. The man's grandiose fur coat contrasts with the woman's refined and polished look, suggesting a juxtaposition of ruggedness and elegance.] —Rachel Syme (2019), "An Irving Penn Portrait for the Coldest Days of Winter," *The New Yorker*

MATHEMATICS

This movie created by the Harvard-led team shows the execution of a 48-logical-qubit circuit, which they say is the most advanced circuit ever executed on a quantum computer. Groups of eight atomic qubits are first brought together and entangled into error-corrected logical qubit blocks, indicated by red ovals. These blocks are then entangled with each other to create a circuit with hundreds of logical gate operations. . . .

At the end of the computation, lasers read out atoms' states: If an atom is in the state that is resonant with the illumination, the light is scattered, but if it's in the other state, there's no scattering.

[*In this image, a grid-like pattern consisting of small green dots arranged in two distinct rectangular groups. The top group has a more extensive and sparse arrangement, while the bottom group appears denser with a more compact arrangement of dots. The background is light, allowing the green dots to stand out clearly.*] —Philip Ball (2024a), "The Best Qubits for Quantum Computing Might Just Be Atoms," *Quanta Magazine*

SCIENCE

A normal *Arabidopsis* seedling (right) bends toward light incoming from the right, while a mutant with water-flooded air channels (left) grows straight upward. Cross sections of the stems show why: Normal air channels create a gradient from brightness to darkness across the plant's cells (shown here using fluorescent methods) that indicates the light's direction. Mutant seedlings with water-flooded channels have no light gradient, and therefore can't sense in which direction to grow.

[*The image shows two elongated plant structures, likely young seedlings or stems, positioned side by side against a black background. Each plant is associated with a magnified circular inset, displaying a close-up of the cellular structure.*

- *Center: The two plant structures are bent differently. The one on the left is relatively straight with a slight curvature at the base, while the one on the right is curved more significantly towards the left side of the image.*
- *Inserts: The circular insets on either side of the plants reveal a green honeycomb-like cellular pattern, suggesting that the cells are being viewed under a microscope, possibly using fluorescence imaging. The left inset shows the structure from the straight plant, and the right one corresponds to the more curved plant.*
- *Label: There is a label on the right side of the image indicating the "Direction of light," with an arrow pointing leftward. This suggests that the curvature in the plant on the right is likely due to phototropism, where plants grow towards a light source.*]

—Asher Elbein (2024), "Plants Find Light Using Gaps Between Their Cells," *Quanta Magazine*

The Fold In (Level 3)

In her English classes, Rebekah has long waged a battle against "the Plop." You've seen it. The Plop is what students do when they know they need evidence but don't know which evidence or how much evidence to use. So, they use it all. They just plop an entire paragraph of evidence into the middle of their writing and leave it there for the reader to trip over.

The Fold In is the remedy for the Plop.

The Fold In is a classic move writers use when they want to provide evidence for their ideas by quoting a source. The Fold In allows writers to segue in and out of a quote without any gap between their ideas and the quote. It's slick and sophisticated and screams authority.

While this move is fairly simple, it requires precision and a solid understanding of punctuation. It also necessitates a comprehensive understanding of the text and how it fits into the writer's ideas. But when used correctly, the Fold In is perfect for writers who need to cite evidence from a text to seamlessly support their ideas. You'll see it pop up again in Quote It to Me (chapter 8, page 123).

This is the basic formula: Ideas + Name the Source + Text Evidence.

POP CULTURE

See figure 7.4 for an annotated mentor text demonstrating this method.

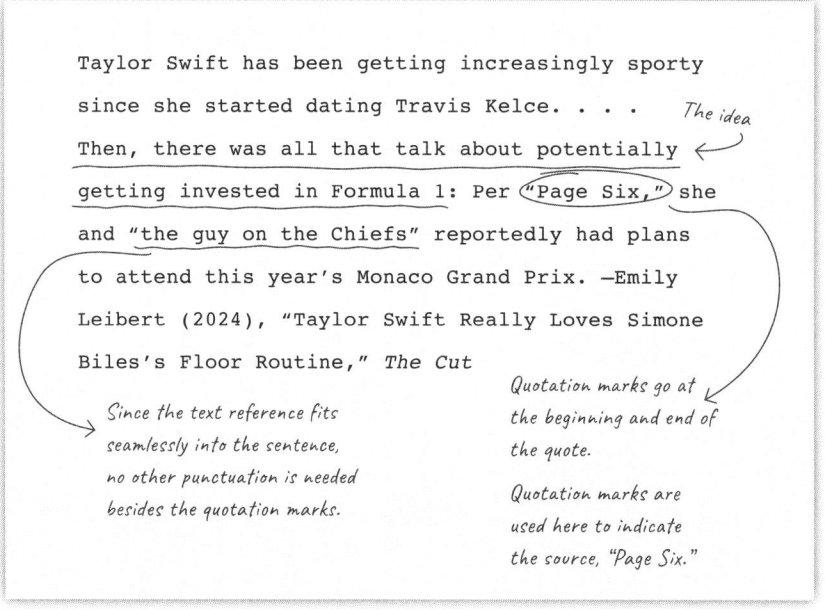

Figure 7.4: The Fold In, annotated mentor text.

Consider this when sharing this move with your students.

» One of the first things we would point out to our students is how short the text reference is. This is a key component of the Fold In—students should be taking small excerpts from a text to weave them into their sentences.

» If read aloud, a text that uses the Fold In move should have no pause between the author's ideas and the text evidence.

» Students may notice that there is no verb of attribution here ("Taylor Swift said . . ."). The seamless flow of the Fold In makes this more formal quotation component unnecessary. However, if students would like to incorporate a verb of attribution, they certainly can. See the following mathematics and science (page 112) mentor texts, which retain the weaving vibe of the Fold In while directly linking the quote to its source.

» One tip we usually give our students as they're trying out this move is to write the sentence or sentences they'd like to use without text evidence. Then, we would advise them to go back through the source they are writing about and choose an excerpt that will, with a little tweaking, fit into what they have already written.

ENGLISH

Christie's home life sputtered at approximately the rate her career took off. She seems to have had a take-it-or-leave-it attitude to motherhood, ditching Rosalind for months at a stretch and neglecting to answer the unhappy girl's letters. Later Christie would describe Rosalind as playing "the valuable role in life of eternally trying to discourage me without success." —Molly Young (2022), "Agatha Christie's Latest Biographer Plumbs a Life of Mystery," *The New York Times*

MATHEMATICS

Convex pentagons that tile the plane were trickier to classify. Reinhardt discovered five families of such pentagons; 50 years later, Richard Kershner found three more. Then in 1975, Martin Gardner wrote about the problem for *Scientific American*, bringing it to the attention of professional and amateur mathematicians alike. One such amateur, a computer programmer named Richard James III, sent Gardner an example of a ninth family, asking, "Do you agree that Kershner missed this one?" He had. —David S. Richeson (2023a), "A Brief History of Tricky Mathematical Tiling," *Quanta Magazine*

SCIENCE

A unique feature of hydrothermal vents is that they form structures composed of billions of minuscule microchambers, each contained and exposed to different conditions and reactants. They constitute a "vast array of simultaneously running semi-independent experiments," Brunk and Marshall described. —Ross Pomeroy (2024), "The Ocean Vents Where Life on Earth Likely Began," *JSTOR Daily*

SOCIAL STUDIES

Unlike most of the anti-slavery movement's white leaders, Birney was a southerner and an enslaver when he joined the cause. To navigate this conflicted position and complicated questions of emancipation and colonization, Birney turned to study. He "read almost every work [he] could lay his hands on" in the winter of 1833 and spring of 1834 and was transformed by what he read. —Marcy Dinius (2024), "The Power of Pamphlets in the Anti-Slavery Movement," *JSTOR Daily*

Paraphrase It (Level 4)

How many times a school year do you have to define *paraphrasing* to your students? We can't even tally it—it's a mind-boggling number. Paraphrasing is the art of rephrasing and repurposing someone else's ideas to use as evidence in your own writing. And it's an incredibly important skill for students to learn, but many students avoid paraphrasing because (1) it's more difficult than quoting directly and (2) they're worried about plagiarizing.

We like to tell our students that paraphrasing goes beyond scrambling up someone else's words (which is what they tend to think it is). Paraphrasing requires the writer to understand how something someone else said fits into their writing and works in conjunction with their ideas. And while there are no strict rules to paraphrasing, if students follow the three paraphrasing guidelines, they will not have to worry about accidentally plagiarizing someone else's work.

1. Paraphrasing should always be used as evidence to support the writer's own ideas.

2. The message of the original text should remain the same, but the words should not.

3. The original author should always be cited, formally and informally.

If your students are like ours, they struggle with rephrasing someone else's words. Here are some tips that we use with our students.

- Read the original text, cover it up, and summarize what it said.
- Write an answer to the question, "How does this information support my point?"
- Write an answer to the question, "What unique information or perspective does this source provide?"
- Try to summarize the original text in half its original length (for instance, if it were four sentences, try to rephrase it in two).

We have included the original text of the paraphrased source above each of the mentor texts. Use these to show students how the author rephrased and repurposed the original text to support their points.

This is the basic formula: Your Idea + Author Name + Phrase of Attribution + Paraphrased Evidence.

POP CULTURE

See figure 7.5 for an example of Paraphrase It.

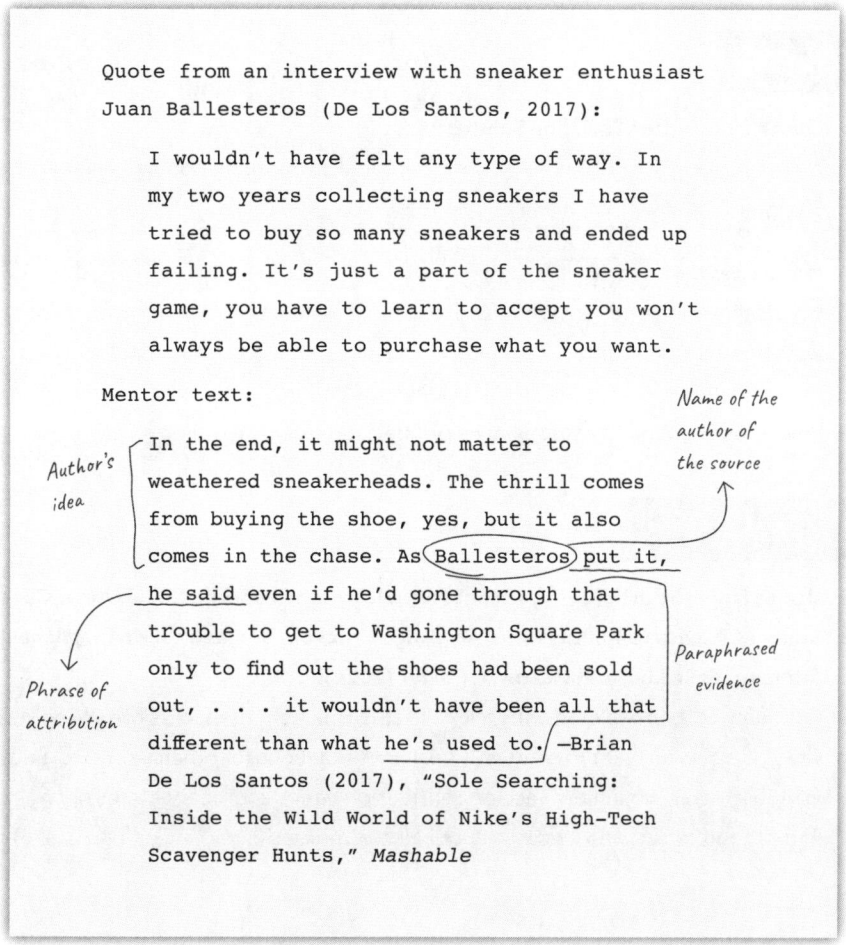

Figure 7.5: Paraphrase It, annotated mentor text.

As you teach this move to your students, here are some things to consider.

- » Students may notice that the author's central idea, "the thrill comes from buying the shoe" and "in the chase," is not exactly how Ballesteros describes his affinity for sneakerdom. This is this author's unique idea—a theory that they have come up with in the course of researching for this piece.
- » The last name of the source is used because the author previously quoted Ballesteros in the piece.
- » The phrase of attribution comes directly before the paraphrase.
- » The paraphrase includes details that Ballesteros does not mention (such as Washington Square Park). Incorporating contextualizing details into the paraphrased evidence is an excellent way for an author to take ownership over the information.
- » Students might notice that the paraphrased evidence has shortened the length of the quote from two sentences to one. Considering how to make the source's information more concise is another great strategy for paraphrasing.
- » The evidence directly supports the author's original idea.

ENGLISH

Quote from writer Christine Schutt:
A story is a circle. —Christine Schutt, personal communication to Julia Phillips, Summer 2014

Mentor text:
I'm paraphrasing a brilliant writer and teacher, Christine Schutt, when I say that this way of structuring a story, returning in the end to the elements that were put in play at the start, is what gives the reader satisfaction. —Julia Phillips (2024), "Julia Phillips on the Writing Lessons of Fairy Tales," *Literary Hub*

MATHEMATICS

Quote from the article "Persistent Homology for Resource Coverage: A Case Study of Access to Polling Sites" by Abigail Hickok, Benjamin Jarman, Michael Johnson, Jiajie Luo, and Mason A. Porter (2024):
Although we have explored a specific case study (namely, the accessibility of polling sites), it is also relevant to conduct similar investigations for other resources, such as public parks, hospitals, vaccine distribution centers, grocery stores, Planned Parenthood clinics, and Department of Motor Vehicles (DMV) locations. (p. 498)

Mentor text:
Topology concerns itself with continuous shapes, and polling sites are at discrete locations. But in recent years, topologists have adapted their tools to work on discrete data by creating graphs of points connected by lines and then analyzing the properties of those graphs. Hickok said these techniques are useful not only for understanding the distribution of polling places but also for studying who has better access to hospitals, grocery stores and parks. —Lyndie Chiou (2024b), "Topologists Tackle the Trouble With Poll Placement," *Quanta Magazine*

SCIENCE

Quote from the book *The Science of Oriental Medicine, Diet and Hygiene* by Li Wing (1902):
When the Chinese commenced to study medicine they went at once to the root of different questions involved by practicing vivisection. Thousands of condemned criminals were taken and cut to pieces for the benefit of the living. In this way the functions of the vital organs, such as the kidneys, the liver, the stomach, the spleen and the heart were studied in the living person. The intensely important questions involved in the digestion of foods were determined as well as the effects of different drugs. These investigations, made while the man was still alive, were a thousand times more thorough and reliable than the guesswork which civilized physicians have practiced for many years by cutting up the bodies of dead men, when heat, motion and life are gone, and death has destroyed every function. (p. 10)

Mentor text:
A 1902 book by Los Angeles Chinese pharmacist Li Wing, *The Science of Oriental Medicine, Diet and Hygiene*, played on white Americans' beliefs about Asian barbarity. It claimed that Chinese doctors understood the human body better than American ones because they practiced vivisection on condemned criminals. —Livia Gershon (2022), "The Allure of Chinese Medicine," *JSTOR Daily*

SOCIAL STUDIES

Quote from "Memorial and Remonstrance Against Religious Assessments" by James Madison (1785):
Whilst we assert for ourselves a freedom to embrace, to profess and to observe the Religion which we believe to be of divine origin, we cannot deny an equal freedom to those whose minds have not yet yielded to the evidence which has convinced us. If this freedom be abused, it is an offence against God, not against man: To God, therefore, not to man, must an account of it be rendered.

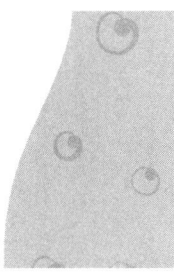

Mentor text:

James Madison believed that an established religion—a church whose doctrines were guaranteed and enforced by state law—did harm both to religion and to free government, and he found it abhorrent to imagine God being twisted to fit political expediency: this was, he said, to throw religion to the wolves. —Elisabeth Sifton (2010), "Church and State in America," *Lapham's Quarterly*

End With Analysis (Level 5)

In the End With Analysis move, writers will present their own idea, follow it up with evidence—usually in the form of a quote from a text—and then analyze how the evidence informs and affects the idea that they have introduced to the reader. It's a classic structure that English teachers have taught for eons because it just works *so* well.

In all our mentor texts, this move takes place within the body of the writing, but it could certainly be used to conclude the entire piece!

We love this move because its components can be neatly broken up into three paragraphs (though they don't have to be), which helps our students visualize the move's structure. This move also offers students a challenge. Ending a discussion of a topic with analysis is more of a risk than ending with evidence—what if the reader doesn't agree? But when writers are able to provide a well-crafted explication of the content, it is arguably the most powerful way to incorporate evidence into their writing.

This is the basic formula: Central Idea + Evidence + Analysis.

POP CULTURE

See figure 7.6 for a mentor text that demonstrates the End With Analysis move.

Some things that we might notice with our students follow.

- » The first paragraph begins with an observation, which allows the writer to easily segue into their topic.

- » The second sentence in the first paragraph is almost like a mini-claim statement. Considering the central idea that they plan to discuss as a mini claim can be a helpful strategy for students as they write.

- » The text evidence here is a quote from a person (John Donahoe) first mentioned in the idea component of the mentor text. The text reference should come from a source that is directly connected to the initial idea.

- » In the pop culture mentor text, the author transitions into their analysis with rhetorical questions, which are used to isolate flaws in Donahoe's line of reasoning.

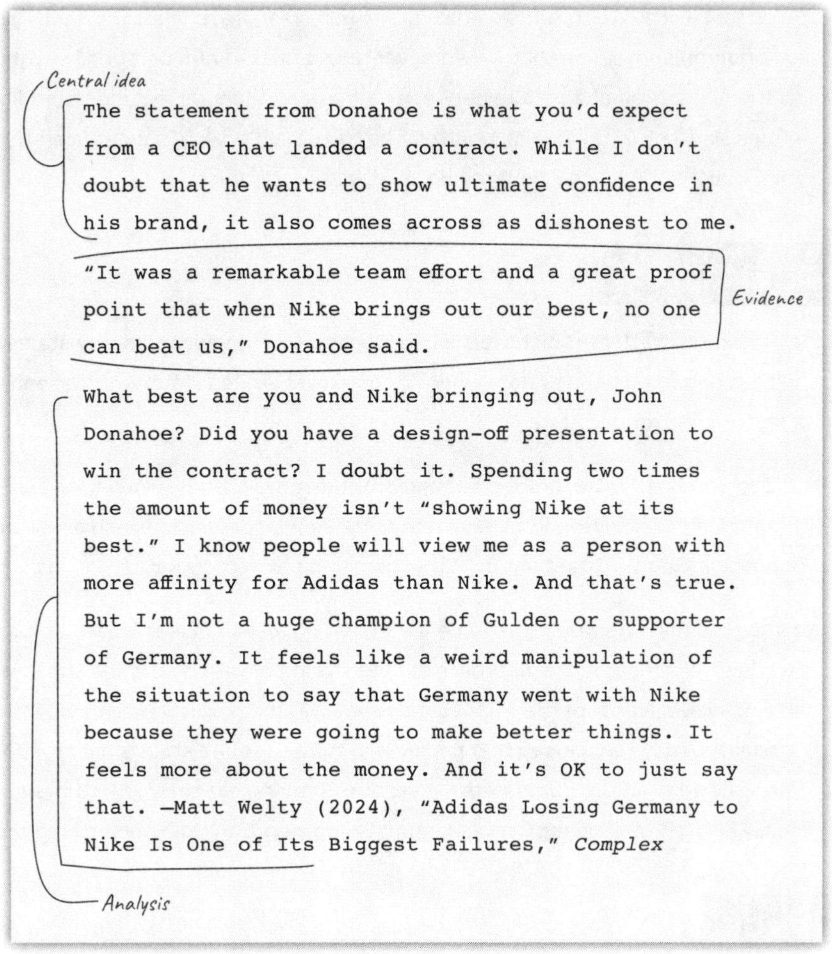

> *Central idea*
>
> The statement from Donahoe is what you'd expect from a CEO that landed a contract. While I don't doubt that he wants to show ultimate confidence in his brand, it also comes across as dishonest to me.
>
> "It was a remarkable team effort and a great proof point that when Nike brings out our best, no one can beat us," Donahoe said. — *Evidence*
>
> What best are you and Nike bringing out, John Donahoe? Did you have a design-off presentation to win the contract? I doubt it. Spending two times the amount of money isn't "showing Nike at its best." I know people will view me as a person with more affinity for Adidas than Nike. And that's true. But I'm not a huge champion of Gulden or supporter of Germany. It feels like a weird manipulation of the situation to say that Germany went with Nike because they were going to make better things. It feels more about the money. And it's OK to just say that. —Matt Welty (2024), "Adidas Losing Germany to Nike Is One of Its Biggest Failures," *Complex* — *Analysis*

Figure 7.6: End With Analysis, annotated mentor text.

» In their analysis, the author acknowledges their own bias and proves why, in this case, it is irrelevant. This technique adds credibility to their argument.

» The final lines of the mentor text tell the reader what their big takeaway about the topic should be and answer the question, "What are you ultimately trying to say about _____?"

ENGLISH

Perhaps even more disturbing than Offred's total erasure is the blasé nature with which the scholars of the epilogue regard the events of the novel. Pieixoto remarks "we must be cautious about passing moral judgment upon the Gileadean. Surely we have learned by now that such judgments are of necessity culture-specific." The professor listened to Offred's description of the tortures that women were subjected to during her time, yet he is reluctant to judge the perpetrators of her suffering. Dr. Pieixoto, as a male scholar, is viewing these historical events from the distant perspective of privilege, and as a result, like many real-life scholars, he is unwilling to condemn something that would never have affected him personally, writing off the oppression of an entire gender as a matter of cultural misunderstanding. —Anna Sheffer (2017), "The Epilogue of 'The Handmaid's Tale' Changes Everything You Thought You Knew About the Book," *Electric Literature*

MATHEMATICS

If we want to better predict the system's properties at various energy states, it helps to understand the system when it's in its least excited state, which scientists refer to as the ground state.

"A lot of chemists, material scientists and quantum physicists are working on finding ground states," said Robert Huang, one of the new paper authors and a research scientist at Google Quantum AI. "It is known to be extremely hard."

It's so hard that after more than a century of work, researchers still haven't found an effective computational approach to determining a system's ground state from first principles. Nor does there appear to be any way for a quantum computer to do it. Scientists have concluded that finding a system's ground state is hard for both classical and quantum computers. —Lakshmi Chandrasekaran (2024), "Physicists Finally Find a Problem That Only Quantum Computers Can Do," *Quanta Magazine*

SCIENCE

Programmed cell death appeared to create usable resources from dead parts. However, this process could only benefit relatives of the dead algae, he found. "It was actually harmful to those of a different species," Durand said. In 2022, another research group confirmed the finding in another algae.

The results possibly explain how cell death can evolve in single-celled creatures. If an organism is surrounded by kin, then its death can provide nutrition and therefore further its relatives' survival. That creates an opening for natural selection to select for the tools for self-induced death. —Veronique Greenwood (2024a), "Cellular Self-Destruction May Be Ancient. But Why?," *Quanta Magazine*

SOCIAL STUDIES

This issue came to a head in 2007 when the *Los Angeles Times* concluded an investigation into the investment practices of foundations by revealing that the Bill and Melinda Gates Foundation funded a polio vaccination clinic in Ebocha, Nigeria,

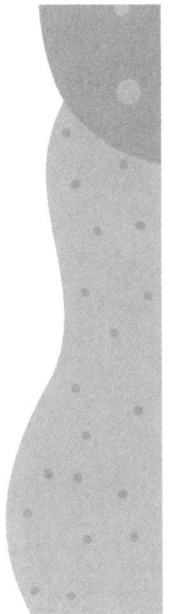

in the shadow of a giant petroleum-processing plant in which the Gates Foundation was invested. The *Los Angeles Times* report states:

> But polio is not the only threat Justice [a Nigerian child] faces. Almost since birth, he has had respiratory trouble. His neighbors call it "the cough." People blame fumes and soot spewing from flames that tower 300 feet into the air over a nearby oil plant. It is owned by the Italian petroleum giant Eni, whose investors include the Bill and Melinda Gates Foundation.

Despite the intense criticism at the time, the Gates Foundation did not change its course. An investigation of the Gates Foundation's tax return for 2013 performed by *The Guardian* revealed that the foundation held $1.4 billion of investment in fossil-fuel companies including BP and Anadarko (the latter of which was recently forced to pay $5 billion in environmental cleanup charges). —Curtis White (2015), "Philanthropy in the End Times," *Lapham's Quarterly*

Use the reproducible "Writing Application Practice: Moves That Provide Evidence" (page 121) to provide evidence.

Student Samples

The following student samples include moves that provide evidence.

This sample uses Hyperlink Layers (level 1):

> Heavy rains, a dam failure, and open floodgates flooded Nigeria on September 10, 2024. For years, villagers who lived near the Alau dam in Nigeria had told the government that the dam was broken and the reservoir behind the dam was too full. Alhaji Bukar Tijani, a government official, assured the worried locals that the dam was not broken. Four days later, water ripped through the Alau dam wall, flooding two-thirds of the city. The Nigerian media found budget records showing that money had been repeatedly given to fix the dam. But local people said nothing had been done to fix it or reduce the pressure it was under. Eight months before the dam collapsed, one of the engineers, Mala Gutti, warned dam officials that the structure was under a lot of pressure and was at risk of catastrophic failure. The officials replied that they already knew of the problem and were taking action. On September 10, because of the floods, hundreds of people died, and nearly half a million were displaced. Although the exact death count has not been released yet, authorities estimate it is almost 1000. On September 28, Agence France-Presse reported that about 2 million people had been affected, whether they died or they were misplaced, and about 50,000 families had been left homeless in Nigeria. The floods also destroyed crops and thousands of acres of farmland, making people

> worried about <u>food security</u>. The bridges connecting the city overflowed, so the two sides of the city were <u>completely disconnected</u>. —Tommy, Seventh Grade

This sample uses The Fold In (level 3):

> The Nigerian government blamed multiple factors for the dam breakage, including climate change. But the real cause of the dam breakage seems to be "years of government failure". —Maya, Seventh Grade

This sample uses End With Analysis (level 5):

> After the Vietnam War, the Vietnamese began the process of collectivization: developing peasant farming communes for the benefit of Vietnam. This policy required farmers to send any surplus of food directly to the government for redistribution elsewhere in the country. This strategy, while appearing successful on the surface, just led to a lack of incentive, as no one had any desire to farm above the bare necessities of what they needed to survive. This, paired with uncompetitive crop pricing, effectively destroyed the Vietnamese farming economy. —William, Eighth Grade

Writing Application Practice: Moves That Provide Evidence

After teaching your students one of these moves—or all of these moves—you'll be looking for an opportunity for them to practice these skills immediately.

For each writing task, we have provided a prompt you could use to get your students writing. They can use this prompt to practice a single move for that writing task or to begin combining, mixing, and matching moves. You can find all writing application practice from the whole book in one place in appendix C (page 275).

Content Area	Writing Application Practice
English	Evaluate how the setting of the novel you most recently read influences or affects one of the characters. Use one of the moves from this chapter to incorporate evidence from the text in your response.
Mathematics	Explain and evaluate how you solved your most recent mathematical problem. Use one of the moves from this chapter to incorporate evidence, either from the textbook or with a visual of your own work, in your response.
Science	Consider the most recent experiment you have conducted or studied in class. Choose one independent variable from the experiment, and explain how the increase or decrease of this variable would affect the results of the experiment. Be sure to include evidence in your response using one of the moves from this chapter.
Social Studies	Evaluate how the most recent event that you learned about in this class affected a person or group of people. Use one of the moves from this chapter to incorporate evidence into your response.

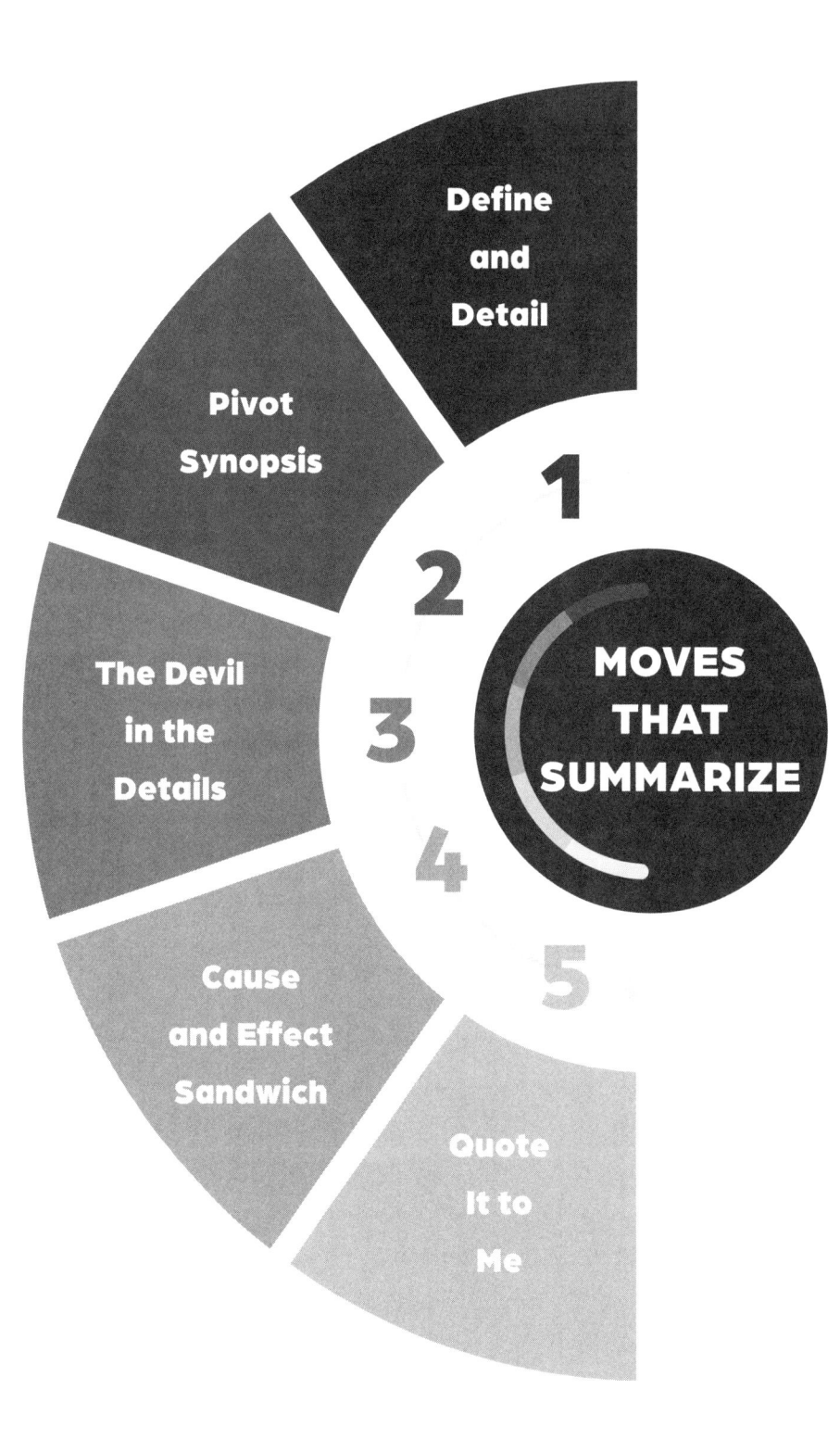

CHAPTER 8

Moves That Summarize

A summary helps a writer briefly share information about an event, place, person, idea, or thing with readers so that the writer can move on to the more complex analysis, synthesis, or argument within the piece.

Summarizing may seem like a basic writing skill—you're just telling someone about something, right? But in our experience, students have a tough time summarizing *well*. A well-written summary requires students to have a nuanced understanding of whatever they're summarizing, the ability to determine importance, and a firm handle on chronology. These are advanced skills! And when we add that we want the summary to sound interesting, too, well, things can get tricky really quickly.

But have no fear—in this chapter, we will look at five moves to help students draft outstanding summaries.

One way we tell our students to measure the success of their summary is to ask themselves if it can stand alone. While a summary may appear anywhere within a piece, students should always be able to remove the summary from the piece and have the summary make complete sense to any reader. Just like any piece of writing, a summary will always have a beginning, middle, and end. And while a summary may not share every single detail or offer up complex analysis every time, it will always give the reader an overview of the topic in question and answer the question, "What is _____ about?" See table 8.1 (page 124) for recommendations as to when summaries would prove most useful when writing.

Define and Detail (Level 1)

Define and Detail is a synopsis technique that allows writers to explain the most essential aspects of a topic while leaving room for a little flare. We love this move for our emerging writers because students can lean on two skills that they likely feel

Table 8.1: Writing Needs and Moves That Summarize

When Writers Need...	Start Here...
To write a brief synopsis	Define and Detail (page 123)
	Pivot Synopsis (page 127)
To summarize an event	Define and Detail (page 123)
	The Devil in the Details (page 129)
	Cause and Effect Sandwich (page 132)
To share something about the topic the reader might not have expected	Pivot Synopsis (page 127)
	Quote It to Me (page 136)
To cite evidence within the summary	The Devil in the Details (page 129)
	Cause and Effect Sandwich (page 132)
	Quote It to Me (page 136)
To tell a more descriptive, analytical story in the summary	The Devil in the Details (page 129)
	Quote It to Me (page 136)
To structure a summary that maintains chronological order	Define and Detail (page 123)
	Pivot Synopsis (page 127)
	Cause and Effect Sandwich (page 132)
To structure a summary that allows room to play with chronological order	The Devil in the Details (page 129)
	Quote It to Me (page 136)

pretty comfortable with—defining and listing. Our more experienced writers will see opportunities for complicating their details in this move with rich vocabulary, on-the-nose descriptions, and chronological play.

This is the basic formula: Name the Topic + Definition + Between Two and Six Details About the Topic.

POP CULTURE

See figure 8.1 for a mentor text that uses the Define and Detail method.

Here are some other features you and your students might consider together.

» The first thing we would point out is the simple construction of the definition sentence. We would remind students that longer, complicated sentences are not always better. Here, rather than crafting a lengthy introductory sentence, the authors add a bit of voice to the writing by personifying "Fortnight" with the verb "has arrived." This gives them room to set up a longer second sentence with a list of details.

» Notice that the first detail sneaks into the second sentence with "Post Malone collab." Modifying nouns in prepositional phrases before the verb can be a great way to succinctly add detail. Plus, teaching this to the class can be a nice moment for a grammar corner.

» The descriptiveness and contextualization of the details provided in the Define and Detail move example, as well as in the following content-area mentor texts, are highly audience specific. The authors of the pop culture mentor text assume their readers know who Post Malone is, so they do not feel the need to explain more about him here. Alternately, in the science mentor text (page 126), the author explains who James Webb was because even scientists might not know this specific reference.

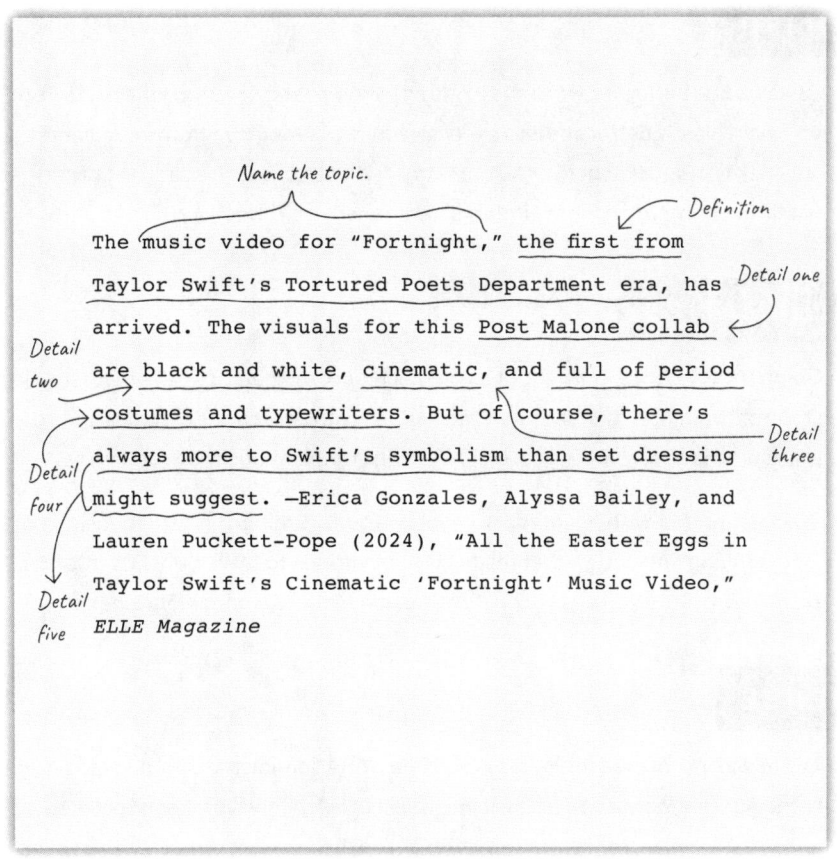

Figure 8.1: Define and Detail, annotated mentor text.

» An author is not going to tell the reader everything they need to know about the topic in this synopsis. This is merely an introduction—something to help the reader get mildly acquainted with the topic so that they can move on to the author's subsequent points.

» Students might ask how this move is different from a move that defines. Answer: It's really not that different! A simple synopsis is basically a definition with a lot of little details.

ENGLISH

Pasta nada is better known to the world as pantry pasta. These are the pasta dishes you make, vastly better and less expensive than ordering out, from ingredients that are already in your kitchen. —Dwight Garner (2024b), "Pasta Nada: The Culinary Art of Making Something From Nothing," *The New York Times*

MATHEMATICS

Graph theory can be thought of as a branch of combinatorics—the mathematical study of counting. Counting what can happen with collections of nodes and edges is, in some sense, a special case of counting combinations more generally.

The year ended with a landmark proof by four prominent mathematicians of a longstanding conjecture that relates combinatorics to the algebraic structure of sets. —Konstantin Kakaes (2023), "The Year in Math," *Quanta Magazine*

SCIENCE

The telescope, named for James Webb, the NASA administrator during the buildup to the Apollo moon landings, is a joint project of NASA, the European Space Agency and the Canadian Space Agency. It was launched on Christmas one year ago—after two trouble-plagued decades and $10 billion—on a mission to observe the universe in wavelengths no human eye can see. —Dennis Overbye (2022), "The Webb Telescope Is Just Getting Started," *The New York Times*

SOCIAL STUDIES

On November 29, 1947, the United Nations General Assembly adopted Resolution 181 (also known as the Partition Resolution) that would divide Great Britain's former Palestinian mandate into Jewish and Arab states in May 1948. Under the resolution, the area of religious significance surrounding Jerusalem would remain under international control administered by the United Nations. The Palestinian Arabs refused to recognize this arrangement, which they regarded as favorable to the Jews and unfair to the Arab population that would remain in Jewish territory under the partition. —Office of the Historian (n.d.), "The Arab-Israeli War of 1948"

Pivot Synopsis (Level 2)

A pivot synopsis contains the basic components of a standard synopsis; it answers the question, "What is this about?" and it gives a big overview of the topic in a few short sentences. But it always includes a pivot word—*but, then, however, except, not only*, and so on—to acknowledge tension, conflict, evolution, or change. This move allows writers to share a brief overview of the topic while acknowledging the topic's complexity.

This is the basic formula: Topic + Topic Overview + Pivot Word + Conflict or Tension Explanation.

POP CULTURE

See figure 8.2 for a mentor text where the Pivot Synopsis proves useful.

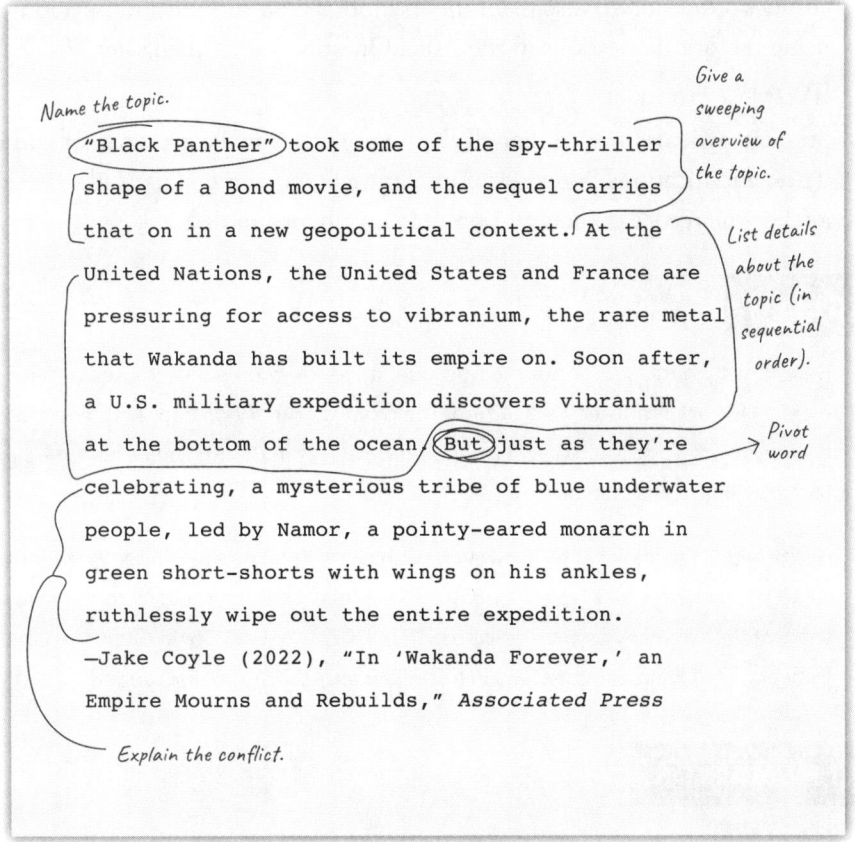

Figure 8.2: Pivot Synopsis, annotated mentor text.

Consider this when sharing this move with your students.

» The first thing we notice in the pop culture example is that it still gives a big overview of the topic. Starting with a bit of background on the first *Black Panther* film, it gives a sequential outline of what we need to know about the *Black Panther* sequel.

» The pivot word "but" allows us to understand something crucial: the conflict that will make *Black Panther: Wakanda Forever* worth watching.

» In the science mentor text, the writer uses a pivot word to ask a rhetorical question. We like to tell our students that when writing about a complicated topic, rhetorical questions are like step stools: They provide a little boost to help us reach something that feels out of our grasp. Here, using a rhetorical question is a great strategy for students who are struggling to identify a conflict or tension to discuss in their synopsis. You can learn more about using rhetorical questions in the Ask a Question move in chapter 10 (page 164).

» Students will also notice that all the mentor texts make great use of names, dates, and locations. Since a synopsis must stand alone, details like these help anchor the reader in facts and prevent misunderstanding.

ENGLISH

Relentlessly harassed about his homosexuality by both schoolmates and his especially harsh mother, Keith Chen, the novel's primary protagonist, flees his hometown of Yongjing to live a freer, bohemian life in Berlin, where he enters a romance with a German named T.

By the end of the first chapter, **however**, Keith reveals that he's murdered T, without saying how or why. After serving his prison sentence, Keith returns to Yongjing for the first time in many years. —Leland Cheuk (2022), "'Ghost Town' Blurs the Line Between the Living and the Dead in Rural Taiwan," *NPR* (emphasis added)

MATHEMATICS

In Christian culture, 6 has a rather dark meaning and 666 is even called the *"Number of the Beast"*. The number 666 appears several times in the Bible, and in other old scripts. The ancient writers probably didn't know that 666 is related to the golden ratio by $\phi = -2\sin(666°) = -2\cos(6\times6\times6°)$, **but** maybe they were aware of some of the following "scary" relationships. —Philipp Legner (2010), "Editorial: 60 Issues of *Eureka*," *Eureka*, p. 4 (emphasis added)

SCIENCE

Time seems linear to us: We remember the past, experience the present and predict the future, moving consecutively from one moment to the next. **But** why is it that way, and could time ultimately be a kind of illusion? In this episode, the Nobel Prize-winning physicist Frank Wilczek speaks with host Steven Strogatz about the many "arrows" of time and why most of them seem irreversible, the essence of what a clock is, how Einstein changed our definition of time, and the unexpected connection between time and our notions of what dark matter might be. —Steven Strogatz (2024), "What Is the Nature of Time?," *Quanta Magazine* (emphasis added)

SOCIAL STUDIES

When Jefferson became president in 1801, he used his first Annual Message to Congress to remind fellow citizens of America's lasting importance as an asylum. America came into existence because emigrants exercised their freedom to form a country of their own. The fight for this freedom was **not only** a convenient origin story—it was America's perpetual purpose. —Stephanie DeGooyer (2022), "The Right to Leave," *Lapham's Quarterly* (emphasis added)

The Devil in the Details (Level 3)

Imagine that you're sitting at the lunch table at work, and your coworker—let's call her Georgia—asks, "Did you hear about the fight Mr. Humphrey and Mr. Williams had in the hallway?" In that moment, you do not want a quick, simple overview of what happened. You want the tea. The full story. Spare no details, honey. But, alas, you have only two minutes before you need to be back in the classroom! How can Georgia give you the full picture of what happened and her own hot takes while still being succinct?

She could use the Devil in the Details move.

The Devil in the Details move is a sophisticated summary in which the writer combines a big-picture overview of the topic with lots of details and analysis. In fact, the analysis might sneak into the details so cleverly that the reader might not notice where the facts end and opinions begin.

This is the basic formula: Observation + Description + Analysis.

POP CULTURE

See figure 8.3 for an annotated mentor text where the Devil in the Details method proves most effective.

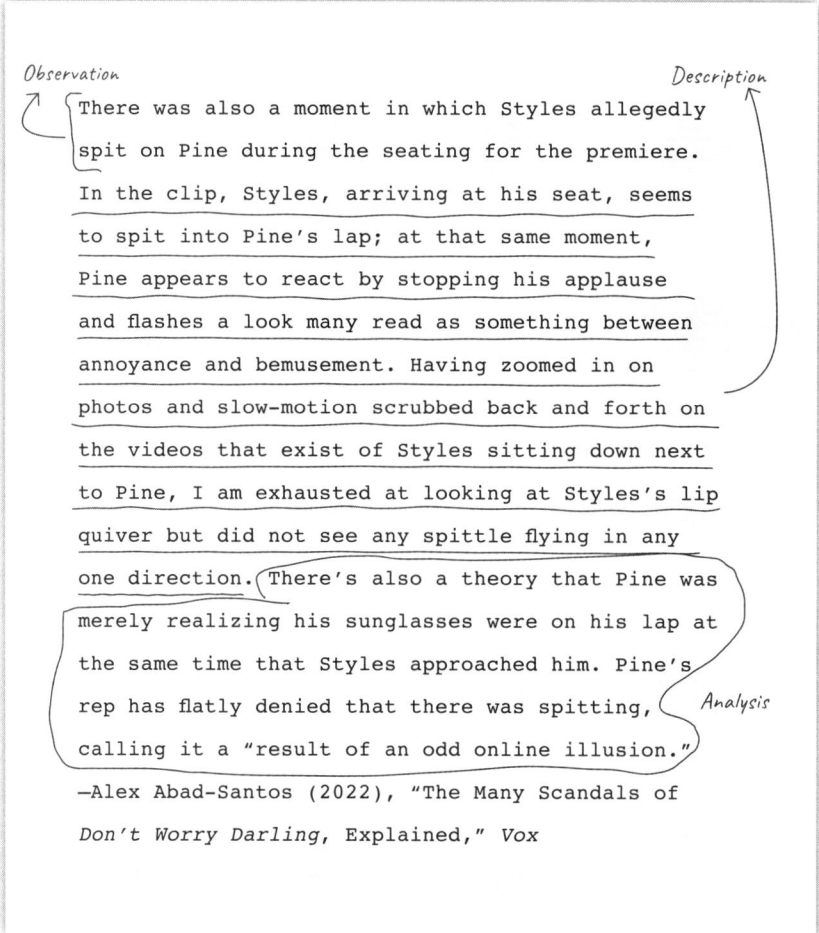

Figure 8.3: The Devil in the Details, annotated mentor text.

Here are some extra tidbits to consider as you share this move with students.

» Students will notice that the initial observation brings us into the scene of the premiere, while the second sentence narrows the focus with a description about Chris Pine's facial expressions. This technique of funneling details until they become almost microscopic—or the size of "spittle"—continues in the analysis. This strategy allows the writer to accomplish the task at hand (summarizing) while bringing a bit of voice to the text.

» This book has a whole chapter on different ways to write descriptions! Check out chapter 6 (page 83) to help your students with this skill.

» In the following English and science (page 132) mentor texts, the writer drops the analysis into a separate paragraph away from the initial parts of the summary. Students who need a bit more support might find this technique helpful, as it reduces the pressure to flow seamlessly from description to analysis. Seeing this move as having separate, distinct parts can help writers chunk information.

» It's worth pointing out to students that the analysis portion of each of the mentor texts is a direct response to the details provided in the observation and description. It's important to remind students that their analysis should directly connect to the information they've already shared about the topic. Otherwise, the reader will be lost.

ENGLISH

The fair, which this year had over 1,000 exhibitors and something like 30,000 visitors, is one of the biggest events of the international publishing calendar. For three days, agents, editors, publishers, scouts and many other people whose jobs are harder to explain gather in a frenzied fashion, primarily to sell and buy foreign rights for English-language books, but also to take temperatures, observe prevailing winds and scheme.

For those who weren't there to close deals, the fair offered the opportunity to map out the minutely graded power structure of the publishing industry. —Rosa Lyster (2024), "Welcome to the London Book Fair, Where Everyone Knows Their Place," *The New York Times*

MATHEMATICS

In string theory, there is a duality symmetry known as T-duality. This is a fundamental ambiguity in the description of the space time background in which the string lives. If the space time has some specific properties (technically, it should possess an isometry and be compact so that its first homotopy class is nontrivial) then there will be two backgrounds that will be related to each other that in ordinary differential geometry will be inequivalent and yet will be indistinguishable from the point of view of the string. These pairs are known as T-duals. This duality is stringy in nature and leads on to the idea of stringy geometry that differs from our usual notion of geometry in that such ideas of T-duality get built in. —George Ellis (2012), "Multiverses and Observational Limits of Cosmology," *Eureka*, p. 69

SCIENCE

For a pathogen to make us sick, it must overcome a lot. First it has to enter the body, bypassing natural barriers such as skin, mucus, cilia and stomach acid. Then it needs to reproduce; some bacteria and parasites can do this virtually anywhere in the body, while viruses and some other pathogens can only do so from within a cell. And all the while, it must parry attacks from the body's immune system.

So while we are constantly inundated by microbes, the number of microbes that enter our bodies is usually too low to get past our defenses. (A tiny enough dose may even serve to remind our immune system of a pathogen's existence, boosting our antibody response to keep us protected against it.) —Tara C. Smith (2023), "How Many Microbes Does It Take to Make You Sick?," *Quanta Magazine*

SOCIAL STUDIES

Take one of the most glaring recent examples, the court's June 2022 decision striking down a century-old New York law requiring gun owners to obtain a permit to carry a gun in public.

New York State Rifle & Pistol Association Inc. v. Bruen was decided 6 to 3, with all the Republican-appointed justices joining the majority opinion by Justice Clarence Thomas. It was the court's most transformative gun rights case since *Heller*, and like that earlier case, it featured the right-wing justices' playing amateur historians, cherry-picking and distorting evidence from decades or centuries ago to justify their existing opinions—a practice real historians refer to derisively as law-office history. —Jesse Wegman (2024), "The Crisis in Teaching Constitutional Law," *The New York Times*

Cause and Effect Sandwich (Level 4)

During the writing of this book, Sam's social studies students were struggling to write meaningful summaries. While some were neglecting to include important details, others were writing down every single fact they knew about an event and getting lost in the weeds. Sam went on a hunt for a strategy she could teach her students that would help them include all the important and relevant information about an event while not writing down every fact. Looking through some mentor texts for a solution, she discovered the Cause and Effect Sandwich.

When we summarize an event, almost no other move works as well as the Cause and Effect Sandwich. This move is a classic and has all the hallmarks of a successful summary—it begins with a quick overview, heavily relies on chronological reasoning, and explains the event from start to finish using analysis.

Just like the Devil in the Details, the Cause and Effect Sandwich begins with a one-sentence observation of the event. But unlike our other moves that summarize in this chapter, after providing that big-picture overview of the event, this move lists causes of the event before providing a brief explanation of the event itself. The move concludes by listing how the event has affected the people involved, the community, the place, and so on.

Students might find it helpful to structure this summary using the following four questions.

1. What is it?
2. Why did this happen?
3. What happened?
4. How did this affect _____?

This is the basic formula: Observation + [Causes + Explanation of the Event + Effects].

POP CULTURE

See figure 8.4 for an annotated mentor text demonstrating this method.

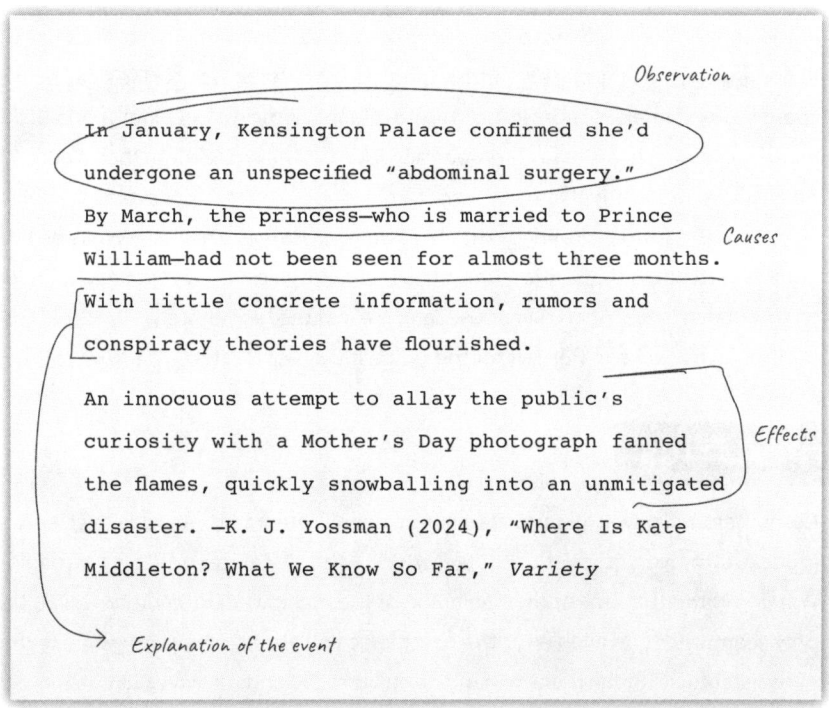

Figure 8.4: Cause and Effect Sandwich, annotated mentor text.

As you teach this move to your students, here are some things to consider.

» One of the first things we like to point out with students is how all the Cause and Effect Sandwich mentor texts heavily rely on dates in every section of the move to chronologically orient the reader. In the pop culture mentor text, the event's timeline is so tight that the author must rely on the names of months and holidays, like Mother's Day, to take the reader through the event from beginning to end.

» Ultimately, even though students may at first find the structure of this summary very familiar, they will quickly notice that discerning cause and effect is an advanced form of analysis—something that historians, scientists, journalists, and other professional writers spend their lives debating.

» To use this move successfully, writers must have a firm grasp of not only the event itself but how the event fits within a larger narrative. For example, in the following social studies mentor text, the author needed a strong understanding of not only the Richmond Bread Riot but also the Civil War and how the Bread Riot connects to the Civil War.

ENGLISH

It makes sense that Peter Freuchen would agree to sign up for such a process: he was nothing if not tough. Freuchen, who was born in 1886, in Denmark, quit school, at the age of twenty, to sail to Greenland, as a stoker on a steamship, after seeing a student play about polar exploration and realizing that it was his life's calling. He spent the next three decades living in and exploring some of the coldest parts of the world. According to his many memoirs and journals (he wrote more than a dozen!), he encountered death at almost every turn. He was trapped for several days in an avalanche. A camp cook almost shot him, thinking he was a bear. . . . While he was stuck, whittling away at the ice, one of his feet froze so severely that he was forced to amputate several of his own toes. Later, he lost the foot entirely. —Rachel Syme (2019), "An Irving Penn Portrait for the Coldest Days of Winter," *The New Yorker*

MATHEMATICS

Computers and powerful calculators are so deeply integrated into today's science—indeed, into every aspect of today's world—that it can be difficult to imagine working without them. At the beginning of the Manhattan Project, however, the only "computers" available for the complex calculations necessary were teams of assistants using mechanical hand calculators. Scientists' wives at Los Alamos were enlisted, the work divided amongst them to maximize efficiency—one dedicated to adding, one to dividing, one to cubing, and so forth. This basic form of calculation worked well initially, but as calculations of neutron mean free paths, critical densities, and shockwave propagation grew ever more complex and time-intensive, it strained to produce results in a timely manner. Further, the scarcity of materials (especially radioactive materials) and scientific manpower [meant] that extensive experimentation was impossible, so theoretical calculations were the only way to test central elements of the bomb designs before the final Trinity test. Los Alamos needed either far more teams of woman "calculators" or some new way of handling extensive calculations. —Office of History and Heritage Resources (n.d.), "The Manhattan Project: An Interactive History"

SCIENCE

CRISPR provides a relatively easy way to release a gene drive. First, researchers insert a CRISPR-powered gene drive into an organism. When the organism mates, its CRISPR-equipped chromosome cleaves the matching chromosome coming from the other parent. The offspring's genetic machinery then attempts to sew up this cut. When it does, it copies over the relevant section of DNA from the first parent—the section that contains the CRISPR gene drive. In this way, the gene drive duplicates itself so that it ends up on both chromosomes, and this will occur with nearly every one of the original organism's offspring. —Brooke Borel (2016), "Genetic Engineering to Clash With Evolution," *Quanta Magazine*

SOCIAL STUDIES

The Richmond Bread Riot, which took place in the Confederate capital of Richmond on April 2, 1863, was the largest and most destructive in a series of civil disturbances throughout the South during the third spring of the American Civil War (1861–1865). By 1863, the Confederate economy was showing signs of serious strain. Congress's passage of an Impressment Act, as well as a tax law deemed "confiscatory," led to hoarding and speculation, and spiraling inflation took its toll, especially on people living in the Confederacy's urban areas. When a group of hungry Richmond women took their complaints to Virginia governor John L. Letcher, he refused to see them. Their anger turned into a street march and attacks on commercial establishments. Only when troops were deployed and authorities threatened to fire on the mob did the rioters disperse. More than sixty men and women were arrested and tried, while the city stepped up its efforts to relieve the suffering of the poor and hungry. —Mary DeCredico (2021), "Bread Riot, Richmond," *Encyclopedia Virginia*

Quote It to Me (Level 5)

One of the most effective and complex ways to summarize is to weave quotations from a source into the summary. Doing so enriches the writing by not only citing evidence directly but also adding another voice or voices to the summary. However, students may struggle with knowing when and how much to quote a source in their summary.

We encourage our students to incorporate a quote into the summary when the quote meets the following criteria.

» It will share a unique perspective or voice that is vital to understanding the topic of the summary.

» It is short.

» It contains information that is difficult to paraphrase.

This means that incorporating a quote into a summary requires precision. Students must be prepared to cut the excess and quote only the most pertinent, unique information from their source.

Besides the quote itself, the Quote It to Me move contains three additional components: (1) students must cite the source by naming both the author and the origins of the quote, (2) they must engage with the quote by contextualizing it further or offering commentary, and (3) they must describe the topic being summarized to answer that essential question of "What?"

As you'll see in the following mentor texts, the order of these components is irrelevant. Students can play around with how they assemble the parts of this move. The result? A sophisticated and unique explanation of a topic.

This is the basic formula: Quote + Source Citation + Quote Context + Topic Description.

POP CULTURE

See figure 8.5 for an example of Quote It to Me.

As we dissect this move with students, here are a few things we might home in on.

» The voice that writers choose to quote in a summary is significant. Including Kate Middleton's voice here is crucial to understanding this event because (1) this whole controversy arose due to her absence from the public and (2) the public debated whether the prose being posted on social media was actually coming from her.

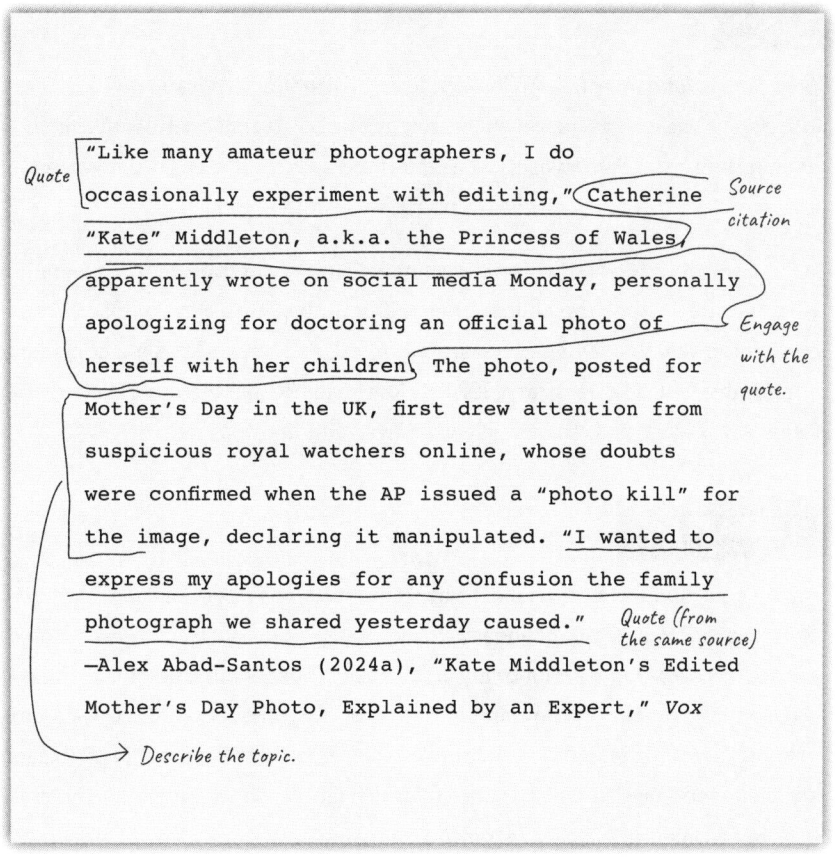

Figure 8.5: Quote It to Me, annotated mentor text.

- » The quote is a complete sentence on its own, but the author weaves it into their commentary. This allows the author to take ownership of the quote and seamlessly blend it into the summary.
- » When providing context for the quote here, the author includes the day of the week to help orient the reader in the chronology within the topic they're summarizing.
- » The description of the photo controversy is brief, just two sentences. The author explains what happened and how it connects to the quote.
- » The author chooses to end the summary with the second portion of the quote that begins the summary. This can be a helpful technique for students who really want to use a longer quote in their summary—break it up!

ENGLISH

Grief here is fundamentally an intense form of attention. Those in power have an incentive to use grief as a spotlight on events that bolster national identity, financial or brand interest, or otherwise, just as they have an incentive not to draw attention to events that could sow discord or upend these interests.

What a society chooses to grieve is ultimately its way of "posing the question of who 'we' are," writes the philosopher Judith Butler. "By asking whose lives are considered valuable, whose lives are mourned, and whose lives are considered ungrievable." —Cody Delistraty (2024), "How Reading Grief Memoirs Helped Cody Delistraty Understand His Loss in New Ways," *Literary Hub*

MATHEMATICS

Nash's equilibrium concept, which earned him a Nobel Prize in economics in 1994, offers a unified framework for understanding strategic behavior not only in economics but also in psychology, evolutionary biology and a host of other fields. Its influence on economic theory "is comparable to that of the discovery of the DNA double helix in the biological sciences," wrote Roger Myerson of the University of Chicago, another economics Nobelist. —Erica Klarreich (2017), "In Game Theory, No Clear Path to Equilibrium," *Quanta Magazine*

SCIENCE

Bothe found that the electric current needed to reach the voltage threshold and trigger a snake's body motor neuron was "way lower than for the rattle motor neurons," he said. "You need to put way more current into the [rattle] neuron for it to fire." And compared to rattle motor neurons, body motor neurons reacted more sluggishly. —Elise Cutts (2024), "Tiny Tweaks to Neurons Can Rewire Animal Motion," *Quanta Magazine*

SOCIAL STUDIES

Hardly anyone noticed this summer when former president Jimmy Carter explained why he had decided to leave the Baptist Church. However "painful and difficult," wrote Carter in an essay that appeared in the *Guardian*, his break with the denomination to which he had belonged for sixty years had begun to seem like the only possible response to past opinions expressed and codified by the Southern Baptist Convention. —Francine Prose (2010), "The Original Sin," *Lapham's Quarterly*

Use the reproducible "Writing Application Practice: Moves That Summarize" (page 141) to summarize.

Student Samples

The following student samples include moves that summarize.

This sample uses Define and Detail (level 1):

> Yusuf Islam, formerly known as Cat Stevens, produced the 1971 anti-war song, "Peace Train." Although it is the last song of his album, Teaser and the Firecat, which was created to bring hope to everyone affected by wars both past and present, it is arguably the best and definitely the most popular. "Peace Train" quickly became Stevens' first US top 10 hit. Released in September of 1971, this song is categorized as soft rock with sounds of violin and acoustic guitar echoing throughout the song. Beginning slow with nothing but the acoustic riffs and the smooth bass lines, it later breaks into an explosion of music as the line "glide on the peace train" repeats.
> —Ellery, Eighth Grade

This sample uses The Devil in the Details (level 3):

> New Deal Reform measures were aimed at fixing the defects and problems in the American economy and ensuring that something as crippling to the economy as the Great Depression would never happen again. The Federal Deposit Insurance Corporation (1933) insured deposit security so that people would never lose their money in the event of a bank failure. The National Labor Relations Act (1935) gave workers the right to form unions and bargain collectively. The Securities and Exchange Commission (1934) was created to watch over the stock market, prevent fraud, and guard against another stock market collapse. But overall, the most important measure of the New Deal was the Social Security Act (1935). It gave workers unemployment insurance, old age pensions, and insurance if they died early. —Conor, Seventh Grade

This sample uses Quote It To Me (level 5):

> In April 1944, Daniels arrived in Auschwitz. She could smell the acrid scent of burning flesh from the crematorium and it was so dark it seemed "like . . . dreaming". She stood in lines while the Nazis separated those too weak to work, and these people were taken straight to the crematoriums. At this point, Daniels was separated from her mother and brother but remained with Eva and her two other cousins. She would never see her mother or brother again; her mother was killed in the crematoriums and her brother died during forced labor. The camp officers shaved Daniels' head,

showered her, and gave her new, "junky", clothes. In the morning they were taken into the concentration camp and given small, cramped barracks.

She spent nearly a month in Auschwitz and was transported to a second concentration camp, Dachau, in the mid to late summer of 1944. In Dachau, she worked with others making ammunition for guns. On September 2, 1945, the war ended and American troops rushed to free the enslaved Jews. When Nazi officers got word that the Americans planned to bomb the factory in Dachau where Daniels and others made ammunition, they forced the remaining prisoners into a death march. When American soldiers finally liberated them at the camp later that year, they were starving, but Daniels said "That was the happiest moment of my life, they were so beautiful". —Stella, Seventh Grade

Writing Application Practice: Moves That Summarize

After teaching your students one of these moves—or all of these moves—you'll be looking for an opportunity for them to practice these skills immediately.

For each writing task, we have provided a prompt you could use to get your students writing. They can use this prompt to practice a single move for that writing task or to begin combining, mixing, and matching moves. You can find all writing application practice from the whole book in one place in appendix C (page 275).

Content Area	Writing Application Practice
English	Choose a character from a book you have recently read, and summarize how they have changed over the course of the book. What details, quotes, or analysis can you share to make your explanation more interesting?
Mathematics	Explain a mathematical concept that you recently learned about (division, subtraction, the quadratic formula, exponents, and so on) to a reader by summarizing it using one (or more) of the moves that summarize.
Science	Write a summary of your most recent lab. Consider the aspects of the lab that you'd like to summarize, from the hypothesis to the results, and choose one of the five summarization moves to help you write your summary.
Social Studies	Find a news article that was published today about an event. Summarize the article using one or more of the moves from this chapter.

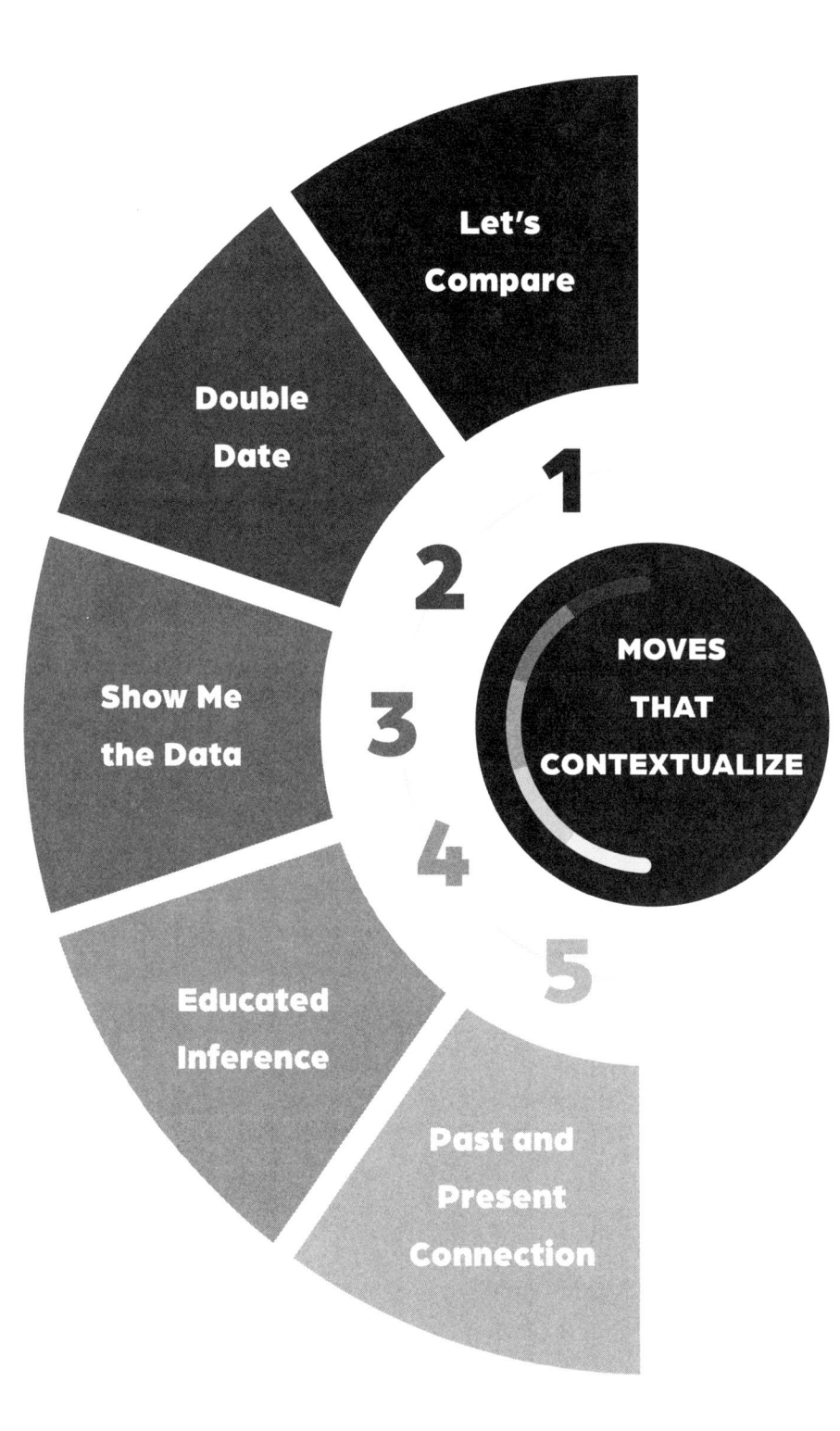

CHAPTER 9

Moves That Contextualize

Contextualizing is an art, but it's one that our students often underappreciate. They refer to it as "background stuff." In that sentence, we used Let's Compare. In the next sentence, we have Educated Inference. We used each of the moves of contextualization in this chapter to contextualize the topic itself.

We have a theory that students tend to shy away from contextualizing because it requires an astute sense of what readers know and what they don't. Unfortunately, most of our students are not clairvoyant, which can make reading their readers' minds rather difficult.

To encourage our student writers to fully explain their ideas, we often tell them never to assume the reader knows *anything*. But, of course, this is a bit of a stretch too—our readers do know *some things*.

Perhaps, instead, we should tell our students never to assume the reader knows *what you're thinking*. And this is really why writers contextualize. In this way, moves that contextualize differ from moves that describe. Writers describe to help their readers imagine; writers contextualize to help their readers understand.

To do this, writers must provide readers with more information. But what information? And how much is enough? How much is too much? In this chapter, we explore five moves that will help students understand when and how to contextualize. These chapters will . . . contextualize . . . the process of contextualizing. See table 9.1 (page 144) for recommendations on when best to use the particular methods for contextualization.

Let's Compare (Level 1)

One of the simplest ways to help a reader understand a writer's line of reasoning is to offer a comparison. Comparisons, especially those using similes, are offerings that say, "Let me help you understand my perspective on _____ by telling you it is like something else that, perhaps, you're more familiar with."

Table 9.1: Writing Needs and Moves That Contextualize

When Writers Need...	Start Here...
To help the reader understand their point by comparing their central idea to something else	Let's Compare (page 143)
	Double Date (page 146)
	Past and Present Connection (page 154)
To help the reader better understand their central idea	Double Date (page 146)
	Past and Present Connection (page 154)
To include numerical information about a topic	Show Me the Data (page 148)
To provide the reader with some background information on a topic that they don't have specific details about	Educated Inference (page 151)
To show a more advanced synthesis in their writing	Show Me the Data (page 148)
	Educated Inference (page 151)
	Past and Present Connection (page 154)

Even if the reader is not very familiar with the comparative element, the author will have provided another example of their central idea for the reader's reference. At a certain point, it is the reader's job to infer.

We love the Let's Compare move for our emerging writers because it is such a natural way of adding context. Being in conversation with someone and having to unpack a topic with the phrase, "It's like _____," is a universal experience. This move translates that universal experience to writing.

This is the basic formula: Your Central Idea + *like* + Comparison.

POP CULTURE

See figure 9.1 for an annotated mentor text demonstrating effective comparison.

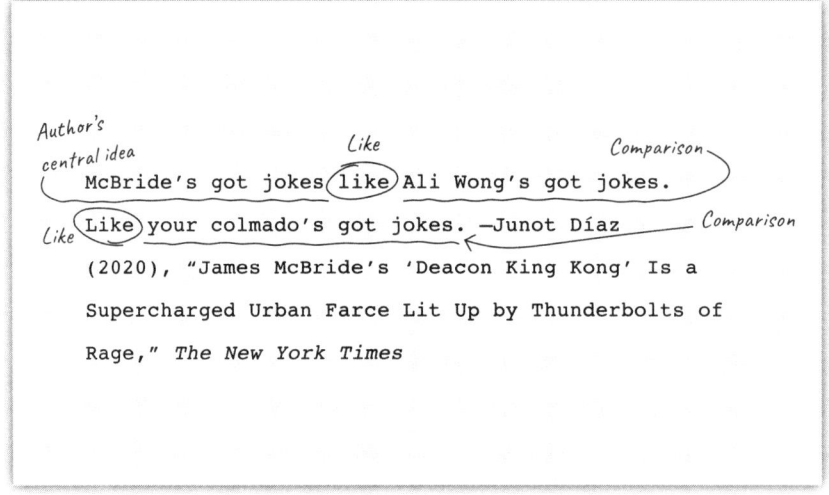

Figure 9.1: Let's Compare, annotated mentor text.

Consider this when sharing this move with your students.

» In most of the mentor texts for this move, the author's central idea comes first. This positions the author's idea as the axis point in the reader's mind—something to which all other ideas can be reflected back.

» Sometimes, the *like* + comparison structure is a simile. Sometimes, it's not—it's simply the word "like" and then a comparative example. This distinction isn't incredibly important to students, but it may come up in your discussion.

» Students might point out that the comparison has the same structure as the central idea. Though not necessary, using parallel structure can be a helpful tool for crafting the Let's Compare move.

» Multiple comparisons are included in this mentor text in concise, rapid-fire sentences. Again, while not necessary, this structure allows the reader more ideas with which to compare the central idea. This can be a great extension for students who are ready to take on a little challenge.

» The comparisons help the reader better understand the writer's message because they are increasingly specific. Here, the first comparison is to a well-known comedian with particular comedy stylings; the second comparison is to a niche concept within the Dominican community.

ENGLISH

Despite the urban setting, this is a village novel, like *Emma* or *Barchester Towers*, an ensemble piece about the way a small community of flawed characters who think they know one another all too well cope with newcomers and their own capacity for change. —Laura Miller (2020), "The Old-Fashioned Warmth of James McBride," *Slate*

MATHEMATICS

Modular arithmetic is often called clock arithmetic, as a 12-hour clock counts in mod 12. This way of thinking about counting around a circle like on a clock suggests that it might be useful for our problem. —Alvin Choy (2023), "The Josephus Problem," *Chalkdust*

SCIENCE

Drawing parallels with successful policies like the "sugar tax" on soft drinks in the United Kingdom, meat taxes could incentivize a reduction in meat production by driving industry reformulation instead of relying on consumer behavior. —Aissa Dearing (2024), "Grilling the Globe," *JSTOR Daily*

SOCIAL STUDIES

Furthermore, daily sin, wealth, and almsgiving were drawn together by a half-hidden homology. Augustine always stressed the way in which daily sin piled up, in and around the human person in a largely unconscious manner—like sand, like drops of water, like fleas. —Peter Brown (2015), "Treasure in Heaven," *Lapham's Quarterly*

Double Date (Level 2)

Time may be a construct, but it is something that we all understand. For this reason, writers use dates to orient readers. In some instances, dates lay out the chronology of events to help readers understand cause and effect like in the Cause and Effect Sandwich move in chapter 8 (page 132). At other times, writers use dates to help situate their readers in a time or place. In the Double Date move, writers isolate the date most central to their topic and then offer an additional date shortly thereafter to provide additional details or comparisons to help the reader better understand the period that they are talking about.

This is the basic formula: Idea and Date It Occurred + Additional Date With Bonus Detail.

POP CULTURE

See figure 9.2 for an annotated mentor text featuring the Double Date method.

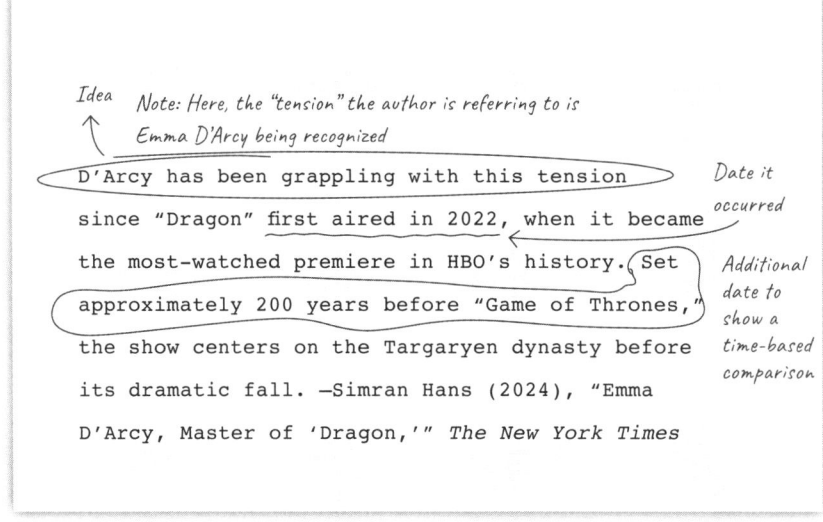

Figure 9.2: Double Date, annotated mentor text.

Here are some other features you and your students might consider together.

» A great way to start with a contextualization mentor text is to ask students to answer the question, "What does the author want us to understand?" If we were to ask our students that question with this mentor text, they might say, "The author wants us to understand that fame is not something new to Emma D'Arcy." This strategy can help writers decide what context they want to include and what they can leave out.

» Ask students, "How do the dates help us understand the idea the author wants to convey?" It's important for students to consider what makes dates meaningful before they begin selecting dates for their own pieces.

» Dates matter. Students might point out that the second date really doesn't have anything to do with Emma D'Arcy—it's describing *House of the Dragon*. But in actuality, it *does* help us understand Emma D'Arcy because that is the central topic of the piece. This date helps the reader understand why the show that D'Arcy is the star of is so incredibly popular and how it relates to its origin show, *Game of Thrones*.

» The first date is a year. This centers the reader in a concrete time.

» The second date is an approximation—"200 years" is not exact. The author does not need this date to be exact because the purpose of this date is not to show a concrete time but to show the reader how *House of the Dragon* corresponds to the larger *Game of Thrones* universe. The following content-area examples show a similar structure.

» Students might notice that the second phrase in each sentence provides further explanation of how the date is relevant to the central topic.

ENGLISH

Known as the Black Tulip, only twelve copies appear to have survived since its publication in July 1827. That one of the last two in private hands is coming to auction this month, not quite two centuries later, marks an historic bibliophilic event. —Bradford Morrow (2024), "In Search of the Rarest Book in American Literature: Edgar Allan Poe's *Tamerlane*," *Literary Hub*

MATHEMATICS

In 1940, from a jailhouse in Rouen, France, André Weil wrote one of the most consequential letters of 20th-century mathematics. He was serving time for refusing to join the French army, and he filled his days in part by writing letters to his sister, Simone, an accomplished philosopher living in London. —Kevin Hartnett (2024b), "A Rosetta Stone for Mathematics," *Quanta Magazine*

SCIENCE

These studies and the keystone idea came to prominence at the same moment that America's environmental conscience was emerging. In 1973, Congress passed the Endangered Species Act, which took a species-focused approach to conserving wildlife. The idea that restoring the population of a single species—a keystone, perhaps—could ensure the biodiversity of an ecological community aligned with this new legal framework. —Lesley Evans Ogden (2024), "Ecologists Struggle to Get a Grip on 'Keystone Species,'" *Quanta Magazine*

SOCIAL STUDIES

During the seven decades of legal Jim Crow segregation from the 1890s through the 1960s, the principal goal of the southern states at the core of red America was defensive: They worked tirelessly to prevent federal interference with state-sponsored segregation but did not seek to impose it on states outside the region. —Ronald Brownstein (2022), "America Is Growing Apart, Possibly for Good," *The Atlantic*

Show Me the Data (Level 3)

Let's be honest; we, as this book's authors, are both humanities teachers. So we get nervous when terms like *data* are bandied about. But even we can agree that, occasionally, to gain a fundamental understanding of a topic, nothing does the job quite like some data.

Sometimes, data serve as evidence. Sometimes, they can launch an idea (see Just-the-Facts in chapter 3, page 28). Data can also contextualize, providing the factual information necessary to set the stakes for why a topic matters and is worthy of our attention.

Just as in Double Date, the details matter here. Roy Peter Clark (2023) cautions that "numbers should be handled carefully in a story. Only the most important numbers should be used, and they should be explained in context" (p. 43). Writers use Show Me the Data when the data truly matter in painting the landscape of the topic and providing the background a reader needs.

This is the basic formula: (Source + Data + Description of Data)Ad Infinitum.

POP CULTURE

See the annotated mentor text demonstrating this method in figure 9.3.

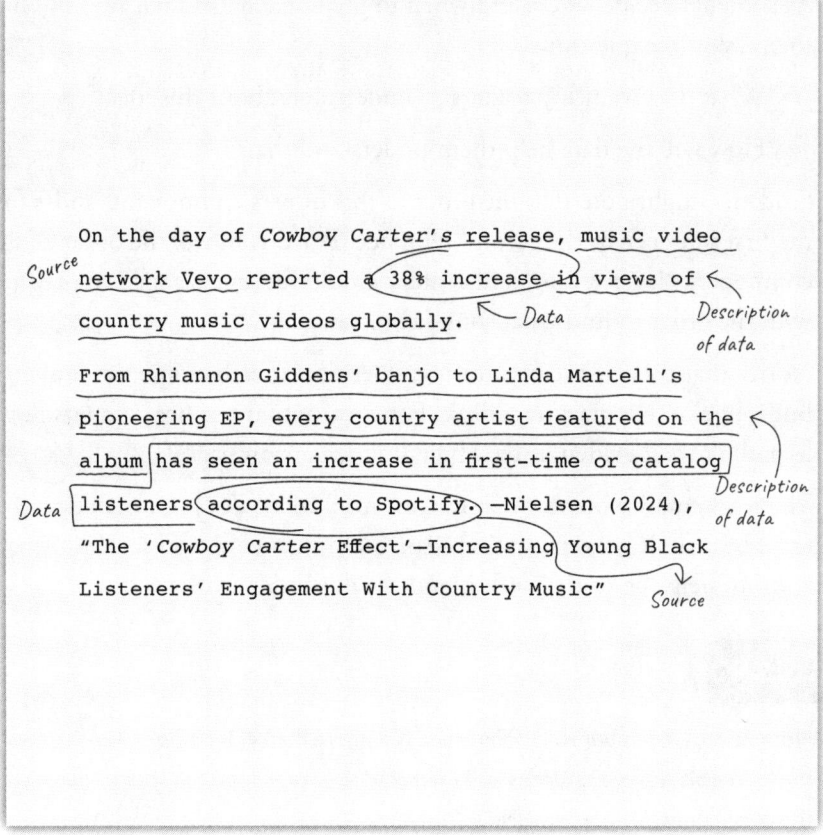

Figure 9.3: Show Me the Data, annotated mentor text.

Here are some extra tidbits to consider as you share this move with students.

» After reading this mentor text aloud with students, we would ask them to answer this prompt: "Based on the information they provided, what does the author want us to understand about *Cowboy Carter*'s release?" Though answers will vary, possible responses might include the following.

  * *Cowboy Carter* has had a positive influence on the country music industry.
  * Country artists who are featured in *Cowboy Carter* have all risen in popularity.

» Then, we would ask students to answer the question, "How do the data help readers understand the author's central idea?" Though answers may vary, possible responses might include the following.

  * If viewership of country music videos increased by 38 percent on the day of *Cowboy Carter*'s release, then there is a clear correlation.
  * People who weren't even listening to these country artists before the release of *Cowboy Carter* are listening to them now for the first time.

» As students decide where and when to include data in their writing, have them ask these questions.

  * "What do I want my readers to understand about this idea?"

  * "How will the data help them understand that?"

» Students might note that the order of this move's components shifts from the first sentence to the second sentence. For this move, the order of the components is irrelevant, and writers should feel encouraged to play around with the order to find what sounds best to them.

» Notice that the science mentor text does not directly name the source, but it does cite it via a hyperlink. For a move that teaches students how to hyperlink their evidence, see Hyperlink Layers on page 102.

» The mathematics mentor text for this mini move does not include a source at all because it uses the statistics surrounding a common scenario (tossing a coin) to help the reader understand the dependency of events.

ENGLISH

From July to December 2023, PEN found that more than 4,300 books were removed from schools across 23 states—a figure that surpassed the number of bans from the entire previous academic year.

The rise in book bans has accelerated in recent years, driven by conservative groups and by new laws and regulations that limit what kinds of books children can access. Since the summer of 2021, PEN has tracked book removals in 42 states and found instances in both Republican- and Democratic-controlled districts. —Alexandra Alter (2024), "Book Bans Continue to Surge in Public Schools," *The New York Times*

MATHEMATICS

The events here are *dependent* upon each other, as opposed to *independent*. In the realm of probability, dependency of events is very important. For example, coin tosses are always independent events. When tossing a fair coin, the probability of it landing on heads, given that it previously landed on heads 10 times in a row, is still 1/2. Even if it lands on heads 1000 times, the chance of it landing on heads on the 1001st toss is still 50%. —Madeleine Hall (2021), "On Conditional Probability: Cards, COVID, and *Crazy Rich Asians*," *Chalkdust*

SCIENCE

Studies have found that some 50% to 70% of patients with major depressive disorder see their symptoms improve after a course of ECT. In comparison, medications aimed at altering brain chemistry help only 10% to 40% of depression patients. —Elizabeth Landau (2024), "Brain's 'Background Noise' May Explain Value of Shock Therapy," *Quanta Magazine*

SOCIAL STUDIES

More than 1.8 million Muslims participated in the hajj this year, 1.6 million of them from outside Saudi Arabia, according to the Saudi General Authority for Statistics. They encountered scorching temperatures that ranged from 108 Fahrenheit to 120, according to preliminary data. —Cassandra Vinograd and Vivian Nereim (2024), "More Than 1,000 Hajj Pilgrims Died. Here's What to Know," *The New York Times*

Educated Inference (Level 4)

Even the best writers cannot know everything. Despite years of research, some questions simply cannot and may not ever be answered. But instead of omitting information from the writing and leaving gaps for the reader, writers supplement what they don't know with what they *do* know by making an educated inference.

In the Educated Inference move, writers identify a question that they cannot answer within their research and then broaden the parameters of that inquiry to make an evidence-based hypothesis about the topic. When writers do make an educated inference about a topic, they use adverbs of probability to signal to readers that they are making a well-researched conjecture. To supplement this conjecture, writers include verifiable evidence about the details they discovered in their research.

The Educated Inference move takes a considerable amount of research to be done correctly. But it is an incredibly helpful tool that will help readers better understand the author's ideas within any piece of writing.

This is the basic formula: Name the Topic + Adverb of Probability + Educated Inference + Verifiable Evidence.

POP CULTURE

See figure 9.4 for an annotated mentor text demonstrating this method.

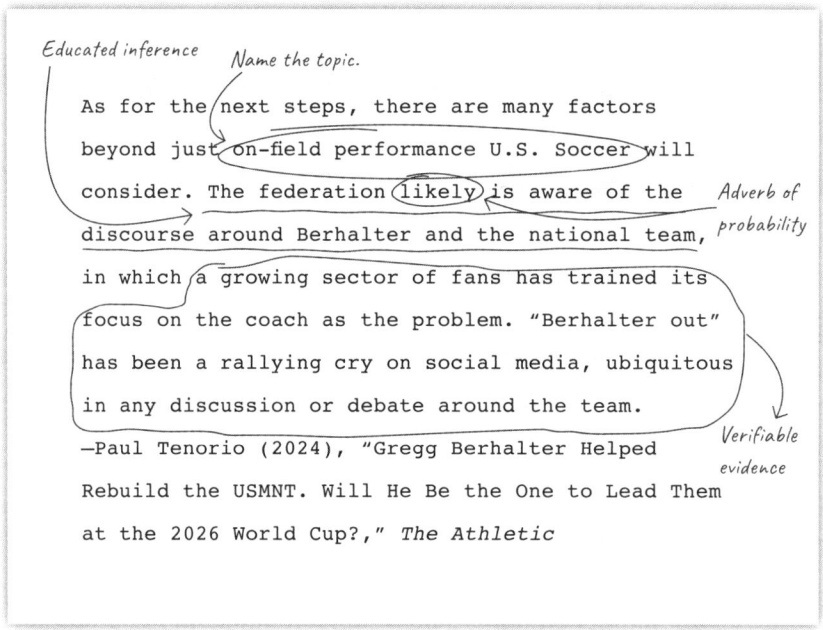

Figure 9.4: Educated Inference, annotated mentor text.

Here are some extra tidbits to consider as you share this move with students.

» Try having your students reverse-engineer the educated inference by hypothesizing about what question the author may be trying to answer. Here, the author is likely trying to answer the question, "Is the U.S. Soccer Federation aware that many fans are displeased with the coach's performance?"

» Students will note that the adverb of probability is "likely" in this mentor text.

» While an educated inference could be made at almost every turn in a piece of writing, writers use this move sparingly. Too many educated inferences can leave a reader feeling unsettled by the lack of concrete evidence to support the author's points.

» Students may identify that the educated inference does not necessarily add credence to the author's argument—it simply helps the reader better understand the argument.

» In the pop culture mentor text, the author supplements the inference about the federation with verifiable evidence concerning the fans' feelings about the coach. It's important to note that the verifiable evidence should always be directly connected and designed to add on to the information shared in the educated inference.

ENGLISH

Plath's most famous poem is **probably** "Daddy," which references her father and his death, but which is absolutely not a biographical poem, and is in many ways a poem about throwing off the influence of powerful men—her father, sure, but also her teachers and certainly her husband, who was a stand-in for both her father and her teachers, throughout their marriage, according to Plath. —Sarah Viren (2024), "A Painful, Urgent Reimagining: Emily van Duyne on Writing a New History of Sylvia Plath's Last Years," *Literary Hub* (emphasis added)

MATHEMATICS

Without the telltale sign of an obviously misshapen district to go by, mathematicians have been developing increasingly powerful statistical methods for finding gerrymanders. These work by comparing a map to an ensemble of thousands or millions of possible maps. If the map results in noticeably more seats for Democrats or Republicans than would be expected from an average map, this is a sign that something fishy **might** have taken place. —Mike Orcutt (2023), "How Math Has Changed the Shape of Gerrymandering," *Quanta Magazine* (emphasis added)

SCIENCE

So it's easy to see why masting trees synchronize their seed production. Understanding how they do it, however, is more complicated. Plants **usually** synchronize their reproduction by timing it to the same weather signals. And warming temperatures and heavy rainfall correlate well with coordinated masting, **suggesting** that the trees synchronize to weather cues. —Meghan Willcoxon (2024), "Across a Continent, Trees Sync Their Fruiting to the Sun," *Quanta Magazine* (emphasis added)

SOCIAL STUDIES

Late in her childhood, Pocahontas **likely** joined Powhatan's large, busy household, where everybody worked, even Powhatan himself. In addition to their daily jobs, members of the household labored to produce grand feasts on important occasions. Pocahontas, meanwhile, **probably** participated in what was traditionally women's work—farming, collecting wild foods and firewood, making utensils, and cooking and cleaning. —Helen Rountree (2024), "Pocahontas (d. 1617)," *Encyclopedia Virginia* (emphasis added)

Past and Present Connection (Level 5)

In the Let's Compare move, students learned how to compare ideas in order to help readers better understand their writing. In the Double Date move, students learned how to use dates as tools to orient readers and connect them to the topic. The Past and Present Connection is the fusion of these two moves.

Here, writers help readers better understand the central topic of their writing by drawing a parallel between something from the past and something from right now. Connecting a current event to a historical topic bridges the past and present for the reader and helps them understand both more coherently.

Notably, the connections that authors make between the past and the present do not always draw parallels between the same ideas or geographic areas. To help the reader make these connections across time, every Past and Present Connection will include "time indicators" for both the historical and present topics. Time indicators are not necessarily dates (although they can be and are for all the following content-area mentor texts) but allusions to a time period that will help situate the reader in a historical or present moment.

Let's be honest; this move is complex (in the best way!). It is nuanced and layered and multifaceted, but the payoff is big, as the Past and Present Connection gives both relevance and depth to its topics.

This is the basic formula: Historical Topic + Time Indicator + Analysis + Transition + Present Topic + Time Indicator + Analysis.

POP CULTURE

See figure 9.5 for an annotated mentor text demonstrating this method.

As you teach this move to your students, here are some things to consider.

» Students might point out that Taylor Swift's *Tortured Poets Department* album is the central topic of this *Rolling Stone* article. We would note that the Past and Present Connection move can be used when the central topic of the piece is current or historical.

» In addition to naming the historical topic, the author defines it for the reader.

» Here, the time indicator is the description of Clara Bow as a "flapper." The concept of a *flapper* is a relatively ubiquitous term; even if the reader didn't know to place it in the 1920s, they would likely understand it to represent a woman in the United States in the early 20th century.

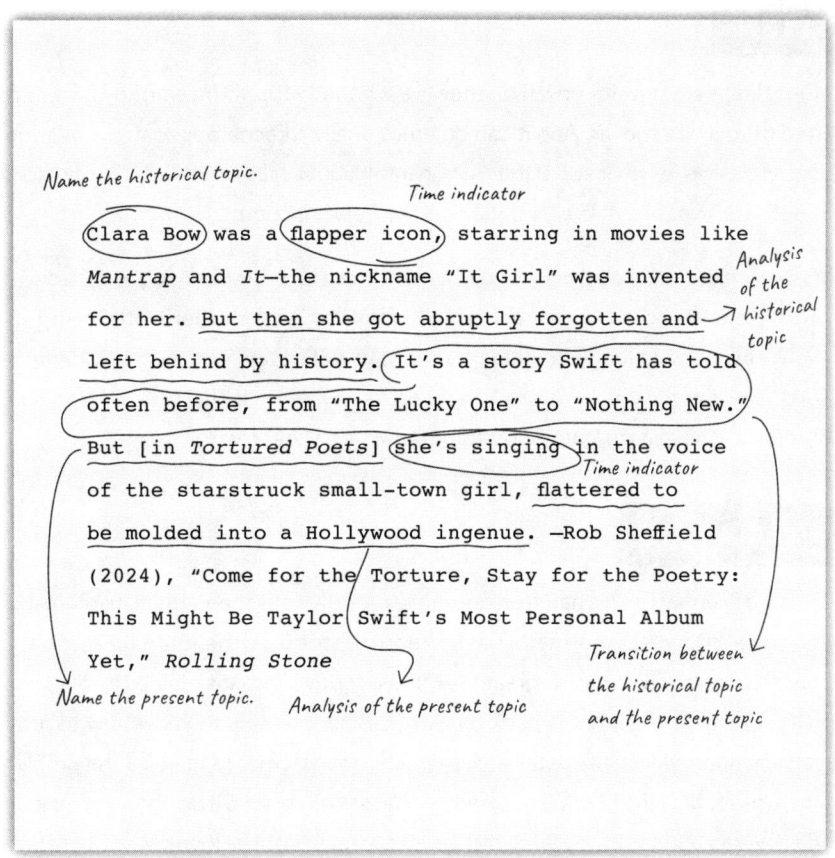

Figure 9.5: Past and Present Connection, annotated mentor text.

» Students might notice that the transition between the historical topic and the present topic identifies a connection between the two and states it explicitly for the reader.

» We would point out to students that the analysis of the historical topic sets up the author's analysis of the present topic by identifying a problem faced in the past and a solution in the present: Clara Bow was forgotten, but now she is remembered in a Taylor Swift song.

ENGLISH

Class leaps are far rarer now than they were in the 1940s, as research by Raj Chetty and others has shown. And it can be emotionally treacherous to move between social classes, or what social theorist Chantal Jaquet calls "transclass" in her recent book *Transclasses: A Theory of Social Non-Reproduction*. . . .

On one hand, Vance's personal narrative is the authentic-seeming apotheosis of Trump's own mostly false story of self-creation. On the other, both Trump and Vance are part of a longer tradition in American writing and entertainment centered on the self-made man. —Alissa Quart (2024), "JD Vance Is the Toxic Byproduct of America's Obsession With Bootstrap Narratives," *Literary Hub*

MATHEMATICS

Pierre de Fermat has his name on one of the most famous theorems in mathematics. For over 300 years, Fermat's Last Theorem stood as the ultimate symbol of unachievable mathematical greatness. In the 1600s, Fermat scribbled a note about his proposed theorem in a book he was reading, claiming to know how to prove it without providing any details. Mathematicians attempted to solve the problem themselves until the 1990s, when Andrew Wiles finally proved it using new techniques discovered hundreds of years after Fermat died. —Patrick Honner (2023b), "Pierre de Fermat's Link to a High School Student's Prime Math Proof," *Quanta Magazine*

SCIENCE

Over 2,500 years ago, Greek philosophers debated whether the nature of reality was impermanence or constant change. Heraclitus was the champion of change, pointing to the march of the seasons and the ebb and flow of the tides. In contrast, Parmenides, a near-contemporary of Heraclitus, claimed that change was illusory and constancy was the rule.

Modern physics has found subatomic examples that support both ways of thinking. For example, the electrons found in your atoms have been unchanged since the Universe began, supporting the constancy conjecture. However, in a clear example of constant change, another form of subatomic particles called neutrinos are in continuous flux, literally changing their identity over and over again. —Don Lincoln (2024), "IceCube Detector Confirms Deep-Space 'Ghost Particle' Phenomenon," *JSTOR Daily*

SOCIAL STUDIES

The first modern Olympic Games took place in Athens in 1896, thanks to the organizational efforts of one Pierre de Coubertin, a French baron who foresaw the value of a multinational sporting competition. "Olympism is not a system," Coubertin once said. "It is a state of mind." Ahead of the Paris 2024 Summer Olympics, here are nine surprising facts about the famed ancient sporting competition that inspired both Coubertin and later iterations of the Games. —Sonja Anderson (2024), "Nine Things You Didn't Know About the Ancient Olympic Games," *Smithsonian Magazine*

Use the reproducible "Writing Application Practice: Moves That Contextualize" (page 158) to contextualize.

Student Samples

The following student samples include moves that contextualize.

This sample uses Let's Compare (level 1):

> The people in the photo look like they are in a cult, making the picture stand out from the others. —Emma, Eighth Grade

This sample uses Show Me the Data (level 3):

> Production of plastic worldwide has increased since the pandemic by 6 million tons. Single-use plastics are the number 1, 2, 3, 4, and 5 most common forms of pollution in Virginia with rivers and beaches being hotspots for the pollution, according to the Virginia Department for Environmental Quality (DEQ). Plastic is so common on beaches in the U.S. because 121.4 billion tons of plastic are produced annually in the United States alone with 50% of that plastic meant for single-use according to Plastic Ocean. These single-use plastics are put into landfills and only 9% are currently recycled. The plastic in these landfills can take anywhere between 20 and 600 years to decompose according to The World Economic Forum. Even when these plastics decompose they leave behind micro plastics that can be digested by sea animals that humans later eat. —Tabor, Eighth Grade

This sample uses Past and Present Connection (level 5):

> Getting up and watching the Sunday Morning show with my Mom has become, in a way, a tradition. But every time I sit down to watch the show there's always a segment on war. War fills the streets in Ukraine. War fills the streets in Israel, Gaza, Palestine, and it never seems to end. It's not all that different looking at pictures of WWII. All of them are black and white, and they all show the same scenes of death, destruction, or people crying. Like the photos I see every Sunday morning, it's depressing. —Camryn, Eighth Grade

Writing Application Practice: Moves That Contextualize

After teaching your students one of these moves—or all of these moves—you'll be looking for an opportunity for them to practice these skills immediately.

For each writing task, we have provided a prompt you could use to get your students writing. They can use this prompt to practice a single move for that writing task or to begin combining, mixing, and matching moves. You can find all writing application practice from the whole book in one place in appendix C (page 275).

Content Area	Writing Application Practice
English	Choose a character from a work of fiction who fits the definition of an antihero (someone who doesn't have conventional hero traits but is still the central character of a story). How might their past experiences have affected their development into an antihero, rather than a typical hero?
Mathematics	Consider the most recent theorem, formula, or mathematical figure that you have learned about in class. In one or two paragraphs, explain the significance of this theorem, formula, or mathematical figure.
Science	Think about an important scientific discovery. Provide the context someone would need to understand this discovery and why it is significant.
Social Studies	Consider the most recent event that you have learned about in class. Briefly, use the moves in this chapter to explain the central causes of this event.

Mini Moves for Every Writer © 2025 Solution Tree Press • SolutionTree.com
Visit **go.SolutionTree.com/literacy/MMEW** to download this free reproducible.

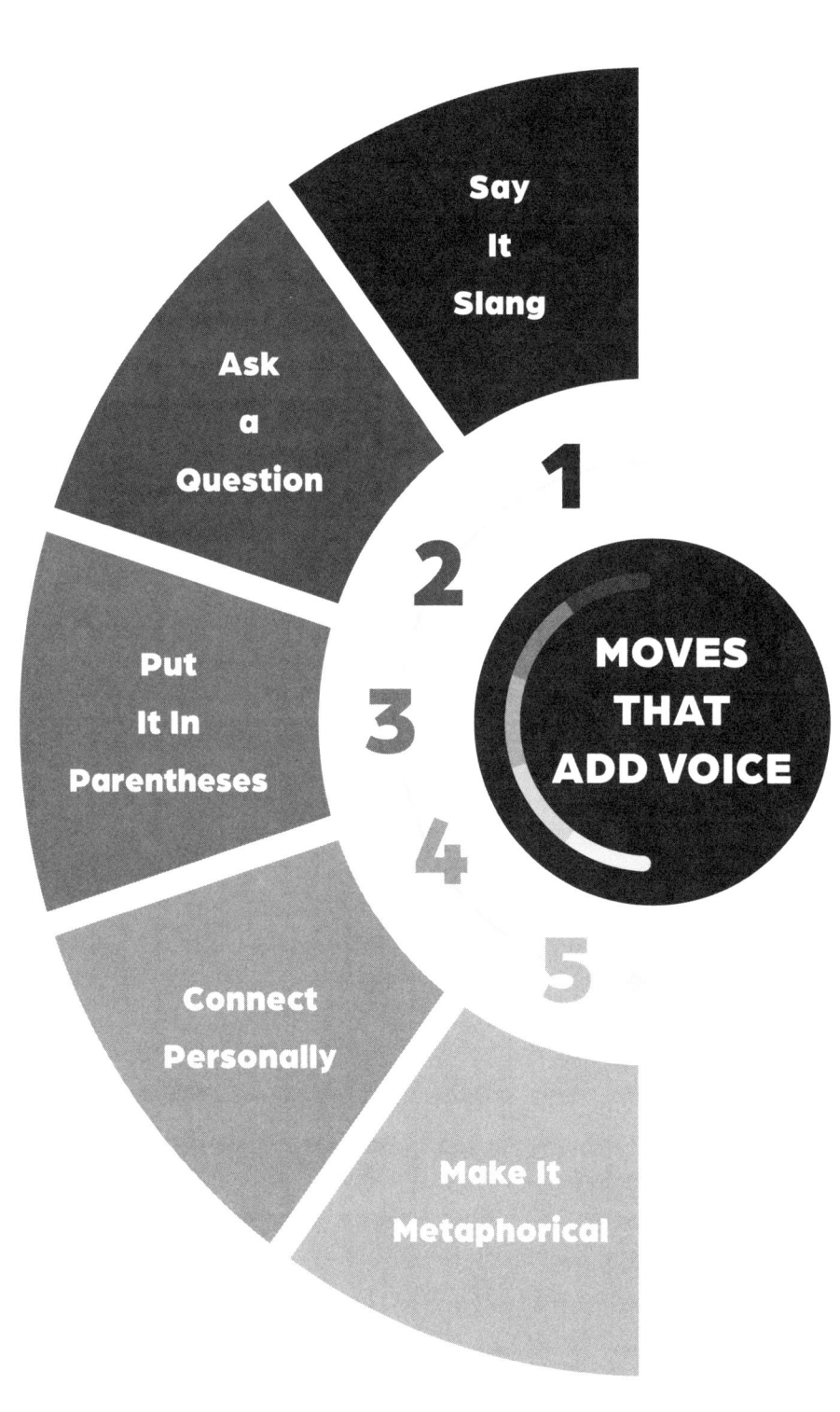

CHAPTER 10

Moves That Add Voice

The difference between the stack of student writing you want to read and the stack of student writing you don't want to read is voice.

Sure, student writing also has a range of interesting ideas and authoritative insights. But the writing that truly engages us as readers has voice. Voice is enigmatic, though. What *is* it? And is it even teachable?

According to the godfather of writing instruction, Donald M. Murray (1985), *voice* is "an individual writer speaking to an individual reader in an individual way" (p. 141). This is what generative AI cannot do.

Adding voice is the freedom and agency of a writer to communicate ideas in a way that feels true and like the real them. It's the personality on the page that reminds readers that a human is behind the writing. And, as you'll see in the mentor texts that follow, writing on absolutely any topic, formal or informal, can be full of voice.

We need to tread carefully when attempting to teach voice, though. In her book *The Anti-Racist Writing Workshop*, author Felicia Rose Chavez (2021) reminds us that asking students to write in their "authentic voice" is "a loaded term for a lot of people of color" (p. 79). Too often, writing with "authentic voice" has meant writing in a code-switched, adopted voice that sounds appealing to those in positions of power. The invitation to write with an authentic voice hasn't always been an honest one. Writer and essayist Matthew Salesses (2021) affirms this in what he says on talking to students about "finding their voice":

> Finding their voice . . . seems more about the cultural constructions that make us say one person has a "voice" and another does not and what kind of voice is acceptable, unique, bold, etc.—or to terms like "quiet" or "demanding" or "hooks you from the very first page," which are often more about our expectations of who should be quiet and who demands our attention. (pp. 92–93)

So, what we aim to offer in this chapter is not a definition of one kind of acceptable voice for writing. Rather, we hope to offer a handful of ways that writers' personalities often peek through their words and speak to the reader. We want you to see a few tools writers use to show voice rather than an evaluation of various writers' voices.

You'll notice that, unlike previous chapters, the moves in this chapter (and in chapter 12, page 195) don't have formulas or the annotations you're used to seeing in the pop culture examples. That's because these moves just don't work that way. Voice is a tangible way a writer's personality shows up on the page—it doesn't happen at a specific time or in a particular place every time. In full-of-voice writing, that personality is anywhere and everywhere.

At first, you and your students might feel a little nervous to proceed without the support of a formula to try or annotations to lean on. (We have included the moves in **bold** in the pop culture examples so that you can easily see what we mean.) You can do it! You've had oodles of writing practice so far, and the good news about not having a formula is that it means you can't do it wrong. Just try! See table 10.1 for recommended ways to begin experimenting.

Table 10.1: Writing Needs and Moves That Add Voice

When Writers Need...	Start Here...
To slip in a quick bit of personality without losing pace	Say It Slang (page 162) Put It in Parentheses (page 166)
To let the reader see the inner workings of their mind	Ask a Question (page 164) Make It Metaphorical (page 172)
To start a conversation with the reader	Ask a Question (page 164)
To tell a personal story	Connect Personally (page 169)

Say It Slang (Level 1)

Bestie, please note that while we're using the term *slang* to name this writing move, we are actually talking about something a little bit broader. Slang, colloquialisms, and idioms are all types of casual, everyday language that we would use when talking to our friends. It's the opposite of formal (iykyk).

When carefully chosen, this language makes writing sound like the writer is literally speaking to the reader. We can hear them! They are in the room! The call is coming from inside the house!

Writers need to use this move judiciously, of course. Some slang is regional or meant for a specific group—that makes it fun (slang establishes a kinship between the writer and the reader) and volatile (slang could possibly ostracize readers who are struggling to understand the nuance of specific words or phrases).

We recommend our young writers employ this move curatorially—meaning they use colloquial language only when it feels pitch-perfect. See the pop culture mentor text for an example.

POP CULTURE

If you need help re-orienting yourself to where things stand, **vis-a-vis** exactly whose noble **keister** now sits the Iron Throne and precisely which royal **chump** got his fool self royally chomped, here's a **handy** refresher. —Glen Weldon (2024), "'House of the Dragon' Season Premiere: I Told You the Rats Would Be a Whole Thing," *NPR* (emphasis added)

Here are some other features you and your students might consider together.

» When choosing slang, colloquialisms, or idioms that not only sound like you but also are comprehensible to the reader, take into consideration the audience.

* When students look at this example, it's possible that "vis-a-vis," "keister," and "chump" might be unfamiliar conversational language. This language is a little bit dated. Talk to your students about this!

* Who might students guess is the audience for this piece based on its subject matter and its place of publication?

* Is the slang accessible to the audience for which it is written? What kind of conversational language would be appropriate for that audience? This is something students need to consider, too.

» Students might notice that conversational language isn't explained in any of the examples here.

* If the terms or phrases needed explanation, they would lose their punch.

* There are hints as to word meanings: The word "keister" is adjacent to "now sits," and the word "chump" is parallel to "fool."

* Conversational language must be considered as a type of diction; students must be able to include it without a definition and still trust that the reader will understand.

ENGLISH

C'est la vie, of course, unless you are some type of time-lord wizard. But novelists *are* wizards, or at least magicians, and one of their favorite tricks is to fit whole narrative worlds inside a single day, book-shaped ships squeezed into bottles. —Leah Greenblatt (2024), "2 Novels Set Over Very Memorable Days," *The New York Times*

MATHEMATICS

The three researchers were trying to show that there couldn't be too many of these points, but so far, all their techniques had come up short.

They seemed to be spinning their wheels. —Erica Klarreich (2024), "Merging Fields, Mathematicians Go the Distance on Old Problem," *Quanta Magazine*

SCIENCE

Its unique hard covering, which may remind you of Taco Tuesday, most likely helped propel it through water, at times upside-down. —Rebecca Dzombak (2024), "Secrets Emerge From a Fossil's Taco Shell-Like Cover," *The New York Times*

SOCIAL STUDIES

When I ran in the House primary in 2009 and got clobbered, I used to wonder: How could I justify going to Washington, DC, for two years and claiming to represent 600,000 people back in Chicago? —Thomas Geoghegan (2020), "In the People's House There Are Many Mansions," *Lapham's Quarterly*

Ask a Question (Level 2)

It's 2068. We hobble into our classrooms (Retirement? In this economy?) and begin to review our most recent batches of student essays. Not one of them begins with a rhetorical question. Like ghosts who have returned to the mortal realm to resolve their unfinished business, we put down our pens and allow our teaching souls to exit our bodies. At last, our work is complete.

This is, perhaps, an exaggeration. (Or a prediction. Who is to say?) But the truth is, random rhetorical questions are writing vibe killers. They offer nothing to the piece. Consider this opening: "Have you ever thought about mitochondria? I know I have." We can't emphasize this enough: No one is thinking about the mitochondria! Rhetorical questions like this feel untethered to reality. They make it seem as if the writer is not reading the room, and good writing is all about reading the room.

However, authentic, clever, and well-placed rhetorical questions can be powerful tools that add voice to a piece of writing. This happens in two ways. First, looking the reader in the eye, so to speak, and asking a question sets up a conversational vibe that makes the reader feel like they are in dialogue with the human behind the writing.

Second, rhetorical questions add voice by letting the reader into the writer's actual thought process. The questions a writer shares reflect what it sounds like to be inside their brain. And, in that way, the reader gets to know the writer better and feel more connected to them. See the example pop culture mentor text.

POP CULTURE

> The candy-store music, the ultra-synthetic animation, the mixture of slow, bobbing movement and relentless editing—watch it for more than a few minutes, and you feel like you're hallucinating. **Where are we? Who are these children?** JJ has only two teeth, but he knows the alphabet and plays soccer. **What sort of baby is this?**
> —Jia Tolentino (2024), "How Cocomelon Captures Our Children's Attention," *The New Yorker* (emphasis added)

Consider this when sharing this move with your students.

» Students might notice that the rhetorical questions here appear in clusters. With only one exception (social studies, page 166), our examples show rhetorical questions strung together in lists. Why? There are a few possibilities.

- Perhaps the writer simply has multiple questions.
- Another possibility is that when we read a list of questions in a row, our pace increases. We read with more intensity. And that intensity mimics the intensity the writer feels about the questions swirling in their head.

» For rhetorical questions to work as a voice move (and not annoy the reader), they have to be authentic. They must be real questions that the reader believes truly come from the writer. This is the same reason why opening with a rhetorical question has become a cheesy cliché. It doesn't feel true or real.

- Here, the author leads into the rhetorical questions with the line "you feel like you're hallucinating." Then, the rhetorical questions mirror this disorientation.
- The author breaks up the question cluster with a description of the absurd to further emphasize their bewilderment.
- The final question becomes a more specific inquiry based on the statement before it.

» Students might notice that the first question includes the plural first-person pronoun, *we*. This strategy draws the reader into the scene with the writer.

ENGLISH

Other writers have persuasively argued for Colwin's ongoing relevance, particularly in regard to the 2021 reissues of her fiction and cooking essays. But my questions were more personal: Would her narratives speak to me nearly 30 years after first reading them? Would I still revel in Colwin's enchantment? Was it finally time to write about her and what she had meant to me? —Mia Manzulli (2024), "In Praise of the Domestic Sensualist: Laurie Colwin at 80," *Literary Hub*

MATHEMATICS

Then Peluse had a thought: What if they ditched the harmonic analysis problem—temporarily, of course—and turned their attention to sets of points in which the distance between any two points is exactly an integer? What possible structures can such sets have? —Erica Klarreich (2024), "Merging Fields, Mathematicians Go the Distance on Old Problem," *Quanta Magazine*

SCIENCE

Over the next century, eclipse expeditions helped settle one of the biggest mysteries in science: Was Mercury's odd orbit due to an undiscovered sun-hugging planet (which would presumably become visible during an eclipse)? Or, as turned out to be the case, was there some problem with Newton's understanding of gravity? —Joshua Sokol (2024), "How the Ancient Art of Eclipse Prediction Became an Exact Science," *Quanta Magazine*

SOCIAL STUDIES

Inside the White House, the subject of immigration, and especially the border, is seen as politically risky; there's a refrain among advisers that a good day for the President is one without immigration in the news. Why, then, did Biden decide to issue a proclamation reasserting that there was a crisis when he'd actually been managing to keep it at bay? —Jonathan Blitzer (2024), "What's Behind Joe Biden's Harsh New Executive Order on Immigration?," *The New Yorker*

Put It in Parentheses (Level 3)

Every teacher will tell you that faculty meetings are the bane of their existence, with endless updates that were already communicated via email, quibbles about policies that will likely never change, and that one person who asks every question that comes into their mind (put your hand down, Reid).

We choose to survive this Sisyphean act of drudgery by supplying our teacher besties with an undercurrent of commentary. So, depending on who you ask, we are actually a lot of fun in faculty meetings. Side comments ("OK, but we all know Alicia didn't turn in her homework"), inside jokes ("*Dragons* starts with a *K*"), and direct messages of praise ("Go off, Wells!") keep us sane.

Parentheses can be employed to add voice as the grammatical equivalents of these asides.

Not all parentheses add voice—some simply add facts or extra information. But the parentheses that *do* add voice are like that faculty meeting buddy, offering colorful bits of personality. This move has similarities to Ask a Question, but it takes a bit more consideration. Rhetorical questions need to be authentic, and in that way, they should come to the writer organically. What goes in the parentheses should be an abbreviated and quippy version of what's in the author's head.

Writers might choose parentheses as a way to add their voice when they want to share a personal opinion that isn't part of their main idea or message. You get the feeling when you read these personality-plus parentheses that the writer just can't resist adding their comment. They just have to squeeze it in somewhere, so they tuck it into parentheses. See the example pop culture mentor text.

POP CULTURE

> And Brenda, as played memorably by Shannen Doherty, who died on Saturday, knew who her peers were. **When she dons a (hideous) hat in Season 1, she is met with derision.** "Hippie witch is out," sneers Kelly (Jennie Garth). —Margaret Lyons (2024), "In 'Beverly Hills, 90210,' Shannen Doherty Redefined Teen TV Drama," *The New York Times* (emphasis added)

You might notice the following as you study this mentor text with your students.

» This pop culture example works well because it highlights the difference between parentheses that add voice—"(hideous)"—and parentheses that don't—"(Jennie Garth)." This is something you'll want to talk about with your students. Consider grabbing a few other examples of non-voice-filled parentheses to show your students all the different things parentheses can do.

» Parentheses can sometimes be associated with snark. That's true here. The parentheses act as a grammatical hand over the mouth as the writer whispers a sarcastic remark.

» But writers can parenthetically show their voice and perspective without humor. Consider the mathematics example. It's still offering an aside, but it's informative rather than snarky. When this move fits the writer, they should use it! But when it doesn't fit the writer, they shouldn't feel compelled to aim for funny.

ENGLISH

But, while many public beaches remained closed, "Beach Read" blew up on TikTok. Cooped-up daughters pressed it on distracted mothers (present company included). The book sailed onto the best-seller list, where it remained for more than a year.

. . . At Henry's request, Chiu outfitted Daphne's free-spirited L. I. (that's romance lingo for love interest) in a pair of yellow Crocs. —Elisabeth Egan (2024), "Emily Henry on Writing Best-Sellers Without Tours or TikTok," *The New York Times*

MATHEMATICS

The first proof of this (there would be several) is commonly attributed to Pythagoras, a 6th-century BCE philosopher, even though none of his writings survive and little is known about him. —Jordana Cepelewicz (2024a), "How the Square Root of 2 Became a Number," *Quanta Magazine*

SCIENCE

To me, a program isn't static code, it's the embodiment of a living creature that follows my instructions to a (hopefully) successful conclusion. I know computers don't physically work this way, but that doesn't stop my metaphorical machine. —Lance Fortnow (2024), "Computation Is All Around Us, and You Can See It If You Try," *Quanta Magazine*

SOCIAL STUDIES

For the next fourteen years he slaved singlemindedly with a team of assistants in a room provided by Clarendon, Oxford's press (no doubt with, in Oxford dialect, his *oak sported*—his door shut firm). —Simon Winchester (2012), "Native Tongues," *Lapham's Quarterly*

Connect Personally (Level 4)

For the most part, we aren't writing this book in the same room. Partly because we might harm each other (just kidding; we are obsessed with each other), but we also have totally opposite schedules when we're not teaching. So, by and large, we have written this book in sections and exchanged them to fuse our voices together.

To supplement this, we have also sent each other codependent text messages about paragraphs, sentences, and naming conventions that made us seem like middle schoolers on the verge of a serious relationship.

I called this move "Double Date." Do you like it?
  a. Yes
  b. No
  c. Maybe
  d. Please leave me alone. It's 2 a.m. on a Wednesday.

Maybe this is unhealthy, but it works. We want to make sure both of us are invested in the writing and connect to it in a personal way.

When a writer connects personally, they take a topic (typically, one that doesn't seem personal) and share a little bit of story to reveal the person behind the ideas on the page. Essentially, they say to the reader, "Here's why I care about this," and that makes the reader care, too. Sometimes, this involves a micro story. Sometimes, it's just a sentence or two that put the writer in their essay alongside their ideas.

No matter how a writer does it, connecting personally makes the writing lively, more interesting, and much more full of voice. See the example pop culture mentor text for an effective demonstration of this method. Please note that, in the following pop culture mentor text, we are not highlighting the move because, really, it's the whole thing!

POP CULTURE

I must tell you that I have been *Ratatouille*'d. Except instead of a rodent making me cook gourmet meals, it's a blonde 4'11" pop star named Sabrina Carpenter controlling my motor functions to make me repeat a phrase that doesn't even make sense: "That's that me espresso."

"We don't have Coke, is Pepsi okay?" That's that me espresso.

"How much do you want to contribute to your 401(k)?" That's that me espresso.

"Sir, do you know why we pulled you over? Do you know how fast you were going?" That's that me espresso.

Like the man Carpenter's singing about in "Espresso," I am up thinking about her every night—and of course her espresso. —Alex Abad-Santos (2024b), "Sabrina Carpenter's 'Espresso,' the Song of the Summer, Explained," *Vox*

As you teach this move to your students, here are some things to consider.

» This pop culture example is gold, isn't it? So much voice. Students will immediately notice the use of first-person pronouns—*I, me, my*. So often, students are told that this is forbidden in their writing at school, but notice that every mentor text we share uses first person! It's a thing real professional writers do in lots of different content areas and in many different kinds of publications! Don't be afraid to let your student writers try it!

» These personal connections take up some real estate in a piece of writing. While they aren't tremendously long, most of our mentor texts have multiple short paragraphs. Here are some guiding questions for students to consider when deciding whether this is the voice move a student wants to use.

* "Is this a longer piece of writing where I have some space to make a meaningful connection?"
* "Is this a piece of writing where concision is key and, perhaps, a different voice move would be better?"

» The trick with this move is for a writer to take something that is somewhat ubiquitous, or at least in the zeitgeist (like Sabrina Carpenter), and tie a specific thread between themselves and it. In this way, the writer claims that thing we all know as their own, and by doing so, helps the reader know them just a bit more.

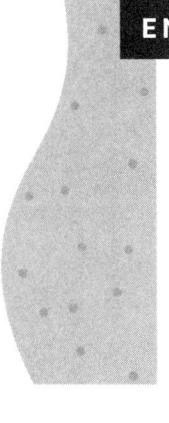

ENGLISH

My idea of hell would be to live with a library that contained only reimaginings of famous novels. It's a wet-brained and dutiful genre, by and large. Or the results are brittle spoofs—to use a word that, according to John Barth, sounds like imperfectly suppressed flatulence—that read as if there are giant scare quotes surrounding the action. Two writers in a hundred walk away unscathed.

"James" is the rarest of exceptions. —Dwight Garner (2024a), "'Huck Finn' Is a Masterpiece. This Retelling Just Might Be, Too," *The New York Times*

MATHEMATICS

This is the "handshake problem," and it's one of my favorites. As a math teacher, I love it because there are so many different ways you can arrive at the solution, and the diversity and interconnectedness of those strategies beautifully illustrate the power of creative thinking in math. —Patrick Honner (2024), "Math That Connects Where We're Going to Where We've Been," *Quanta Magazine*

SCIENCE

As a geologist, I have had the extraordinary opportunity to work on both the Curiosity and Perseverance rover missions. Yet as much as scientists are learning from them, it will take another robotic mission to figure out if Mars has ever hosted life. That mission will bring Martian rocks back to Earth for analysis. Then—hopefully—we will have an answer.

While so much remains mysterious about Mars, there is one thing I am confident about. Amid the thousands of pictures both rovers are taking, I'm quite sure no alien bears or meerkats will show up in any of them. Most scientists doubt the surface of Mars, or its near-surface, could currently sustain even single-celled organisms, much less complex forms of life. —Amy J. Williams (2024), "NASA's Search for Life on Mars," *JSTOR Daily*

SOCIAL STUDIES

I became newly worried about the state of democracy when, a few years ago, my mother was elected president of her neighborhood garden club.

Her election wasn't my worry—far from it. At the time, I was trying to resolve a conflict on a large email group I had created. Someone, inevitably, was being a jerk on the internet. I had the power to remove them, but did I have the right? I realized that the garden club had in its bylaws something I had never seen in nearly all the online communities I had been part of: basic procedures to hold people with power accountable to everyone else.

The internet has yet to catch up to my mother's garden club. —Nathan Schneider (2024), "Why the Future of Democracy Could Depend on Your Group Chats," *The Conversation*

Make It Metaphorical (Level 5)

Even if your school is lucky enough to have a librarian, you have not been lucky enough to have Mary Carpenter. Mary Carpenter is the Harold Hill of books, except instead of conning a small town into buying musical equipment for a turn-of-the-century boy band, she convinces screen-obsessed middle school students into believing that they love books. She doesn't even have to read a book to them—she just talks about it. And suddenly, they decide that they must have it.

> "Oh, The Hunger Games? I can't believe you haven't read it. This book is a fight to the death with a little bit of kissing."

> "To All the Boys I've Loved Before? You will love this book and it will love you back. You need to read it."

And while our library may not have Broadway-style musical productions (although we have seen Mary stand on a bookshelf and sing "One Day More"), just like in the finale of *The Music Man* when the children play music to the delight of their parents, our students come to realize that they do, in fact, love to read.

Mary's gift in life is figurative language. And this move teaches us how to use figurative language to bring voice to our writing.

"Wait a minute," you may be thinking. "This move feels familiar. Haven't we already used figurative language as a move in this book?"

Yes. Yes, we have. Chapter 6 highlights Figurative Language Comparison (page 93) as a move writers use to add description. And it's true! Figurative language can help writers describe things so readers understand them in brand-new ways.

But figurative language—metaphors, similes, analogies—can also be used to show voice because it reveals the unique inner workings of the writer's mind. The associations a writer's mind makes when writing metaphorically tell us a lot about that writer's personality. See the pop culture mentor text for an effective example of this method.

POP CULTURE

Eilish is known for taking her time in a song, sometimes crawling through a melody **as though it were a bowl of molasses**, and she often chooses to sing in a whisper, letting a note hang in the air before it dissipates entirely. **Her vocal style reminds me of an evanescing cloud of smoke after someone blows out a cluster of birthday candles—beautiful, fleeting, a little bit haunted.** —Amanda Petrusich (2024), "The Anxious Love Songs of Billie Eilish," *The New Yorker* (emphasis added)

Here are some ideas worth noting as you share this move with your students.

» Notice how the writer here (and in the following mentor texts) writes their figurative comparison and then adds a little phrase to connect that figurative language to the topic about which they are writing. They explain it a tiny bit. In the pop culture example, writer Amanda Petrusich (2024) compares Billie Eilish's vocal style to "an evanescing cloud of smoke after someone blows out a cluster of birthday candles" and then explicitly says what she means by that. Both the cloud of smoke and Billie Eilish's voice are "beautiful, fleeting, a little bit haunted."

» It's worth sharing multiple mentor texts with your students. Ask them to make inferences—what can they guess about the writer's personality based on the figurative language they choose? This will help students see the connection between writerly personality and metaphorical language.

» Writers successfully use this move with varying degrees of formality and a range of different tones. That's voice, right? Notice how some of the mentor texts here are pretty casual and conversational. Others are fairly formal. This is another great chat to have with your students!

ENGLISH

Forgotten on Sunday is a *pain au chocolat* of a book—flaky but buttery, with a sweet center. This sentimental soul-soother is further sweetened by the knowledge that several of the characters are named, at least in part, after Perrin's grandparents, including Helene Hel's lost-and-found great love, Lucien Perrin. —Heller McAlpin (2024), "'Forgotten on Sunday' Evokes the Heartwarming Whimsy of the Movie 'Amélie,'" *NPR*

MATHEMATICS

Just as the software of your laptop runs without having to keep track of all the microscale information about the electrons in the computer circuitry, so emergent phenomena are governed by macroscale rules that seem self-contained, without heed to what the component parts are doing.

Using a mathematical formalism called computational mechanics, the researchers identified criteria for determining which systems have this kind of hierarchical structure. . . . They tested these criteria on several model systems known to display emergent-type phenomena, including neural networks and Game-of-Life-style cellular automata. —Philip Ball (2024c), "The New Math of How Large-Scale Order Emerges," *Quanta Magazine*

SCIENCE

Previously, all known ribosome-disrupting hibernation factors worked passively: They waited for a ribosome to finish building a protein and then prevented it from starting a new one. Balon, however, pulls the emergency brake. It stuffs itself into every ribosome in the cell, even interrupting active ribosomes in the middle of their work. —Dan Samorodnitsky (2024), "Most Life on Earth Is Dormant, After Pulling an 'Emergency Brake,'" *Quanta Magazine*

SOCIAL STUDIES

America's democracy is divided resentfully against itself across the frontiers of race, gender, ethnicity, and class. Vicious slander streams through the hydra-headed portals of the internet, goading quorums of non-law-abiding citizens to hate instead of help, love, or talk to one another. —Lewis H. Lapham (2024), "Power Outage," *Lapham's Quarterly*

Use the reproducible "Writing Application Practice: Moves That Add Voice" to add voice.

Student Samples

The following student samples include moves that add voice.

This sample uses Say It Slang (level 1):

> The Articles of Confederation were also a massive influence on the U.S. Constitution . . . These articles were a fail because they did not have a strong enough central government. So, the U.S. needed something better. —Anna, Eighth Grade

This sample uses Put It in Parentheses (level 3):

> The reason why I liked these lyrics is not because they were talking about mental problems in NF's head. (Trust me, I'm not a psychopath). It was because when he slid into the two rap verses, it was like feeling a third lung come up out of my mouth, making me hear the words, begging me to sing. —Danny, Seventh Grade

This sample uses Make It Metaphorical (level 5):

> It felt like I had just slipped from a cliff. I had been climbing a tree and living in it for so long, ignoring the signs like the falling leaves and broken branches. But I never expected the tree to split, and for me to fall off the cliff I was next to. —Sophie, Eighth Grade

Writing Application Practice: Moves That Add Voice

Voice moves can be used anytime and anywhere to elevate the personality of a piece of writing. Instead of four individual writing exercises, here is a single idea that allows students to practice a move while demonstrating how moves that use voice can be employed differently and uniquely by each author.

Consider the last piece of writing you did in class. Reread it, and revise it to include at least one of the voice moves used in this chapter. Then, exchange your writing with someone in your class who has chosen the same move. Read what they have written, and answer the question, "What do the author's choices with regard to the move reflect about their personality?" Exchange papers and share your reflections.

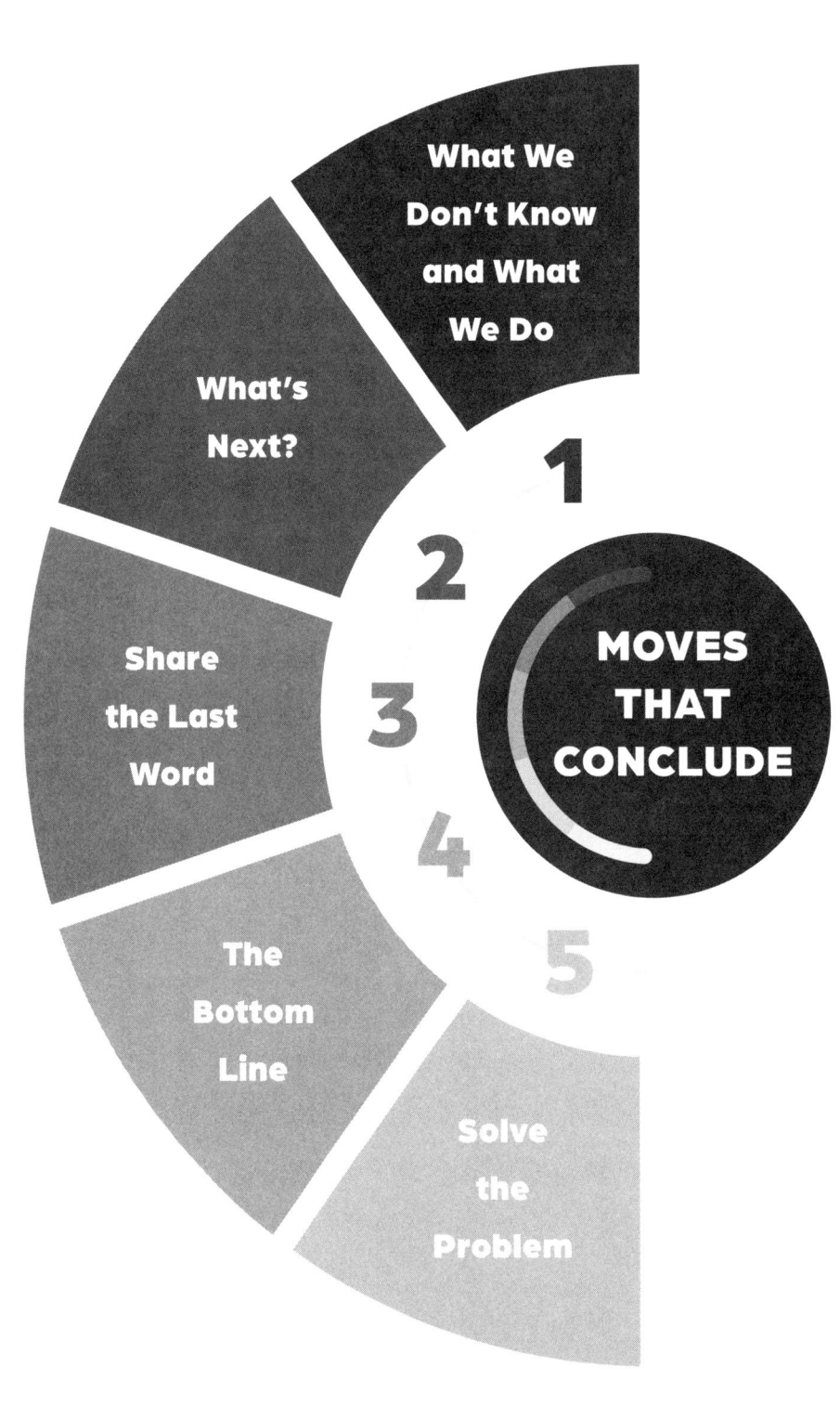

CHAPTER 11

Moves That Conclude

While getting started is difficult, figuring out how to wrap things up is, arguably, even harder. What else is there to say? And how do you say it in a way that isn't just rehashing everything you've said before in different words?

Our middle schoolers don't just struggle to conclude their writing; they struggle to conclude their conversations with us. While we were writing this book, our student Bridget recounted her summer escapades to us. We listened as best we could to her journey to the Outer Banks with her family, but by the mention of her sixth summer crush's name, we got a bit lost. Bridget eventually read the room and realized that she *might* be occupying a bit too much of our free time. Rather than bringing her story to a natural close, she laughed and shouted, "OK. I think I shared too much! *Bye!*" and left the room.

While this was certainly a decisive way to conclude the story, there, perhaps, was a better way to sum up her beach-filled escapades.

Sometimes, students know that they are "supposed to" conclude, but they struggle to see the purpose in a conclusion. And so they panic in the face of concluding—so much so that, in our classes, sometimes, they just *don't*. They just stop writing and press Submit. Bridget's "laugh, shout, and run away" tactic was the real-life version of this.

So why do writers write conclusions? Writers actually have lots of different potential goals when concluding.

- » To simplify something complex
- » To open up their ideas for next steps and forward movement
- » To share an expert's final take on the ideas the writer has presented
- » To acknowledge what's missing from the writer's understanding
- » To reiterate what is known in the face of remaining questions

» To provide possible answers and solutions to the questions and problems that have been proposed elsewhere in the piece

Conclusions can matter. The five conclusion moves in this chapter will help your writers do more than repeat their previous ideas so that they craft conclusions that resonate. See table 11.1 for recommendations on how best to conclude depending on writers' goals and circumstances.

Table 11.1: Writing Needs and Moves That Conclude

When Writers Need...	Start Here...
To ask more questions or complicate	What We Don't Know and What We Do (page 178)
	What's Next? (page 181)
	Solve the Problem (page 188)
To wrap things up neatly or simplify	Share the Last Word (page 183)
	The Bottom Line (page 186)
	Solve the Problem (page 188)
To write a conclusion that looks back	The Bottom Line (page 186)
	Solve the Problem (page 188)
To write a conclusion that looks forward	What We Don't Know and What We Do (page 178)
	What's Next? (page 181)

What We Don't Know and What We Do (Level 1)

Most writing is spent telling the reader what the writer knows or believes. This can be exhausting and intimidating for emerging writers. How are they supposed to know everything?

Quite simply, they are not expected to know everything. And a conclusion is a great place to review what the writer knows and what they don't (yet). When a writer uses this type of conclusion, they very directly and simply state what they know. Then, they wrap up the piece by acknowledging what they don't know. This might be information about the future (which no writer can predict), or what they don't know might just be missing pieces of information that the writer could not find.

A What We Don't Know and What We Do conclusion has a flair of authenticity as the writer plainly shares, "Even now that I'm finished writing, here's what I don't know yet," and then doubles down by summarizing (usually in a single sentence!) what they *do* know to be true.

This is the basic formula: What We Know + What We Still Don't Know. Or, What We Still Don't Know + *but* + What We Know.

POP CULTURE

See figure 11.1 for an effective example of this method.

As you teach this move to your students, here are some things you might discuss.

» The first thing we notice when we look at this conclusion is that the first sentence is very long. (Your students might even say, "That's a run-on

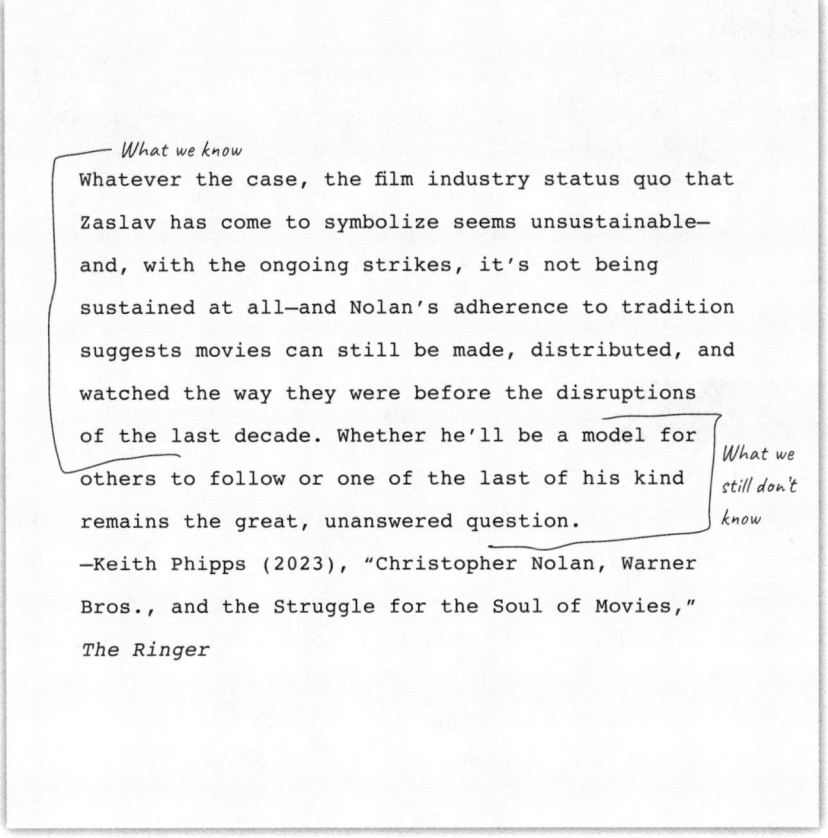

Figure 11.1: What We Don't Know and What We Do, annotated mentor text.

sentence," simply because of the length!) It's a good opportunity to talk about how very long sentences work well sometimes.

» What the writer knows is largely a reiteration of what they have said prior to the conclusion of the piece.

» Almost all our mentor texts here use some sort of language to indicate to the reader that they are segueing into what they don't know. Here, the author notes that this is an "unanswered question." Students can use this strategy in their own writing.

» Students might notice that the two parts of this move are interchangeable. If you look at all the mentor texts here, you'll see that some writers put "what we know" first, and some writers put "what we don't know" first. It works both ways! Students can play around with this, trying it both ways to see which they like best.

» The following mathematics and social studies examples (page 180) posit the "what we don't know" portion as a question. This is another option students can try on.

ENGLISH

Late Bloomers doesn't show how seeing, or rather, *learning to resee*, takes time. All the same, implicit in the novel's gardening motif is a modest message: we seldom care for ourselves with the same determination as for our plants. About the things we care most—namely, ourselves—we lie. And what in turn eludes us is the emergence of new buds within ourselves, blooms that lay dormant for years before opening to the sun. —Rajat Singh (2023), "I Became a Writer When I Needed a Fresh Start," *Electric Literature*

MATHEMATICS

Meanwhile, another question looms: To create a black hole of three spatial dimensions, must an object be compressed in all three directions, as Thorne insisted, or could compression in two directions or even just one be enough? All evidence points to Thorne's statement being true, Khuri said, though it is not yet proved. Indeed, it is just one of many open questions that persist about black holes after they first manifested more than a century ago in a German soldier's notebook. —Steve Nadis (2023), "Math Proof Draws New Boundaries Around Black Hole Formation," *Quanta Magazine*

SCIENCE

Even if we learn all the answers to what's happening to the body in a heat wave, Shandas said we still don't understand "a lot of the human face of heat," as in, how people actually cope. What scientists do understand is that this is just the beginning of these consequences playing out on a global scale. It's only going to get hotter from here. —Rebecca Leber (2023), "The Invisible Consequences of Heat on the Body and Mind," *Vox*

SOCIAL STUDIES

Even today, Sam continues to evolve—and Claire Jerry, a curator at the National Museum of American History, says that there is an ongoing conversation among historians and archivists about whether it's time for him to get yet another makeover. The question, as Jerry puts it, is: "How can he in fact symbolize the whole country?" Perhaps he can't—but one possible answer is to portray Uncle Sam as multiracial, and over the past decade, there has been increasing interest in creating a Black Uncle Sam. As Jerry says: "Uncle Sam will evolve along with us." —Brandon Tensley (2023), "Meet Brother Jonathan, the Predecessor to Uncle Sam," *Smithsonian Magazine*

What's Next? (Level 2)

We often wrap up one class period by previewing what we will do next class: "Next time, we'll return to this doc and discuss as a group, so make sure you put it somewhere safe," we might say to students before they promptly leave the paper on their desks.

A What's Next? conclusion does the same thing (the preview part, we mean)—it acknowledges that the topic of the essay isn't finished just because the essay is. Something else will happen in the future. In a What's Next? conclusion, the writer defies wrapping things up in a neat little bow by suggesting what will happen after the essay concludes. What's next for these people? What's next for this area of scholarship? What's next in tackling this question or problem? The writer often gives immediate next steps that project their idea into the future or asks questions for further contemplation.

This is the basic formula: Current Status of the Topic + Explanation of What's Next.

POP CULTURE

See figure 11.2 for an effective example of this method.

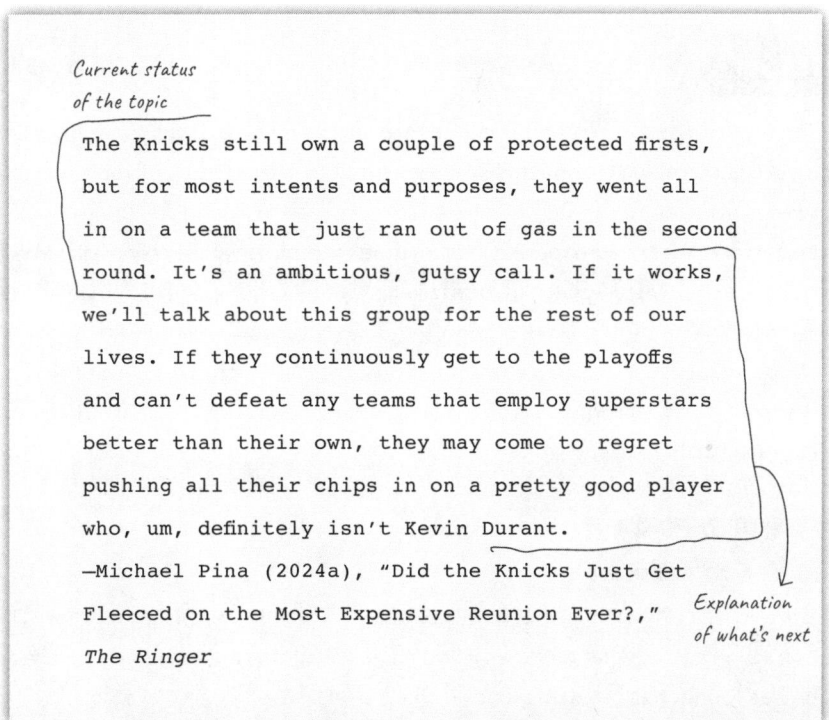

Figure 11.2: What's Next?, annotated mentor text.

Consider this when sharing this move with your students.

» The writer begins by stating the current state of affairs. (In this case, the Knicks spent all their money and still didn't do well in the playoffs.)

» To answer the question, "What's next?" Michael Pina (2024a) actually suggests two possibilities of what might be next for the Knicks beginning with the word "if." We can borrow this structure: "If _____. If _____."

» Writers use this move in different ways. In this example, the "What's next?" is speculative. Other writers in the following examples ask a key question that will need to be answered in the future, state next steps for the future, or suggest how we might move forward. The focus on the future is what all these writers have in common.

» We love the voice in the preceding pop culture example. Check out that last sentence—it sounds like we are hanging out with Michael Pina, chatting about the team. He achieves this by using conversational language and including "um," making the writing feel like he's actually speaking aloud.

ENGLISH

The urge to indulge this outrage can seem overpowering, and I still sometimes find myself succumbing to thoughts like "I can't wait to see all the awful replies to that tweet." Still, more often than not, I can turn away, and my life has become infinitely better for it. I'm not sure I believe that institutional change alone is enough to keep each new social media platform from falling prey to the worst side of human nature. Is it possible for us, the users of the internet, to learn how to simply *not go there*? I hope so, because that may be what it takes to get us out of Rose-Stockwell's dark valley and back into the sun. —Laura Miller (2023), "How to Short-Circuit the Outrage Machine," *Slate*

MATHEMATICS

Socolar, as a physicist, has begun exploring the tilings' material properties. The diffraction pattern that emerges if you shine a light through one of these tilings, he has found, has the same kind of sharp peaks researchers have observed in quasicrystals. Even so, the hat tiling "looks to me to be different from anything else I've seen before," he said.

Meanwhile, Smith isn't done with his "tricky little tile." He intends to explore its artistic possibilities and figure out how to use colors to bring out the patterns the tile appears to insist upon. —Erica Klarreich (2023b), "Hobbyist Finds Math's Elusive 'Einstein' Tile," *Quanta Magazine*

SCIENCE

Our research group and other scientists are using computer simulations and numerical "larvae" to investigate how temperature, salinity and other factors may affect transport of marine organisms. With better understanding of these surf-zone conveyor belts, we aim to help keep swimmers safe and assess how rip currents affect aquatic ecosystems near the shore. —Emma Shie Nuss, Audrey Casper, Christine M. Baker, Melissa Moulton, and Walter Torres (2023), "Rip Currents Are Dangerous for Swimmers but Also Ecologically Important—Here's How Scientists Are Working to Understand These 'Rivers of the Sea,'" *The Conversation*

SOCIAL STUDIES

Israel struck Beirut on Tuesday, targeting the official it blamed for Saturday's attack. Whatever Israel does next, it should be calculated to advance the national interests on all these fronts. If that means postponing a fuller response to explain its rationale, necessity and goal, so much the better. —Bret Stephens (2024), "Israel's Five Wars," *The New York Times*

Share the Last Word (Level 3)

By the time we've reached the end of a piece of writing, we've said *a lot*. We might even be tired of the (written) sound of our own voice. It's also possible that someone else could just put a pin in things better than we can.

And so, sometimes, the best way to end a piece of writing is by giving the last word, that last sound bite, to someone else. Ending a piece of writing with a resonant quote from someone else—typically an authoritative, expert voice—is a powerful note with which to leave the reader.

This is the basic formula: Final Idea + Quote From an Authoritative Voice.

POP CULTURE

See figure 11.3 (page 184) for an effective example of this method.

> {Final idea} Biles has also said she's focused less on external judgment. In Tokyo, some viewers reacted negatively to Biles's decision to pull out of competition, and if athletes—including her—make similar decisions in Paris, it's possible it could engender that same response from certain observers.
>
> *Quote from an authoritative voice*
>
> "I think it has to be for us, because it can't be for anybody else because that's not why we do it. We do it for ourselves, and the love for this sport, and the love for representing the US," Biles said in the press briefing. —Li Zhou (2024), "Simone Biles Is So Back," *Vox*

Figure 11.3: Share the Last Word, annotated mentor text.

You and your students might notice the following.

- » A writer using this move to conclude needs to find a really strong quote—not just any quote—that communicates the idea the writer wants to end on.

- » Students will notice that in this mentor text, the author is discussing Simone Biles's comeback. And who better to talk about Simone Biles's comeback than Simone Biles? Students can mimic this in their own writing; if the piece is about a person, they may give this figure the last word.

- » Here, Li Zhou (and two other mentor text writers) separates the Share the Last Word conclusion into two short paragraphs. Paragraph one contains the writer's final idea; paragraph two contains only the quote. This way works! Or the two parts can be put together in a single paragraph as other writers have done.

- » In the English example, the quote isn't from a person—it's from the literary text being discussed! Students could replicate this with a quote from a song, movie, TV show, or video game.

- » The source of the quote needs to be cited in some way. Our mentors state the name of the source before or after the quote so that the reader knows who said it.

ENGLISH

Imelda drives, one dark afternoon, into the countryside and finds that the yellow hills, the old landmarks, all Ireland, provide no answer to the problems that plague her: "At the crossroads a shuttered pub a blackened sign Guinness Time the country gazes back at you like a mirror with nothing in it." —Dan Kois (2023), "A Novel That Strives to Engage the World on Every Single Page," *Slate*

MATHEMATICS

But he also pointed out that pseudorandom processes are powerful tools, and projects like constructing primes are just one way of using them to connect ideas from mathematics, computer science, information theory and other areas.

"It's exciting to try and think where else these brilliant observations will lead," Tell said. —Stephen Ornes (2023), "How to Build a Big Prime Number," *Quanta Magazine*

SCIENCE

But LTT 9779 b may just be the benchmark for such ultrahot Neptunes. The more the team learns, the more they realize how rare it really is. "It's a super important world," Dr. Jenkins said, adding that the diversity of planets in the cosmos stretches far beyond those found in our own solar system. "Hopefully, we'll stumble across another." —Katrina Miller (2023), "Titanium Clouds Engulf This Ultrahot Neptune-Like Planet," *The New York Times*

SOCIAL STUDIES

The lunar poles are thought to be where most commercial activity will take place as they're thought to contain billions of litres of water ice, vital for manned stations. It could get crowded.

As Ye Peijian, head of China's lunar exploration programme, recently said: "If we don't go there now, even though we are capable of doing so, then we will be blamed by our descendants. If others go, they will take over and you won't be able to go even if you want to." —Tim Marshall (2023), "The Future of Geography and Rise of Astropolitics," *Geographical*

The Bottom Line (Level 4)

When writers use the Bottom Line move to conclude a piece of writing, their goal isn't to repeat all they've said before because they can't think of anything else to say. The goal is to reiterate the central claim of the piece—first in a way that shows the complexity of their argument and then in a way that simplifies those ideas by boiling them down to their essentials and saying them plainly. Writers zoom out and away from the minutiae of their ideas and hover above them to show the big idea that's really at the heart of their piece.

That bottom-line idea or lesson learned becomes a logline for the whole piece—a takeaway for the reader. What's this piece about? Well, here's the Bottom Line.

This is the basic formula: Complex Claim + Simplified Claim.

POP CULTURE

See figure 11.4 for an effective example.

Complex claim

> In a gaming landscape where nearly every open world game can, eventually, be reduced into a simple set of chores on a map, the first 20 hours of Tears of the Kingdom are a revelation. No game since Elden Ring has sparked our sense of discovery so strongly—and where that game over-awed with scale and mystery, this latest Zelda game does something similar with an energetic sense of play. If the phrase "The WarioWare of Zelda games" makes sense to you, you understand what we're trying to convey here; if not, then we'll put it in simpler language: One of the most talented video game design teams on the planet has let their imaginations go with this one, and the results are impeccable. We can't wait to play more. —William Hughes (2023), "First Impressions: *Zelda: Tears of the Kingdom* Is the Most Purely Fun Nintendo Game in a Decade," *AV Club*

Simplified claim

Figure 11.4: The Bottom Line, annotated mentor text.

Here are some other features you and your students might consider together.

» This conclusion opens with two long sentences (including comparisons and allusions to other games) that describe the video game in a variety of ways before the conclusion puts it into "simpler language."

- We would encourage our writers to remember that they are not simply restating an earlier claim in this move. Readers who visit the *AV Club* to read this engaging piece will notice that writer William Hughes (2023) offers a version of these claims at the top of the piece: "The brilliance of *Tears of the Kingdom*, then, is this: It sets out to—and, impossibly, succeeds at—making players like us feel like high-flying demented geniuses like them."
- While the central argument of this claim aligns with what we see in the conclusion in its message, the configuration of the ideas is vastly different.

» Hughes acknowledges that it might be hard for the reader to understand what he is trying to say. Offering to "put it in simpler language" is a phrase we can borrow for our own conclusions.

» Look at that colon in the penultimate sentence. It acts like a drumroll propelling the reader into the Bottom Line. We could borrow that, too: "Let's put it in simpler language for you: [*bottom-line statement*]."

» While the first two sentences focus on details that make the game excellent, the Bottom Line zooms up and out, thinking about the quality of both the design team and the game overall: The design team is "one of the most talented" and the game is "impeccable." These relatively simple statements take in the totality of the topic.

ENGLISH

Black Leopard, Red Wolf and *Moon Witch, Spider King* can be disorienting and confusing books whose narratives jump around in time and treat such bizarre phenomenon as lightning vampires as if they need little explanation. Their difficulty will (and has) put off some readers, but for those who persevere, the two novels show how who you are shapes the kind of story you tell about the world around you, a world made new with every teller. —Laura Miller (2022), "The 'African *Game of Thrones*' Just Keeps Getting Better," *Slate*

MATHEMATICS

Imai is an expert witness for the plaintiffs in the pending Supreme Court case. The plaintiffs are arguing, using the ensembles he generated, that Alabama's districts violate the Voting Rights Act by disenfranchising Black voters. But the state of Alabama, which is being sued, is using his ensembles to argue that the map is fairly drawn. Whatever the court decides, it shows that, when it comes to elections, mathematics will always need to contend with politics. —Mike Orcutt (2023), "How Math Has Changed the Shape of Gerrymandering," *Quanta Magazine*

SCIENCE

Most of all, remember that having sharks around is a rare victory for conservation and—as we learn to live with them—human communities. These animals help sustain the ecosystems that support us all. —Benji Jones (2023a), "New York's Shark-Infested Waters Are a Good Thing. Yes, Really," *Vox*

SOCIAL STUDIES

The long history of vaccination and its opposition has taught us that the benefits of vaccines, which have become extremely safe, far outweigh the risks. But it also suggests that attending to the concerns of the targets and beneficiaries of public health initiatives is vital to the success of any policy to contain communicable diseases—which will always be with us, precisely because germs do not recognize the individual's right to bodily autonomy. —Nadja Durbach (2023), "Our Medical Liberties," *Lapham's Quarterly*

Solve the Problem (Level 5)

Solve the Problem appears in many state curricula as a ubiquitous text structure students should be able to identify and create themselves. This makes sense because all writers know that problems are launching pads for all kinds of writing. While an entire piece of writing can be built around a problem and potential solutions, writers sometimes condense that entire text structure into just the conclusion paragraph.

A Solve the Problem conclusion is satisfying. Like the Bottom Line conclusion, it *does* put a bow on the entire piece by arriving at an answer to a question that has been posed. Writers seem to use this type of conclusion in two different writing circumstances. Sometimes, this type of conclusion is used in a piece that uses a problem-solution text structure overall. The mathematics (page 190) and science (page 191) examples come from pieces like this. The entire article presents a problem and a solution, and then the conclusion does it again but in a tighter, briefer way.

The other time writers tend to use this kind of conclusion is when their essay is more of a journey that explores an idea. You can see examples of this kind of piece in the following pop culture, English (page 190), and social studies (page 191) examples. In this situation, a writer meanders a bit as they explore an idea. Then, at the end, they conclude by essentially saying, "Now that I've explored this idea, I'm realizing that this was the problem all along. And this is the solution."

This is the basic formula: Problem + Solution.

POP CULTURE

See figure 11.5 for an effective example of this method.

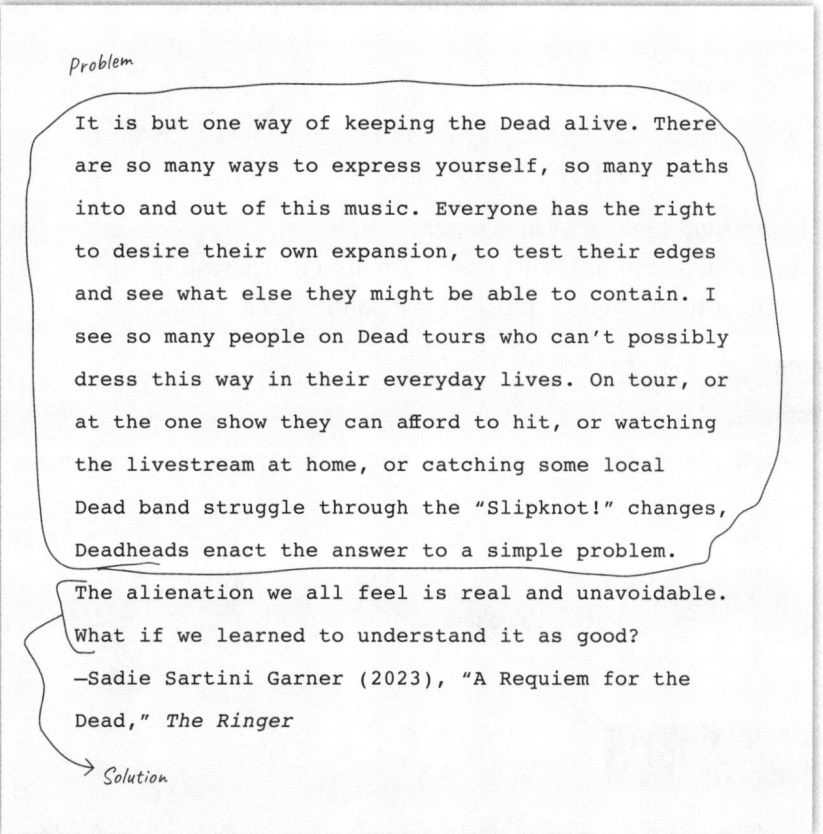

Figure 11.5: Solve the Problem, annotated mentor text.

As you study this move with your students, here are a few other items worth noting.

» This conclusion paragraph begins with a Hinge Transition (chapter 12, page 198). It's fun for students to begin to see the mixing and matching of writing moves in different pieces of writing as they are introduced to them!

» This writer, Sadie Sartini Garner, explicitly states that she is about to present a "simple problem." The writers of the following mentor texts don't do this quite as explicitly. This gives us two different methods for student writers to try.

» If students visited *The Ringer* to read the entirety of Garner's article, they would discover that this problem is the essay's central topic.

  * The first few sentences are a review of the essay's central points and act as a segue into the solution Garner presents.
  * Not all the mentor texts provided here do this. In the English mentor text, for example, the author presents the problem in the form of a question.
  * Encourage students to play with the varying structures for this move until they find what feels right for them.

» Interestingly, maybe even counterintuitively, the answer is presented as a rhetorical question: "What if we learned to understand it as good?" This might require a bit of discussion if it confuses some students.

ENGLISH

So how do we define ourselves in the age of Instagram and Reality TV? Maybe we don't. Maybe we date who we love and plant a garden in our backyard, and when the finale of *Love Is Blind* comes out, we sit on the couch, watch with our limbs intertwined, and laugh and smile and cringe and gasp. Maybe it's as simple as that. —Grace Kennedy (2023), "Searching for 'The One' in the Age of Social Media and Reality TV," *Electric Literature*

MATHEMATICS

Sailors facing an imminent storm don't have years to study the growing waves around them, but the new framework represents small steps toward the long-term goal for rogue wave prediction—machinery that scans the ocean and sounds the alarm when it's time to batten down the hatches. LDT tools, once they're modified for the open ocean, could be one way for those on boats like the München to know the moment a rogue wave starts focusing. —Charlie Wood (2020), "The Grand Unified Theory of Rogue Waves," *Quanta Magazine*

SCIENCE

There is no doubt that managing retail returns is a difficult task. To make the process more sustainable, retailers need to help customers make choices that limit the need for a return or that minimize the impact of a return on the environment and, of course, the retailer's bottom line. —Christopher Faires and Robert Overstreet (2023), "Just in Time for Back-to-School Shopping: How Retailers Can Alter Customer Behavior to Encourage More Sustainable Returns," *The Conversation*

SOCIAL STUDIES

What it has wrought is the institutionalization of criminality . . . What can be done? We start with the lawyers, who are not only invested with the monopolistic right to be attorneys for clients but should also be obliged, as officers of the court subject to their code of professional ethics, to be the sentinels for the administration of justice. Some are heroically assuming this august obligation to the people. But far too few of the 1.3 million lawyers in America see the rule of law for the myth it is; too few see the rule of power for the lawlessness it creates. More of them must assume the higher significance of their calling, to respond to the silent cries for justice—which nearly two centuries ago Senator Daniel Webster called "the great interest of man on Earth" and "the ligament which holds civilized beings and civilized nations together." —Ralph Nader (2018), "Land of the Lawless," *Lapham's Quarterly*

Use the reproducible "Writing Application Practice: Moves That Conclude" (page 193) to conclude.

Student Samples

The following student samples include moves that conclude.

This sample uses What We Don't Know and What We Do (level 1):

> While we don't know exactly who took this photograph, we do know that they were working for a Russian press company called Fototeca Storica Nazionale. In English, this means National Photo Library. The National Photo Library constitutes one of the richest, most important, and most complex state photographic collections of the 20th century. —Jack, Eighth Grade

This sample uses Share the Last Word (level 3):

> I was in my room crying, and that is when I realized this surgery can help me in many ways even though I gave up a sport for it. "Life doesn't get easier or more forgiving. We just get stronger and more resilient" (Steve Maraboli). —Maddi, Eighth Grade

This sample uses Solve the Problem (level 5):

It's not always easy to handle the weight of my two worlds. So how can I control the way they collide into each other? Maybe I don't. Maybe I don't always need to focus on the small task at hand and instead I could look at the big picture. Maybe I should run through the doubt of it all and realize that I put this weight on myself knowing I can handle it all. I am just like a heavy lifter, hands writing on a piece of paper, tying up my running shoes. —Addy, Eighth Grade

Writing Application Practice: Moves That Conclude

After teaching your students one of these moves—or all of these moves—you'll be looking for an opportunity for them to practice these skills immediately.

For each writing task, we have provided a prompt you could use to get your students writing. They can use this prompt to practice a single move for that writing task or to begin combining, mixing, and matching moves. You can find all writing application practice from the whole book in one place in appendix C (page 275).

Content Area	Writing Application Practice
English	Choose a conclusion move to help wrap up the reading that you have done today in class.
Mathematics	Think about a problem you worked on today in class. Use one of the conclusion moves to sum up your experience working on that problem.
Science	A science experiment always ends in the scientist drawing a conclusion about their hypothesis. Consider a recent experiment in science class. How might you use one of these conclusion moves to help you reflect on the outcome of your experiment?
Social Studies	We're willing to bet at least one of your classmates was absent today. (If not, we can pretend!) Use one of the conclusion moves to wrap up what you learned in class today for a classmate who was absent.

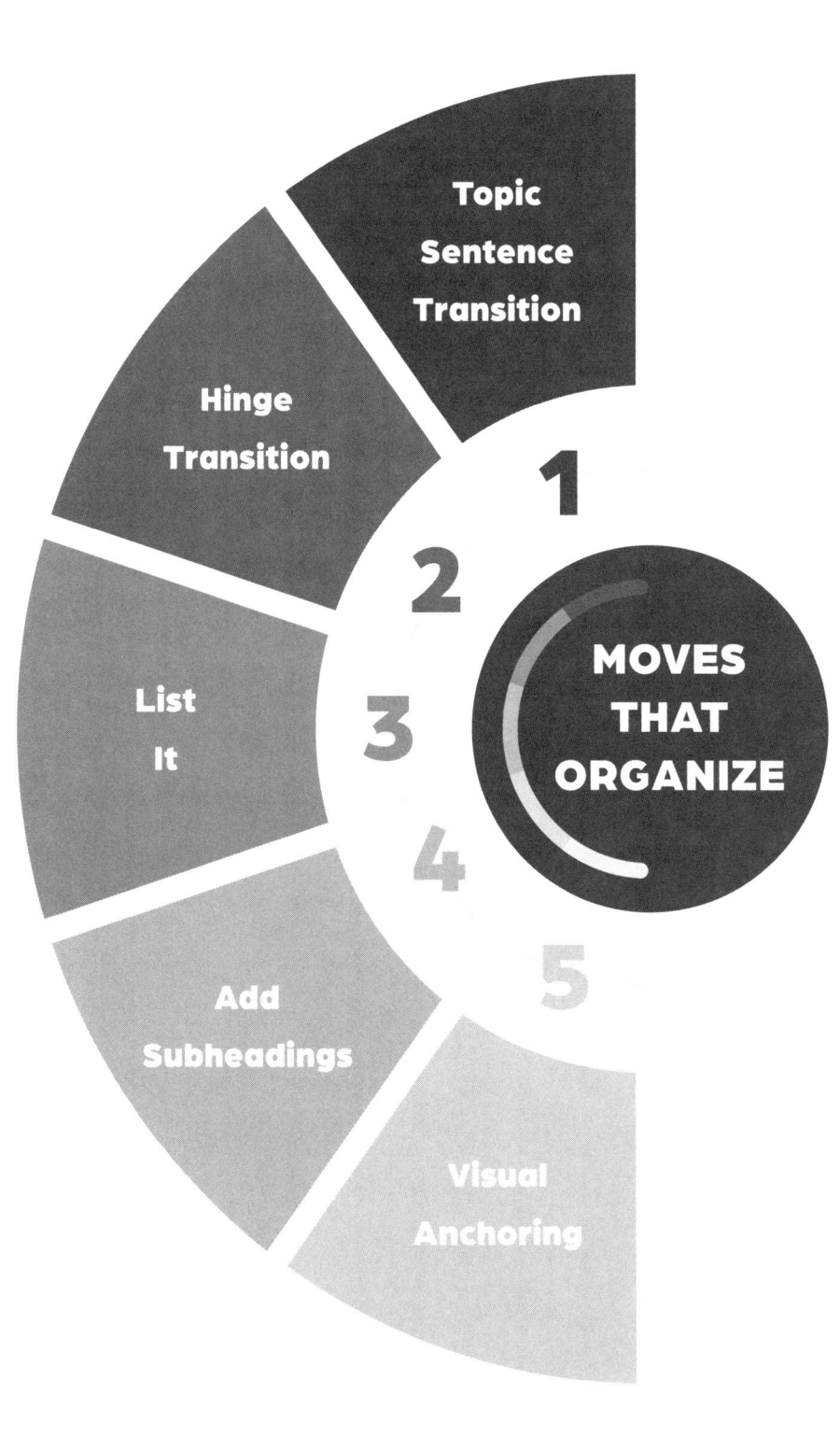

CHAPTER 12

Moves That Organize

When we talk about organization in writing (or *structure*, a term we will use almost synonymously with *organization*), we are thinking about fitting our ideas into the right spaces within the larger piece of writing so that the writing has a logical flow and is easily comprehensible to a reader. In this chapter, we're not talking about commonly taught and tested text structures (think cause and effect, problem-solution, description, and so on). We're talking about a writer's ability to take their ideas and arrange them in a way that is organic, authentic, and meaningful.

Trusting students to organize and structure their writing makes teachers nervous. We've all seen students turn in giant, multipage non-paragraphs filled with stream-of-consciousness information. And we fear that if we don't provide our students with organizational templates to follow, they will be completely adrift.

But when we provide students with organizational templates, we limit not only their choice but also their ability to ever learn how to organize their ideas for themselves. Instead of providing students with templates, we need to provide them with tools so that when they leave our classes and face new writing challenges, they are able to meet them on their own.

Just like in chapter 10 (page 161), you will not see a basic formula offered in this chapter. Organizational moves don't work quite like that. They aren't formulas you pick up, write into, and potentially innovate. They are building blocks you move and stack within the walls of the essay. So, the mentor texts themselves also look a little different from what you've seen in previous chapters. See table 12.1 (page 196) for recommendations on when to employ these moves.

Table 12.1: Writing Needs and Moves That Organize

When Writers Need...	Start Here...
To link ideas together	Topic Sentence Transition (page 196)
	Hinge Transition (page 198)
To make organization visible	List It (page 200)
	Add Subheadings (page 203)
	Visual Anchoring (page 205)
To help orient themselves inside their own writing	Add Subheadings (page 203)
	Visual Anchoring (page 205)
To quickly chunk information so the reader can process it more easily	List It (page 200)
	Visual Anchoring (page 205)

Topic Sentence Transition (Level 1)

The first writing lesson Rebekah ever taught when student teaching more than two decades ago was how to write a topic sentence. "A topic sentence states the main idea and is the first sentence of each body paragraph," she undoubtedly told her students. True. But also reductive and oversimplified.

Indeed, topic sentences do provide structure to paragraphs. But some topic sentences can do even more—simultaneously acting as both a topic sentence and a transition from the previous idea.

When writers use a topic sentence transition, they borrow a word or idea from the end of the previous paragraph and weave it into the language of the topic sentence of the next paragraph. We've highlighted these borrowed words and phrases in **bold** so you can see them more easily. See the pop culture mentor text for an effective example of this method.

POP CULTURE

Written 200 years ago, the "Ode" is crafted like the **best of pop songs**, with easily hummable, simple phrases that use the same techniques you hear in a Taylor Swift hit today.

But the "Ode" is **more than pop**. It's a supranational anthem that aspires to a world in which "all men become brothers," as its lyrics say. —Joshua Barone (2024), "Why We Still Want to Hear the 'Ode to Joy,' 200 Years Later," *The New York Times* (emphasis added)

As you study this move with your students, you might notice the following.

» In the pop culture example, the writer borrows the idea of pop music to show contrast. "Ode to Joy" is catchy, like pop music. But then the writer presents a contrast: It's also more than just pop music.

» Writers might borrow the same exact words for the topic sentence transition, but they might also use synonyms (like "wasn't clear" and "ambiguity" in the mathematics mentor text). Have students play with both. Here are some guiding questions we might share with our students.

* What words or terms in your current paragraph might connect to the topic of your next paragraph?
* When does it feel powerful to repeat the exact same term?
* When does it add nuance to use synonymous terms instead?
* How is the topic of your next paragraph different from the topic of your current paragraph?

ENGLISH

My mother also believed that **writing** was the highest possible calling, so she read *Pride and Prejudice*, her favorite Jane Austen novel, aloud to me in the womb.

She wanted me to hear the **words**, the magnificent prose; to enjoy the wit; to appreciate the insights; to value exemplary work. —Jane Cleland (2021), "Jane Austen and Me," *CrimeReads* (emphasis added)

MATHEMATICS

The modern notation for square roots came into use in the 16th and 17th centuries. But still, there was something slippery about them. Does $\sqrt{2}$ exist in the same way that 2 does? It **wasn't clear**.

Mathematicians continued to live with that **ambiguity**. Then, in the mid-1800s, Richard Dedekind, among others, realized that calculus—which had been developed 200 years earlier by Isaac Newton and Gottfried Leibniz—stood on a shaky foundation. —Jordana Cepelewicz (2024a), "How the Square Root of 2 Became a Number," *Quanta Magazine* (emphasis added)

SCIENCE

Turing machines perform computations by reading and writing 0s and 1s on an infinite tape divided into square cells, using a "head" that operates on one cell at a time. Every machine has a unique set of **rules** that governs its behavior.

Each of these **rules** specifies what the head should do when it moves into a new cell, depending on whether it encounters a 0 or a 1 already there. —Ben Brubaker (2024), "With Fifth Busy Beaver, Researchers Approach Computation's Limits," *Quanta Magazine* (emphasis added)

> **SOCIAL STUDIES**
>
> Dueling factions representing starkly different constituencies, policies and worldviews had come together in New York City's Madison Square Garden to **tear each other apart with no plans for reconciliation or compromise**.
>
> The **divisions** within the party were so profound that fights broke out on the convention floor and across the New York metropolitan area. —Eli Wizevich (2024b), "Why the 1924 Democratic National Convention Was the Longest and Most Chaotic of Its Kind in U.S. History," *Smithsonian Magazine* (emphasis added)

Hinge Transition (Level 2)

We're willing to bet that at some point in your own school experience, someone handed you a list of *transition words*—usually ordinals like *first*, *last*, and *next*—and encouraged you to choose from the list so that your writing had adequate transitions. Chances are good that you, as we did, randomly chose from that list, slapped those magical words onto the beginning of paragraphs, and called it a day.

Transitions are important because they tell the reader how different ideas fit together. And, believe it or not, there are better ways to do this than by selecting a transition word from a list. One way we can do this is by using a hinge.

In the real world, a hinge is a small piece of metal that joins two objects together while still allowing movement. We can think about this organizational move in the same way—a small transition that joins two ideas together while allowing the essay to move forward.

A hinge transition is a mini paragraph—one sentence to three short sentences max. It communicates with the idea that has come before it while presenting a new idea that will move the piece forward. See the pop culture mentor text for an effective example of hinge transitions.

> **POP CULTURE**
>
> He was no longer as sculpted and vibrant as his glory days. Yet, somehow, he was no less statuesque.
>
> **His aura was still 60 feet. His presence still kingly.**
>
> I couldn't call my dad, who'd passed away by the time of my encounter. So I called his oldest brother, who I knew would comprehend my awe. —Marcus Thompson II (2024), "Willie Mays Is a Monument to an Era of Black Baseball Gone but Never Forgotten," *The Athletic* (emphasis added)

As you teach this move to your students, here are some things to consider.

» Imagine stepping stones across a pond. That's what this organizational pattern feels like. The Hinge Transition move is a way of bridging two bigger ideas like a stepping stone can help you cross water between two pieces of land.

» Even though this organizational move only deals with ideas between paragraphs, it's still rather rigorous because there isn't just one way to do this.

* Sometimes, the hinge is a statement. Sometimes, the hinge is a series of short statements. Sometimes, it's a question.

* The hinge transition feels like it could be part of the previous paragraph, but it has been cut off and bumped to its own tiny paragraph. (Your writers might even practice it this way. Take that last thought from the end of a paragraph, bump it to its own paragraph, and connect it to the next idea. Does it work?)

» The hinge transition definitely evokes a sense of drama. Those short paragraphs demand the reader's attention, so a writer might want to save this move for a time in which they want to strongly push the focus from one idea to the next.

ENGLISH

At one end of the spectrum is the therapeutic confessional, where the need or wish is a subconscious, complicated thing; at the other end is the diary of the politician or other public figure, where the need or wish—to be read—is the whole point of writing the thing in the first place.

But could it be that a hitherto unrecognized literary law dictates that the less a person expects others to read a diary, the more interesting it will be?

Political diaries certainly prove the point. —Helen Fielding (2024), "Helen Fielding on *Bridget Jones* and the Subtle Art of Diary Keeping," *Literary Hub* (emphasis added)

MATHEMATICS

The mathematicians ended up with what they called a smooth fractal snowflake—an infinite and delicate self-similar structure.

It had nonnegative Ricci curvature at every point. And it had an infinite number of holes. They had disproved Milnor's conjecture.

"It's more complicated than all the previous constructions" of manifolds with nonnegative Ricci curvature, said Guofang Wei of the University of California, Santa Barbara. —Jordana Cepelewicz (2024b), "Strangely Curved Shapes Break 50-Year-Old Geometry Conjecture," *Quanta Magazine* (emphasis added)

SCIENCE

These competitions were marked by baby steps, and the researchers had little reason to think that 2020 would be any different.

They were wrong about that.

That week, a relative newcomer to the protein science community named John Jumper had presented a new artificial intelligence tool, AlphaFold2, which had emerged from the offices of Google DeepMind, the tech company's artificial intelligence arm in London. —Yasemin Saplakoglu (2024), "How AI Revolutionized Protein Science, but Didn't End It," *Quanta Magazine* (emphasis added)

SOCIAL STUDIES

"These artifacts likely haven't seen the light of day since before the American Revolution, perhaps forgotten when George Washington departed Mount Vernon to take command of the Continental Army," Bradburn added.

That was in 1775.

Archaeologists revisited the site as part of a privately funded $40 million preservation project, aimed at ensuring Mount Vernon's structural integrity and slated for completion in 2026—just in time for America's 250th birthday. —Rachel Treisman (2024), "Centuries-Old Cherries Were Found at George Washington's Home. What Can They Tell Us?," *NPR* (emphasis added)

List It (Level 3)

Writers use lists "to compile the most important information in a meaningful order" (Clark, 2023, p. 71). But really, lists are liberating. They embody order as they gently flood the reader with concise information while simultaneously freeing both the writer and readers from the heavy weight of traditional paragraphs.

Lists organize information by slowing it down and putting it into an order so that a reader is able to digest it. It's a move that's as much about pacing as it is about structuring. Writers might turn to a bulleted list when they have a large amount of information they want to communicate quickly, when they want to preview information they will discuss at greater length later in the piece, or when they want to change the pace of reading. See the pop culture mentor text for effective listing.

POP CULTURE

Once you've identified a burn, Njoroge says, it's crucial to soothe and treat any inflammation. Severe burns might need medical attention but, for milder cases, "anything that can reduce the skin's temperature," she says, "will reduce discomfort and potentially reduce post-inflammatory hyperpigmentation." Here, her favorite, cooling post-sun routine:
- Put Farmacy's Honey Potion Plus, a hydrating mask with skin-soothing antioxidants, in the fridge for an hour and then apply it to your face for 10 to 15 minutes. (Aloe gel is a cost-friendly alternative.)
- Shower in cool water and dry yourself by gently patting, rather than rubbing, your skin to avoid aggravating it further.
- Apply a cool compress to irritated areas for up to 10 minutes.
- Wear free-flowing clothes until your skin has healed

—Nia Decaille (2024), "Are You Wearing Sunscreen the Right Way?," *The New York Times Style Magazine*

Consider this when sharing this move with your students.

» Lists are connected to paragraphs. Look at the mentor texts. The writer begins a new paragraph focused on one idea. Then, they introduce a list with a colon. That list breaks down smaller parts of that big idea.

» Lists have parallel structure. Notice in the pop culture example, each item in the list begins with a verb. Using bulleted lists is the perfect opportunity to teach this concept and practice this skill.

» Lists can be formatted in different ways. In the mentor texts we share here, we see bulleted lists, lists with no visual indicator, and numbered lists.

» The order of a list does matter! But there are lots of different ways to organize it. Roy Peter Clark (2023) suggests that readers pay most attention to the first item and the last item in a list. You might find a different way to order the list items, like chronologically. Play around with the order and really think about which method will have the biggest impact on the reader.

ENGLISH

Except not all fairy tales actually conclude this way. In my go-to collection of Brothers Grimm stories, sure, some tales have it, but many end on a last line with a decidedly different tenor:

> "All of them were executed as payment for their villainy."
>
> "That was how Hans lost his bride."
>
> "And since nobody could get out, they were all burned to death."
>
> "The duplicity of the stepmother and her daughter was now clear as day, and they were cast into the forest to be devoured by wild animals."
>
> "Watch out!"

—Julia Phillips (2024), "Julia Phillips on the Writing Lessons of Fairy Tales," *Literary Hub*

MATHEMATICS

For example, let's say we have two tiles, A and B, and two rules for putting them together:

1. Next to an A, on either side you can only place a B.
2. Next to a B, on either side you can only place an A.

—Patrick Honner (2023a), "Math Patterns That Go On Forever but Never Repeat," *Quanta Magazine*

SCIENCE

In addition to the high ocean heat content, research has shown other environmental factors need to typically align for rapid intensification to occur. These include:

- Low vertical wind shear, where the winds steering the hurricane do not change much in strength or direction over the depth of the storm. Strong wind shear makes it difficult for a storm to stay organized and maintain its strength.
- A moist atmosphere surrounding the storm, with heavy precipitation encircling the developing eye.

—Brian Tang (2024), "Hurricane Beryl's Rapid Intensification, Category 5 Winds So Early in a Season Were Alarming: Here's Why More Tropical Storms Are Exploding in Strength," *The Conversation*

SOCIAL STUDIES

Our research, published in the *International Journal of Heritage Studies*, identified four key themes:
- locals don't want heritage reconstruction to be privileged over security
- they want local religious sites rebuilt as much as significant non-religious sites
- they want heritage sites transformed into more useful structures for the community
- and they want control and agency over the future of their own heritage.

—Benjamin Isakhan and Lynn Meskell (2024), "Reconstructing Heritage After War: What We Learned From Asking 1,600 Syrians About Rebuilding Aleppo," *The Conversation*

Add Subheadings (Level 4)

Subheadings are a kind of magic in the best way. Writers who struggle with the high level of executive function needed to mentally organize their ideas suddenly thrive when they add subheadings to their writing. But why?

Subheadings essentially take the A-level outline of a piece of writing and make it visible on the page. This helps the writer because they can see and remember where they have been and where they are going in a piece of writing. Some of the mental load is reduced through this breadcrumb idea trail on the page.

Subheadings help readers for the exact same reasons. It's easier to follow the writer's train of thought when they signal that flow to the reader through subheadings.

Now, obviously, not every type of writing has subheadings in the wild (personal essays, memoirs, short op-eds, and letters, for example). Even so, many (dare we say, most) writers benefit from using subheadings to stay organized while drafting and revising. They can always remove the subheadings at the very end, if their teacher or editor is fundamentally against them.

For each of the following mentor texts, we've shared the list of subheadings in bullet points beneath its title. Even without reading the article, students should get a sense of the structure.

POP CULTURE

"How 'Not Like Us' became an anti-Drake anthem: The Drake vs. Kendrick Lamar feud, explained"
- Who's beefing with who?
- Who is Drake dissing on "Push Ups"?
- Drake's latest round with Kendrick took a particularly dark turn
- Drake has previously thrived in beefs—but can he win when the whole industry is against him?

—Kyndall Cunningham (2024), "How 'Not Like Us' Became an Anti-Drake Anthem," *Vox*

Here are some other features you and your students might consider together.

» Subheadings are typically brief, but they can take different forms—questions, complete sentences, phrases.

» Subheadings can be more or less abstract. In the pop culture example, the reader pretty much understands the entire article from the subheadings alone. But in the English example, while the reader can understand the general arc of information, the subheadings themselves are more abstract and less literal.

» Students might notice that three seems to be a minimum number for subheadings. This makes sense: beginning, middle, and end.

» All the subheadings match the topic of the piece in either tone, diction, or concept. In the pop culture mentor text, the author uses slang appropriate for a piece on a feud between rap icons. In the science example, the author chooses words like "frozen," "thick," and "cell" to tether the reader to the essay's analysis of water as a scientific substance.

» Something you can't see here is that subheadings belong in the body of a piece of writing. If you open up these mentor texts, you'll see each has a little introductory section before the first subheading and a conclusion following a final section.

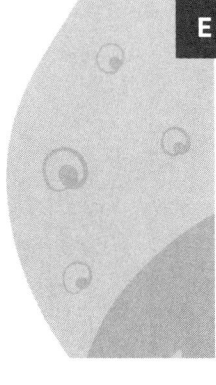

ENGLISH

"The Secret History of *One Hundred Years of Solitude*"
- Leaving Home
- A Sheet of Paper
- Mind on Fire
- The Altercation
- Perfect Marriage

—Paul Elie (2015), "The Secret History of *One Hundred Years of Solitude*," *Vanity Fair*

MATHEMATICS

"A.I.'s Latest Challenge: The Math Olympics"
- The big jump
- Proof of concept
- Soulful solutions

—Siobhan Roberts (2024), "A.I.'s Latest Challenge: The Math Olympics," *The New York Times*

SCIENCE

"The Physics of Cold Water May Have Jump-Started Complex Life"
- A Frozen Paradox
- Life in Thick Water
- A Cell's Perspective

—Veronique Greenwood (2024b), "The Physics of Cold Water May Have Jump-Started Complex Life," *Quanta Magazine*

SOCIAL STUDIES

"The Real Story Behind the Star-Spangled Banner, the Flag That Inspired the National Anthem"
- The flag's beginnings
- The missing pieces
- Preserving a national icon at the Smithsonian

—Cate Lineberry and Meilan Solly (2024), "The Real Story Behind the Star-Spangled Banner, the Flag That Inspired the National Anthem," *Smithsonian Magazine*

Visual Anchoring (Level 5)

In chapter 7 (page 101), we shared how writers reference visuals as a different kind of evidence. Visuals—images, screenshots of social media posts, videos, and so on—also provide an organizing pattern writers can rely on to help them structure their writing.

When we think about visuals as organizational anchors in a piece of writing, we can see they work in two ways. Sometimes, writers make a point and then follow it with a visual that demonstrates that point. (Yep. That's evidence.) Then they move to a new idea.

But other times, writers make a point, share a visual, and then use that visual as both a landmark and a launching pad for further discussion. With a visual present, the writer now has a new direction to pursue as they journey through their idea.

While Visual Anchoring could be used once or twice in a piece of writing, we think it works best as a way to organize the entire piece. All the mentor texts selected for this chapter use visuals as an organizational tool throughout the writing.

Writers should exercise a little bit of caution when using this move because a visual anchor isn't just any visual. It's not just a pretty picture. It's not just a clip of last night's game. It's a cairn built and left as a landmark throughout the piece of writing.

In figure 12.2, you'll notice that once again (just like in chapter 7, page 101), we have annotated a social studies mentor text, rather than the pop culture example. (Darn you, copyrights!) We think this article on tennis icon Arthur Ashe's legacy in Richmond, Virginia, does a beautiful job with this move and will serve as a solid example for your students.

When you share the other mentor texts for this move, we encourage you to pull up the original examples so that students can see the visual anchors in the text. While we aren't able to show them here, letting your students see them is important because it helps them see the difference between a visual that exists for interest and a visual that exists as an organizational anchor.

```
Ashe died on February 6, 1993. His body lay in honor in the
capitol building in Richmond, the first person so honored
since 1863, when Confederate general Thomas J. "Stonewall"
Jackson died. About 6,000 people attended his funeral. He
was later buried at Woodland Cemetery in Richmond.

Still, the legacy of Arthur Ashe was not complete.
Richmond's historic tree-lined Monument Avenue was at the
time home to five monuments, all to prominent Confederates
including Robert E. Lee, Jefferson Davis, and Jackson. In
1995, the city voted to erect a sixth—to Ashe. In what became the "Battle of Monument
Avenue," locating the monument there became a divisive issue taking months of debate
before its unveiling on July 10, 1996, or what would have been Ashe's fifty-third
birthday. The twelve-foot statue on a forty-four-ton stone column depicts Ashe facing
west, surrounded by children, holding a tennis racket in one hand and carrying books in
the other. —Boyd Childress (2023), "Arthur Ashe (1943–1993)," Encyclopedia Virginia
```

Figure 12.1: Visual Anchoring, annotated mentor text.

Here are some extra tidbits to consider as you share this move with students.

» We would begin by taking our students to Boyd Childress's (2023) article on Arthur Ashe for *Encyclopedia Virginia* and scrolling through the images. We would ask them, "Based on the images, what do you think each section of the article discusses?" Students should be able to answer this question for each of the following mentor texts. This exercise will help demonstrate for students that this move is the visual version of Add Subheadings.

» For a visual to be an organizational move, the writer needs to discuss it—either before the visual is shared or directly after. In the social studies example here, Ashe is introduced, the visual (of the Ashe statue) is shared, and then the statue is discussed.

» Anchoring visuals should be chosen with care. Writers might ask themselves, "What could an image reveal that my words alone cannot?"

» Students might notice that the visual acts as a pivot point or a transition within the writing. Here, Childress is discussing Ashe's death and uses the picture of Ashe's monument as a way to segue into the tennis icon's legacy.

POP CULTURE

Now a combined 74 years old, Team USA's all-time leaders in points and assists still looked like giants; their combined shot chart is excellence everlasting:

[*Diagram of Team USA's shot chart*]

As a whole, Team USA made 56 percent of its 3s and 68 percent of its 2s. Steph Curry's screens induced chaos, Anthony Edwards's athleticism ignited fast-break opportunities, Devin Booker's outside stroke punctured a game plan that packed the paint, and Jrue Holiday, Bam Adebayo, Anthony Davis, and Derrick White put on a defensive clinic. —Michael Pina (2024b), "Team USA Looks Unstoppable, but It's Not a Dream Team Yet," *The Ringer*

ENGLISH

Then, midway through the book, after the wise woman gives our hero one truth about dragons—basically that they're all like Smaug from *The Hobbit*, sitting on piles of treasure and shooting flames at trespassers—the little boy steps over and out of the border of the first story, and straight into another.

[*Image of an illustration in the book with a boy standing next to an elderly woman: The woman has her arm around the boy's shoulder. They sit on the porch of a cabin in a forest with large green trees and the text "You may also journey into another forest . . ."*]

Now the illustrations are airy and cool—greens and blues replace the warm reds and browns of yore. The borders have disappeared. The oak trees have been uprooted by a bamboo forest. The child is guided by nine-tailed foxes, ghostly maidens, and the white rabbit who dwells on the moon. —Samantha Balaban (2024), "To Learn 'The Truth About Dragons,' Go on a Quest Through This Kids' Book," *NPR*

MATHEMATICS

For example, you can use scissors congruence to compute the area of a pentagon. Since area is preserved if you cut the pentagon up into smaller triangles, you can instead find the area of these triangles (using "½ base × height") and add them up to get the answer.

[*Illustration of a pentagon broken into five smaller triangles that are then added together*] —Maxine Calle and Mona Merling (2023), "A Brief Illustrated Guide to 'Scissors Congruence'—an Ancient Geometric Idea That's Still Fueling Cutting-Edge Mathematical Research," *The Conversation*

SCIENCE

The current bleaching event in the wider Caribbean region is longer and more severe than any previous bleaching episode recorded since the first global one in 1998. I study large-scale climate and ocean dynamics and am analyzing how biological connections between coral reefs—sometimes extending over great distances—may help reefs recover from heat stress.

[*YouTube video clip of a news segment showing coral bleaching*] —Annalisa Bracco (2024), "The World's Fourth Mass Coral Bleaching Is Underway, but Well-Connected Reefs May Have a Better Chance to Recover," *The Conversation*

SOCIAL STUDIES

Rissech's discovery could cast doubt on the idea that the order was exclusive to men. This woman almost certainly fought—and died—alongside the male warrior monks. Her bones show no signs of regrowth or healing around her injuries.

[*Screenshot of a tweet from the university leading the research showing the bones*]

One hypothesis suggests this mystery woman was a servant called to arms out of desperation to defend the castle against the order's Muslim opponents. Evidence of lower protein consumption than her male counterparts supports the claim that she was from a lower social class. —Eli Wizevich (2024a), "Was This Mysterious Woman a Medieval Warrior?," *Smithsonian Magazine*

Use the reproducible "Writing Application Practice: Moves That Organize" to organize.

Writing Application Practice: Moves That Organize

Like moves that add voice, moves that organize can be used at any point in a piece of writing. These moves are used to build a sound structure. They can even be used in conjunction with one another. Instead of four individual writing exercises, here is a single idea that allows students to practice the moves while demonstrating how moves that organize can be employed differently and uniquely by each author.

Consider the last piece of writing you did in class. Reread it, and organize all or a portion of it using a move from this chapter. (If using a digital doc, turn on the mode that lets you see your changes. If writing by hand, use a different-colored pen than you originally wrote with.) Then, exchange papers with someone else in the class who chose to revise their writing with a different move. Read what they have written, and answer the question, "How did this organizational move affect my understanding of this section or piece of writing?" When finished, share your answers with each other and reflect.

Epilogue

It's the Sunday before the first day of school. Fall's cool breath is whispering into the air like it has a secret it doesn't want the sun to know. The world is quiet.

But tomorrow won't be.

Tomorrow will be filled with the metal crinkle of a hundred backpacks unzipping; the smell of strong, earthy coffee; the eager shuffle of little bodies as they bump into one another to sit in blue plastic chairs; and the high-pitched laughter of a dozen adolescent reunions in vinyl hallways.

And tomorrow, no matter who they are or what class they are in, students will be writing. Whether it's with a freshly sharpened pencil, black ink, a keyboard, or a brick red crayon (because they've already lost all their other writing utensils), students will be authoring ideas in their English language arts, mathematics, science, and social studies classes. Because of this, no matter what class we teach, we have to teach our students how to write. All of us. Separately and together.

But, luckily, you're ready. You've got a book of *fifty* strategies, workbook pages, and videos that you can use to increase content literacy, multiply your instructional capacity, and elevate students' voices in your classroom.

And, luckily, these strategies don't just apply to your class. The beauty of the mini-move framework is that it can be used in any core discipline. We know that when writing instruction happens across the curriculum, schools will see a collective surge in writing skill development and content literacy (Childs, 2020; Gallagher, 2017). So we encourage you—bring mini moves to every writer *and* every teacher!

Whether it's used in your classroom, throughout your school, or across your district, the *Mini Moves for Every Writer* framework will provide a path to successful writing instruction for you and your students, like it has for ours.

We wish you and yours happy writing.

APPENDIX A

Mini-Move Lesson Plan Templates

We have shared lots of ideas and even more mentor texts with you over the course of this book. The appendices are here to help you put them all into action in your classroom! The most important classroom resource doesn't live inside this book, though. It's online. At **go.SolutionTree.com/literacy/MMEW**, you'll find a complete workbook for each content area that will guide your students through the noticing and practicing habits of mini-move instruction. In many ways, these workbook pages are the only thing you need to teach your students to use mini moves in their own writing!

In this appendix, you'll find the following tools.

» **Reproducible "Progression of Chapters" (page 215):** Just as the moves follow a progression from easier and more straightforward to more nuanced and challenging, the chapters themselves have a similar progression. Some writing tasks—like introducing and concluding—are easier places for students to start, while other moves—like contextualizing and providing evidence—are heavier lifts. This chart helps you strategize about where your students might begin their mini-move journey.

» **Mini-move lesson plan templates:** In chapter 2 (page 23), we shared ideas for what mini-move instruction might look like in your classroom. The lesson plan templates in this appendix walk you through three different instructional modes: (1) direct instruction, (2) student-driven inquiry, and (3) independent student work. Use the following templates as guides and scaffolds to start mini moves in your own classroom.

* Reproducible "Mini-Move Lesson Plan Template: Direct Instruction" (page 216)
* Reproducible "Mini-Move Lesson Plan Template: Student-Driven Inquiry" (page 218)
* Reproducible "Student Organizer for Mini-Mentor Text Stations" (page 220)
* Reproducible "Mini-Move Lesson Plan Template: Independent Student Work" (page 221)

Progression of Chapters

Just as every chapter has a progression of skills that increase in challenge, the writing tasks featured in each chapter also progress from less challenging to more challenging. The following image shows a progression of the chapters starting at entry-level moves, moving through intermediate moves, and concluding with the most challenging moves. This progression might help guide the order in which you teach the chapters' tasks to your students.

Entry-Level Moves → **Intermediate Moves** → **Challenging Moves**

Entry-Level Moves	Intermediate Moves	Challenging Moves
Moves That Introduce Chapter 3	**Moves That Make a Claim** Chapter 4	**Moves That Provide Evidence** Chapter 7
Moves That Define Chapter 5	**Moves That Summarize** Chapter 8	**Moves That Contextualize** Chapter 9
Moves That Describe Chapter 6	**Moves That Organize** Chapter 12	**Moves That Add Voice** Chapter 10
Moves That Conclude Chapter 11		

Mini-Move Lesson Plan Template: Direct Instruction

You can use this lesson plan template anytime you want to quickly and directly teach a move to students—a whole class, a small group, or an individual. This is the model you'll see in our Mini Moves for Writers videos, too! This form is an organizing tool to help include relevant Common Core State Standards.

Lesson Duration
10–20 minutes

Lesson Objectives
Students will:

» Understand why a writer might use this move
» Learn the name of the move writers use
» Read a mentor text using the move
» Understand how to use the move in their own writing
» Understand the effect of the move on a reader or a piece of writing
» Try the move on their own

Materials

» Mini-mentor text that includes the mini move you wish to teach
» Optional materials:
  * Computer with projector
  * Mini-move video

Procedure

1. **Highlight a writing need this lesson will address.**

   * Say, "Sometimes, in a piece of writing, a writer needs to _____. One way that professional writers do this is by _____."

2. **Name the move you will be teaching.**

   * Say, "Today, we are going to learn a move called _____ that will help us do this in our own writing."

3. **Share a mini-mentor text that uses the move.**

   * Say, "Let's look at how one writer uses this move."
   * Share the mini-mentor text with students. Read it aloud for them.
     › The mini-mentor text might be projected on the board, written on the board, or printed on paper for students to keep in their binder or writer's notebook.

4. **Discuss how the move is used and its effect.**

   * Say, "In this mentor text, I notice the writer is _____. The writer is using this move because _____."
     › When you notice aloud what the writer is doing, go slow. You want to unpack the choices the writer is making step by step so that students can see the steps they will need to take to use the move themselves.
     › When you discuss the effect of the move, you might find that you are highlighting an effect on the reader or an effect on the writing itself. Either is helpful to student writers! The goal here is to highlight what this move is accomplishing so that student writers will understand when the move might benefit their own writing.

5. **Set students free to try the move in their own writing.**
    * Say, "OK, think for a minute: Where is a place you could try this move in your own writing? Let's try it and see what happens!"
    * There are lots of ways to do this. Students can try the move in a piece of existing writing they are currently working on in class, try it in a piece of older writing, connect the move to current class content as they try it, or quickly come up with an original example in their notebook.
    * Since students are learning and trying this move for the first time, informal assessment is key. You can check on student understanding in a few different ways.
        › Peek over students' shoulders as they write.
        › Use a Google Form to have students submit their first attempt.
        › Ask students to publish their attempt on a Padlet or sticky note on the classroom wall or via a quick notebook gallery walk.

Mini-Move Lesson Plan Template: Student-Driven Inquiry

Use this lesson plan template when students have had some experience with mini moves and are ready to lead the learning themselves. This inquiry lesson template has the added advantage of getting students physically engaged in the lesson.

This template is a great next step for students, as it exposes them to multiple mini-mentor texts at the same time. You could approach this in one of two ways: (1) with multiple mentor texts that use the same mini move, or, for an even greater challenge (and greater efficiency in teaching students a range of moves!), (2) with multiple mentor texts that address the same writing need, each highlighting a different mini move. See the reproducible "Student Organizer for Mini-Mentor Text Stations" (page 220) for organizers to manage the mini-mentor text stations and to include relevant Common Core State Standards.

Lesson Duration
15–30 minutes

Lesson Objectives
Students will:

- Understand why a writer might use this move
- Learn the name of the move writers use
- Read a mentor text using the move
- Understand how to use the move in their own writing
- Understand the effect of the move on a reader or a piece of writing
- Try the move on their own

Materials
Three to five mini-mentor texts using the same mini move written on chart paper or printed and posted around the room

Procedure

1. **Highlight a writing need this lesson will address.**
   - Say, "Sometimes, in a piece of writing, a writer needs to _____. Today, we're going to look at some mentor texts and figure out what moves writers make to address that need."

2. **Share mini-mentor texts that use a writing move that addresses that need.**
   - Set up stations around the room, each with a mini-mentor text written or printed on a piece of paper.
   - Divide students into small groups or partnerships, and invite them to study each mentor text and record what they notice. They might use an organizer like the reproducible "Student Organizer for Mini-Mentor Text Stations" (page 220) to jot down their thinking.
   - When students have visited each mini-mentor text, have them return to their seats.

3. **Discuss how the move is used and its effect.**
   - Debrief students' learning as a class. You might ask the following questions.
     - What did you notice?
     - What patterns did you see as you visited each mini-mentor text?
     - How did you see the writing need being addressed?
     - What steps did each writer take to address the writing need?
   - As you discuss students' noticings, you might project the mini-mentor texts and annotate them on the board or create a list on chart paper.
   - If you are using mentor texts that address the writing need in different ways and use different moves, you will want to ask, "What are the different ways we see writers addressing this writing need? How are these similar? How are these different?"

4. **Name the move you will be teaching.**
    - Say, "OK! We have noticed a lot about these mini-mentor texts. Based on what we have seen, what might we name this move? We want something simple that describes what the writer is doing and something we can remember."
    - Solicit potential names from the students.
        - A fun way to do this is to put students into small teams to develop a name for the move. Everyone writes their name on the board, and then the class votes on the name that best represents the move.
    - If you are using mentor texts that address the writing need in different ways and use different moves, you will need to develop names for all the moves. This is most efficiently accomplished by assigning each small group a move and letting them develop the name themselves.

5. **Set students free to try the move in their own writing.**
    - Say, "OK, think for a minute: Where is a place you could try this move in your own writing? Let's try it and see what happens!"
    - There are lots of ways to do this. Students can try the move in a piece of existing writing they are currently working on in class, try it in a piece of older writing, connect the move to current class content as they try it, or quickly come up with an original example in their notebook.
    - Since students are learning and trying this move for the first time, informal assessment is key. You can check on student understanding in a few different ways.
        - Peek over students' shoulders as they write.
        - Use a Google Form to have students submit their first attempt.
        - Ask students to publish their attempt on a Padlet or sticky note on the classroom wall or via a quick notebook gallery walk.

Student Organizer for Mini-Mentor Text Stations

For small groups and partnered work, have students use this organizer to jot down their thinking.

Writing need we are investigating: _____

Mini-Mentor Text	What I Notice

Name that move:

Mini-Move Lesson Plan Template: Independent Student Work

Inviting students to independently work with mini moves is one of the ultimate goals of our teaching; we want students to be able to do this on their own in the future with any text they might find helpful and inspiring.

Use this lesson plan template with students who need to work on their own, with students who have had a good bit of practice using mini-mentor texts and identifying moves, or with students who need a little extra challenge. Here, you will see a procedural breakdown of activities and materials based on the kind of instruction given.

Lesson Duration
10–30 minutes

Lesson Objectives
Students will:

- Understand why a writer might use this move
- Learn the name of the move writers use
- Read a mentor text using the move
- Understand how to use the move in their own writing
- Understand the effect of the move on a reader or a piece of writing
- Try the move on their own

Materials

- Guided independent practice: Teacher-selected mini-move videos (a single video or a few videos from which students can choose)
- Independent inquiry practice: Mini-mentor texts that highlight a teacher-selected mini move
- Fully independent practice: Student-selected mini-mentor texts

Procedure
Follow the steps based on your practice.

Guided Independent Practice

Follow along.

1. Teacher highlights a writing need this lesson will address.
2. Teacher shows selected mini-moves video.
3. Teacher shares a mini-mentor text that uses the move.
4. Teacher discusses how the move is used and its effect.
5. Student tries the move.

Independent Inquiry Practice

Follow along.

1. Teacher highlights a writing need this lesson will address.
2. Teacher shares mini-mentor texts that use a writing move that addresses that need.
3. Student studies the mini-mentor texts to identify the move and its effect.
4. Student names the move.
5. Student tries the move.

Fully Independent Practice

Follow along.

1. Student identifies a need in their writing and a mini-mentor text that can inspire their work.
2. Student studies the mini-mentor text to identify a move the writer is making.
3. Student names the move.
4. Student tries the move.

APPENDIX B

All Moves by Content Area

This concise, keep-on-the-corner-of-your-desk appendix puts all the mini moves and mentor texts for your content area in one place! The following are your go-to tools for identifying the moves your students need and teaching them quickly.

- » Reproducible "All Pop Culture Moves" (page 224)
- » Reproducible "All English Moves" (page 234)
- » Reproducible "All Mathematics Moves" (page 244)
- » Reproducible "All Science Moves" (page 254)
- » Reproducible "All Social Studies Moves" (page 264)

All Pop Culture Moves

Please see the following tables to view all pop culture mentor texts pertaining to each mini move.

Moves That Introduce: Pop Culture

Move	Mini-Mentor Text
Just-the-Facts	In what was the second highest profile legal deliberation this week, jurors determined on Thursday that Gwyneth Paltrow was not liable for damages in a ski crash between her and a retired optometrist, Terry Sanderson, causing him, he alleged, a traumatic brain injury. Mr. Sanderson was denied the $300,000 he sued for, and Ms. Paltrow, whose net worth is reportedly north of $200 million, was awarded the amount she requested in a countersuit: $1. —Elizabeth Spiers (2023), "In the Utah Ski Trial, We Are All Gwynnocent," *The New York Times*
Make the Case	The future of sports is female, folks. The NCAA Women's Basketball Tournament this year shattered viewership records for the First Four round, Sweet 16, Elite 8 and Final Four matches, per ESPN. After the title game, *Forbes* ran the following headline: "March Madness Finals Ratings Set A Record High For Women, Record Low For Men." Powered in part by the historic play of Iowa's Caitlin Clark, who helped her team all the way to the championship round, the NCAA Women's Basketball Tournament Final drew an average of 9.9 million viewers, making it the most watched women's college basketball game ever. —Michael Stahl (2023), "The Upcoming World Cup Could Be the Most Valuable Women's Tournament in History," *InsideHook*
What They Said	Ana de Armas made her *Saturday Night Live* debut last night with a monologue that took full advantage of her bilingual capabilities. De Armas greeted the audience in Spanish, before explaining a bit about her background. "I speak English," De Armas said. "But I didn't when I first got to the U.S. I was born in Cuba." She revealed that she learned English "the way everyone who comes to this country does: by watching *Friends*." Stars—they're just like us! —Charu Sinha (2023), "Ana de Armas Goes Bilingual in *SNL* Monologue," *Vulture*
Scene-Drop	They're all here waiting. Anxiously swaying on the Sabbath. Impatiently jostling for better sight lines. Blinking with the neuroses that begin to take root when the face of the messiah will never be revealed, no matter how many months of rent are sacrificed for a "Jester on Dice" Homer pendant studded with nine lab-grown diamonds and 18 karats of gold. Zoom in (3x) on the TikTok sorority blonds with the matching jean shorts and white Chucks and "I <3 Frank Ocean" baby tees. The Cobra Kai-headbanded and Jokic-jerseyed consultants who scrawled "Frankchella" on their Jeep Wranglers before plodding east from Venice. The sensitive pilgrims with twice as many stick-and-poke lyric tattoos as their idol has albums, traveling thousands of miles for the resurrection, who crouched like sprinters at the starter's block and stampeded to the front of the stage as soon as the Coachella gates opened at noon. —Jeff Weiss (2023), "What's a God to a Machine?," *The Ringer*
Then-and-Now	If you thought Taylor Swift was going to shake off the moody melancholy of "Folklore" and "Evermore"—the double dose of alluring alt-folkiness that she gave us in 2020—think again. "Midnights"—the pop superstar's much-anticipated new album that, after arriving at the stroke of midnight on Friday, will be keeping Swifties up all night—is designed for the quiet of the dark. Indeed, Swift's 10th album—which comes almost exactly 10 years after she began to make her play for pop dominance with 2012's "Red"—is a far grayer shade of the 32-year-old singer-songwriter. —Chuck Arnold (2022), "Taylor Swift Goes Dark on New Album 'Midnights,'" *New York Post*

Moves That Make a Claim: Pop Culture

Move	Mini-Mentor Text
The Big Idea	In both its incarnations, "All Too Well" is a song about the weaponization of memory. —Lindsay Zoladz (2021), "Taylor Swift's 'All Too Well' and the Weaponization of Memory," *The New York Times*
Outline It	But this song represents the moment that everything the Beatles did best came together in rich, glorious harmony—studio innovation, pop sensibility, and avant-garde ambition all struck at once and left to ring out like the most stirring chord imaginable. —Lindsay Zoladz (2019), "'A Day in the Life,'" *The Ringer*
This-and-That	The vivid bloodletting "Traitor" was alternately coffeehouse quiet and arena bombastic, and equally persuasive in both modes. —Jon Caramanica (2022), "Olivia Rodrigo's Punky Heartbreak Revue," *The New York Times*
Not-This-But-That	But the song isn't really "about" Bruno in the same way the movie isn't really "about" magic. Instead, the movie is actually about unresolved intergenerational trauma (especially in migrant and politically oppressed cultures), while the song actually lays bare the characters' own frustrations, shortcomings, and prejudices. —Chris White (2022), "Why 'We Don't Talk About Bruno' Is the Biggest Disney Hit Since 'Let It Go,'" *Slate*
Synthesize It	Beyoncé is to millennials what Christianity was to our grandparents; there's a societal expectation that you'll be involved and occasionally perform conspicuous acts of piety, though as a Christmas-and-Easter-type Beyoncéist, my faith is hardly integral to my identity. —Michael Baumann (2018), "Beyoncé Sings 'Halo' at a Hospital," *The Ringer*

Moves That Define: Pop Culture

Move	Mini-Mentor Text
It Is What It Is	Ballet is an otherworldly art, more than a few cool moves strung together by a trendy choreographer. —Gia Kourlas (2024), "What Is Ballet in the 21st Century? It's All Over the Place," *The New York Times*
Say My Name	When "Inside Out 2" opens, Joy is still running the show with Sadness, Anger (Lewis Black), Fear (Tony Hale) and Disgust (Liza Lapira) inside a bright tower called headquarters. —Manohla Dargis (2024), "'Inside Out 2' Review: PUBERTY! OMG! LOL! IYKYK!," *The New York Times*
Keep It Appositive	It was that same friend, she said, who coaxed her into trying what's known as aggressive or in-line street skating, a style heavy on tricks and stunts like grinding curbs, skidding on railings and spinning along half-pipes. —Max Berlinger (2023), "At More Skate Parks, an 'Aggressive' Takeover," *The New York Times*
Gimme an Example	Cringe: the ultimate insult of our era. It implies a kind of pathetic attachment to hope, to sincerity, to possibility. Cringe is not exclusively female; the musical "Hamilton," written by a man, Lin-Manuel Miranda, is definitely cringe. —Lydia Polgreen (2023), "Why Is Everyone Suddenly Listening to a Staple of My Angsty Adolescence?," *The New York Times*
Engage With Etymology	Nostalgia is derived from the Greek words for "homecoming" and "pain," and before it referred to a yearning for the past, it was a psychopathological disorder, describing a homesickness so severe it could actually kill. Nostalgia itself represented a form of traumatic stress, and now pseudo-therapeutic treatments have made their way into our cultural retrospectives. So while Serena Williams appears on MasterClass to teach tennis, and Ringo Starr to teach drumming, Clinton arrives to school us on "the power of resilience." —Amanda Hess (2021), "Victory Speech (Hillary's Version)," *The New York Times*

Moves That Describe: Pop Culture

Move	Mini-Mentor Text
Describing Lists	Most of us have an idea of what Major League Baseball games are supposed to feel like. Crowded stands. Calls for *peanuts*! Fans commiserating pleasantly like picnickers at a city park. —Dan Moore (2023), "The Long, Sad Story of the Stealing of the Oakland A's," *The Ringer*
Say It Again, But Make It Specific	Barbecue's ability to reflect whatever might be hot at the time (from reality TV to the taco craze) isn't new; in fact, barbecue has a long history of permeation, perhaps best experienced by the ongoing barbecue feud that plagues the South. From the Atlantic to the Gulf, bordered by the western outposts of Texas and Kansas City, the area of the United States known as the "barbecue belt" houses four distinct barbecue traditions—Carolina, Texas, Memphis and Kansas City. —Natasha Geiling (2023), "The Evolution of American Barbecue," *Smithsonian Magazine*
Dash That Describes	The growing tension in the second verse—when the drums kick in and the piano becomes more forceful, like a film score foreshadowing a pivotal moment—took me right back to when Rodrigo and producer Dan Nigro used the same trick on her 2021 breakout hit, "drivers license." —Justin Curto (2023), "Olivia Rodrigo Is Perfecting the Formula on 'vampire,'" *Vulture*
Let's Imagine . . .	Imagine that the most important part of your job were so difficult to accomplish that your boss would be happy if you succeeded once every 40 tries. What if you got a major bonus if you could do it twice that often? That's life for an NFL pass rusher. The scarcity of sacks is what makes rushing the passer such a sought-after skill—one that's probably second only to a quarterback's ability to throw—and why the best players at the position are earning the same money as the league's top wide receivers. —Diante Lee (2024), "Which NFL Teams Have the Best Pass-Rushing Corps?," *The Ringer*
Figurative Language Comparison	She remembers infraction after infraction, and her vocal performance races from rueful rumination to bitter crescendo, the piano galloping alongside her, and the song feels like it's approaching liftoff. The pre-chorus has a dreamy lightheadedness to it that's quickly become a Rodrigo trademark—as has her way with a punch to the gut. —Laura Snapes (2023), "Olivia Rodrigo: Vampire Review—A Brilliant, Biting Comeback," *The Guardian*

Moves That Provide Evidence: Pop Culture

Move	Mini-Mentor Text
Hyperlink Layers	Beyoncé did warn us. *Cowboy Carter* is bigger than a country album—it's a Beyoncé album. The follow-up to 2022's Renaissance is an odyssey through American history and music, stacked with just as many references as its counterpart, covering everything from classic rock to opera to rap. —Justin Curto (2024), "Two-Steppin' Our Way Through *Cowboy Carter*: The People, Songs, and History Behind Beyoncé's Americana Odyssey," *Vulture*
Reference a Visual	Michelle Yeoh looks like a classic movie star at the Balenciaga Couture show in this floor-length leather trench and oversize sunnies. I want to channel this energy every time I leave the house. [*The image that would be provided alongside the writing in this figure shows Michelle Yeoh wearing a long black leather coat with a belt at the waist. She is also wearing large, dark sunglasses. The scene appears to be outside, likely at an event or a gathering, as there are photographers and people around her taking pictures. Her hair is short and dark. She is confident, while a crowd of onlookers and security personnel surround her. The overall atmosphere suggests a high-profile event.*] —Brooke LaMantia (2024), "What Michelle Yeoh, Tyler, the Creator, and Paris Hilton Wore This Week," *The Cut*
The Fold In	Taylor Swift has been getting increasingly sporty since she started dating Travis Kelce.... Then, there was all that talk about potentially getting invested in Formula 1: Per "Page Six," she and "the guy on the Chiefs" reportedly had plans to attend this year's Monaco Grand Prix. —Emily Leibert (2024), "Taylor Swift Really Loves Simone Biles's Floor Routine," *The Cut*
Paraphrase It	**Quote from an interview with sneaker enthusiast Juan Ballesteros (De Los Santos, 2024):** "I wouldn't have felt any type of way. In my two years collecting sneakers I have tried to buy so many sneakers and ended up failing. It's just a part of the sneaker game, you have to learn to accept you won't always be able to purchase what you want." **Mentor text:** In the end, it might not matter to weathered sneakerheads. The thrill comes from buying the shoe, yes, but it also comes in the chase. As Ballesteros put it, he said even if he'd gone through that trouble to get to Washington Square Park only to find out the shoes had been sold out,... it wouldn't have been all that different than what he's used to. —Brian De Los Santos (2017), "Sole Searching: Inside the Wild World of Nike's High-Tech Scavenger Hunts," *Mashable*
End With Analysis	The statement from Donahoe is what you'd expect from a CEO that landed a contract. While I don't doubt that he wants to show ultimate confidence in his brand, it also comes across as dishonest to me. "It was a remarkable team effort and a great proof point that when Nike brings out our best, no one can beat us," Donahoe said. What best are you and Nike bringing out, John Donahoe? Did you have a design-off presentation to win the contract? I doubt it. Spending two times the amount of money isn't "showing Nike at its best." I know people will view me as a person with more affinity for Adidas than Nike. And that's true. But I'm not a huge champion of Gulden or supporter of Germany. It feels like a weird manipulation of the situation to say that Germany went with Nike because they were going to make better things. It feels more about the money. And it's OK to just say that. —Matt Welty (2024), "Adidas Losing Germany to Nike Is One of Its Biggest Failures," *Complex*

Moves That Summarize: Pop Culture

Move	Mini-Mentor Text
Define and Detail	The music video for "Fortnight," the first from Taylor Swift's *Tortured Poets Department* era, has arrived. The visuals for this Post Malone collab are black and white, cinematic, and full of period costumes and typewriters. But of course, there's always more to Swift's symbolism than set dressing might suggest. —Erica Gonzales, Alyssa Bailey, and Lauren Puckett-Pope (2024), "All the Easter Eggs in Taylor Swift's Cinematic 'Fortnight' Music Video," *ELLE Magazine*
Pivot Synopsis	"Black Panther" took some of the spy-thriller shape of a Bond movie, and the sequel carries that on in a new geopolitical context. At the United Nations, the United States and France are pressuring for access to vibranium, the rare metal that Wakanda has built its empire on. Soon after, a U.S. military expedition discovers vibranium at the bottom of the ocean. But just as they're celebrating, a mysterious tribe of blue underwater people, led by Namor, a pointy-eared monarch in green short-shorts with wings on his ankles, ruthlessly wipe out the entire expedition. —Jake Coyle (2022), "In 'Wakanda Forever,' an Empire Mourns and Rebuilds," *Associated Press*
The Devil in the Details	There was also a moment in which Styles allegedly spit on Pine during the seating for the premiere. In the clip, Styles, arriving at his seat, seems to spit into Pine's lap; at that same moment, Pine appears to react by stopping his applause and flashes a look many read as something between annoyance and bemusement. Having zoomed in on photos and slow-motion scrubbed back and forth on the videos that exist of Styles sitting down next to Pine, I am exhausted at looking at Styles's lip quiver but did not see any spittle flying in any one direction. There's also a theory that Pine was merely realizing his sunglasses were on his lap at the same time that Styles approached him. Pine's rep has flatly denied that there was spitting, calling it a "result of an odd online illusion." —Alex Abad-Santos (2022), "The Many Scandals of *Don't Worry Darling*, Explained," *Vox*
Cause and Effect Sandwich	In January, Kensington Palace confirmed she'd undergone an unspecified "abdominal surgery." By March, the princess—who is married to Prince William—had not been seen for almost three months. With little concrete information, rumors and conspiracy theories have flourished. An innocuous attempt to allay the public's curiosity with a Mother's Day photograph fanned the flames, quickly snowballing into an unmitigated disaster. —K. J. Yossman (2024), "Where Is Kate Middleton? What We Know So Far," *Variety*
Quote It to Me	"Like many amateur photographers, I do occasionally experiment with editing," Catherine "Kate" Middleton, a.k.a. the Princess of Wales, apparently wrote on social media Monday, personally apologizing for doctoring an official photo of herself with her children. The photo, posted for Mother's Day in the UK, first drew attention from suspicious royal watchers online, whose doubts were confirmed when the AP issued a "photo kill" for the image, declaring it manipulated. "I wanted to express my apologies for any confusion the family photograph we shared yesterday caused." —Alex Abad-Santos (2024a), "Kate Middleton's Edited Mother's Day Photo, Explained by an Expert," *Vox*

Moves That Contextualize: Pop Culture

Move	Mini-Mentor Text
Let's Compare	McBride's got jokes like Ali Wong's got jokes. Like your colmado's got jokes. —Junot Díaz (2020), "James McBride's 'Deacon King Kong' Is a Supercharged Urban Farce Lit Up by Thunderbolts of Rage," *The New York Times*
Double Date	D'Arcy has been grappling with this tension since "Dragon" first aired in 2022, when it became the most-watched premiere in HBO's history. Set approximately 200 years before "Game of Thrones," the show centers on the Targaryen dynasty before its dramatic fall. —Simran Hans (2024), "Emma D'Arcy, Master of 'Dragon,'" *The New York Times*
Show Me the Data	On the day of *Cowboy Carter*'s release, music video network Vevo reported a 38% increase in views of country music videos globally. From Rhiannon Giddens' banjo to Linda Martell's pioneering EP, every country artist featured on the album has seen an increase in first-time or catalog listeners according to Spotify. —Nielsen (2024), "The '*Cowboy Carter* Effect'—Increasing Young Black Listeners' Engagement With Country Music"
Educated Inference	As for the next steps, there are many factors beyond just on-field performance U.S. Soccer will consider. The federation likely is aware of the discourse around Berhalter and the national team, in which a growing sector of fans has trained its focus on the coach as the problem. "Berhalter out" has been a rallying cry on social media, ubiquitous in any discussion or debate around the team. —Paul Tenorio (2024), "Gregg Berhalter Helped Rebuild the USMNT. Will He Be the One to Lead Them at the 2026 World Cup?," *The Athletic*
Past and Present Connection	Clara Bow was a flapper icon, starring in movies like *Mantrap* and *It*—the nickname "It Girl" was invented for her. But then she got abruptly forgotten and left behind by history. It's a story Swift has told often before, from "The Lucky One" to "Nothing New." But [in *Tortured Poets*] she's singing in the voice of the starstruck small-town girl, flattered to be molded into a Hollywood ingenue. —Rob Sheffield (2024), "Come for the Torture, Stay for the Poetry: This Might Be Taylor Swift's Most Personal Album Yet," *Rolling Stone*

Moves That Add Voice: Pop Culture

Move	Mini-Mentor Text
Say It Slang	If you need help re-orienting yourself to where things stand, vis-a-vis exactly whose noble keister now sits the Iron Throne and precisely which royal chump got his fool self royally chomped, here's a handy refresher. —Glen Weldon (2024), "'House of the Dragon' Season Premiere: I Told You the Rats Would Be a Whole Thing," *NPR*
Ask a Question	The candy-store music, the ultra-synthetic animation, the mixture of slow, bobbing movement and relentless editing—watch it for more than a few minutes, and you feel like you're hallucinating. Where are we? Who are these children? JJ has only two teeth, but he knows the alphabet and plays soccer. What sort of baby is this? —Jia Tolentino (2024), "How Cocomelon Captures Our Children's Attention," *The New Yorker*
Put It in Parentheses	And Brenda, as played memorably by Shannen Doherty, who died on Saturday, knew who her peers were. When she dons a (hideous) hat in Season 1, she is met with derision. "Hippie witch is out," sneers Kelly (Jennie Garth). —Margaret Lyons (2024), "In 'Beverly Hills, 90210,' Shannen Doherty Redefined Teen TV Drama," *The New York Times*
Connect Personally	I must tell you that I have been *Ratatouille*'d. Except instead of a rodent making me cook gourmet meals, it's a blonde 4'11" pop star named Sabrina Carpenter controlling my motor functions to make me repeat a phrase that doesn't even make sense: "That's that me espresso." "We don't have Coke, is Pepsi okay?" That's that me espresso. "How much do you want to contribute to your 401(k)?" That's that me espresso. "Sir, do you know why we pulled you over? Do you know how fast you were going?" That's that me espresso. Like the man Carpenter's singing about in "Espresso," I am up thinking about her every night—and of course her espresso. —Alex Abad-Santos (2024b), "Sabrina Carpenter's 'Espresso,' the Song of the Summer, Explained," *Vox*
Make It Metaphorical	Eilish is known for taking her time in a song, sometimes crawling through a melody as though it were a bowl of molasses, and she often chooses to sing in a whisper, letting a note hang in the air before it dissipates entirely. Her vocal style reminds me of an evanescing cloud of smoke after someone blows out a cluster of birthday candles—beautiful, fleeting, a little bit haunted. —Amanda Petrusich (2024), "The Anxious Love Songs of Billie Eilish," *The New Yorker*

Moves That Conclude: Pop Culture

Move	Mini-Mentor Text
What We Don't Know and What We Do	Whatever the case, the film industry status quo that Zaslav has come to symbolize seems unsustainable—and, with the ongoing strikes, it's not being sustained at all—and Nolan's adherence to tradition suggests movies can still be made, distributed, and watched the way they were before the disruptions of the last decade. Whether he'll be a model for others to follow or one of the last of his kind remains the great, unanswered question. —Keith Phipps (2023), "Christopher Nolan, Warner Bros., and the Struggle for the Soul of Movies," *The Ringer*
What's Next?	The Knicks still own a couple of protected firsts, but for most intents and purposes, they went all in on a team that just ran out of gas in the second round. It's an ambitious, gutsy call. If it works, we'll talk about this group for the rest of our lives. If they continuously get to the playoffs and can't defeat any teams that employ superstars better than their own, they may come to regret pushing all their chips in on a pretty good player who, um, definitely isn't Kevin Durant. —Michael Pina (2024a), "Did the Knicks Just Get Fleeced on the Most Expensive Reunion Ever?," *The Ringer*
Share the Last Word	Biles has also said she's focused less on external judgment. In Tokyo, some viewers reacted negatively to Biles's decision to pull out of competition, and if athletes—including her—make similar decisions in Paris, it's possible it could engender that same response from certain observers. "I think it has to be for us, because it can't be for anybody else because that's not why we do it. We do it for ourselves, and the love for this sport, and the love for representing the US," Biles said in the press briefing. —Li Zhou (2024), "Simone Biles Is So Back," *Vox*
The Bottom Line	In a gaming landscape where nearly every open world game can, eventually, be reduced into a simple set of chores on a map, the first 20 hours of *Tears of the Kingdom* are a revelation. No game since *Elden Ring* has sparked our sense of discovery so strongly—and where that game over-awed with scale and mystery, this latest *Zelda* game does something similar with an energetic sense of play. If the phrase "The *WarioWare* of *Zelda* games" makes sense to you, you understand what we're trying to convey here; if not, then we'll put it in simpler language: One of the most talented video game design teams on the planet has let their imaginations go with this one, and the results are impeccable. We can't wait to play more. —William Hughes (2023), "First Impressions: *Zelda: Tears of the Kingdom* Is the Most Purely Fun Nintendo Game in a Decade," *AV Club*
Solve the Problem	It is but one way of keeping the Dead alive. There are so many ways to express yourself, so many paths into and out of this music. Everyone has the right to desire their own expansion, to test their edges and see what else they might be able to contain. I see so many people on Dead tours who can't possibly dress this way in their everyday lives. On tour, or at the one show they can afford to hit, or watching the livestream at home, or catching some local Dead band struggle through the "Slipknot!" changes, Deadheads enact the answer to a simple problem. The alienation we all feel is real and unavoidable. What if we learned to understand it as good? —Sadie Sartini Garner (2023), "A Requiem for the Dead," *The Ringer*

Moves That Organize: Pop Culture

Move	Mini-Mentor Text
Topic Sentence Transition	Written 200 years ago, the "Ode" is crafted like the best of pop songs, with easily hummable, simple phrases that use the same techniques you hear in a Taylor Swift hit today. But the "Ode" is more than pop. It's a supranational anthem that aspires to a world in which "all men become brothers," as its lyrics say. —Joshua Barone (2024), "Why We Still Want to Hear the 'Ode to Joy,' 200 Years Later," *The New York Times*
Hinge Transition	He was no longer as sculpted and vibrant as his glory days. Yet, somehow, he was no less statuesque. His aura was still 60 feet. His presence still kingly. I couldn't call my dad, who'd passed away by the time of my encounter. So I called his oldest brother, who I knew would comprehend my awe. —Marcus Thompson II (2024), "Willie Mays Is a Monument to an Era of Black Baseball Gone but Never Forgotten," *The Athletic*
List It	Once you've identified a burn, Njoroge says, it's crucial to soothe and treat any inflammation. Severe burns might need medical attention but, for milder cases, "anything that can reduce the skin's temperature," she says, "will reduce discomfort and potentially reduce post-inflammatory hyperpigmentation." Here, her favorite, cooling post-sun routine: - *Put Farmacy's Honey Potion Plus, a hydrating mask with skin-soothing antioxidants, in the fridge for an hour and then apply it to your face for 10 to 15 minutes. (Aloe gel is a cost-friendly alternative.)* - *Shower in cool water and dry yourself by gently patting, rather than rubbing, your skin to avoid aggravating it further.* - *Apply a cool compress to irritated areas for up to 10 minutes.* - *Wear free-flowing clothes until your skin has healed.* —Nia Decaille (2024), "Are You Wearing Sunscreen the Right Way?," *The New York Times Style Magazine*
Add Subheadings	Subheadings: - *Who's beefing with who?* - *Who is Drake dissing on "Push Ups"?* - *Drake's latest round with Kendrick took a particularly dark turn* - *Drake has previously thrived in beefs—but can he win when the whole industry is against him?* —Kyndall Cunningham (2024), "How 'Not Like Us' Became an Anti-Drake Anthem," *Vox*
Visual Anchoring	Now a combined 74 years old, Team USA's all-time leaders in points and assists still looked like giants; their combined shot chart is excellence everlasting: [*Diagram of Team USA's shot chart*] As a whole, Team USA made 56 percent of its 3s and 68 percent of its 2s. Steph Curry's screens induced chaos, Anthony Edwards's athleticism ignited fast-break opportunities, Devin Booker's outside stroke punctured a game plan that packed the paint, and Jrue Holiday, Bam Adebayo, Anthony Davis, and Derrick White put on a defensive clinic. —Michael Pina (2024b), "Team USA Looks Unstoppable, but It's Not a Dream Team Yet," *The Ringer*

All English Moves

Please see the following tables to view all English mentor texts pertaining to each mini move.

Moves That Introduce: English

Move	Mini-Mentor Text
Just-the-Facts	Climate activist Greta Thunberg who, at age 15, led school strikes every Friday in her home country of Sweden—a practice that caught on globally—has now, at 20, managed to bring together more than 100 scientists, environmental activists, journalists and writers to lay out exactly how and why it's clear that the climate crisis is happening. —Barbara J. King (2023), "Greta Thunberg's 'The Climate Book' Urges World to Keep Climate Justice Out Front," *NPR*
Make the Case	Dennis Lehane's *Small Mercies* may take place in Boston's Southie neighborhood in 1974—but the topics it deals with are incredibly timely. At once a crime novel, a deep, unflinching look at racism, and a heart-wrenching story about a mother who has lost everything, this narrative delves into life in the projects at a time when the city of Boston struggled with the desegregation of its public school system—and a lot [of] residents were showing their worst side. —Gabino Iglesias (2023), "Dennis Lehane's 'Small Mercies' Is a Crime Thriller That Spotlights Rampant Racism," *NPR*
What They Said	*Parable of the Sower* was first published in October 1993. It tells the story of 15-year-old Lauren Olamina, a young Black woman living through a time of severe societal collapse. She creates (through observation and deduction) a new religion, Earthseed, which she expounds between her diary entries in simple verses that are both axiomatic and richly open-ended: "The Self must create / Its own reason for being. / To shape God, / Shape Self." —Roz Dineen (2024), "On the Simple Prophecy of Octavia Butler's *Parable of the Sower*," *Literary Hub*
Scene-Drop	The small, sickly African girl who arrived in Boston on a seafaring vessel in 1761 had already been stripped of her family and her home. She missed her father, who suffered after having his young child "snatched," she would later lament in writing. She longed for her mother, whose morning libations to the sun had imprinted on her an enduring memory. She was naked beneath her only physical covering, a "dirty carpet." She owned nothing, not even herself. A little over a decade later, this same girl, named Phillis Wheatley after the slave ship that had transported her (the Phillis) and the enslavers who had purchased her (Susanna and John Wheatley), was an author. Her widely read 1773 book of verse, *Poems on Various Subjects, Religious and Moral*, was striking in its creativity and spoke up for Black humanity. In his erudite, enlightening new biography, *The Odyssey of Phillis Wheatley*, the historian David Waldstreicher points out that the remarkable and unlikely story of this Revolutionary-era Black celebrity, who was both highlighted and castigated for her race, turns on such reversals and contradictions. Wheatley emerges in these pages as a literary marvel. Waldstreicher's comprehensive account is a monument to her prowess. —Tiya Miles (2023), "The Great American Poet Who Was Named After a Slave Ship," *The Atlantic*
Then-and-Now	Back in 1995, Russia's two major art museums, in St. Petersburg and Moscow, mounted exhibitions a month apart that attracted considerable attention. Not so much because of the art, although much of it was spectacular, but because Russia openly identified it as art looted from Nazi Germany at the end of World War II. . . . . . . Last month, those "twice saved" treasures came to mind with the news that a German government delegation had traveled to Nigeria to return 20 precious artifacts, a tiny portion of the vast trove of what are known as Benin Bronzes, plundered by British colonial soldiers from what was the West African kingdom of Benin. (The kingdom is now part of Nigeria; modern Benin is a separate, neighboring state.) —Serge Schmemann (2023), "'She Comes Back to Where She Belongs,'" *The New York Times*

Moves That Make a Claim: English

Move	Mini-Mentor Text
The Big Idea	Dennis Lehane's *Small Mercies* is a crime thriller that spotlights rampant racism. —Gabino Iglesias (2023), "Dennis Lehane's 'Small Mercies' Is a Crime Thriller That Spotlights Rampant Racism," *NPR*
Outline It	While *Fledgling* explores a host of far-reaching themes—racial anxiety, codependency, memory (or a lack thereof)—Butler seems most keen on examining power and intimacy. —Lovia Gyarkye (2022), "The Octavia Butler Novel for Our Times," *The Atlantic*
This-and-That	By her presence, Moreno teaches us how to approach this movie, as both an affectionate tribute and a gentle corrective. —Justin Chang (2021), "Steven Spielberg's 'West Side Story' Will Make You Believe in Movies Again," *NPR*
Not-This-But-That	[Clarence Thomas's] efforts at reconciliation ultimately illustrate the extent to which "originalism" is merely a process of exploiting history to justify conservative policy preferences, and not a neutral philosophical framework. —Adam Serwer (2023), "The Most Baffling Argument a Supreme Court Justice Has Ever Made," *The Atlantic*
Synthesize It	*Freedom Song*, Amit Chaudhuri's third novel, is set in Calcutta in 1993. The book is pointillist in form, capturing both the inner and outer voices of its many characters. If Dylan Thomas, with his uncanny ear for unspoken thoughts, had written *Under Milk Wood* set not in a Welsh village but in an Indian city, this might be it. —Wendy Doniger (2024), "A Quiet Roar: Wendy Doniger on Amit Chaudhuri's *Freedom Song*," *Literary Hub*

Moves That Define: English

Move	Mini-Mentor Text
It Is What It Is	Of course, it is Breyer's patience for sifting through the most finicky details that made him such a scrupulous jurist. He is dedicated, precise and deliberate. —Jennifer Szalai (2024), "The Retired Justice Who Doesn't Understand the Supreme Court," *The New York Times*
Say My Name	Here, hurricanes and tides have made building collapse a constant danger, the freeway is visible only on low-tide days, food is government rations, the wealthy have fled "upriver to scattered little freshwater townships," and gigantic birds called rook cranes are everywhere. —Jessamine Chan (2024), "In Téa Obreht's Latest, a Refugee Seeks Home in a Ruined World," *The New York Times*
Keep It Appositive	*The Talk* explores the question of how people—in this case, a precocious, geeky, and artistic young man, the child of a white mother and Black father—know what they know. —Tahneer Oksman (2023b), "'The Talk' Is an Epic Portrait of an Artist Making His Way Through Hardships," *NPR*
Gimme an Example	And so it starts with being an altar boy for those Masses in Enniscorthy, the stained glass, the light, the Cathedral, the choir, the amazing choir singing Mozart . . . all of that mattered enormously, as did later at St. Peter's, which was half a seminary and half a Diocesan school where a lot of the real influences on, certainly on me, were priests. —Caoilinn Hughes (2024), "Colm Tóibín on James Baldwin's Enduring, International Influence," *Literary Hub*
Engage With Etymology	Loneliness is a compound or multidimensional emotion: It contains elements of sadness and anxiety, fear and heartache. The experience of it is inherently, intensely subjective, as any chronically lonely person can tell you. A clerk at a crowded grocery store can be wildly lonely, just as a wizened hermit living in a cave can weather solitude in perfect bliss. (If you want to infuriate an expert in loneliness, try confusing the word "isolation" with "loneliness.") For convenience's sake, most researchers still use the definition coined nearly three decades ago, in the early 1980s, by the social psychologists Daniel Perlman and Letitia Anne Peplau, who described loneliness as "a discrepancy between one's desired and achieved levels of social relations." Unfortunately, that definition is pretty subjective, too. —Matthew Shaer (2024), "Why Is the Loneliness Epidemic So Hard to Cure?," *The New York Times*

Moves That Describe: English

Move	Mini-Mentor Text
Describing Lists	I wanted to find what she discovers in our borderlands, to see if it's as dearly held as my memory of a childhood bedroom window opening southward to a daily breeze of blended language, barking dogs and Grandmother's whistled greetings to her neighbors. —Marcela Davison Avilés (2023), "'The Wind Knows My Name' Is a Reference and a Refrain in the Search for Home," *NPR*
Say It Again, But Make It Specific	Britell deftly captures the emotional dissonance at the heart of the show. His score's dual capacity for harmony and dissonant chords underlines the nuanced nature of so many interactions, as affection is clouded by trauma, jealousy, and anger. —Ali Royals (2023), "Hereditary Venom: On Nicholas Britell's 'Succession: Season 4' Soundtrack," *Los Angeles Review of Books*
Dash That Describes	*The Wind Knows My Name* is a tale of two child immigrants—a boy who escapes Nazi occupied Vienna in 1938 and a girl who escapes military gangs in El Salvador in 2019. —Marcela Davison Avilés (2023), "'The Wind Knows My Name' Is a Reference and a Refrain in the Search for Home," *NPR*
Let's Imagine . . .	Few delights bring as much comfort as good food, so imagine how cheering a good cup of coffee and a fresh donut would have been to soldiers on the front lines in World War II. But also imagine how women recruited to serve food to soldiers might view the value of their contribution when they see the life-and-death sacrifices those men had to make. That's one of the animating conflicts in the heartfelt novel *Good Night, Irene* from Pulitzer Prize finalist Luis Alberto Urrea. —Michael Magras (2023), "*Good Night, Irene* by Luis Alberto Urrea," *BookPage*
Figurative Language Comparison	Seemingly overnight, Bridget was to digital correspondence what Chandler Bing was to comic timing: a fresh metronome for the last gasp of the 20th century. —Elisabeth Egan (2023), "Bridget Jones Deserved Better. We All Did," *The New York Times*

Moves That Provide Evidence: English

Move	Mini-Mentor Text
Hyperlink Layers	It's a minor-league mind that chooses to make sport of sports. Not that there aren't major-league authors who do so, among them George Orwell ("Serious sport is war minus the shooting") and H. L. Mencken ("It is impossible to imagine Goethe or Beethoven being good at billiards or golf"). Their thinking hurts the ball club. As a nation, it is through the prism of sports that we frame our ethical values, remember our history, envision our future, and find the figures of speech that create our common culture and define our national identity. Walt Whitman once whimsically described American democracy as "athletic"; history has borne out his observation in more ways than he could have foreseen. —Simon Apter (2010), "Wordplay," *Lapham's Quarterly*
Reference a Visual	Behold the hulking Arctic explorer Peter Freuchen and his chic wife, Dagmar, in an unforgettable picture from 1947. . . . . . . For one thing, look at the proportions! He is so *large*, swaddled in a colossal polar-bear coat, and she is so *tiny*, in her pert black suit and pearls, her one extravagance (a hat with a bow and netting, the millinery trend in those days) dwarfed by his opulent pelage. And then there are their expressions. His: leathered and intimidating, as if he were staring down a predator he intends to harpoon. [*The image is a black-and-white photograph featuring two individuals, a man and a woman, who are both dressed in distinctive attire.* • *Man on the left: He is standing and wearing an oversized, heavy fur coat that almost engulfs him, making him appear larger and more imposing. The fur coat is thick and covers him from his shoulders down to his ankles. The man's facial expression is serious, with a full beard, adding to his rugged appearance.* • *Woman on the right: She is seated on what appears to be a draped fabric or cushion. She is dressed elegantly in a dark, formal outfit with a knee-length dress and heels. She is also wearing a stylish hat with a decorative element, which adds to the sophisticated look. Her pose is composed, with one leg crossed over the other and her hands resting on her lap.* *The photograph likely has a historical or artistic context, with the contrasting appearances of the two subjects creating a striking visual effect. The man's grandiose fur coat contrasts with the woman's refined and polished look, suggesting a juxtaposition of ruggedness and elegance.*] —Rachel Syme (2019), "An Irving Penn Portrait for the Coldest Days of Winter," *The New Yorker*
The Fold In	Christie's home life sputtered at approximately the rate her career took off. She seems to have had a take-it-or-leave-it attitude to motherhood, ditching Rosalind for months at a stretch and neglecting to answer the unhappy girl's letters. Later Christie would describe Rosalind as playing "the valuable role in life of eternally trying to discourage me without success." —Molly Young (2022), "Agatha Christie's Latest Biographer Plumbs a Life of Mystery," *The New York Times*
Paraphrase It	**Quote from writer Christine Schutt:** A story is a circle. —Christine Schutt, personal communication to Julia Phillips, Summer 2014 **Mentor text:** I'm paraphrasing a brilliant writer and teacher, Christine Schutt, when I say that this way of structuring a story, returning in the end to the elements that were put in play at the start, is what gives the reader satisfaction. —Julia Phillips (2024), "Julia Phillips on the Writing Lessons of Fairy Tales," *Literary Hub*
End With Analysis	Perhaps even more disturbing than Offred's total erasure is the blasé nature with which the scholars of the epilogue regard the events of the novel. Pieixoto remarks "we must be cautious about passing moral judgment upon the Gileadean. Surely we have learned by now that such judgments are of necessity culture-specific." The professor listened to Offred's description of the tortures that women were subjected to during her time, yet he is reluctant to judge the perpetrators of her suffering. Dr. Pieixoto, as a male scholar, is viewing these historical events from the distant perspective of privilege, and as a result, like many real-life scholars, he is unwilling to condemn something that would never have affected him personally, writing off the oppression of an entire gender as a matter of cultural misunderstanding. —Anna Sheffer (2017), "The Epilogue of 'The Handmaid's Tale' Changes Everything You Thought You Knew About the Book," *Electric Literature*

Moves That Summarize: English

Move	Mini-Mentor Text
Define and Detail	Pasta nada is better known to the world as pantry pasta. These are the pasta dishes you make, vastly better and less expensive than ordering out, from ingredients that are already in your kitchen. —Dwight Garner (2024b), "Pasta Nada: The Culinary Art of Making Something From Nothing," *The New York Times*
Pivot Synopsis	Relentlessly harassed about his homosexuality by both schoolmates and his especially harsh mother, Keith Chen, the novel's primary protagonist, flees his hometown of Yongjing to live a freer, bohemian life in Berlin, where he enters a romance with a German named T. By the end of the first chapter, however, Keith reveals that he's murdered T, without saying how or why. After serving his prison sentence, Keith returns to Yongjing for the first time in many years. —Leland Cheuk (2022), "'Ghost Town' Blurs the Line Between the Living and the Dead in Rural Taiwan," *NPR*
The Devil in the Details	The fair, which this year had over 1,000 exhibitors and something like 30,000 visitors, is one of the biggest events of the international publishing calendar. For three days, agents, editors, publishers, scouts and many other people whose jobs are harder to explain gather in a frenzied fashion, primarily to sell and buy foreign rights for English-language books, but also to take temperatures, observe prevailing winds and scheme. For those who weren't there to close deals, the fair offered the opportunity to map out the minutely graded power structure of the publishing industry. —Rosa Lyster (2024), "Welcome to the London Book Fair, Where Everyone Knows Their Place," *The New York Times*
Cause and Effect Sandwich	It makes sense that Peter Freuchen would agree to sign up for such a process: he was nothing if not tough. Freuchen, who was born in 1886, in Denmark, quit school, at the age of twenty, to sail to Greenland, as a stoker on a steamship, after seeing a student play about polar exploration and realizing that it was his life's calling. He spent the next three decades living in and exploring some of the coldest parts of the world. According to his many memoirs and journals (he wrote more than a dozen!), he encountered death at almost every turn. He was trapped for several days in an avalanche. A camp cook almost shot him, thinking he was a bear.... While he was stuck, whittling away at the ice, one of his feet froze so severely that he was forced to amputate several of his own toes. Later, he lost the foot entirely. —Rachel Syme (2019), "An Irving Penn Portrait for the Coldest Days of Winter," *The New Yorker*
Quote It to Me	Grief here is fundamentally an intense form of attention. Those in power have an incentive to use grief as a spotlight on events that bolster national identity, financial or brand interest, or otherwise, just as they have an incentive not to draw attention to events that could sow discord or upend these interests. What a society chooses to grieve is ultimately its way of "posing the question of who 'we' are," writes the philosopher Judith Butler. "By asking whose lives are considered valuable, whose lives are mourned, and whose lives are considered ungrievable." —Cody Delistraty (2024), "How Reading Grief Memoirs Helped Cody Delistraty Understand His Loss in New Ways," *Literary Hub*

Moves That Contextualize: English

Move	Mini-Mentor Text
Let's Compare	Despite the urban setting, this is a village novel, like *Emma* or *Barchester Towers*, an ensemble piece about the way a small community of flawed characters who think they know one another all too well cope with newcomers and their own capacity for change. —Laura Miller (2020), "The Old-Fashioned Warmth of James McBride," *Slate*
Double Date	Known as the Black Tulip, only twelve copies appear to have survived since its publication in July 1827. That one of the last two in private hands is coming to auction this month, not quite two centuries later, marks an historic bibliophilic event. —Bradford Morrow (2024), "In Search of the Rarest Book in American Literature: Edgar Allan Poe's *Tamerlane*," *Literary Hub*
Show Me the Data	From July to December 2023, PEN found that more than 4,300 books were removed from schools across 23 states—a figure that surpassed the number of bans from the entire previous academic year. The rise in book bans has accelerated in recent years, driven by conservative groups and by new laws and regulations that limit what kinds of books children can access. Since the summer of 2021, PEN has tracked book removals in 42 states and found instances in both Republican- and Democratic-controlled districts. —Alexandra Alter (2024), "Book Bans Continue to Surge in Public Schools," *The New York Times*
Educated Inference	Plath's most famous poem is probably "Daddy," which references her father and his death, but which is absolutely not a biographical poem, and is in many ways a poem about throwing off the influence of powerful men—her father, sure, but also her teachers and certainly her husband, who was a stand-in for both her father and her teachers, throughout their marriage, according to Plath. —Sarah Viren (2024), "A Painful, Urgent Reimagining: Emily van Duyne on Writing a New History of Sylvia Plath's Last Years," *Literary Hub*
Past and Present Connection	Class leaps are far rarer now than they were in the 1940s, as research by Raj Chetty and others has shown. And it can be emotionally treacherous to move between social classes, or what social theorist Chantal Jaquet calls "transclass" in her recent book *Transclasses: A Theory of Social Non-Reproduction*. . . . On one hand, Vance's personal narrative is the authentic-seeming apotheosis of Trump's own mostly false story of self-creation. On the other, both Trump and Vance are part of a longer tradition in American writing and entertainment centered on the self-made man. —Alissa Quart (2024), "JD Vance Is the Toxic Byproduct of America's Obsession With Bootstrap Narratives," *Literary Hub*

Moves That Add Voice: English

Move	Mini-Mentor Text
Say It Slang	C'est la vie, of course, unless you are some type of time-lord wizard. But novelists are wizards, or at least magicians, and one of their favorite tricks is to fit whole narrative worlds inside a single day, book-shaped ships squeezed into bottles. —Leah Greenblatt (2024), "2 Novels Set Over Very Memorable Days," *The New York Times*
Ask a Question	Other writers have persuasively argued for Colwin's ongoing relevance, particularly in regard to the 2021 reissues of her fiction and cooking essays. But my questions were more personal: Would her narratives speak to me nearly 30 years after first reading them? Would I still revel in Colwin's enchantment? Was it finally time to write about her and what she had meant to me? —Mia Manzulli (2024), "In Praise of the Domestic Sensualist: Laurie Colwin at 80," *Literary Hub*
Put It in Parentheses	But, while many public beaches remained closed, "Beach Read" blew up on TikTok. Cooped-up daughters pressed it on distracted mothers (present company included). The book sailed onto the best-seller list, where it remained for more than a year. . . . At Henry's request, Chiu outfitted Daphne's free-spirited L. I. (that's romance lingo for love interest) in a pair of yellow Crocs. —Elisabeth Egan (2024), "Emily Henry on Writing Best-Sellers Without Tours or TikTok," *The New York Times*
Connect Personally	My idea of hell would be to live with a library that contained only reimaginings of famous novels. It's a wet-brained and dutiful genre, by and large. Or the results are brittle spoofs—to use a word that, according to John Barth, sounds like imperfectly suppressed flatulence—that read as if there are giant scare quotes surrounding the action. Two writers in a hundred walk away unscathed. "James" is the rarest of exceptions. —Dwight Garner (2024a), "'Huck Finn' Is a Masterpiece. This Retelling Just Might Be, Too," *The New York Times*
Make It Metaphorical	*Forgotten on Sunday* is a *pain au chocolat* of a book—flaky but buttery, with a sweet center. This sentimental soul-soother is further sweetened by the knowledge that several of the characters are named, at least in part, after Perrin's grandparents, including Helene Hel's lost-and-found great love, Lucien Perrin. —Heller McAlpin (2024), "'Forgotten on Sunday' Evokes the Heartwarming Whimsy of the Movie 'Amélie,'" *NPR*

Moves That Conclude: English

Move	Mini-Mentor Text
What We Don't Know and What We Do	*Late Bloomers* doesn't show how seeing, or rather, *learning to resee*, takes time. All the same, implicit in the novel's gardening motif is a modest message: we seldom care for ourselves with the same determination as for our plants. About the things we care most—namely, ourselves—we lie. And what in turn eludes us is the emergence of new buds within ourselves, blooms that lay dormant for years before opening to the sun. —Rajat Singh (2023), "I Became a Writer When I Needed a Fresh Start," *Electric Literature*
What's Next?	I'm not sure I believe that institutional change alone is enough to keep each new social media platform from falling prey to the worst side of human nature. Is it possible for us, the users of the internet, to learn how to simply *not go there*? I hope so, because that may be what it takes to get us out of Rose-Stockwell's dark valley and back into the sun. —Laura Miller (2023), "How to Short-Circuit the Outrage Machine," *Slate*
Share the Last Word	Imelda drives, one dark afternoon, into the countryside and finds that the yellow hills, the old landmarks, all Ireland, provide no answer to the problems that plague her: "At the crossroads a shuttered pub a blackened sign Guinness Time the country gazes back at you like a mirror with nothing in it." —Dan Kois (2023), "A Novel That Strives to Engage the World on Every Single Page," *Slate*
The Bottom Line	*Black Leopard, Red Wolf* and *Moon Witch, Spider King* can be disorienting and confusing books whose narratives jump around in time and treat such bizarre phenomenon as lightning vampires as if they need little explanation. Their difficulty will (and has) put off some readers, but for those who persevere, the two novels show how who you are shapes the kind of story you tell about the world around you, a world made new with every teller. —Laura Miller (2022), "The 'African *Game of Thrones*' Just Keeps Getting Better," *Slate*
Solve the Problem	So how do we define ourselves in the age of Instagram and Reality TV? Maybe we don't. Maybe we date who we love and plant a garden in our backyard, and when the finale of *Love Is Blind* comes out, we sit on the couch, watch with our limbs intertwined, and laugh and smile and cringe and gasp. Maybe it's as simple as that. —Grace Kennedy (2023), "Searching for 'The One' in the Age of Social Media and Reality TV," *Electric Literature*

Moves That Organize: English

Move	Mini-Mentor Text
Topic Sentence Transition	My mother also believed that writing was the highest possible calling, so she read *Pride and Prejudice*, her favorite Jane Austen novel, aloud to me in the womb. She wanted me to hear the words, the magnificent prose; to enjoy the wit; to appreciate the insights; to value exemplary work. —Jane Cleland (2021), "Jane Austen and Me," *CrimeReads*
Hinge Transition	At one end of the spectrum is the therapeutic confessional, where the need or wish is a subconscious, complicated thing; at the other end is the diary of the politician or other public figure, where the need or wish—to be read—is the whole point of writing the thing in the first place. But could it be that a hitherto unrecognized literary law dictates that the less a person expects others to read a diary, the more interesting it will be? Political diaries certainly prove the point. —Helen Fielding (2024), "Helen Fielding on *Bridget Jones* and the Subtle Art of Diary Keeping," *Literary Hub*

List It	Except not all fairy tales actually conclude this way. In my go-to collection of Brothers Grimm stories, sure, some tales have it, but many end on a last line with a decidedly different tenor
	    "*All of them were executed as payment for their villainy.*"
	    "*That was how Hans lost his bride.*"
	    "*And since nobody could get out, they were all burned to death.*"
	    "*The duplicity of the stepmother and her daughter was now clear as day, and they were cast into the forest to be devoured by wild animals.*"
	    "*Watch out!*"
	—Julia Phillips (2024), "Julia Phillips on the Writing Lessons of Fairy Tales," *Literary Hub*

Add Subheadings	Subheadings: • Leaving Home • A Sheet of Paper • Mind on Fire • The Altercation • Perfect Marriage —Paul Elie (2015), "The Secret History of *One Hundred Years of Solitude*," *Vanity Fair*
Visual Anchoring	Then, midway through the book, after the wise woman gives our hero one truth about dragons—basically that they're all like Smaug from *The Hobbit*, sitting on piles of treasure and shooting flames at trespassers—the little boy steps over and out of the border of the first story, and straight into another. [*Image of an illustration in the book with a boy standing next to an elderly woman: The woman has her arm around the boy's shoulder. They sit on the porch of a cabin in a forest with large green trees and the text "You may also journey into another forest..."*] Now the illustrations are airy and cool—greens and blues replace the warm reds and browns of yore. The borders have disappeared. The oak trees have been uprooted by a bamboo forest. The child is guided by nine-tailed foxes, ghostly maidens, and the white rabbit who dwells on the moon. —Samantha Balaban (2024), "To Learn 'The Truth About Dragons,' Go on a Quest Through This Kids' Book," *NPR*

All Mathematics Moves

Please see the following tables to view all mathematics mentor texts pertaining to each mini move.

Moves That Introduce: Mathematics

Move	Mini-Mentor Text
Just-the-Facts	In the 1950s, four decades before he won a Nobel Prize for his contributions to game theory and his story inspired the book and film "A Beautiful Mind," the mathematician John Nash proved one of the most remarkable results in all of geometry. Among other features, it implied that you could crumple a sphere down to a ball of any size without ever creasing it. He made this possible by inventing a new type of geometric object called an "embedding," which situates a shape inside a larger space—not unlike fitting a two-dimensional poster into a three-dimensional tube. —Mordechai Rorvig (2021), "Mathematicians Identify Threshold at Which Shapes Give Way," *Quanta Magazine*
Make the Case	In a new proof, a long-neglected mathematical object has finally gotten its moment in the spotlight. At first glance, modular forms—functions whose abundant symmetries have intrigued mathematicians for centuries—seem to have garnered more than enough attention. They crop up in all sorts of problems: They were a key ingredient in Andrew Wiles' 1994 proof of Fermat's Last Theorem, which resolved one of the biggest open questions in number theory. They play a central role in the Langlands program, an ongoing effort to develop "a grand unified theory of mathematics." They've even been used to study models in string theory and quantum physics. —Jordana Cepelewicz (2023b), "New Proof Distinguishes Mysterious and Powerful 'Modular Forms,'" *Quanta Magazine*
What They Said	"For me, mathematics exists in the space between us," Emmy Murphy wrote in accepting the 2020 New Horizons in Mathematics Prize. That space, for her, is a realm of art, perhaps even more than science. And like an artist, she is most fulfilled when exploring the fertile ground where constraint meets creation. The objects she studies are "beautiful to me in the same way that architecture or fashion or expensive furniture is beautiful—the way they are both highly constrained by their geometry and also highly flexible," she told *Quanta*. —Erica Klarreich (2023a), "Emmy Murphy Is a Mathematician Who Finds Beauty in Flexibility," *Quanta Magazine*
Scene-Drop	A few minutes into a 2018 talk at the University of Michigan, Ian Tobasco picked up a large piece of paper and crumpled it into a seemingly disordered ball of chaos. He held it up for the audience to see, squeezed it for good measure, then spread it out again. "I get a wild mass of folds that emerge, and that's the puzzle," he said. "What selects this pattern from another, more orderly pattern?" He then held up a second large piece of paper—this one pre-folded into a famous origami pattern of parallelograms known as the Miura-ori—and pressed it flat. The force he used on each sheet of paper was about the same, he said, but the outcomes couldn't have been more different. The Miura-ori was divided neatly into geometric regions; the crumpled ball was a mess of jagged lines. —Stephen Ornes (2022), "The New Math of Wrinkling," *Quanta Magazine*
Then-and-Now	In the fourth century, the Greek mathematician Pappus of Alexandria praised bees for their "geometrical forethought." The hexagonal structure of their honeycomb seemed like the optimal way to partition two-dimensional space into cells of equal area and minimal perimeter—allowing the insects to cut down on how much wax they needed to produce, and to spend less time and energy building their hive. Or so Pappus and others hypothesized. For millennia, nobody could prove that hexagons were optimal—until finally, in 1999, the mathematician Thomas Hales showed that no other shape could do better. Today, mathematicians still don't know which shapes can tile three or more dimensions with the smallest possible surface area. —Jordana Cepelewicz (2023a), "Mathematicians Complete Quest to Build 'Spherical Cubes,'" *Quanta Magazine*

Moves That Make a Claim: Mathematics

Move	Mini-Mentor Text
The Big Idea	In a 912-page paper posted online on May 30, Szeftel, Elena Giorgi of Columbia University and Sergiu Klainerman of Princeton University have proved that slowly rotating Kerr black holes are indeed stable. —Steve Nadis (2022a), "At Long Last, Mathematical Proof That Black Holes Are Stable," *Quanta Magazine*
Outline It	Four Fields Medals were awarded for major breakthroughs in geometry, combinatorics, statistical physics and number theory, even as mathematicians continued to wrestle with how computers are changing the discipline. —Konstantin Kakaes (2022), "The Year in Math," *Quanta Magazine*
This-and-That	But it turns out that shapes with nonnegative Ricci curvature are more flexible and less well behaved than mathematicians had expected—complicating their understanding of the relationship between local geometric properties and global topological ones. —Jordana Cepelewicz (2024b), "Strangely Curved Shapes Break 50-Year-Old Geometry Conjecture," *Quanta Magazine*
Not-This-But-That	General relativity has transformed our understanding of gravity, depicting it not as an attractive force between massive objects, as had long been held, but rather as a consequence of the way space and time curve in the presence of mass and energy. —Steve Nadis (2022b), "Mass and Angular Momentum, Left Ambiguous by Einstein, Get Defined," *Quanta Magazine*
Synthesize It	What we do know is that the mathematical technique now known as the Chinese remainder theorem was devised sometime between the third and fifth centuries CE by the Chinese mathematician Sun Tzu (not to be confused with Sun Tzu who wrote *The Art of War* almost 1,000 years earlier).... ... Sun Tzu never proved this formally, but later the Indian mathematician and astronomer Aryabhata developed a process for solving any given instance of the theorem. —Lakshmi Chandrasekaran (2021), "How Ancient War Trickery Is Alive in Math Today," *Quanta Magazine*

Moves That Define: Mathematics

Move	Mini-Mentor Text
It Is What It Is	To formalize how close to a square a rectangle is, mathematicians use a number called the aspect ratio. It is simply the length divided by the width. —Kevin Hartnett (2024a), "Mathematicians Identify the Best Versions of Iconic Shapes," *Quanta Magazine*
Say My Name	This process, called the unfolding of the billiard path, allows the ball to continue in a straight-line trajectory. —David S. Richeson (2024), "Unfolding the Mysteries of Polygonal Billiards," *Quanta Magazine*
Keep It Appositive	Alongside this came the work of Christopher Clavius—a German Jesuit astronomer who helped Pope Gregory XIII to introduce the Gregorian calendar—and other mathematicians on fractions. —Madeleine S. Killacky (2023), "Shakespeare by Numbers: How Mathematical Breakthroughs Influenced the Bard's Plays," *The Conversation*
Gimme an Example	In general, a set is a group if it comes with some operation that, like addition, combines two elements into a third element in a way that satisfies some basic requirements. —Leila Sloman (2023), "Probability and Number Theory Collide—in a Moment," *Quanta Magazine*
Engage With Etymology	The term *tally* comes from the French verb *tailler*, "to cut," like the English word *tailor*; the root is seen in the Latin *taliare*, meaning "to cut." It is also interesting to note that the English word *write* can be traced to the Anglo-Saxon *writan*, "to scratch," or "to notch." . . . Counts were maintained by making scratches on stones, by cutting notches in wooden sticks or pieces of bone, or by tying knots in strings of different colors or lengths. —David M. Burton (2011), *The History of Mathematics: An Introduction*, p. 2

Moves That Describe: Mathematics

Move	Mini-Mentor Text
Describing Lists	Wantzel used his results to resolve other classical problems by proving that they can't be solved—it is impossible to trisect some angles, it is impossible to double the cube and it is impossible to construct certain regular polygons. —David S. Richeson (2023b), "How Math Achieved Transcendence," *Quanta Magazine*
Say It Again, But Make It Specific	Let's call $g(x)$ the new quadratic function we get when we replace x with $x + 4$. In other words, let $g(x) = f(x + 4)$. —Patrick Honner (2023c), "The Symmetry That Makes Solving Math Equations Easy," *Quanta Magazine*
Dash That Describes	Still, the impact on payments for undergraduates is relatively modest—an addition of about $2 a month on a $5,500 loan (the first-year maximum borrowing amount), with a standard 10-year repayment term. —Ann Carrns (2023), "Expect Interest Rates on Federal Student Loans to Rise," *The New York Times*
Let's Imagine . . .	For example, let's say we have two tiles, A and B, and two rules for putting them together: 1. Next to an A, on either side you can only place a B. 2. Next to a B, on either side you can only place an A. Can we tile the line with these tiles and these rules? Absolutely. Suppose we put an A down first. —Patrick Honner (2023a), "Math Patterns That Go On Forever but Never Repeat," *Quanta Magazine*
Figurative Language Comparison	These classical problems could go down in infamy as sirens whose songs lured mathematicians to crash on the rocky shores of impossibility. But I see them as muses who inspired generations of creative thinkers. —David S. Richeson (2020), "When Math Gets Impossibly Hard," *Quanta Magazine*

Moves That Provide Evidence: Mathematics

Move	Mini-Mentor Text
Hyperlink Layers	After the start of the pandemic, Yang-Hui He, a researcher at the London Institute for Mathematical Sciences, decided to take on some new challenges. He had been a physics major in college, and had gotten his doctorate from the Massachusetts Institute of Technology in mathematical physics. But he was increasingly interested in number theory, and given the increasing capabilities of artificial intelligence, he thought he'd try his hand at using AI as a tool for finding unexpected patterns in numbers. (He had already been using machine learning to classify Calabi-Yau manifolds, mathematical structures that are widely used in string theory.) —Lyndie Chiou (2024a), "Elliptic Curve 'Murmurations' Found With AI Take Flight," *Quanta Magazine*
Reference a Visual	This movie created by the Harvard-led team shows the execution of a 48-logical-qubit circuit, which they say is the most advanced circuit ever executed on a quantum computer. Groups of eight atomic qubits are first brought together and entangled into error-corrected logical qubit blocks, indicated by red ovals. These blocks are then entangled with each other to create a circuit with hundreds of logical gate operations.... At the end of the computation, lasers read out atoms' states: If an atom is in the state that is resonant with the illumination, the light is scattered, but if it's in the other state, there's no scattering. [*In this image, a grid-like pattern consisting of small green dots arranged in two distinct rectangular groups. The top group has a more extensive and sparse arrangement, while the bottom group appears denser with a more compact arrangement of dots. The background is light, allowing the green dots to stand out clearly.*] —Philip Ball (2024a), "The Best Qubits for Quantum Computing Might Just Be Atoms," *Quanta Magazine*
The Fold In	Convex pentagons that tile the plane were trickier to classify. Reinhardt discovered five families of such pentagons; 50 years later, Richard Kershner found three more. Then in 1975, Martin Gardner wrote about the problem for *Scientific American*, bringing it to the attention of professional and amateur mathematicians alike. One such amateur, a computer programmer named Richard James III, sent Gardner an example of a ninth family, asking, "Do you agree that Kershner missed this one?" He had. —David S. Richeson (2023a), "A Brief History of Tricky Mathematical Tiling," *Quanta Magazine*
Paraphrase It	**Quote from the article "Persistent Homology for Resource Coverage: A Case Study of Access to Polling Sites" by Abigail Hickok, Benjamin Jarman, Michael Johnson, Jiajie Luo, and Mason A. Porter (2024):** Although we have explored a specific case study (namely, the accessibility of polling sites), it is also relevant to conduct similar investigations for other resources, such as public parks, hospitals, vaccine distribution centers, grocery stores, Planned Parenthood clinics, and Department of Motor Vehicles (DMV) locations. (p. 498) **Mentor text:** Topology concerns itself with continuous shapes, and polling sites are at discrete locations. But in recent years, topologists have adapted their tools to work on discrete data by creating graphs of points connected by lines and then analyzing the properties of those graphs. Hickok said these techniques are useful not only for understanding the distribution of polling places but also for studying who has better access to hospitals, grocery stores and parks. —Lyndie Chiou (2024b), "Topologists Tackle the Trouble With Poll Placement," *Quanta Magazine*
End With Analysis	If we want to better predict the system's properties at various energy states, it helps to understand the system when it's in its least excited state, which scientists refer to as the ground state. "A lot of chemists, material scientists and quantum physicists are working on finding ground states," said Robert Huang, one of the new paper authors and a research scientist at Google Quantum AI. "It is known to be extremely hard." It's so hard that after more than a century of work, researchers still haven't found an effective computational approach to determining a system's ground state from first principles. Nor does there appear to be any way for a quantum computer to do it. Scientists have concluded that finding a system's ground state is hard for both classical and quantum computers. —Lakshmi Chandrasekaran (2024), "Physicists Finally Find a Problem That Only Quantum Computers Can Do," *Quanta Magazine*

Moves That Summarize: Mathematics

Move	Mini-Mentor Text
Define and Detail	Graph theory can be thought of as a branch of combinatorics—the mathematical study of counting. Counting what can happen with collections of nodes and edges is, in some sense, a special case of counting combinations more generally. The year ended with a landmark proof by four prominent mathematicians of a longstanding conjecture that relates combinatorics to the algebraic structure of sets. —Konstantin Kakaes (2023), "The Year in Math," *Quanta Magazine*
Pivot Synopsis	In Christian culture, 6 has a rather dark meaning and 666 is even called the *"Number of the Beast"*. The number 666 appears several times in the Bible, and in other old scripts. The ancient writers probably didn't know that 666 is related to the golden ratio by $\phi = -2 \sin(666°) = -2 \cos(6 \times 6 \times 6°)$, but maybe they were aware of some of the following "scary" relationships. —Philipp Legner (2010), "Editorial: 60 Issues of *Eureka*," *Eureka*, p. 4
The Devil in the Details	In string theory, there is a duality symmetry known as T-duality. This is a fundamental ambiguity in the description of the space time background in which the string lives. If the space time has some specific properties (technically, it should possess an isometry and be compact so that its first homotopy class is nontrivial) then there will be two backgrounds that will be related to each other that in ordinary differential geometry will be inequivalent and yet will be indistinguishable from the point of view of the string. These pairs are known as T-duals. This duality is stringy in nature and leads on to the idea of stringy geometry that differs from our usual notion of geometry in that such ideas of T-duality get built in. —George Ellis (2012), "Multiverses and Observational Limits of Cosmology," *Eureka*, p. 69
Cause and Effect Sandwich	Computers and powerful calculators are so deeply integrated into today's science—indeed, into every aspect of today's world—that it can be difficult to imagine working without them. At the beginning of the Manhattan Project, however, the only "computers" available for the complex calculations necessary were teams of assistants using mechanical hand calculators. Scientists' wives at Los Alamos were enlisted, the work divided amongst them to maximize efficiency—one dedicated to adding, one to dividing, one to cubing, and so forth. This basic form of calculation worked well initially, but as calculations of neutron mean free paths, critical densities, and shockwave propagation grew ever more complex and time-intensive, it strained to produce results in a timely manner. Further, the scarcity of materials (especially radioactive materials) and scientific manpower [meant] that extensive experimentation was impossible, so theoretical calculations were the only way to test central elements of the bomb designs before the final Trinity test. Los Alamos needed either far more teams of woman "calculators" or some new way of handling extensive calculations. —Office of History and Heritage Resources (n.d.), "The Manhattan Project: An Interactive History"
Quote It to Me	Nash's equilibrium concept, which earned him a Nobel Prize in economics in 1994, offers a unified framework for understanding strategic behavior not only in economics but also in psychology, evolutionary biology and a host of other fields. Its influence on economic theory "is comparable to that of the discovery of the DNA double helix in the biological sciences," wrote Roger Myerson of the University of Chicago, another economics Nobelist. —Erica Klarreich (2017), "In Game Theory, No Clear Path to Equilibrium," *Quanta Magazine*

Moves That Contextualize: Mathematics

Move	Mini-Mentor Text
Let's Compare	Modular arithmetic is often called clock arithmetic, as a 12-hour clock counts in mod 12. This way of thinking about counting around a circle like on a clock suggests that it might be useful for our problem. —Alvin Choy (2023), "The Josephus Problem," *Chalkdust*
Double Date	In 1940, from a jailhouse in Rouen, France, André Weil wrote one of the most consequential letters of 20th-century mathematics. He was serving time for refusing to join the French army, and he filled his days in part by writing letters to his sister, Simone, an accomplished philosopher living in London. —Kevin Hartnett (2024b), "A Rosetta Stone for Mathematics," *Quanta Magazine*
Show Me the Data	The events here are dependent upon each other, as opposed to independent. In the realm of probability, dependency of events is very important. For example, coin tosses are always independent events. When tossing a fair coin, the probability of it landing on heads, given that it previously landed on heads 10 times in a row, is still 1/2. Even if it lands on heads 1000 times, the chance of it landing on heads on the 1001st toss is still 50%. —Madeleine Hall (2021), "On Conditional Probability: Cards, COVID, and *Crazy Rich Asians*," *Chalkdust*
Educated Inference	Without the telltale sign of an obviously misshapen district to go by, mathematicians have been developing increasingly powerful statistical methods for finding gerrymanders. These work by comparing a map to an ensemble of thousands or millions of possible maps. If the map results in noticeably more seats for Democrats or Republicans than would be expected from an average map, this is a sign that something fishy might have taken place. —Mike Orcutt (2023), "How Math Has Changed the Shape of Gerrymandering," *Quanta Magazine*
Past and Present Connection	Pierre de Fermat has his name on one of the most famous theorems in mathematics. For over 300 years, Fermat's Last Theorem stood as the ultimate symbol of unachievable mathematical greatness. In the 1600s, Fermat scribbled a note about his proposed theorem in a book he was reading, claiming to know how to prove it without providing any details. Mathematicians attempted to solve the problem themselves until the 1990s, when Andrew Wiles finally proved it using new techniques discovered hundreds of years after Fermat died. —Patrick Honner (2023b), "Pierre de Fermat's Link to a High School Student's Prime Math Proof," *Quanta Magazine*

Moves That Add Voice: Mathematics

Move	Mini-Mentor Text
Say It Slang	The three researchers were trying to show that there couldn't be too many of these points, but so far, all their techniques had come up short. They seemed to be spinning their wheels. —Erica Klarreich (2024), "Merging Fields, Mathematicians Go the Distance on Old Problem," *Quanta Magazine*
Ask a Question	Then Peluse had a thought: What if they ditched the harmonic analysis problem—temporarily, of course—and turned their attention to sets of points in which the distance between any two points is exactly an integer? What possible structures can such sets have? —Erica Klarreich (2024), "Merging Fields, Mathematicians Go the Distance on Old Problem," *Quanta Magazine*
Put It in Parentheses	The first proof of this (there would be several) is commonly attributed to Pythagoras, a 6th-century BCE philosopher, even though none of his writings survive and little is known about him. —Jordana Cepelewicz (2024a), "How the Square Root of 2 Became a Number," *Quanta Magazine*
Connect Personally	This is the "handshake problem," and it's one of my favorites. As a math teacher, I love it because there are so many different ways you can arrive at the solution, and the diversity and interconnectedness of those strategies beautifully illustrate the power of creative thinking in math. —Patrick Honner (2024), "Math That Connects Where We're Going to Where We've Been," *Quanta Magazine*
Make It Metaphorical	Just as the software of your laptop runs without having to keep track of all the microscale information about the electrons in the computer circuitry, so emergent phenomena are governed by macroscale rules that seem self-contained, without heed to what the component parts are doing. Using a mathematical formalism called computational mechanics, the researchers identified criteria for determining which systems have this kind of hierarchical structure.... They tested these criteria on several model systems known to display emergent-type phenomena, including neural networks and Game-of-Life-style cellular automata. —Philip Ball (2024c), "The New Math of How Large-Scale Order Emerges," *Quanta Magazine*

Moves That Conclude: Mathematics

Move	Mini-Mentor Text
What We Don't Know and What We Do	Meanwhile, another question looms: To create a black hole of three spatial dimensions, must an object be compressed in all three directions, as Thorne insisted, or could compression in two directions or even just one be enough? All evidence points to Thorne's statement being true, Khuri said, though it is not yet proved. Indeed, it is just one of many open questions that persist about black holes after they first manifested more than a century ago in a German soldier's notebook. —Steve Nadis (2023), "Math Proof Draws New Boundaries Around Black Hole Formation," *Quanta Magazine*
What's Next?	Socolar, as a physicist, has begun exploring the tilings' material properties. The diffraction pattern that emerges if you shine a light through one of these tilings, he has found, has the same kind of sharp peaks researchers have observed in quasicrystals. Even so, the hat tiling "looks to me to be different from anything else I've seen before," he said. Meanwhile, Smith isn't done with his "tricky little tile." He intends to explore its artistic possibilities and figure out how to use colors to bring out the patterns the tile appears to insist upon. —Erica Klarreich (2023b), "Hobbyist Finds Math's Elusive 'Einstein' Tile," *Quanta Magazine*
Share the Last Word	But he also pointed out that pseudorandom processes are powerful tools, and projects like constructing primes are just one way of using them to connect ideas from mathematics, computer science, information theory and other areas. "It's exciting to try and think where else these brilliant observations will lead," Tell said. —Stephen Ornes (2023), "How to Build a Big Prime Number," *Quanta Magazine*
The Bottom Line	Imai is an expert witness for the plaintiffs in the pending Supreme Court case. The plaintiffs are arguing, using the ensembles he generated, that Alabama's districts violate the Voting Rights Act by disenfranchising Black voters. But the state of Alabama, which is being sued, is using his ensembles to argue that the map is fairly drawn. Whatever the court decides, it shows that, when it comes to elections, mathematics will always need to contend with politics. —Mike Orcutt (2023), "How Math Has Changed the Shape of Gerrymandering," *Quanta Magazine*
Solve the Problem	Sailors facing an imminent storm don't have years to study the growing waves around them, but the new framework represents small steps toward the long-term goal for rogue wave prediction—machinery that scans the ocean and sounds the alarm when it's time to batten down the hatches. LDT tools, once they're modified for the open ocean, could be one way for those on boats like the München to know the moment a rogue wave starts focusing. —Charlie Wood (2020), "The Grand Unified Theory of Rogue Waves," *Quanta Magazine*

Moves That Organize: Mathematics

Move	Mini-Mentor Text
Topic Sentence Transition	The modern notation for square roots came into use in the 16th and 17th centuries. But still, there was something slippery about them. Does √2 exist in the same way that 2 does? It wasn't clear. Mathematicians continued to live with that ambiguity. Then, in the mid-1800s, Richard Dedekind, among others, realized that calculus—which had been developed 200 years earlier by Isaac Newton and Gottfried Leibniz—stood on a shaky foundation. —Jordana Cepelewicz (2024a), "How the Square Root of 2 Became a Number," *Quanta Magazine*
Hinge Transition	The mathematicians ended up with what they called a smooth fractal snowflake—an infinite and delicate self-similar structure. It had nonnegative Ricci curvature at every point. And it had an infinite number of holes. They had disproved Milnor's conjecture. "It's more complicated than all the previous constructions" of manifolds with nonnegative Ricci curvature, said Guofang Wei of the University of California, Santa Barbara. —Jordana Cepelewicz (2024b), "Strangely Curved Shapes Break 50-Year-Old Geometry Conjecture," *Quanta Magazine*
List It	For example, let's say we have two tiles, A and B, and two rules for putting them together: Next to an A, on either side you can only place a B. Next to a B, on either side you can only place an A. —Patrick Honner (2023a), "Math Patterns That Go On Forever but Never Repeat," *Quanta Magazine*
Add Subheadings	Subheadings: • *The big jump* • *Proof of concept* • *Soulful solutions* —Siobhan Roberts (2024), "A.I.'s Latest Challenge: The Math Olympics," *The New York Times*
Visual Anchoring	For example, you can use scissors congruence to compute the area of a pentagon. Since area is preserved if you cut the pentagon up into smaller triangles, you can instead find the area of these triangles (using "½ base × height") and add them up to get the answer. [*Illustration of a pentagon broken into five smaller triangles that are then added together*] —Maxine Calle and Mona Merling (2023), "A Brief Illustrated Guide to 'Scissors Congruence'—an Ancient Geometric Idea That's Still Fueling Cutting-Edge Mathematical Research," *The Conversation*

All Science Moves

Please see the following tables to view all science mentor texts pertaining to each mini move.

Moves That Introduce: Science

Move	Mini-Mentor Text
Just-the-Facts	On Feb. 3 a train carrying hazardous materials derailed in East Palestine, Ohio. Some of the contents immediately caught fire. Three days later authorities released and burned off additional material from five tankers. These fires caused elevated levels of harmful chemicals in the local air, although the Environmental Protection Agency says that the pollution wasn't severe enough to cause long-term health damage. —Paul Krugman (2023), "Conspiracy Theorizing Goes off the Rails," *The New York Times*
Make the Case	Speaking two languages provides the enviable ability to make friends in unusual places. A new study suggests that bilingualism may also come with another benefit: improved memory in later life. Studying hundreds of older patients, researchers in Germany found that those who reported using two languages daily from a young age scored higher on tests of learning, memory, language and self-control than patients who spoke only one language. The findings, published in the April issue of the journal *Neurobiology of Aging*, add to two decades of work suggesting that bilingualism protects against dementia and cognitive decline in older people. —Jaya Padmanabhan (2023), "Bilingualism May Stave Off Dementia, Study Suggests," *The New York Times*
What They Said	"As I imagine it," Carl Sagan once said, "there will be a multilayered message. First there is a beacon, an announcement signal, something that says, *Pay attention. This is not some natural astronomical phenomenon. This is a signal from intelligent beings* . . . Then, the next layer is one that says, *This message is directed specifically to you guys on Earth. It isn't directed to anybody else.* And the third part of the message is the real content, which is a very complex set of data in a new language, which is also explained." He was describing his novel, *Contact*, a 370-or-so-page answer, literally or in spirit, to every question we can ask about how finding alien intelligence might go. Yes, there's conflict and strife—acts of terrorism, government obstruction, frustration and loss and death—but at its core the story promises an inviting cosmos. A door opening to a galactic community. We're not only not alone but also welcomed. This hope is central to the idealistic origins of the search for extraterrestrial intelligence (SETI), to Sagan's motivations as a scientist and communicator. It also makes it especially weird that the novel ends with its heroine finding proof that God is real, but we'll get to that. —Jaime Green (2023), "Why Does *Contact* Say So Much About God?," *The Atlantic*
Scene-Drop	The giant new spaceship was all fueled up and ready to go. Its stainless-steel exterior gleamed in the South Texas sun. Everyone gathered at the launch site was elated to witness the first uncrewed test flight of Starship, the futuristic spacecraft that Elon Musk wants to someday use to take people to Mars. The crowd erupted in cheers as the 33-engine rocket booster below the spacecraft ignited its engines and rose from the launchpad, generating twice the thrust of the Saturn V rocket that propelled Apollo astronauts to the moon more than 50 years ago. But as Starship climbed higher, toward the edge of space and the next move in the sequence, something went wrong. The spaceship and the rocket booster failed to separate as intended, and started tumbling. Four minutes after a beautiful liftoff, Starship exploded over the Gulf of Mexico. —Marina Koren (2023), "Elon Musk's Explosive Day," *The Atlantic*
Then-and-Now	Alex Wiltschko began collecting perfumes as a teenager. His first bottle was Azzaro Pour Homme, a timeless cologne he spotted on the shelf at a T.J. Maxx department store. He recognized the name from *Perfumes: The Guide*, a book whose poetic descriptions of aroma had kick-started his obsession. Enchanted, he saved up his allowance to add to his collection. "I ended up going absolutely down the rabbit hole," he said. More recently, as an olfactory neuroscientist for Google Research's Brain Team, Wiltschko used machine learning to dissect our most ancient and least understood sense. Sometimes he looked almost longingly at his colleagues studying the other senses. "They have these beautiful intellectual structures, these cathedrals of knowledge," he said, that explain the visual and auditory world, shaming what we know about olfaction. —Allison Parshall (2022), "Machine Learning Highlights a Hidden Order in Scents," *Quanta Magazine*

Moves That Make a Claim: Science

Move	Mini-Mentor Text
The Big Idea	Though we can't see them, X-rays are widespread in outer space. —Carlyn Kranking (2024), "See 25 Stunning Images of the Cosmos From the Chandra X-Ray Observatory as It Celebrates 25 Years in Space," *Smithsonian Magazine*
Outline It	And once the real MOMA gets to Mars, approximately in 2030, Brinckerhoff and his colleagues will use the prototype—as well as a pristine copy kept in a Mars-like environment at NASA—to test tweaks to experimental protocols, troubleshoot issues that come up during the mission and facilitate interpretation of Mars data. —Carmen Drahl (2023), "The Mission That Could Transform Our Understanding of Mars," *Smithsonian Magazine*
This-and-That	The measurements of mutation rates could be critically useful in calibrating the gene-based molecular clocks that biologists use to determine when species diverged, and they offer useful tests of several theories about how evolution works. —Yasemin Saplakoglu (2023), "Animal Mutation Rates Reveal Traits That Speed Evolution," *Quanta Magazine*
Not-This-But-That	Biodiversity might hinge on what species have in common, not their particular niches. —Veronique Greenwood (2023b), "A New Explanation for One of Ecology's Most Debated Ideas," *The Atlantic*
Synthesize It	COVID-19 has disrupted everyday life worldwide. It is the first disease event since the 1918–20 H1N1 Spanish influenza (flu) pandemic to demand an urgent global healthcare response, propagated by the speed and likelihood of potential transmission. —Grace E. Patterson, K. Marie McIntyre, Helen E. Clough, and Jonathan Rushton (2021), "Societal Impacts of Pandemics: Comparing COVID-19 With History to Focus Our Response," *Frontiers in Public Health*

Moves That Define: Science

Move	Mini-Mentor Text
It Is What It Is	Cosmologists' reigning model of the universe identifies dark energy as the energy of space itself and pegs it at 70% of the universe's contents. —Liz Kruesi (2024), "Fresh X-Rays Reveal a Universe as Clumpy as Cosmology Predicts," *Quanta Magazine*
Say My Name	The powerhouse organelles called mitochondria are dutifully churning out energy. —Veronique Greenwood (2024a), "Cellular Self-Destruction May Be Ancient. But Why?," *Quanta Magazine*
Keep It Appositive	All of the characteristics of the odd ants—the wings, the social behaviors and the reproductive traits—were caused by what geneticists call a supergene, a collection of genes that are inherited as a unit and are highly resistant to being broken up. —Viviane Callier (2023), "A Mutation Turned Ants Into a Parasite in One Generation," *Quanta Magazine*
Gimme an Example	Venus has more than volcanic outbursts; the planet also sinks in places, like the chest of a recumbent giant exhaling. This process is called subduction, a phenomenon that also occurs on Earth, albeit by a different mechanism. —Shi En Kim (2024), "The Six Most Amazing Discoveries We've Made by Exploring Venus," *Smithsonian Magazine*
Engage With Etymology	The word "apocalypse" is derived from the Latin for "revelation," and our current predicament draws out the irony of that double meaning, as we mistake obsessing about the "end of the world" for acting on it. —Amanda Hess (2022), "Apocalypse When? Global Warming's Endless Scroll," *The New York Times*

Moves That Describe: Science

Move	Mini-Mentor Text
Describing Lists	More than four decades ago, field ecologists set out to quantify the diversity of trees on a forested plot on Barro Colorado Island in Panama, one of the most intensively studied tracts of forest on the planet. They began counting every tree with a trunk wider than a centimeter. They identified the species, measured the trunks and calculated the biomass of each individual. They put ladders up the trees, examined saplings and recorded it all in sprawling spreadsheets. —Veronique Greenwood (2023a), "The Key to Species Diversity May Be in Their Similarities," *Quanta Magazine*
Say It Again, But Make It Specific	Research indicates that these chemicals can be dangerous. Exposure to PFAS is linked to cancers, weakened immune systems among children, weight gain, and a wide range of other health problems. —Benji Jones (2023b), "You Probably Have 'Forever Chemicals' in Your Body. Here's What That Means," *Vox*
Dash That Describes	Of the 100 trillion neutrinos that pass through you every second, most come from the sun or Earth's atmosphere. But a smattering of the particles—those moving much faster than the rest—traveled here from powerful sources farther away. —Thomas Lewton (2023), "A New Map of the Universe, Painted With Cosmic Neutrinos," *Quanta Magazine*
Let's Imagine . . .	Bjånes likens the setup of their brain-machine interface to a football game. Imagine that your brain is the football stadium, and each of the neurons is a person in that stadium. The electrodes are the microphones you lower into the stadium to listen in. "We hope that we place those near the coach, or maybe an announcer, or near some person in the audience that really knows what's going on," he explains. "And then we're trying to understand what's happening on the field. When we hear a roar of the crowd, is that a touchdown? Was that a pass play? Was that the quarterback getting sacked? We're trying to understand the rules of the game, and the more information we can get, the better our device will be." —Marla Broadfoot (2023), "The Brain-Computer Interfaces That Could Give Locked-In Patients a Voice," *Smithsonian Magazine*
Figurative Language Comparison	We make an analogy to an orchestra. The musicians need to play in synchrony for the music to work. When you lose the cellos and the woodwinds, the remaining musicians can't deliver the piece as effectively as when all players are present. Similarly, when brain tumors hijack the areas surrounding it, the brain is less able to effectively function. —Saritha Krishna and Shawn Hervey-Jumper (2023), "Brain Tumors Are Cognitive Parasites—How Brain Cancer Hijacks Neural Circuits and Causes Cognitive Decline," *The Conversation*

Moves That Provide Evidence: Science

Move	Mini-Mentor Text
Hyperlink Layers	The age of dinosaurs was probably longer than you think. T. rex lived at the end of the Cretaceous period, just before the dinosaur-killing asteroid strike 66 million years ago. Stegosaurus, and other popular Jurassic dinosaurs such as Diplodocus, lived around 150 million years ago. —Abi Crane (2024), "Five Things You Probably Have Wrong About the T. rex," JSTOR Daily
Reference a Visual	A normal *Arabidopsis* seedling (right) bends toward light incoming from the right, while a mutant with water-flooded air channels (left) grows straight upward. Cross sections of the stems show why: Normal air channels create a gradient from brightness to darkness across the plant's cells (shown here using fluorescent methods) that indicates the light's direction. Mutant seedlings with water-flooded channels have no light gradient, and therefore can't sense in which direction to grow. [*The image shows two elongated plant structures, likely young seedlings or stems, positioned side by side against a black background. Each plant is associated with a magnified circular inset, displaying a close-up of the cellular structure.* • *Center: The two plant structures are bent differently. The one on the left is relatively straight with a slight curvature at the base, while the one on the right is curved more significantly towards the left side of the image.* • *Inserts: The circular insets on either side of the plants reveal a green honeycomb-like cellular pattern, suggesting that the cells are being viewed under a microscope, possibly using fluorescence imaging. The left inset shows the structure from the straight plant, and the right one corresponds to the more curved plant.* • *Label: There is a label on the right side of the image indicating the "Direction of light," with an arrow pointing leftward. This suggests that the curvature in the plant on the right is likely due to phototropism, where plants grow towards a light source.*] —Asher Elbein (2024), "Plants Find Light Using Gaps Between Their Cells," Quanta Magazine
The Fold In	A unique feature of hydrothermal vents is that they form structures composed of billions of minuscule microchambers, each contained and exposed to different conditions and reactants. They constitute a "vast array of simultaneously running semi-independent experiments," Brunk and Marshall described. —Ross Pomeroy (2024), "The Ocean Vents Where Life on Earth Likely Began," JSTOR Daily
Paraphrase It	**Quote from the book *The Science of Oriental Medicine, Diet and Hygiene* by Li Wing (1902):** When the Chinese commenced to study medicine they went at once to the root of different questions involved by practicing vivisection. Thousands of condemned criminals were taken and cut to pieces for the benefit of the living. In this way the functions of the vital organs, such as the kidneys, the liver, the stomach, the spleen and the heart were studied in the living person. The intensely important questions involved in the digestion of foods were determined as well as the effects of different drugs. These investigations, made while the man was still alive, were a thousand times more thorough and reliable than the guesswork which civilized physicians have practiced for many years by cutting up the bodies of dead men, when heat, motion and life are gone, and death has destroyed every function. (p. 10) **Mentor text:** A 1902 book by Los Angeles Chinese pharmacist Li Wing, *The Science of Oriental Medicine, Diet and Hygiene,* played on white Americans' beliefs about Asian barbarity. It claimed that Chinese doctors understood the human body better than American ones because they practiced vivisection on condemned criminals. —Livia Gershon (2022), "The Allure of Chinese Medicine," JSTOR Daily
End With Analysis	Programmed cell death appeared to create usable resources from dead parts. However, this process could only benefit relatives of the dead algae, he found. "It was actually harmful to those of a different species," Durand said. In 2022, another research group confirmed the finding in another algae. The results possibly explain how cell death can evolve in single-celled creatures. If an organism is surrounded by kin, then its death can provide nutrition and therefore further its relatives' survival. That creates an opening for natural selection to select for the tools for self-induced death. —Veronique Greenwood (2024a), "Cellular Self-Destruction May Be Ancient. But Why?," Quanta Magazine

Moves That Summarize: Science

Move	Mini-Mentor Text
Define and Detail	The telescope, named for James Webb, the NASA administrator during the buildup to the Apollo moon landings, is a joint project of NASA, the European Space Agency and the Canadian Space Agency. It was launched on Christmas one year ago—after two trouble-plagued decades and $10 billion—on a mission to observe the universe in wavelengths no human eye can see. —Dennis Overbye (2022), "The Webb Telescope Is Just Getting Started," *The New York Times*
Pivot Synopsis	Time seems linear to us: We remember the past, experience the present and predict the future, moving consecutively from one moment to the next. But why is it that way, and could time ultimately be a kind of illusion? In this episode, the Nobel Prize-winning physicist Frank Wilczek speaks with host Steven Strogatz about the many "arrows" of time and why most of them seem irreversible, the essence of what a clock is, how Einstein changed our definition of time, and the unexpected connection between time and our notions of what dark matter might be. —Steven Strogatz (2024), "What Is the Nature of Time?," *Quanta Magazine*
The Devil in the Details	For a pathogen to make us sick, it must overcome a lot. First it has to enter the body, bypassing natural barriers such as skin, mucus, cilia and stomach acid. Then it needs to reproduce; some bacteria and parasites can do this virtually anywhere in the body, while viruses and some other pathogens can only do so from within a cell. And all the while, it must parry attacks from the body's immune system. So while we are constantly inundated by microbes, the number of microbes that enter our bodies is usually too low to get past our defenses. (A tiny enough dose may even serve to remind our immune system of a pathogen's existence, boosting our antibody response to keep us protected against it.) —Tara C. Smith (2023), "How Many Microbes Does It Take to Make You Sick?," *Quanta Magazine*
Cause and Effect Sandwich	CRISPR provides a relatively easy way to release a gene drive. First, researchers insert a CRISPR-powered gene drive into an organism. When the organism mates, its CRISPR-equipped chromosome cleaves the matching chromosome coming from the other parent. The offspring's genetic machinery then attempts to sew up this cut. When it does, it copies over the relevant section of DNA from the first parent—the section that contains the CRISPR gene drive. In this way, the gene drive duplicates itself so that it ends up on both chromosomes, and this will occur with nearly every one of the original organism's offspring. —Brooke Borel (2016), "Genetic Engineering to Clash With Evolution," *Quanta Magazine*
Quote It to Me	Bothe found that the electric current needed to reach the voltage threshold and trigger a snake's body motor neuron was "way lower than for the rattle motor neurons," he said. "You need to put way more current into the [rattle] neuron for it to fire." And compared to rattle motor neurons, body motor neurons reacted more sluggishly. —Elise Cutts (2024), "Tiny Tweaks to Neurons Can Rewire Animal Motion," *Quanta Magazine*

Moves That Contextualize: Science

Move	Mini-Mentor Text
Let's Compare	Drawing parallels with successful policies like the "sugar tax" on soft drinks in the United Kingdom, meat taxes could incentivize a reduction in meat production by driving industry reformulation instead of relying on consumer behavior. —Aissa Dearing (2024), "Grilling the Globe," *JSTOR Daily*
Double Date	These studies and the keystone idea came to prominence at the same moment that America's environmental conscience was emerging. In 1973, Congress passed the Endangered Species Act, which took a species-focused approach to conserving wildlife. The idea that restoring the population of a single species—a keystone, perhaps—could ensure the biodiversity of an ecological community aligned with this new legal framework. —Lesley Evans Ogden (2024), "Ecologists Struggle to Get a Grip on 'Keystone Species,'" *Quanta Magazine*
Show Me the Data	Studies have found that some 50% to 70% of patients with major depressive disorder see their symptoms improve after a course of ECT. In comparison, medications aimed at altering brain chemistry help only 10% to 40% of depression patients. —Elizabeth Landau (2024), "Brain's 'Background Noise' May Explain Value of Shock Therapy," *Quanta Magazine*
Educated Inference	So it's easy to see why masting trees synchronize their seed production. Understanding how they do it, however, is more complicated. Plants usually synchronize their reproduction by timing it to the same weather signals. And warming temperatures and heavy rainfall correlate well with coordinated masting, suggesting that the trees synchronize to weather cues. —Meghan Willcoxon (2024), "Across a Continent, Trees Sync Their Fruiting to the Sun," *Quanta Magazine*
Past and Present Connection	Over 2,500 years ago, Greek philosophers debated whether the nature of reality was impermanence or constant change. Heraclitus was the champion of change, pointing to the march of the seasons and the ebb and flow of the tides. In contrast, Parmenides, a near-contemporary of Heraclitus, claimed that change was illusory and constancy was the rule. Modern physics has found subatomic examples that support both ways of thinking. For example, the electrons found in your atoms have been unchanged since the Universe began, supporting the constancy conjecture. However, in a clear example of constant change, another form of subatomic particles called neutrinos are in continuous flux, literally changing their identity over and over again. —Don Lincoln (2024), "IceCube Detector Confirms Deep-Space 'Ghost Particle' Phenomenon," *JSTOR Daily*

Moves That Add Voice: Science

Move	Mini-Mentor Text
Say It Slang	Its unique hard covering, which may remind you of Taco Tuesday, most likely helped propel it through water, at times upside-down. —Rebecca Dzombak (2024), "Secrets Emerge From a Fossil's Taco Shell-Like Cover," *The New York Times*
Ask a Question	Over the next century, eclipse expeditions helped settle one of the biggest mysteries in science: Was Mercury's odd orbit due to an undiscovered sun-hugging planet (which would presumably become visible during an eclipse)? Or, as turned out to be the case, was there some problem with Newton's understanding of gravity? —Joshua Sokol (2024), "How the Ancient Art of Eclipse Prediction Became an Exact Science," *Quanta Magazine*
Put It in Parentheses	To me, a program isn't static code, it's the embodiment of a living creature that follows my instructions to a (hopefully) successful conclusion. I know computers don't physically work this way, but that doesn't stop my metaphorical machine. —Lance Fortnow (2024), "Computation Is All Around Us, and You Can See It If You Try," *Quanta Magazine*
Connect Personally	As a geologist, I have had the extraordinary opportunity to work on both the Curiosity and Perseverance rover missions. Yet as much as scientists are learning from them, it will take another robotic mission to figure out if Mars has ever hosted life. That mission will bring Martian rocks back to Earth for analysis. Then—hopefully—we will have an answer. While so much remains mysterious about Mars, there is one thing I am confident about. Amid the thousands of pictures both rovers are taking, I'm quite sure no alien bears or meerkats will show up in any of them. Most scientists doubt the surface of Mars, or its near-surface, could currently sustain even single-celled organisms, much less complex forms of life. —Amy J. Williams (2024), "NASA's Search for Life on Mars," *JSTOR Daily*
Make It Metaphorical	Previously, all known ribosome-disrupting hibernation factors worked passively: They waited for a ribosome to finish building a protein and then prevented it from starting a new one. Balon, however, pulls the emergency brake. It stuffs itself into every ribosome in the cell, even interrupting active ribosomes in the middle of their work. —Dan Samorodnitsky (2024), "Most Life on Earth Is Dormant, After Pulling an 'Emergency Brake,'" *Quanta Magazine*

Moves That Conclude: Science

Move	Mini-Mentor Text
What We Don't Know and What We Do	Even if we learn all the answers to what's happening to the body in a heat wave, Shandas said we still don't understand "a lot of the human face of heat," as in, how people actually cope. What scientists do understand is that this is just the beginning of these consequences playing out on a global scale. It's only going to get hotter from here. —Rebecca Leber (2023), "The Invisible Consequences of Heat on the Body and Mind," *Vox*
What's Next?	Our research group and other scientists are using computer simulations and numerical "larvae" to investigate how temperature, salinity and other factors may affect transport of marine organisms. With better understanding of these surf-zone conveyor belts, we aim to help keep swimmers safe and assess how rip currents affect aquatic ecosystems near the shore. —Emma Shie Nuss, Audrey Casper, Christine M. Baker, Melissa Moulton, and Walter Torres (2023), "Rip Currents Are Dangerous for Swimmers but Also Ecologically Important—Here's How Scientists Are Working to Understand These 'Rivers of the Sea,'" *The Conversation*
Share the Last Word	But LTT 9779 b may just be the benchmark for such ultrahot Neptunes. The more the team learns, the more they realize how rare it really is. "It's a super important world," Dr. Jenkins said, adding that the diversity of planets in the cosmos stretches far beyond those found in our own solar system. "Hopefully, we'll stumble across another." —Katrina Miller (2023), "Titanium Clouds Engulf This Ultrahot Neptune-Like Planet," *The New York Times*
The Bottom Line	Most of all, remember that having sharks around is a rare victory for conservation and—as we learn to live with them—human communities. These animals help sustain the ecosystems that support us all. —Benji Jones (2023a), "New York's Shark-Infested Waters Are a Good Thing. Yes, Really," *Vox*
Solve the Problem	There is no doubt that managing retail returns is a difficult task. To make the process more sustainable, retailers need to help customers make choices that limit the need for a return or that minimize the impact of a return on the environment and, of course, the retailer's bottom line. —Christopher Faires and Robert Overstreet (2023), "Just in Time for Back-to-School Shopping: How Retailers Can Alter Customer Behavior to Encourage More Sustainable Returns," *The Conversation*

Moves That Organize: Science

Move	Mini-Mentor Text
Topic Sentence Transition	Turing machines perform computations by reading and writing 0s and 1s on an infinite tape divided into square cells, using a "head" that operates on one cell at a time. Every machine has a unique set of rules that governs its behavior. Each of these rules specifies what the head should do when it moves into a new cell, depending on whether it encounters a 0 or a 1 already there. —Ben Brubaker (2024), "With Fifth Busy Beaver, Researchers Approach Computation's Limits," *Quanta Magazine*
Hinge Transition	These competitions were marked by baby steps, and the researchers had little reason to think that 2020 would be any different. They were wrong about that. That week, a relative newcomer to the protein science community named John Jumper had presented a new artificial intelligence tool, AlphaFold2, which had emerged from the offices of Google DeepMind, the tech company's artificial intelligence arm in London. —Yasemin Saplakoglu (2024), "How AI Revolutionized Protein Science, but Didn't End It," *Quanta Magazine*
List It	In addition to the high ocean heat content, research has shown other environmental factors need to typically align for rapid intensification to occur. These include: - *Low vertical wind shear, where the winds steering the hurricane do not change much in strength or direction over the depth of the storm. Strong wind shear makes it difficult for a storm to stay organized and maintain its strength.* - *A moist atmosphere surrounding the storm, with heavy precipitation encircling the developing eye.* —Brian Tang (2024), "Hurricane Beryl's Rapid Intensification, Category 5 Winds So Early in a Season Were Alarming: Here's Why More Tropical Storms Are Exploding in Strength," *The Conversation*
Add Subheadings	Subheadings: - *A Frozen Paradox* - *Life in Thick Water* - *A Cell's Perspective* —Veronique Greenwood (2024b), "The Physics of Cold Water May Have Jump-Started Complex Life," *Quanta Magazine*
Visual Anchoring	The current bleaching event in the wider Caribbean region is longer and more severe than any previous bleaching episode recorded since the first global one in 1998. I study large-scale climate and ocean dynamics and am analyzing how biological connections between coral reefs—sometimes extending over great distances—may help reefs recover from heat stress. [YouTube video clip of a news segment showing coral bleaching] —Annalisa Bracco (2024), "The World's Fourth Mass Coral Bleaching Is Underway, but Well-Connected Reefs May Have a Better Chance to Recover," *The Conversation*

All Social Studies Moves

Please see the following tables to view all social studies mentor texts pertaining to each mini move.

Moves That Introduce: Social Studies

Move	Mini-Mentor Text
Just-the-Facts	A nearly 60-foot replica of a 4,000-year-old boat—complete with a sail made from goat hair—recently launched off the coast of Abu Dhabi, the capital of the United Arab Emirates. According to a statement from Zayed University, the vessel passed numerous trials over two days at sea. It journeyed 50 nautical miles in the Arabian Gulf, reaching speeds of up to 5.6 knots (6.4 miles per hour). —Julia Binswanger (2024), "This Bronze Age Ship Replica, Made From Reeds and Goat Hair, Just Sailed 50 Nautical Miles," *Smithsonian Magazine*
Make the Case	President Biden's most significant failure during his first two years in office is the lack of progress on the truly domestic portion of his domestic agenda. Earlier in the pandemic, the federal government did more to help parents than it ever did before. Washington temporarily mandated paid leave for many workers, it gave billions of dollars in aid to child care businesses, and for several glorious months in 2021, it even expanded the child tax credit to provide assistance to most families with children. —Binyamin Appelbaum (2023), "And Child Care for All," *The New York Times*
What They Said	"Millennials are many things, but above all, they are murderers," *Mashable* noted in 2017, introducing a list of 70 items and institutions that Millennials were purported to have "killed," including napkins, breakfast cereal, department stores, the 9-to-5 workday, and marriage. The list was tongue-in-cheek—the cereal aisle persists—but it captured something essential about a generation that has reshaped old habits of American life. Even amid this slaughter of tradition, Millennials are best known for another characteristic: how broke they are. Millennials, it's often said, are the first American generation that will do worse than its parents financially. —Jean M. Twenge (2023), "The Myth of the Broke Millennial," *The Atlantic*
Scene-Drop	The sky above the Mississippi River stretched out like a song. The river was still in the windless afternoon, its water a yellowish-brown from the sediment it carried across thousands of miles of farmland, cities, and suburbs on its way south. At dusk, the lights of the Crescent City Connection, a pair of steel cantilever bridges that cross the river and connect the east and west banks of New Orleans, flickered on. Luminous bulbs ornamented the bridges' steel beams like a congregation of fireflies settling onto the backs of two massive, unbothered creatures. A tugboat made its way downriver, pulling an enormous ship in its wake. The sounds of the French Quarter, just behind me, pulsed through the brick sidewalk underfoot. . . . After the transatlantic slave trade was outlawed in 1808, about a million people were transported from the upper South to the lower South. More than one hundred thousand of them were brought down the Mississippi River and sold in New Orleans. —Clint Smith (2021), *How the Word Is Passed: A Reckoning With the History of Slavery Across America*, p. 3
Then-and-Now	When up to 190,000 Russian soldiers invaded Ukraine last February, even its most ardent foreign supporters expected the nation's far more limited defenses would collapse within days. But one year later, Russia has lost a reported 200,000 men, including many high-ranking military officials, and President Vladimir Putin has been embarrassed by the Ukrainian Army's successes and the resilience of Ukraine's many citizen militias. —Christina Pazzanese (2023), "One Year Later: How Does Ukraine War End?," *The Harvard Gazette*

Moves That Make a Claim: Social Studies

Move	Mini-Mentor Text
The Big Idea	Washington's message was this mandate: We must guard our inheritance. —Alexis Coe (2023), "How George Washington Wrote His Farewell Address," *Smithsonian Magazine*
Outline It	The history of American barbecue is as diverse as the variations themselves, charting the path of a Caribbean cooking style brought north by Spanish conquistadors, moved westward by settlers, and seasoned with the flavors of European cultures. —Natasha Geiling (2023), "The Evolution of American Barbecue," *Smithsonian Magazine*
This-and-That	This spindly labyrinth of a swamp holds both the costs of slavery and the prices paid to resist it. —Lex Pryor (2022), "The Hidden and Eternal Spirit of the Great Dismal Swamp," *The Ringer*
Not-This-But-That	What should have been a moment of political danger for Trump instead has become another stage for him to demonstrate his dominance within the party. —Ronald Brownstein (2023), "Why Trump Might Just Roll to the Presidential Nomination," *The Atlantic*
Synthesize It	Instead of following the Soviet model of development, which leaned heavily towards industry alone, China would "walk on two legs": the peasant masses were mobilized to transform both agriculture and industry at the same time, converting a backward economy into a modern communist society of plenty for all. —Frank Dikötter (2011), *Mao's Great Famine: The History of China's Most Devastating Catastrophe, 1958-1962*, p. xi

Moves That Define: Social Studies

Move	Mini-Mentor Text
It Is What It Is	The Great Chain of Being is, perhaps, the most ancient metaphorical device for organizing nature and society. God and the angels sit on top with matter in all its forms scaled downward: humans in order of their ranks and occupations; followed by birds, fish, and beasts; then trees and other plants; and finally rocks and earthen things. —Steven Stoll (2008), "Pattern Recognition," *Lapham's Quarterly*
Say My Name	Until the early 20th century, it was standard practice to assemble all-female juries, called "juries of matrons," to determine whether a woman was pregnant and could therefore avoid hanging for capital offenses. —Alice Neikirk (2024b), "How All-Female 'Juries of Matrons' Shaped Legal History," *The Conversation*
Keep It Appositive	The great French historian and resistance martyr, Marc Bloch, is supposed to have said that history was like a knife: You can cut bread with it, but you could also kill. —Fritz Stern (2008), "Imperial Hubris," *Lapham's Quarterly*
Gimme an Example	A large number were public figures—influential lawyers, journalists, playwrights or physicians, some of whom were the only women in their fields—and often had their names in the papers for the work they were performing. —Laura Kiniry (2024), "The All-Woman Secret Society That Paved the Way for Modern Feminism," *Smithsonian Magazine*
Engage With Etymology	As the industrial historian S. Martin Gaskell [1980] writes in an article titled "Gardens for the Working Class: Victorian Practical Pleasure," the word "garden" denoted: on the one hand, something that was the personal and private preserve of the upper classes, whether in immediate proximity to the great house or in locked London square, or, on the other, a place of gratification and amusement, frequently associated with a drinking establishment, nearly always a scene of dissipation, and more than usually of ill-repute. These competing interpretations—one gesturing toward the hidden and secretive, one toward a general debauchery—made gardens a suitable locale for crime and detective fiction, genres that, aside from providing suspense and intrigue, have long been concerned with exploring the darker sides of industrialization, urbanization, and modernization—and indeed humanity itself. —Tim Brinkhof (2024), "What Do Gardens and Murder Have in Common?," *JSTOR Daily*

Moves That Describe: Social Studies

Move	Mini-Mentor Text
Describing Lists	The parade included parents who had served prison terms for noncompliance, a cart filled with unvaccinated children, an open hearse bearing a child's coffin inscribed ANOTHER VICTIM OF VACCINATION, doctors riding backward on cows, and an effigy of vaccine pioneer Edward Jenner that was eventually hanged and decapitated. —Nadja Durbach (2023), "Our Medical Liberties," *Lapham's Quarterly*
Say It Again, But Make It Specific	The old representative democracy is starting to crack up. In its place there is a digital or direct democracy. By email or tweet, small bands of vigilantes can track down our representatives and cling, Fury-like, until they vote the right way. —Thomas Geoghegan (2020), "In the People's House There Are Many Mansions," *Lapham's Quarterly*
Dash That Describes	After the first day of battle, Meade replaced Abner Doubleday, commander of I Corps and a staunch Republican, with a more junior Democratic officer—a move that prompted criticism from within his own ranks. —Nicholas Liu (2023), "After Winning the Battle of Gettysburg, George Meade Fought With—and Lost to—the Press," *Smithsonian Magazine*
Let's Imagine . . .	Imagine a heated prehistoric game of basketball where the two teams, the Skins and the Furs, use an inflated mammoth bladder for the ball. One player jams his finger and notes that it is pointing sideways. Instinctively, he yanks on it and successfully realigns the dislocation. Next week a teammate incurs the same injury, and the experienced one performs the same restorative maneuver. Over time he continues to learn from experience and achieves local acclaim as the go-to bonesetter. These skills are then passed down to his children. These bonesetters, along with shamans, midwives, and herbalists, developed in many cultures, including ancient Egypt and early Hawaii. —Roy A. Meals (2020), "A Brief History of Surgeons," *Lapham's Quarterly*
Figurative Language Comparison	Celebrity culture is religion in disguise. It pretends to be junk while giving us the sustenance that we need. Celebrities live like gods; they act like gods. They dwell in the dark recesses of our souls where we crave the images of gods. In the aisles of the supermarkets they stare down at us like the saints and gargoyles that once crowded the cornices of medieval cathedrals with the iconography of suffering, or like sculptures in Hindu temples that celebrate birth, sex, death, rebirth. —Stephen Marche (2011), "Consumer Products," *Lapham's Quarterly*

Moves That Provide Evidence: Social Studies

Move	Mini-Mentor Text
Hyperlink Layers	When it comes to war, American leaders have a long history of deceiving the public. In light of the Congressional introduction of the Executive Accountability Act in 2009, scholar Louis Fisher examines a record of misleading statements by US presidents used to justify conflicts, including the Mexican-American, Spanish-American, Vietnam, and Iraq wars. —Matthew Wills (2024), "Using False Claims to Justify War," *JSTOR Daily*
Reference a Visual	Ahead of the first workshop … SNCC organizers also disseminated cartoon storybooks in an effort to reach those unable to read. The storybooks used simple, hand-drawn figures to depict the responsibilities of county officeholders and to describe the potential power of African American elected officials. The cartoon about the sheriff showed a black police officer reviewing jailhouse records with the public and appointing black poll inspectors. —Hasan Kwame Jeffries (2010), *Bloody Lowndes: Civil Rights and Black Power in Alabama's Black Belt*, p. 155 [This cartoon's top-left panel shows a hand paying "$1.00 for making finger prints." The top-right panel illustrates a hand signing multiple ballots, with the caption indicating the sheriff keeps a record of his work and gets his money. The middle-left panel shows a man and a group of voters, with the caption stating, "The sheriff helps with the county, state and federal elections." The middle-right panel reads that the "sheriff probate judge and the circuit clerk are the election appointing board for the courts." The bottom-left panel shows a man telling a group of people, "I need some people to help with the election!" while another says, "We'll help!" The bottom-right panel shows a man surrounded by others, saying, "Are all of you registered?" with the caption, "Those appointed must be registered voters" (Gemini, 2025).]
The Fold In	Unlike most of the anti-slavery movement's white leaders, Birney was a southerner and an enslaver when he joined the cause. To navigate this conflicted position and complicated questions of emancipation and colonization, Birney turned to study. He "read almost every work [he] could lay his hands on" in the winter of 1833 and spring of 1834 and was transformed by what he read. —Marcy Dinius (2024), "The Power of Pamphlets in the Anti-Slavery Movement," *JSTOR Daily*
Paraphrase It	**Quote from "Memorial and Remonstrance Against Religious Assessments" by James Madison (1785):** Whilst we assert for ourselves a freedom to embrace, to profess and to observe the Religion which we believe to be of divine origin, we cannot deny an equal freedom to those whose minds have not yet yielded to the evidence which has convinced us. If this freedom be abused, it is an offence against God, not against man: To God, therefore, not to man, must an account of it be rendered. **Mentor text:** James Madison believed that an established religion—a church whose doctrines were guaranteed and enforced by state law—did harm both to religion and to free government, and he found it abhorrent to imagine God being twisted to fit political expediency: this was, he said, to throw religion to the wolves. —Elisabeth Sifton (2010), "Church and State in America," *Lapham's Quarterly*
End With Analysis	This issue came to a head in 2007 when the *Los Angeles Times* concluded an investigation into the investment practices of foundations by revealing that the Bill and Melinda Gates Foundation funded a polio vaccination clinic in Ebocha, Nigeria, in the shadow of a giant petroleum-processing plant in which the Gates Foundation was invested. The *Los Angeles Times* report states: > But polio is not the only threat Justice [a Nigerian child] faces. Almost since birth, he has had respiratory trouble. His neighbors call it "the cough." People blame fumes and soot spewing from flames that tower 300 feet into the air over a nearby oil plant. It is owned by the Italian petroleum giant Eni, whose investors include the Bill and Melinda Gates Foundation. Despite the intense criticism at the time, the Gates Foundation did not change its course. An investigation of the Gates Foundation's tax return for 2013 performed by *The Guardian* revealed that the foundation held $1.4 billion of investment in fossil-fuel companies including BP and Anadarko (the latter of which was recently forced to pay $5 billion in environmental cleanup charges). —Curtis White (2015), "Philanthropy in the End Times," *Lapham's Quarterly*

Moves That Summarize: Social Studies

Move	Mini-Mentor Text
Define and Detail	On November 29, 1947, the United Nations General Assembly adopted Resolution 181 (also known as the Partition Resolution) that would divide Great Britain's former Palestinian mandate into Jewish and Arab states in May 1948. Under the resolution, the area of religious significance surrounding Jerusalem would remain under international control administered by the United Nations. The Palestinian Arabs refused to recognize this arrangement, which they regarded as favorable to the Jews and unfair to the Arab population that would remain in Jewish territory under the partition. —Office of the Historian (n.d.), "The Arab-Israeli War of 1948"
Pivot Synopsis	When Jefferson became president in 1801, he used his first Annual Message to Congress to remind fellow citizens of America's lasting importance as an asylum. America came into existence because emigrants exercised their freedom to form a country of their own. The fight for this freedom was not only a convenient origin story—it was America's perpetual purpose. —Stephanie DeGooyer (2022), "The Right to Leave," *Lapham's Quarterly*
The Devil in the Details	Take one of the most glaring recent examples, the court's June 2022 decision striking down a century-old New York law requiring gun owners to obtain a permit to carry a gun in public. *New York State Rifle & Pistol Association Inc. v. Bruen* was decided 6 to 3, with all the Republican-appointed justices joining the majority opinion by Justice Clarence Thomas. It was the court's most transformative gun rights case since *Heller*, and like that earlier case, it featured the right-wing justices' playing amateur historians, cherry-picking and distorting evidence from decades or centuries ago to justify their existing opinions—a practice real historians refer to derisively as law-office history. —Jesse Wegman (2024), "The Crisis in Teaching Constitutional Law," *The New York Times*
Cause and Effect Sandwich	The Richmond Bread Riot, which took place in the Confederate capital of Richmond on April 2, 1863, was the largest and most destructive in a series of civil disturbances throughout the South during the third spring of the American Civil War (1861–1865). By 1863, the Confederate economy was showing signs of serious strain. Congress's passage of an Impressment Act, as well as a tax law deemed "confiscatory," led to hoarding and speculation, and spiraling inflation took its toll, especially on people living in the Confederacy's urban areas. When a group of hungry Richmond women took their complaints to Virginia governor John L. Letcher, he refused to see them. Their anger turned into a street march and attacks on commercial establishments. Only when troops were deployed and authorities threatened to fire on the mob did the rioters disperse. More than sixty men and women were arrested and tried, while the city stepped up its efforts to relieve the suffering of the poor and hungry. —Mary DeCredico (2021), Bread Riot, Richmond," *Encyclopedia Virginia*
Quote It to Me	Hardly anyone noticed this summer when former president Jimmy Carter explained why he had decided to leave the Baptist Church. However "painful and difficult," wrote Carter in an essay that appeared in the *Guardian*, his break with the denomination to which he had belonged for sixty years had begun to seem like the only possible response to past opinions expressed and codified by the Southern Baptist Convention. —Francine Prose (2010), "The Original Sin," *Lapham's Quarterly*

Moves That Contextualize: Social Studies

Move	Mini-Mentor Text
Let's Compare	Furthermore, daily sin, wealth, and almsgiving were drawn together by a half-hidden homology. Augustine always stressed the way in which daily sin piled up, in and around the human person in a largely unconscious manner—like sand, like drops of water, like fleas. —Peter Brown (2015), "Treasure in Heaven," *Lapham's Quarterly*
Double Date	During the seven decades of legal Jim Crow segregation from the 1890s through the 1960s, the principal goal of the southern states at the core of red America was defensive: They worked tirelessly to prevent federal interference with state-sponsored segregation but did not seek to impose it on states outside the region. —Ronald Brownstein (2022), "America Is Growing Apart, Possibly for Good," *The Atlantic*
Show Me the Data	More than 1.8 million Muslims participated in the hajj this year, 1.6 million of them from outside Saudi Arabia, according to the Saudi General Authority for Statistics. They encountered scorching temperatures that ranged from 108 Fahrenheit to 120, according to preliminary data. —Cassandra Vinograd and Vivian Nereim (2024), "More Than 1,000 Hajj Pilgrims Died. Here's What to Know," *The New York Times*
Educated Inference	Late in her childhood, Pocahontas likely joined Powhatan's large, busy household, where everybody worked, even Powhatan himself. In addition to their daily jobs, members of the household labored to produce grand feasts on important occasions. Pocahontas, meanwhile, probably participated in what was traditionally women's work—farming, collecting wild foods and firewood, making utensils, and cooking and cleaning. —Helen Rountree (2024), "Pocahontas (d. 1617)," *Encyclopedia Virginia*
Past and Present Connection	The first modern Olympic Games took place in Athens in 1896, thanks to the organizational efforts of one Pierre de Coubertin, a French baron who foresaw the value of a multinational sporting competition. "Olympism is not a system," Coubertin once said. "It is a state of mind." Ahead of the Paris 2024 Summer Olympics, here are nine surprising facts about the famed ancient sporting competition that inspired both Coubertin and later iterations of the Games. —Sonja Anderson (2024), "Nine Things You Didn't Know About the Ancient Olympic Games," *Smithsonian Magazine*

Moves That Add Voice: Social Studies

Move	Mini-Mentor Text
Say It Slang	When I ran in the House primary in 2009 and got clobbered, I used to wonder: How could I justify going to Washington, DC, for two years and claiming to represent 600,000 people back in Chicago? —Thomas Geoghegan (2020), "In the People's House There Are Many Mansions," *Lapham's Quarterly*
Ask a Question	Inside the White House, the subject of immigration, and especially the border, is seen as politically risky; there's a refrain among advisers that a good day for the President is one without immigration in the news. Why, then, did Biden decide to issue a proclamation reasserting that there was a crisis when he'd actually been managing to keep it at bay? —Jonathan Blitzer (2024), "What's Behind Joe Biden's Harsh New Executive Order on Immigration?," *The New Yorker*
Put It in Parentheses	For the next fourteen years he slaved singlemindedly with a team of assistants in a room provided by Clarendon, Oxford's press (no doubt with, in Oxford dialect, his *oak sported*—his door shut firm). —Simon Winchester (2012), "Native Tongues," *Lapham's Quarterly*
Connect Personally	I became newly worried about the state of democracy when, a few years ago, my mother was elected president of her neighborhood garden club. Her election wasn't my worry—far from it. At the time, I was trying to resolve a conflict on a large email group I had created. Someone, inevitably, was being a jerk on the internet. I had the power to remove them, but did I have the right? I realized that the garden club had in its bylaws something I had never seen in nearly all the online communities I had been part of: basic procedures to hold people with power accountable to everyone else. The internet has yet to catch up to my mother's garden club. —Nathan Schneider (2024), "Why the Future of Democracy Could Depend on Your Group Chats," *The Conversation*
Make It Metaphorical	America's democracy is divided resentfully against itself across the frontiers of race, gender, ethnicity, and class. Vicious slander streams through the hydra-headed portals of the internet, goading quorums of non-law-abiding citizens to hate instead of help, love, or talk to one another. —Lewis H. Lapham (2024), "Power Outage," *Lapham's Quarterly*

Moves That Conclude: Social Studies

Move	Mini-Mentor Text
What We Don't Know and What We Do	Even today, Sam continues to evolve—and Claire Jerry, a curator at the National Museum of American History, says that there is an ongoing conversation among historians and archivists about whether it's time for him to get yet another makeover. The question, as Jerry puts it, is: "How can he in fact symbolize the whole country?" Perhaps he can't—but one possible answer is to portray Uncle Sam as multiracial, and over the past decade, there has been increasing interest in creating a Black Uncle Sam. As Jerry says: "Uncle Sam will evolve along with us." —Brandon Tensley (2023), "Meet Brother Jonathan, the Predecessor to Uncle Sam," *Smithsonian Magazine*
What's Next?	Israel struck Beirut on Tuesday, targeting the official it blamed for Saturday's attack. Whatever Israel does next, it should be calculated to advance the national interests on all these fronts. If that means postponing a fuller response to explain its rationale, necessity and goal, so much the better. —Bret Stephens (2024), "Israel's Five Wars," *The New York Times*
Share the Last Word	The lunar poles are thought to be where most commercial activity will take place as they're thought to contain billions of litres of water ice, vital for manned stations. It could get crowded. As Ye Peijian, head of China's lunar exploration programme, recently said: "If we don't go there now, even though we are capable of doing so, then we will be blamed by our descendants. If others go, they will take over and you won't be able to go even if you want to." —Tim Marshall (2023), "The Future of Geography and Rise of Astropolitics," *Geographical*
The Bottom Line	The long history of vaccination and its opposition has taught us that the benefits of vaccines, which have become extremely safe, far outweigh the risks. But it also suggests that attending to the concerns of the targets and beneficiaries of public health initiatives is vital to the success of any policy to contain communicable diseases—which will always be with us, precisely because germs do not recognize the individual's right to bodily autonomy. —Nadja Durbach (2023), "Our Medical Liberties," *Lapham's Quarterly*
Solve the Problem	What it has wrought is the institutionalization of criminality . . . What can be done? We start with the lawyers, who are not only invested with the monopolistic right to be attorneys for clients but should also be obliged, as officers of the court subject to their code of professional ethics, to be the sentinels for the administration of justice. Some are heroically assuming this august obligation to the people. But far too few of the 1.3 million lawyers in America see the rule of law for the myth it is; too few see the rule of power for the lawlessness it creates. More of them must assume the higher significance of their calling, to respond to the silent cries for justice—which nearly two centuries ago Senator Daniel Webster called "the great interest of man on Earth" and "the ligament which holds civilized beings and civilized nations together." —Ralph Nader (2018), "Land of the Lawless," *Lapham's Quarterly*

Moves That Organize: Social Studies

Move	Mini-Mentor Text
Topic Sentence Transition	Dueling factions representing starkly different constituencies, policies and worldviews had come together in New York City's Madison Square Garden to tear each other apart with no plans for reconciliation or compromise. The divisions within the party were so profound that fights broke out on the convention floor and across the New York metropolitan area. —Eli Wizevich (2024b), "Why the 1924 Democratic National Convention Was the Longest and Most Chaotic of Its Kind in U.S. History," *Smithsonian Magazine*
Hinge Transition	"These artifacts likely haven't seen the light of day since before the American Revolution, perhaps forgotten when George Washington departed Mount Vernon to take command of the Continental Army," Bradburn added. That was in 1775. Archaeologists revisited the site as part of a privately funded $40 million preservation project, aimed at ensuring Mount Vernon's structural integrity and slated for completion in 2026—just in time for America's 250th birthday. —Rachel Treisman (2024), "Centuries-Old Cherries Were Found at George Washington's Home. What Can They Tell Us?," *NPR*
List It	Our research, published in the *International Journal of Heritage Studies*, identified four key themes: • locals don't want heritage reconstruction to be privileged over security • they want local religious sites rebuilt as much as significant non-religious sites • they want heritage sites transformed into more useful structures for the community • and they want control and agency over the future of their own heritage. —Benjamin Isakhan and Lynn Meskell (2024), "Reconstructing Heritage After War: What We Learned From Asking 1,600 Syrians About Rebuilding Aleppo," *The Conversation*
Add Subheadings	Subheadings: • The flag's beginnings • The missing pieces • Preserving a national icon at the Smithsonian —Cate Lineberry and Meilan Solly (2024), "The Real Story Behind the Star-Spangled Banner, the Flag That Inspired the National Anthem," *Smithsonian Magazine*
Visual Anchoring	Rissech's discovery could cast doubt on the idea that the order was exclusive to men. This woman almost certainly fought—and died—alongside the male warrior monks. Her bones show no signs of regrowth or healing around her injuries. [*Screenshot of a tweet from the university leading the research showing the bones*] One hypothesis suggests this mystery woman was a servant called to arms out of desperation to defend the castle against the order's Muslim opponents. Evidence of lower protein consumption than her male counterparts supports the claim that she was from a lower social class. —Eli Wizevich (2024a), "Was This Mysterious Woman a Medieval Warrior?," *Smithsonian Magazine*

APPENDIX C

Writing Application Practice

This appendix features all our writing application practice ideas in one place.

- » Reproducible "English Writing Application Practice" (page 276)
- » Reproducible "Mathematics Writing Application Practice" (page 277)
- » Reproducible "Science Writing Application Practice" (page 278)
- » Reproducible "Social Studies Writing Application Practice" (page 279)

English Writing Application Practice

Moves That Introduce	Choose one of the moves that introduce, and use it to introduce a book you've recently read to someone who has not yet read it.
Moves That Make a Claim	Choose one of the moves that make a claim, and write a claim statement about the current book you're reading.
Moves That Define	Think of a topic you know everything about—a topic you could discuss for an hour without getting bored. Now, what's a term within that topic that most people wouldn't know? Write a few sentences telling a friend about your topic. Include that term you've identified, and choose one of the definition moves to include a definition.
Moves That Describe	Describe a moment from your life—just a few minutes—that has left a powerful imprint on your memory. Which moves that describe can help you bring this moment to life for a reader?
Moves That Provide Evidence	Evaluate how the setting of the novel you most recently read influences or affects one of the characters. Use one of the moves from this chapter to incorporate evidence from the text in your response.
Moves That Summarize	Choose a character from a book you have recently read, and summarize how they have changed over the course of the book. What details, quotes, or analysis can you share to make your explanation more interesting?
Moves That Contextualize	Choose a character from a work of fiction who fits the definition of an antihero (someone who doesn't have conventional hero traits but is still the central character of a story). How might their past experiences have affected their development into an antihero, rather than a typical hero?
Moves That Add Voice	Consider the last piece of writing you did in class. Reread it, and revise it to include at least one of the voice moves used in this chapter. Then, exchange your writing with someone in your class who has chosen the same move. Read what they have written, and answer the question, "What do the author's choices with regard to the move reflect about their personality?" Exchange papers and share your reflections.
Moves That Conclude	Choose a conclusion move to help wrap up the reading that you have done today in class.
Moves That Organize	Consider the last piece of writing you did in class. Reread it, and organize all or a portion of it using a move from this chapter. (If using a digital doc, turn on suggesting mode. If writing by hand, use a different-colored pen than you originally wrote with.) Then, exchange papers with someone else in the class who chose to revise their writing with a different move. Read what they have written, and answer the question, "How did this organizational move affect my understanding of this section or piece of writing?" When finished, share your answers with each other and reflect.

Mathematics Writing Application Practice

Moves That Introduce	What did you learn or practice today in class? Use a move that introduces to introduce the topic to a parent or friend.
Moves That Make a Claim	Consider your current unit in mathematics class. What is the most important mathematical concept to understand in order to be successful in this unit? Write a claim making that argument.
Moves That Define	Think of a new and significant term in your current mathematics unit. Explain what you have been learning using that term, and be sure to include a definition using one of the moves that define.
Moves That Describe	Describe how you solved the hardest problem in last night's mathematics homework. Find a move (or moves) that describes to help you.
Moves That Provide Evidence	Explain and evaluate how you solved your most recent mathematical problem. Use one of the moves from this chapter to incorporate evidence, either from the textbook or with a visual of your own work, in your response.
Moves That Summarize	Explain a mathematical concept that you recently learned about (division, subtraction, the quadratic formula, exponents, and so on) to a reader by summarizing it using one (or more) of the moves that summarize.
Moves That Contextualize	Consider the most recent theorem, formula, or mathematical figure that you have learned about in class. In one or two paragraphs, explain the significance of this theorem, formula, or mathematical figure.
Moves That Add Voice	Consider the last piece of writing you did in class. Reread it, and revise it to include at least one of the voice moves used in this chapter. Then, exchange your writing with someone in your class who has chosen the same move. Read what they have written, and answer the question, "What do the author's choices with regard to the move reflect about their personality?" Exchange papers and share your reflections.
Moves That Conclude	Think about a problem you worked on today in class. Use one of the conclusion moves to sum up your experience working on that problem.
Moves That Organize	Consider the last piece of writing you did in class. Reread it, and organize all or a portion of it using a move from this chapter. (If using a digital doc, turn on suggesting mode. If writing by hand, use a different-colored pen than you originally wrote with.) Then, exchange papers with someone else in the class who chose to revise their writing with a different move. Read what they have written, and answer the question, "How did this organizational move affect my understanding of this section or piece of writing?" When finished, share your answers with each other and reflect.

Science Writing Application Practice

Moves That Introduce	Pretend you are rewriting a chapter from your science textbook. Write a brief introduction to your current unit using one of the moves that introduce.
Moves That Make a Claim	What is the most important issue facing scientists today? Write a claim that makes that argument.
Moves That Define	Choose one word from science class today that you believe is the most important word for understanding today's class. Write a few sentences explaining what you learned today. Be sure to include that most important word and its definition using one of the moves that define.
Moves That Describe	Describe the process you used to conduct an experiment or lab. How might the moves that describe help you make your process clear and vivid to a reader?
Moves That Provide Evidence	Consider the most recent experiment you have conducted or studied in class. Choose one independent variable from the experiment, and explain how the increase or decrease of this variable would affect the results of the experiment. Be sure to include evidence in your response using one of the moves from this chapter.
Moves That Summarize	Write a summary of your most recent lab. Consider the aspects of the lab that you'd like to summarize, from the hypothesis to the results, and choose one of the five summarization moves to help you write your summary.
Moves That Contextualize	Think about an important scientific discovery. Provide the context someone would need to understand this discovery and why it is significant.
Moves That Add Voice	Consider the last piece of writing you did in class. Reread it, and revise it to include at least one of the voice moves used in this chapter. Then, exchange your writing with someone in your class who has chosen the same move. Read what they have written, and answer the question, "What do the author's choices with regard to the move reflect about their personality?" Exchange papers and share your reflections.
Moves That Conclude	A science experiment always ends in the scientist drawing a conclusion about their hypothesis. Consider a recent experiment in science class. How might you use one of these conclusion moves to help you reflect on the outcome of your experiment?
Moves That Organize	Consider the last piece of writing you did in class. Reread it, and organize all or a portion of it using a move from this chapter. (If using a digital doc, turn on suggesting mode. If writing by hand, use a different-colored pen than you originally wrote with.) Then, exchange papers with someone else in the class who chose to revise their writing with a different move. Read what they have written, and answer the question, "How did this organizational move affect my understanding of this section or piece of writing?" When finished, share your answers with each other and reflect.

Social Studies Writing Application Practice

Moves That Introduce	Who is the most significant figure in the unit you are now studying in class? Introduce this person by using one of the moves that introduce.
Moves That Make a Claim	What event did you last study in your social studies class? Write a claim statement that explains the significance of this event within your current unit of study.
Moves That Define	Take sixty seconds to write down as many vocabulary terms as you can that are connected to your current unit. Then, write a paragraph describing your unit in which you define at least one of the key terms using one of the moves that define.
Moves That Describe	Use the Library of Congress or another database to locate a primary source that relates to a current topic you have studied in social studies. Use a move or multiple moves that describe to help your reader see that source.
Moves That Provide Evidence	Evaluate how the most recent event that you learned about in this class affected a person or group of people. Use one of the moves from this chapter to incorporate evidence into your response.
Moves That Summarize	Find a news article that was published today about an event. Summarize the article using one or more of the moves from this chapter.
Moves That Contextualize	Consider the most recent event that you have learned about in class. Briefly, use the moves in this chapter to explain the central causes of this event.
Moves That Add Voice	Consider the last piece of writing you did in class. Reread it, and revise it to include at least one of the voice moves used in this chapter. Then, exchange your writing with someone in your class who has chosen the same move. Read what they have written, and answer the question, "What do the author's choices with regard to the move reflect about their personality?" Exchange papers and share your reflections.
Moves That Conclude	We're willing to bet at least one of your classmates was absent today. (If not, we can pretend!) Use one of the conclusion moves to wrap up what you learned in class today for a classmate who was absent.
Moves That Organize	Consider the last piece of writing you did in class. Reread it, and organize all or a portion of it using a move from this chapter. (If using a digital doc, turn on suggesting mode. If writing by hand, use a different-colored pen than you originally wrote with.) Then, exchange papers with someone else in the class who chose to revise their writing with a different move. Read what they have written, and answer the question, "How did this organizational move affect my understanding of this section or piece of writing?" When finished, share your answers with each other and reflect.

APPENDIX D

Moves Remix

As you begin to teach your students the moves in this book, they will start to notice similarities between them. For instance, as you introduce Show Me the Data as a contextualization move, your students might say, "Hey! This is like Just-the-Facts for introductions!" And they're right.

To help you see connections between moves across writing tasks, we've created a few remix lists. We know that building on prior knowledge and developing associations between concepts deepens and strengthens long-term learning (CAST, 2024). The reproducible tool "Moves Remix Lists" (page 282) will help you discuss these connections in your classroom.

Moves Remix Lists

You and your students will likely develop connections beyond those listed here. Continue to add to the lists.

Moves That Use Facts, Numbers, and Data Just-the-Facts (Chapter 3) Double Date (Chapter 9) Show Me the Data (Chapter 9)	**Moves That Use Narrative Techniques** Scene-Drop (Chapter 3) Gimme an Example (Chapter 5) Let's Imagine . . . (Chapter 6) Connect Personally (Chapter 10)	**Moves That Make Arguments** Make the Case (Chapter 3) The Big Idea (Chapter 4) Outline It (Chapter 4) This-and-That (Chapter 4) Not-This-But-That (Chapter 4) Synthesize It (Chapter 4) End With Analysis (Chapter 7) Educated Inference (Chapter 9) Past and Present Connection (Chapter 9)
Moves That Use Quotes What They Said (Chapter 3) Quote It to Me (Chapter 8) Share the Last Word (Chapter 11)	**Moves That Use Time or Chronology** Then-and-Now (Chapter 3) Cause and Effect Sandwich (Chapter 8) Double Date (Chapter 9) Past and Present Connection (Chapter 9)	**Moves That Present Contrasts** Then-and-Now (Chapter 3) Not-This-But-That (Chapter 4) Pivot Synopsis (Chapter 8) What We Don't Know and What We Do (Chapter 11)
Moves That Make Comparisons Then-and-Now (Chapter 3) Figurative Language Comparison (Chapter 6) Let's Compare (Chapter 9) Past and Present Connection (Chapter 9) Make It Metaphorical (Chapter 10)	**Moves That List** Outline It (Chapter 4) Describing Lists (Chapter 6) List It (Chapter 12)	**Moves That Rely on Punctuation** Keep It Appositive (Chapter 5) Dash That Describes (Chapter 6) Put It in Parentheses (Chapter 10)
Moves That Use Figurative Language Figurative Language Comparison (Chapter 6) Make It Metaphorical (Chapter 10)	**Moves That Use Visuals** Reference a Visual (Chapter 7) Visual Anchoring (Chapter 12)	**Moves That Ask or Imply Questions** Educated Inference (Chapter 9) Ask a Question (Chapter 10) What We Don't Know and What We Do (Chapter 11)
Moves That Use Research Just-the-Facts (Chapter 3) What They Said (Chapter 3) Then-and-Now (Chapter 3) Synthesize It (Chapter 4) Engage With Etymology (Chapter 5) Hyperlink Layers (Chapter 7) Reference a Visual (Chapter 7) Paraphrase It (Chapter 7) Quote It to Me (Chapter 8) Double Date (Chapter 9) Show Me the Data (Chapter 9) Educated Inference (Chapter 9) Past and Present Connection (Chapter 9) What's Next? (Chapter 11) Share the Last Word (Chapter 11) Visual Anchoring (Chapter 12)		

APPENDIX E

Standards and Mini Moves Connected

This appendix plainly illustrates that whether you teach English, social studies, mathematics, or science, teaching students to practice using mini moves in their writing is not just one more demand on your already-packed curriculum. Rather, mini moves are built into your standards.

For the purposes of the illustration, we have used the Common Core State Standards (CCSS) for English language arts and literacy in history/social studies, science, and technical subjects and for mathematics. While most U.S. states use the Common Core, we know that your state, like ours, might not; you have your own standards. However, since the Common Core standards were created through the synthesis of the "highest, most effective standards from states across the United States and countries around the world" (Common Core State Standards Initiative, n.d.), they provide a useful foundation for us to utilize together. Even if these aren't your exact standards, yours are likely extremely similar.

Not only do the following standards reveal that the writing tasks accomplished through mini moves align with standards we are required to teach, but the Common Core State Standards also include guidance for what writing should look like in the classroom. According to the standards for English language arts and literacy in history/social studies, science, and technical subjects, students should "write routinely over extended time frames (time for research, reflection, and revision) and shorter time frames (a single sitting or a day or two) for a range of discipline-specific tasks, purposes, and audiences" (W.3.10; National Governors Association Center for Best Practices & Council of Chief State School Officers, 2010a).

This means that consistent, focused writing practice, the kind of writing instruction we advocate for in this book, is also supported by and aligned to our standards.

In short, mini moves aren't something extra. They are part of the instruction our standards already demand.

So, how might you use this document?

- » If you teach in a state that uses the Common Core State Standards, use this appendix as a checklist, matching mini moves to standards you need to teach.

- » If you do not teach in a CCSS state, compare your standards to these—we promise, they will match up!—and use the moves suggested to teach your similar standards.

- » Print and share this appendix as you communicate with colleagues, parents, and administrators about teaching with mini moves. Showing that this kind of instruction perfectly aligns with standards you already need to teach gives you excellent support!

The following reproducibles will help.

- » "English Language Arts Standards"

- » "Grades 6–12 Literacy in History/Social Studies, Science, and Technical Subjects" (page 287)

- » "Standards for Mathematical Practice" (page 290)

English Language Arts Standards

Writing Tasks: Making a Claim, Providing Evidence, Organizing		
CCSS.ELA-LITERACY.W.6.1.A: Introduce claim(s) and organize the reasons and evidence clearly.		

Moves That Make a Claim:
  The Big Idea
  Outline It
  This-and-That
  Not-This-But-That
  Synthesize It
	Moves That Provide Evidence:
	  Hyperlink Layers
	  Reference a Visual
	  The Fold In
	  Paraphrase It
	  End With Analysis
		Moves That Organize:
		  Topic Sentence Transition
		  Hinge Transition
		  List It
		  Add Subheadings
		  Visual Anchoring

Writing Tasks: Introducing, Defining, Organizing		
CCSS.ELA-LITERACY.W.6.2.A: Introduce a topic; organize ideas, concepts, and information, using strategies such as definition, classification, comparison/contrast, and cause/effect; include formatting (e.g., headings), graphics (e.g., charts, tables), and multimedia when useful to aiding comprehension.		

Moves That Introduce:
  Just-the-Facts
  Make the Case
  What They Said
  Scene-Drop
  Then-and-Now
	Moves That Define:
	  It Is What It Is
	  Say My Name
	  Keep It Appositive
	  Gimme an Example
	  Engage With Etymology
		Moves That Organize:
		  Topic Sentence Transition
		  Hinge Transition
		  List It
		  Add Subheadings
		  Visual Anchoring

Writing Tasks: Making a Claim, Providing Evidence		
CCSS.ELA-LITERACY.W.6.1.B: Support claim(s) with clear reasons and relevant evidence, using credible sources and demonstrating an understanding of the topic or text.		

Moves That Make a Claim:
  The Big Idea
  Outline It
  This-and-That
  Not-This-But-That
  Synthesize It
	Moves That Provide Evidence:
	  Hyperlink Layers
	  Reference a Visual
	  The Fold In
	  Paraphrase It
	  End With Analysis	

Writing Task: Concluding		
CCSS.ELA-LITERACY.W.6.1.E: Provide a concluding statement or section that follows from the argument presented. CCSS.ELA-LITERACY.W.6.2.F: Provide a concluding statement or section that follows from the information or explanation presented. CCSS.ELA-LITERACY.W.6.3.E: Provide a conclusion that follows from the narrated experiences or events.		

Moves That Conclude:
  What We Don't Know and What We Do
  What's Next?
  Share the Last Word
  The Bottom Line
  Solve the Problem		

Writing Tasks: Defining, Describing, Providing Evidence, Summarizing		
CCSS.ELA-LITERACY.W.6.2.B: Develop the topic with relevant facts, definitions, concrete details, quotations, or other information and examples.		

Moves That Define:	Moves That Describe:	Moves That Provide Evidence:	Moves That Summarize:
It Is What It Is	Describing Lists	Hyperlink Layers	Define and Detail
Say My Name	Say It Again, But Make It Specific	Reference a Visual	Pivot Synopsis
Keep It Appositive	Dash That Describes	The Fold In	The Devil in the Details
Gimme an Example	Let's Imagine . . .	Paraphrase It	Cause and Effect Sandwich
Engage With Etymology	Figurative Language Comparison	End With Analysis	Quote It to Me

Writing Tasks: Contextualizing, Organizing

CCSS.ELA-LITERACY.W.6.3.A: Engage and orient the reader by establishing a context and introducing a narrator and/or characters; organize an event sequence that unfolds naturally and logically.

Moves That Contextualize:	Moves That Organize:
Let's Compare	Topic Sentence Transition
Double Date	Hinge Transition
Show Me the Data	List It
Educated Inference	Add Subheadings
Past and Present Connection	Visual Anchoring

Writing Task: Describing

CCSS.ELA-LITERACY.W.6.3.B: Use narrative techniques, such as dialogue, pacing, and description, to develop experiences, events, and/or characters.

Moves That Describe:
- Describing Lists
- Say It Again, But Make It Specific
- Dash That Describes
- Let's Imagine . . .
- Figurative Language Comparison

Writing Task: Providing Evidence

CCSS.ELA-LITERACY.W.6.9: Draw evidence from literary or informational texts to support analysis, reflection, and research.

Moves That Provide Evidence:
- Hyperlink Layers
- Reference a Visual
- The Fold In
- Paraphrase It
- End With Analysis

Writing Task: Organizing

CCSS.ELA-LITERACY.W.6.2.C: Use appropriate transitions to clarify the relationships among ideas and concepts.
CCSS.ELA-LITERACY.W.6.3.C: Use a variety of transition words, phrases, and clauses to convey sequence and signal shifts from one time frame or setting to another.

Moves That Organize:
- Topic Sentence Transition
- Hinge Transition
- List It
- Add Subheadings
- Visual Anchoring

Source for standards: National Governors Association Center for Best Practices & Council of Chief State School Officers. (2010). Common Core State Standards for English language arts and literacy in history/social studies, science, and technical subjects. Authors. Accessed at https://corestandards.org/wp-content/uploads/2023/09/ELA_Standards1.pdf on November 13, 2024.

Grades 6–12 Literacy in History/Social Studies, Science, and Technical Subjects

Writing Task: Making a Claim
CCSS.ELA-LITERACY.WHST.6-8.1.A: Introduce claim(s) about a topic or issue, acknowledge and distinguish the claim(s) from alternate or opposing claims, and organize the reasons and evidence logically. CCSS.ELA-LITERACY.WHST.9-10.1.A: Introduce precise claim(s), distinguish the claim(s) from alternate or opposing claims, and create an organization that establishes clear relationships among the claim(s), counterclaims, reasons, and evidence. CCSS.ELA-LITERACY.WHST.11-12.1.A: Introduce precise, knowledgeable claim(s), establish the significance of the claim(s), distinguish the claim(s) from alternate or opposing claims, and create an organization that logically sequences the claim(s), counterclaims, reasons, and evidence.

Moves That Make a Claim:
    The Big Idea
    Outline It
    This-and-That
    Not-This-But-That
    Synthesize It

Writing Tasks: Making a Claim, Providing Evidence
CCSS.ELA-LITERACY.WHST.6-8.1.B: Support claim(s) with logical reasoning and relevant, accurate data and evidence that demonstrate an understanding of the topic or text, using credible sources. CCSS.ELA-LITERACY.WHST.9-10.1.B: Develop claim(s) and counterclaims fairly, supplying data and evidence for each while pointing out the strengths and limitations of both claim(s) and counterclaims in a discipline-appropriate form and in a manner that anticipates the audience's knowledge level and concerns. CCSS.ELA-LITERACY.WHST.11-12.1.B: Develop claim(s) and counterclaims fairly and thoroughly, supplying the most relevant data and evidence for each while pointing out the strengths and limitations of both claim(s) and counterclaims in a discipline-appropriate form that anticipates the audience's knowledge level, concerns, values, and possible biases.

Moves That Make a Claim: *Moves That Provide Evidence:*
    The Big Idea   Hyperlink Layers
    Outline It   Reference a Visual
    This-and-That   The Fold In
    Not-This-But-That   Paraphrase It
    Synthesize It   End With Analysis

Writing Task: Organizing
CCSS.ELA-LITERACY.WHST.6-8.1.C: Use words, phrases, and clauses to create cohesion and clarify the relationships among claim(s), counterclaims, reasons, and evidence. CCSS.ELA-LITERACY.WHST.9-10.1.C: Use words, phrases, and clauses to link the major sections of the text, create cohesion, and clarify the relationships between claim(s) and reasons, between reasons and evidence, and between claim(s) and counterclaims. CCSS.ELA-LITERACY.WHST.11-12.1.C: Use words, phrases, and clauses as well as varied syntax to link the major sections of the text, create cohesion, and clarify the relationships between claim(s) and reasons, between reasons and evidence, and between claim(s) and counterclaims.

Moves That Organize:
    Topic Sentence Transition
    Hinge Transition
    List It
    Add Subheadings
    Visual Anchoring

Writing Task: Concluding
CCSS.ELA-LITERACY.WHST.6–8.1.E: Provide a concluding statement or section that follows from and supports the argument presented. CCSS.ELA-LITERACY.WHST.6–8.2.F: Provide a concluding statement or section that follows from and supports the information or explanation presented. CCSS.ELA-LITERACY.WHST.9–10.1.E: Provide a concluding statement or section that follows from or supports the argument presented. CCSS.ELA-LITERACY.WHST.9–10.2.F: Provide a concluding statement or section that follows from and supports the information or explanation presented (e.g., articulating implications or the significance of the topic). CCSS.ELA-LITERACY.WHST.11–12.1.E: Provide a concluding statement or section that follows from or supports the argument presented. CCSS.ELA-LITERACY.WHST.11–12.2.E: Provide a concluding statement or section that follows from and supports the information or explanation provided (e.g., articulating implications or the significance of the topic).

Moves That Conclude:
    What We Don't Know and What We Do
    What's Next?
    Share the Last Word
    The Bottom Line
    Solve the Problem

Writing Tasks: Introducing, Organizing
CCSS.ELA-LITERACY.WHST.6–8.2.A: Introduce a topic clearly, previewing what is to follow; organize ideas, concepts, and information into broader categories as appropriate to achieving purpose; include formatting (e.g., headings), graphics (e.g., charts, tables), and multimedia when useful to aiding comprehension. CCSS.ELA-LITERACY.WHST.9–10.2.A: Introduce a topic and organize ideas, concepts, and information to make important connections and distinctions; include formatting (e.g., headings), graphics (e.g., figures, tables), and multimedia when useful to aiding comprehension. CCSS.ELA-LITERACY.WHST.11–12.2.A: Introduce a topic and organize complex ideas, concepts, and information so that each new element builds on that which precedes it to create a unified whole; include formatting (e.g., headings), graphics (e.g., figures, tables), and multimedia when useful to aiding comprehension.

Moves That Introduce:	*Moves That Organize:*
Just-the-Facts	Topic Sentence Transition
Make the Case	Hinge Transition
What They Said	List It
Scene-Drop	Add Subheadings
Then-and-Now	Visual Anchoring

Writing Tasks: Describing, Providing Evidence
CCSS.ELA-LITERACY.WHST.6–8.2.B: Develop the topic with relevant, well-chosen facts, definitions, concrete details, quotations, or other information and examples. CCSS.ELA-LITERACY.WHST.9–10.2.B: Develop the topic with well-chosen, relevant, and sufficient facts, extended definitions, concrete details, quotations, or other information and examples appropriate to the audience's knowledge of the topic. CCSS.ELA-LITERACY.WHST.11–12.2.B: Develop the topic thoroughly by selecting the most significant and relevant facts, extended definitions, concrete details, quotations, or other information and examples appropriate to the audience's knowledge of the topic.

Moves That Describe:	Moves That Provide Evidence:
Describing Lists	Hyperlink Layers
Say It Again, But Make It Specific	Reference a Visual
Dash That Describes	The Fold In
Let's Imagine . . .	Paraphrase It
Figurative Language Comparison	End With Analysis

Writing Task: Organizing

CCSS.ELA-LITERACY.WHST.6–8.2.C: Use appropriate and varied transitions to create cohesion and clarify the relationships among ideas and concepts.

CCSS.ELA-LITERACY.WHST.9–10.2.C: Use varied transitions and sentence structures to link the major sections of the text, create cohesion, and clarify the relationships among ideas and concepts.

CCSS.ELA-LITERACY.WHST.11–12.2.C: Use varied transitions and sentence structures to link the major sections of the text, create cohesion, and clarify the relationships among complex ideas and concepts.

Moves That Organize:
- Topic Sentence Transition
- Hinge Transition
- List It
- Add Subheadings
- Visual Anchoring

Writing Task: Describing

Note to the standards: In history/social studies, students must be able to incorporate narrative accounts into their analyses of individuals or events of historical import. In science and technical subjects, students must be able to write precise enough descriptions of the step-by-step procedures they use in their investigations or technical work that others can replicate them and (possibly) reach the same results.

Moves That Describe:
- Describing Lists
- Say It Again, But Make It Specific
- Dash That Describes
- Let's Imagine . . .
- Figurative Language Comparison

Source for standards: National Governors Association Center for Best Practices & Council of Chief State School Officers. (2010). Common Core State Standards for English language arts and literacy in history/social studies, science, and technical subjects. Authors. Accessed at https://corestandards.org/wp-content/uploads/2023/09/ELA_Standards1.pdf on November 13, 2024.

Standards for Mathematical Practice

Writing Tasks: Making a Claim, Defining, Describing, Concluding
CCSS.MATH.PRACTICE.MP3: Construct viable arguments and critique the reasoning of others. Mathematically proficient students understand and use stated assumptions, definitions, and previously established results in constructing arguments. They make conjectures and build a logical progression of statements to explore the truth of their conjectures. They are able to analyze situations by breaking them into cases, and can recognize and use counterexamples. They justify their conclusions, communicate them to others, and respond to the arguments of others. They reason inductively about data, making plausible arguments that take into account the context from which the data arose.

Moves That Make a Claim:	*Moves That Define:*	*Moves That Describe:*	*Moves That Conclude:*
The Big Idea	It Is What It Is	Describing Lists	What We Don't Know and What We Do
Outline It	Say My Name	Say It Again, But Make It Specific	What's Next?
This-and-That	Keep It Appositive	Dash That Describes	Share the Last Word
Not-This-But-That	Gimme an Example	Let's Imagine . . .	The Bottom Line
Synthesize It	Engage With Etymology	Figurative Language Comparison	Solve the Problem

Writing Task: Defining
CCSS.MATH.PRACTICE.MP6: Attend to precision. Mathematically proficient students try to communicate precisely to others. They try to use clear definitions in discussion with others and in their own reasoning. They state the meaning of the symbols they choose, including using the equal sign consistently and appropriately. They are careful about specifying units of measure, and labeling axes to clarify the correspondence with quantities in a problem. They calculate accurately and efficiently, express numerical answers with a degree of precision appropriate for the problem context. In the elementary grades, students give carefully formulated explanations to each other. By the time they reach high school they have learned to examine claims and make explicit use of definitions.

Moves That Define:
    It Is What It Is
    Say My Name
    Keep It Appositive
    Gimme an Example
    Engage With Etymology

Source for standards: National Governors Association Center for Best Practices & Council of Chief State School Officers. (2010). *Common Core State Standards for mathematics. Authors.* Accessed at https://corestandards.org/wp-content/uploads/2023/09/Math_Standards1.pdf on November 13, 2024.

References and Resources

Abad-Santos, A. (2022, September 26). The many scandals of *Don't Worry Darling*, explained. *Vox*. Accessed at www.vox.com/culture/2022/9/6/23339631/dont-worry-darling-wilde-pugh-feud-explained on September 24, 2024.

Abad-Santos, A. (2024a, March 12). Kate Middleton's edited Mother's Day photo, explained by an expert. *Vox*. Accessed at www.vox.com/culture/24098724/kate-middleton-editing-photo-explained on September 23, 2024.

Abad-Santos, A. (2024b, August 23). Sabrina Carpenter's "Espresso," the song of the summer, explained. *Vox*. Accessed at www.vox.com/culture/2024/5/14/24155699/sabrina-carpenter-espresso-career-olivia-rodrigo-explained on September 23, 2024.

Alter, A. (2024, April 16). Book bans continue to surge in public schools. *The New York Times*. Accessed at www.nytimes.com/2024/04/16/books/book-bans-public-schools.html on September 23, 2024.

Anderson, S. (2024, July 15). Nine things you didn't know about the ancient Olympic Games. *Smithsonian Magazine*. Accessed at www.smithsonianmag.com/history/nine-things-you-didnt-know-about-the-ancient-olympic-games-180984672 on September 23, 2024.

Appelbaum, B. (2023, March 1). And child care for all [Editorial]. *The New York Times*. Accessed at www.nytimes.com/2023/03/01/opinion/editorials/and-child-care-for-all.html on September 23, 2024.

Apter, S. (2010, Summer). Wordplay. *Lapham's Quarterly*, *III*(3). Accessed at www.laphamsquarterly.org/sports-games/wordplay on September 23, 2024.

Arnold, C. (2022, October 21). Taylor Swift goes dark on new album 'Midnights' [Review of the musical album *Midnights*, by T. Swift]. *New York Post*. Accessed at https://nypost.com/2022/10/21/taylor-swift-goes-dark-on-new-album-midnights on September 23, 2024.

Balaban, S. (2024, July 27). To learn 'The Truth About Dragons,' go on a quest through this kids' book. *NPR*. Accessed at www.npr.org/2024/07/26/nx-s1-5001940/the-truth-about-dragons-julie-leung-hanna-cha on September 23, 2024.

Ball, P. (2024a, March 25). The best qubits for quantum computing might just be atoms. *Quanta Magazine*. Accessed at www.quantamagazine.org/the-best-qubits-for-quantum-computing-might-just-be-atoms-20240325 on September 23, 2024.

Ball, P. (2024b, February 14). A 'lobby' where a molecule mob tells genes what to do. *Quanta Magazine*. Accessed at www.quantamagazine.org/a-lobby-where-a-molecule-mob-tells-genes-what-to-do-20240214 on September 25, 2024.

Ball, P. (2024c, June 10). The new math of how large-scale order emerges. *Quanta Magazine*. Accessed at www.quantamagazine.org/the-new-math-of-how-large-scale-order-emerges-20240610 on September 23, 2024.

Barone, J. (2024, July 2). Why we still want to hear the 'Ode to Joy,' 200 years later. *The New York Times*. Accessed at www.nytimes.com/2024/07/02/arts/music/ode-to-joy-beethoven.html on September 23, 2024.

Baumann, M. (2018, April 20). Beyoncé sings "Halo" at a hospital. In Ringer Staff, The best Beyoncé videos on the internet. *The Ringer*. Accessed at www.theringer.com/music/2018/4/20/17261124/best-beyonce-videos-online on September 23, 2024.

Berlinger, M. (2023, June 8). At more skate parks, an 'aggressive' takeover. *The New York Times*. Accessed at www.nytimes.com/2023/06/08/style/aggressive-inline-skating-rollerblading.html on September 23, 2024.

Berne, J. (2009). Setting up and managing the writing workshop. In *The writing-rich high school classroom: Engaging students in the writing workshop* (pp. 10–26). Guilford Press.

Binswanger, J. (2024, July 22). This Bronze Age ship replica, made from reeds and goat hair, just sailed 50 nautical miles. *Smithsonian Magazine*. Accessed at www.smithsonianmag.com/smart-news/this-bronze-age-ship-replica-made-from-reeds-and-goat-hair-just-sailed-50-nautical-miles-180984728 on September 23, 2024.

Blitzer, J. (2024, June 8). What's behind Joe Biden's harsh new executive order on immigration? *The New Yorker*. Accessed at www.newyorker.com/news/daily-comment/whats-behind-joe-bidens-harsh-new-executive-order-on-immigration on September 23, 2024.

Borel, B. (2016, September 8). Genetic engineering to clash with evolution. *Quanta Magazine*. Accessed at www.quantamagazine.org/gene-drives-will-clash-with-evolution-20160908 on September 23, 2024.

Bracco, A. (2024, June 26). The world's fourth mass coral bleaching is underway, but well-connected reefs may have a better chance to recover. *The Conversation*. Accessed at https://theconversation.com/the-worlds-fourth-mass-coral-bleaching-is-underway-but-well-connected-reefs-may-have-a-better-chance-to-recover-230755 on September 23, 2024.

Brinkhof, T. (2024, March 6). What do gardens and murder have in common? *JSTOR Daily*. Accessed at https://daily.jstor.org/gardens-murder-mysteries on September 23, 2024.

Broadfoot, M. (2023, May 26). The brain-computer interfaces that could give locked-in patients a voice. *Smithsonian Magazine*. Accessed at www.smithsonianmag.com/innovation/brain-computer-interfaces-that-could-give-locked-in-patients-voice-180982254 on September 23, 2024.

Brown, P. (2015, Summer). Treasure in heaven. *Lapham's Quarterly, VIII*(3). Accessed at www.laphamsquarterly.org/philanthropy/treasure-heaven on September 23, 2024.

Brownstein, R. (2022, June 24). America is growing apart, possibly for good. *The Atlantic*. Accessed at www.theatlantic.com/politics/archive/2022/06/red-and-blue-state-divide-is-growing-michael-podhorzer-newsletter/661377 on September 23, 2024.

Brownstein, R. (2023, June 15). Why Trump might just roll to the presidential nomination. *The Atlantic*. Accessed at www.theatlantic.com/politics/archive/2023/06/what-it-would-take-to-beat-trump-in-the-primaries/674413 on September 23, 2024.

Brubaker, B. (2024, July 2). With fifth busy beaver, researchers approach computation's limits. *Quanta Magazine*. Accessed at www.quantamagazine.org/amateur-mathematicians-find-fifth-busy-beaver-turing-machine-20240702 on September 23, 2024.

Burton, D. M. (2011). *The history of mathematics: An introduction* (7th ed.). McGraw-Hill.

Calle, M., & Merling, M. (2023, August 9). A brief illustrated guide to 'scissors congruence'—an ancient geometric idea that's still fueling cutting-edge mathematical research. *The Conversation*. Accessed at https://theconversation.com/a-brief-illustrated-guide-to-scissors-congruence-an-ancient-geometric-idea-thats-still-fueling-cutting-edge-mathematical-research-210612 on September 23, 2024.

Callier, V. (2023, May 8). A mutation turned ants into parasites in one generation. *Quanta Magazine*. Accessed at www.quantamagazine.org/a-mutation-turned-ants-into-parasites-in-one-generation-20230508 on September 23, 2024.

Caramanica, J. (2022, April 6). Olivia Rodrigo's punky heartbreak revue [Review of the *Sour* musical tour, by O. Rodrigo]. *The New York Times*. Accessed at www.nytimes.com/2022/04/06/arts/music/olivia-rodrigo-sour-tour-review.html on September 23, 2024.

Carrns, A. (2023, May 19). Expect interest rates on federal student loans to rise. *The New York Times*. Accessed at www.nytimes.com/2023/05/19/your-money/interest-rates-federal-student-loans.html on September 23, 2024.

Carter, M. (2007, February). Ways of knowing, doing, and writing in the disciplines. *College Composition and Communication, 58*(3), 385–418.

CAST. (2024). *The UDL guidelines*. Accessed at https://udlguidelines.cast.org on September 23, 2024.

Cepelewicz, J. (2023a, February 10). Mathematicians complete quest to build 'spherical cubes.' *Quanta Magazine*. Accessed at www.quantamagazine.org/mathematicians-complete-quest-to-build-spherical-cubes-20230210 on September 23, 2024.

Cepelewicz, J. (2023b, March 9). New proof distinguishes mysterious and powerful 'modular forms.' *Quanta Magazine*. Accessed at www.quantamagazine.org/long-sought-math-proof-unlocks-more-mysterious-modular-forms-20230309 on September 23, 2024.

Cepelewicz, J. (2024a, June 21). How the square root of 2 became a number. *Quanta Magazine*. Accessed at www.quantamagazine.org/how-the-square-root-of-2-became-a-number-20240621 on September 23, 2024.

Cepelewicz, J. (2024b, May 14). Strangely curved shapes break 50-year-old geometry conjecture. *Quanta Magazine*. Accessed at www.quantamagazine.org/strangely-curved-shapes-break-50-year-old-geometry-conjecture-20240514 on September 23, 2024.

Chan, J. (2024, March 18). In Téa Obreht's latest, a refugee seeks home in a ruined world [Review of the book *The Morningside*, by T. Obreht]. *The New York Times*. Accessed at www.nytimes.com/2024/03/18/books/review/tea-obreht-morningside.html on September 23, 2024.

Chandrasekaran, L. (2021, September 14). How ancient war trickery is alive in math today. *Quanta Magazine*. Accessed at www.quantamagazine.org/how-ancient-war-trickery-is-alive-in-math-today-20210914 on September 23, 2024.

Chandrasekaran, L. (2024, March 12). Physicists finally find a problem that only quantum computers can do. *Quanta Magazine*. Accessed at www.quantamagazine.org/physicists-finally-find-a-problem-only-quantum-computers-can-do-20240312 on September 23, 2024.

Chang, J. (2021, December 9). Steven Spielberg's 'West Side Story' will make you believe in movies again [Review of the film *West Side story*, by S. Spielberg, Dir.]. *NPR*. Accessed at www.npr.org/2021/12/09/1062380664/steven-spielbergs-west-side-story-review on September 23, 2024.

Chavez, F. R. (2021). *The anti-racist writing workshop: How to decolonize the creative classroom*. Haymarket Books.

Cheuk, L. (2022, November 13). 'Ghost Town' blurs the line between the living and the dead in rural Taiwan [Review of the book *Ghost town*, by K. Chen]. *NPR*. Accessed at www.npr.org/2022/11/13/1135093196/ghost-town-kevin-chen-book-review on September 23, 2024.

Childress, B. (2023, July 5). Arthur Ashe (1943–1993). In *Encyclopedia Virginia*. Accessed at https://encyclopediavirginia.org/entries/ashe-arthur-1943-1993 on September 23, 2024.

Childs, K. R. (2020). Write away: Writing across the curriculum and beyond. *Texas Association for Literacy Education Yearbook*, *7*, 44–48. Accessed at https://files.eric.ed.gov/fulltext/EJ1286844.pdf on September 23, 2024.

Chiou, L. (2024a, March 5). Elliptic curve 'murmurations' found with AI take flight. *Quanta Magazine*. Accessed at www.quantamagazine.org/elliptic-curve-murmurations-found-with-ai-take-flight-20240305 on September 23, 2024.

Chiou, L. (2024b, March 26). Topologists tackle the trouble with poll placement. *Quanta Magazine*. Accessed at www.quantamagazine.org/topologists-tackle-the-trouble-with-poll-placement-20240326 on September 23, 2024.

Choy, A. (2023, December 6). The Josephus problem. *Chalkdust*, *18*. Accessed at https://chalkdustmagazine.com/features/josephus-problem on September 23, 2024.

Clark, R. P. (2023). *Tell it like it is: A guide to clear and honest writing*. Little, Brown Spark.

Clayton, H. (2021). Planning and teaching mini-lessons. *Just ASK's Making the Standards Come Alive!*, *X*(1). Accessed at https://justaskpublications.com/just-ask-resource-center/e-newsletters/msca/planning-and-teaching-mini-lessons on September 23, 2024.

Cleland, J. (2021, December 17). Jane Austen and me. *CrimeReads*. Accessed at https://crimereads.com/jane-austen-and-me on September 23, 2024.

Coe, A. (2023, July/August). How George Washington wrote his farewell address. *Smithsonian Magazine*. Accessed at www.smithsonianmag.com/smithsonian-institution/how-george-washington-wrote-farewell-address-180982346 on September 23, 2024.

Common Core State Standards Initiative. (n.d.). *About the standards*. Accessed at www.thecorestandards.org/about-the-standards on September 23, 2024.

Confessore, N. (2024, January 20). 'America is under attack': Inside the anti-D.E.I. crusade. *The New York Times*. Accessed at www.nytimes.com/interactive/2024/01/20/us/dei-woke-claremont-institute.html on January 9, 2025.

Coyle, J. (2022, November 8). In 'Wakanda Forever,' an empire mourns and rebuilds. *Associated Press*. Accessed at https://apnews.com/article/black-panther-wakanda-forever-film-reviews-entertainment-ryan-coogler-chadwick-boseman-424bcbf6ee3c730e80e25d153328eb8e on September 23, 2024.

Crane, A. (2024, January 11). Five things you probably have wrong about the *T. rex*. *JSTOR Daily*. Accessed at https://daily.jstor.org/five-things-you-probably-have-wrong-about-the-t-rex on September 23, 2024.

Cunningham, K. (2024, June 20). How "Not Like Us" became an anti-Drake anthem. *Vox*. Accessed at www.vox.com/culture/24132396/drake-beef-explained-kendrick-lamar-the-heart-part-6-euphoria-meet-the-grahams-taylor on September 23, 2024.

Curto, J. (2023, June 30). Olivia Rodrigo is perfecting the formula on 'vampire' [Review of the song "vampire," by O. Rodrigo]. *Vulture*. Accessed at www.vulture.com/2023/06/olivia-rodrigo-vampire-review.html on September 23, 2024.

Curto, J. (2024, April 1). Two-steppin' our way through *Cowboy Carter*: The people, songs, and history behind Beyoncé's Americana odyssey. *Vulture*. Accessed at www.vulture.com/article/beyonce-cowboy-carter-country-guests-references.html on September 23, 2024.

Cutts, E. (2024, March 11). Tiny tweaks to neurons can rewire animal motion. *Quanta Magazine*. Accessed at www.quantamagazine.org/tiny-tweaks-to-neurons-can-rewire-animal-motion-20240311 on September 23, 2024.

Dargis, M. (2024, June 12). 'Inside Out 2' review: PUBERTY! OMG! LOL! IYKYK! [Review of the film *Inside out 2*, by K. Mann, Dir.]. *The New York Times*. Accessed at www.nytimes.com/2024/06/12/movies/inside-out-2-review.html on September 23, 2024.

Davison Avilés, M. (2023, June 10). 'The Wind Knows My Name' is a reference and a refrain in the search for home [Review of the book *The wind knows my name*, by I. Allende]. *NPR*. Accessed at www.npr.org/2023/06/10/1180103464/book-review-isabel-allende-novel-the-wind-knows-my-name on September 23, 2024.

Dearing, A. (2024, February 1). Grilling the globe. *JSTOR Daily*. Accessed at https://daily.jstor.org/meat-tax on September 23, 2024.

Decaille, N. (2024, May 24). Are you wearing sunscreen the right way? *The New York Times Style Magazine*. Accessed at www.nytimes.com/article/spf-sunscreen-skin-care-routine.html on September 23, 2024.

DeCredico, M. (2021, February 5). Bread Riot, Richmond. In *Encyclopedia Virginia*. Accessed at https://encyclopediavirginia.org/entries/bread-riot-richmond on September 23, 2024.

DeGooyer, S. (2022, April/May). The right to leave. *Lapham's Quarterly*, *XIV*(3). Accessed at www.laphamsquarterly.org/migration/right-leave on September 24, 2024.

Delistraty, C. (2024, June 25). How reading grief memoirs helped Cody Delistraty understand his loss in new ways. *Literary Hub*. Accessed at https://lithub.com/how-reading-grief-memoirs-helped-cody-delistraty-understand-his-loss-in-new-ways on September 23, 2024.

De Los Santos, B. (2017, August 6). Sole searching: Inside the wild world of Nike's high-tech scavenger hunts. *Mashable*. Accessed at https://mashable.com/feature/nike-snkrs-app-drops on September 23, 2024.

Diamond, J. (1999). *Guns, germs, and steel: The fates of human societies*. Norton.

Díaz, J. (2020, February 29). James McBride's 'Deacon King Kong' is a supercharged urban farce lit up by thunderbolts of rage [Review of the book *Deacon King Kong*, by J. McBride]. *The New York Times*. Accessed at www.nytimes.com/2020/02/29/books/review/deacon-king-kong-james-mcbride.html on September 23, 2024.

Dikötter, F. (2011). *Mao's great famine: The history of China's most devastating catastrophe, 1958–1962*. Bloomsbury USA.

Dineen, R. (2024, July 22). On the simple prophecy of Octavia Butler's *Parable of the Sower*. *Literary Hub*. Accessed at https://lithub.com/on-the-simple-prophecy-of-octavia-butlers-parable-of-the-sower on September 23, 2024.

Dinius, M. (2024, March 25). The power of pamphlets in the anti-slavery movement. *JSTOR Daily*. Accessed at https://daily.jstor.org/the-power-of-pamphlets-in-the-anti-slavery-movementavery-pamphlets on September 23, 2024.

Doniger, W. (2024, May 15). A quiet roar: Wendy Doniger on Amit Chaudhuri's *Freedom Song*. *Literary Hub*. Accessed at https://lithub.com/a-quiet-roar-wendy-doniger-on-amit-chaudhuris-freedom-song on September 23, 2024.

Drahl, C. (2023, May 10). The mission that could transform our understanding of Mars. *Smithsonian Magazine*. Accessed at www.smithsonianmag.com/science-nature/the-mission-that-could-transform-our-understanding-of-mars-180982144 on September 23, 2024.

Durbach, N. (2023, Spring). Our medical liberties. *Lapham's Quarterly*, *XV*(1). Accessed at www.laphamsquarterly.org/freedom/our-medical-liberties on September 23, 2024.

Dzombak, R. (2024, July 23). Secrets emerge from a fossil's taco shell-like cover. *The New York Times*. Accessed at www.nytimes.com/2024/07/23/science/taco-shell-fossil.html on September 23, 2024.

Egan, E. (2023, June 30). Bridget Jones deserved better. We all did. [Review of the book *Bridget Jones's diary*, by H. Fielding]. *The New York Times*. Accessed at www.nytimes.com/2023/06/30/books/review/bridget-joness-diary-helen-fielding.html on September 23, 2024.

Egan, E. (2024, June 27). Emily Henry on writing best-sellers without tours or TikTok. *The New York Times*. Accessed at www.nytimes.com/2024/06/27/books/emily-henry-funny-story-tiktok.html on September 23, 2024.

Elbein, A. (2024, January 31). Plants find light using gaps between their cells. *Quanta Magazine*. Accessed at www.quantamagazine.org/plants-find-light-using-gaps-between-their-cells-20240131 on September 23, 2024.

Elie, P. (2015, December 9). The secret history of *One Hundred Years of Solitude*. *Vanity Fair*. Accessed at www.vanityfair.com/culture/2015/12/gabriel-garcia-marquez-one-hundred-years-of-solitude-history on September 23, 2024.

Ellis, G. (2012, December). Multiverses and observational limits of cosmology. *Eureka*, *62*, 58–64. Accessed at https://static.mathigon.org/eureka-62.pdf on September 23, 2024.

Evans Ogden, L. (2024, April 24). Ecologists struggle to get a grip on 'keystone species.' *Quanta Magazine*. Accessed at www.quantamagazine.org/ecologists-struggle-to-get-a-grip-on-keystone-species-20240424 on September 24, 2024.

Faires, C., & Overstreet, R. (2023, July 19). Just in time for back-to-school shopping: How retailers can alter customer behavior to encourage more sustainable returns. *The Conversation.* Accessed at https://theconversation.com/just-in-time-for-back-to-school-shopping-how-retailers-can-alter-customer-behavior-to-encourage-more-sustainable-returns-206164 on September 23, 2024.

Fielding, H. (2024, June 26). Helen Fielding on *Bridget Jones* and the subtle art of diary keeping. *Literary Hub.* Accessed at https://lithub.com/helen-fielding-on-bridget-jones-and-the-subtle-art-of-diary-keeping on September 23, 2024.

Fisher, D., & Frey, N. (2021). *Better learning through structured teaching: A framework for the gradual release of responsibility* (3rd ed.). ASCD.

Fortnow, L. (2024, June 12). Computation is all around us, and you can see it if you try. *Quanta Magazine.* Accessed at www.quantamagazine.org/computation-is-all-around-us-and-you-can-see-it-if-you-try-20240612 on September 23, 2024.

Gabriel, R. (2023). *Doing disciplinary literacy: Teaching reading and writing across the content areas.* Teachers College Press.

Gallagher, K. (2017, February 1). The writing journey. *Educational Leadership, 74*(5). Accessed at https://ascd.org/el/articles/the-writing-journey on September 24, 2024.

Garner, D. (2024a, March 11). 'Huck Finn' is a masterpiece. This retelling just might be, too [Review of the book *James*, by P. Everett]. *The New York Times.* Accessed at www.nytimes.com/2024/03/11/books/review/percival-everett-james.html on September 24, 2024.

Garner, D. (2024b, June 12). Pasta nada: The culinary art of making something from nothing. *The New York Times.* Accessed at www.nytimes.com/2024/06/12/dining/pasta-nada.html on September 24, 2024.

Gaskell, S. M. (1980). Gardens for the working class: Victorian practical pleasure. *Victorian Studies, 23*(4), 479–501.

Gayle Morris Sweetland Center for Writing. (n.d.). *How do I effectively integrate textual evidence?* University of Michigan. Accessed at https://lsa.umich.edu/sweetland/undergraduates/writing-guides/how-do-i-effectively-integrate-textual-evidence-.html on September 24, 2024.

Geiling, N. (2023, July 3). The evolution of American barbecue. *Smithsonian Magazine.* Accessed at www.smithsonianmag.com/arts-culture/the-evolution-of-american-barbecue-13770775 on September 24, 2024.

Geoghegan, T. (2020, Fall). In the People's House there are many mansions. *Lapham's Quarterly, XIII*(4). Accessed at www.laphamsquarterly.org/democracy/peoples-house-there-are-many-mansions on September 24, 2024.

Gershon, L. (2022, November 20). The allure of Chinese medicine. *JSTOR Daily.* Accessed at https://daily.jstor.org/the-allure-of-chinese-medicine on September 24, 2024.

Gonzales, E., Bailey, A., & Puckett-Pope, L. (2024, April 19). All the Easter eggs in Taylor Swift's cinematic 'Fortnight' music video. *ELLE Magazine.* Accessed at www.elle.com/culture/music/a60551319/taylor-swift-fortnight-music-video-easter-eggs on September 24, 2024.

Green, J. (2023, April 17). Why does *Contact* say so much about God? *The Atlantic.* Accessed at www.theatlantic.com/science/archive/2023/04/carl-sagan-contact-book-alien-intelligence/673748 on September 24, 2024.

Greenblatt, L. (2024, June 24). 2 novels set over very memorable days. *The New York Times*. Accessed at www.nytimes.com/2024/06/22/books/novels-set-over-one-single-day.html on September 24, 2024.

Greenwood, V. (2023a, June 26). The key to species diversity may be in their similarities. *Quanta Magazine*. Accessed at www.quantamagazine.org/the-key-to-species-diversity-may-be-in-their-similarities-20230626 on September 24, 2024.

Greenwood, V. (2023b, July 4). A new explanation for one of ecology's most debated ideas. *The Atlantic*. Accessed at www.theatlantic.com/science/archive/2023/07/ecology-niche-theory-biodiversity/674614 on February 18, 2025.

Greenwood, V. (2024a, March 6). Cellular self-destruction may be ancient. But why? *Quanta Magazine*. Accessed at www.quantamagazine.org/cellular-self-destruction-may-be-ancient-but-why-20240306 on September 24, 2024.

Greenwood, V. (2024b, July 24). The physics of cold water may have jump-started complex life. *Quanta Magazine*. Accessed at www.quantamagazine.org/the-physics-of-cold-water-may-have-jump-started-complex-life-20240724 on September 24, 2024.

Gyarkye, L. (2022, February 1). The Octavia Butler novel for our times. *The Atlantic*. Accessed at www.theatlantic.com/books/archive/2022/02/fledgling-octavia-butler-reissue-consent/621420 on September 24, 2024.

Hall, M. (2021, May 1). On conditional probability: Cards, COVID, and *Crazy Rich Asians*. *Chalkdust*, *13*. Accessed at https://chalkdustmagazine.com/features/on-conditional-probability-cards-covid-and-crazy-rich-asians on September 24, 2024.

Hannah, M. A., & Saidy, C. (2014, September). Locating the terms of engagement: Shared language development in secondary to postsecondary writing transitions. *College Composition and Communication*, *66*(1), 120–144. Accessed at www.jstor.org/stable/43490904 on September 24, 2024.

Hans, S. (2024, June 17). Emma D'Arcy, master of 'Dragon.' *The New York Times*. Accessed at www.nytimes.com/2024/06/14/arts/television/emma-darcy-house-of-the-dragon.html on September 24, 2024.

Hartnett, K. (2024a, January 5). Mathematicians identify the best versions of iconic shapes. *Quanta Magazine*. Accessed at www.quantamagazine.org/mathematicians-identify-the-best-versions-of-iconic-shapes-20240105 on September 24, 2024.

Hartnett, K. (2024b, May 6). A Rosetta stone for mathematics. *Quanta Magazine*. Accessed at www.quantamagazine.org/a-rosetta-stone-for-mathematics-20240506 on September 24, 2024.

Harvard College Writing Program. (n.d.). Summarizing, paraphrasing, and quoting. In *Harvard guide to using sources*. Harvard University. Accessed at https://usingsources.fas.harvard.edu/summarizing-paraphrasing-and-quoting-0 on September 24, 2024.

Hess, A. (2021, December 23). Victory speech (Hillary's version). *The New York Times*. Accessed at www.nytimes.com/2021/12/22/arts/hillary-clinton-masterclass.html on September 24, 2024.

Hess, A. (2022, February 3). Apocalypse when? Global warming's endless scroll. *The New York Times*. Accessed at www.nytimes.com/2022/02/03/arts/climate-change-doomsday-culture.html on September 24, 2024.

Hickok, A., Jarman, B., Johnson, M., Luo, J., & Porter, M. A. (2024). Persistent homology for resource coverage: A case study of access to polling sites. *SIAM Review, 66*(3), 481–500.

Honner, P. (2023a, May 23). Math patterns that go on forever but never repeat. *Quanta Magazine.* Accessed at www.quantamagazine.org/math-that-goes-on-forever-but-never-repeats-20230523 on September 24, 2024.

Honner, P. (2023b, November 22). Pierre de Fermat's link to a high school student's prime math proof. *Quanta Magazine.* Accessed at www.quantamagazine.org/pierre-de-fermats-link-to-a-high-school-students-prime-math-proof-20231122 on September 24, 2024.

Honner, P. (2023c, March 24). The symmetry that makes solving math equations easy. *Quanta Magazine.* Accessed at www.quantamagazine.org/the-symmetry-that-makes-solving-math-equations-easy-20230324 on September 24, 2024.

Honner, P. (2024, March 22). Math that connects where we're going to where we've been. *Quanta Magazine.* Accessed at www.quantamagazine.org/math-that-connects-where-were-going-to-where-weve-been-20240322 on September 24, 2024.

Hughes, C. (2024, August 2). Colm Tóibín on James Baldwin's enduring, international influence. *Literary Hub.* Accessed at https://lithub.com/colm-toibin-on-james-baldwins-enduring-international-influence on September 24, 2024.

Hughes, W. (2023, May 17). First impressions: *Zelda: Tears of the Kingdom* is the most purely fun Nintendo game in a decade. *AV Club.* Accessed at www.avclub.com/zelda-tears-of-the-kingdom-is-the-most-purely-fun-nint-1850444146 on September 24, 2024.

Iglesias, G. (2023, April 28). Dennis Lehane's 'Small Mercies' is a crime thriller that spotlights rampant racism [Review of the book *Small mercies*, by D. Lehane]. *NPR.* Accessed at www.npr.org/2023/04/28/1172426738/book-review-dennis-lehane-small-mercies on September 24, 2024.

International Literacy Association. (2017). *Content area and disciplinary literacy: Strategies and frameworks* (Literacy Leadership Brief No. 9429). Author. Accessed at www.literacyworldwide.org/docs/default-source/where-we-stand/ila-content-area-disciplinary-literacy-strategies-frameworks.pdf on September 25, 2024.

Isakhan, B., & Meskell, L. (2024, June 13). Reconstructing heritage after war: What we learned from asking 1,600 Syrians about rebuilding Aleppo. *The Conversation.* Accessed at https://theconversation.com/reconstructing-heritage-after-war-what-we-learned-from-asking-1-600-syrians-about-rebuilding-aleppo-229627 on September 26, 2024.

Jeffries, H. K. (2010). *Bloody Lowndes: Civil rights and Black power in Alabama's Black Belt.* New York University Press.

Jones, B. (2023a, August 8). New York's shark-infested waters are a good thing. Yes, really. *Vox.* Accessed at www.vox.com/down-to-earth/23789849/new-york-shark-attacks-rockaway-long-island-beach on September 24, 2024.

Jones, B. (2023b, June 23). You probably have "forever chemicals" in your body. Here's what that means. *Vox.* Accessed at www.vox.com/2022/8/25/23318667/pfas-forever-chemicals-safety-drinking-water on September 24, 2024.

Kakaes, K. (2022, December 22). The year in math. *Quanta Magazine.* Accessed at www.quantamagazine.org/the-biggest-math-breakthroughs-in-2022-20221222 on September 24, 2024.

Kakaes, K. (2023, December 22). The year in math. *Quanta Magazine*. Accessed at www.quanta magazine.org/the-biggest-discoveries-in-math-in-2023-20231222 on September 24, 2024.

Kang, I. (2024, February 5). The dark delights of a millennial "Mr. and Mrs. Smith." *The New Yorker*. Accessed at www.newyorker.com/culture/on-television/the-dark-delights-of-a-millennial-mr-and-mrs-smith on September 26, 2024.

Kennedy, G. (2023, May 3). Searching for "The One" in the age of social media and reality TV. *Electric Literature*. Accessed at https://electricliterature.com/searching-for-the-one-in-the-age-of-social-media-and-reality-tv on September 24, 2024.

Killacky, M. S. (2023, April 20). Shakespeare by numbers: How mathematical breakthroughs influenced the Bard's plays. *The Conversation*. Accessed at https://theconversation.com/shakespeare-by-numbers-how-mathematical-breakthroughs-influenced-the-bards-plays-202020 on September 24, 2024.

Kim, S. E. (2024, February 14). The six most amazing discoveries we've made by exploring Venus. *Smithsonian Magazine*. Accessed at www.smithsonianmag.com/science-nature/the-six-most-amazing-discoveries-weve-made-by-exploring-venus-180983787 on September 24, 2024.

King, B. J. (2023, February 9). Greta Thunberg's 'The Climate Book' urges world to keep climate justice out front. [Review of the book *The climate book*, by G. Thunberg]. *NPR*. Accessed at www.npr.org/2023/02/09/1150729582/greta-thunbergs-the-climate-book-urges-world-to-keep-climate-justice-out-front on September 24, 2024.

Kiniry, L. (2024, March 25). The all-woman secret society that paved the way for modern feminism. *Smithsonian Magazine*. Accessed at www.smithsonianmag.com/history/the-all-woman-secret-society-that-paved-the-way-for-modern-feminism-180983989 on September 24, 2024.

Kittle, P. (2008). *Write beside them: Risk, voice, and clarity in high school writing*. Heinemann.

Klarreich, E. (2017, July 18). In game theory, no clear path to equilibrium. *Quanta Magazine*. Accessed at www.quantamagazine.org/in-game-theory-no-clear-path-to-equilibrium-20170718 on September 24, 2024.

Klarreich, E. (2023a, March 27). Emmy Murphy is a mathematician who finds beauty in flexibility. *Quanta Magazine*. Accessed at www.quantamagazine.org/emmy-murphy-is-a-mathematician-who-finds-beauty-in-flexibility-20230327 on September 24, 2024.

Klarreich, E. (2023b, April 4). Hobbyist finds math's elusive 'einstein' tile. *Quanta Magazine*. Accessed at www.quantamagazine.org/hobbyist-finds-maths-elusive-einstein-tile-20230404 on September 24, 2024.

Klarreich, E. (2024, April 1). Merging fields, mathematicians go the distance on old problem. *Quanta Magazine*. Accessed at www.quantamagazine.org/merging-fields-mathematicians-go-the-distance-on-old-problem-20240401 on September 24, 2024.

Kois, D. (2023, August 10). A novel that strives to engage the world on every single page [Review of the book *The bee sting*, by P. Murray]. *Slate*. Accessed at https://slate.com/culture/2023/08/paul-murray-the-bee-sting-novel-review.html on September 24, 2024.

Koren, M. (2023, April 20). Elon Musk's explosive day. *The Atlantic*. Accessed at www.theatlantic.com/science/archive/2023/04/musk-spacex-starship-test-launch-explosion/673802 on September 24, 2024.

Kourlas, G. (2024, June 13). What is ballet in the 21st century? It's all over the place. *The New York Times*. Accessed at www.nytimes.com/2024/06/13/arts/dance/ballet-21st-century.html on September 24, 2024.

Kranking, C. (2024, July 23). See 25 stunning images of the cosmos from the Chandra X-Ray Observatory as it celebrates 25 years in space. *Smithsonian Magazine*. Accessed at www.smithsonianmag.com/smart-news/see-25-stunning-images-of-the-cosmos-from-the-chandra-x-ray-observatory-as-it-celebrates-25-years-in-space-180984745 on September 24, 2024.

Krishna, S., & Hervey-Jumper, S. (2023, June 7). Brain tumors are cognitive parasites—How brain cancer hijacks neural circuits and causes cognitive decline. *The Conversation*. Accessed at https://theconversation.com/brain-tumors-are-cognitive-parasites-how-brain-cancer-hijacks-neural-circuits-and-causes-cognitive-decline-205901 on September 24, 2024.

Kruesi, L. (2024, March 4). Fresh X-rays reveal a universe as clumpy as cosmology predicts. *Quanta Magazine*. Accessed at www.quantamagazine.org/fresh-x-rays-reveal-a-universe-as-clumpy-as-cosmology-predicts-20240304 on September 24, 2024.

Krugman, P. (2023, February 27). Conspiracy theorizing goes off the rails [Editorial]. *The New York Times*. Accessed at www.nytimes.com/2023/02/27/opinion/east-palestine-train-derailment-conspiracy-theories.html on September 24, 2024.

LaMantia, B. (2024, June 28). What Michelle Yeoh, Tyler, the Creator, and Paris Hilton wore this week. *The Cut*. Accessed at www.thecut.com/article/what-michelle-yeoh-and-more-wore-this-week.html on September 24, 2024.

Landau, E. (2024, March 18). Brain's 'background noise' may explain value of shock therapy. *Quanta Magazine*. Accessed at www.quantamagazine.org/brains-background-noise-may-explain-value-of-shock-therapy-20240318 on September 24, 2024.

Lapham, L. H. (2024, Winter). Power outage. *Lapham's Quarterly*, *XV*(2). Accessed at www.laphamsquarterly.org/energy/power-outage on September 24, 2024.

Leber, R. (2023, July 21). The invisible consequences of heat on the body and mind. *Vox*. Accessed at www.vox.com/climate/2023/7/21/23799004/invisible-consequences-extreme-heat-physical-mental-health on September 24, 2024.

Lee, D. (2024, August 27). Which NFL teams have the best pass-rushing corps? *The Ringer*. Accessed at www.theringer.com/nfl/2024/8/27/24229351/ranking-best-pass-rush-units-2024-myles-garrett-maxx-crosby-micah-parsons on September 24, 2024.

Lee, H. (2020, July 21). How Earth's climate changes naturally (and why things are different now). *Quanta Magazine*. Accessed at www.quantamagazine.org/how-earths-climate-changes-naturally-and-why-things-are-different-now-20200721 on February 19, 2025.

Legner, P. (2010). Editorial: 60 Issues of *Eureka* [Editorial]. *Eureka*, *60*, 4–5. Accessed at https://static.mathigon.org/eureka-60.pdf on September 24, 2024.

Leibert, E. (2024, June 30). Taylor Swift really loves Simone Biles's floor routine. *The Cut*. Accessed at www.thecut.com/article/taylor-swift-loves-simone-biles-floor-routine.html on September 24, 2024.

Lewton, T. (2023, June 29). A new map of the universe, painted with cosmic neutrinos. *Quanta Magazine*. Accessed at www.quantamagazine.org/a-new-map-of-the-universe-painted-with-cosmic-neutrinos-20230629 on September 24, 2024.

Lincoln, D. (2024, June 6). IceCube detector confirms deep-space "ghost particle" phenomenon. *JSTOR Daily*. Accessed at https://daily.jstor.org/icecube-detector-confirms-deep-space-ghost-particle-phenomenon on September 24, 2024.

Lineberry, C., & Solly, M. (2024, July 1). The real story behind the Star-Spangled Banner, the flag that inspired the national anthem. *Smithsonian Magazine*. Accessed at www.smithsonianmag.com/history/real-story-behind-star-spangled-banner-flag-inspired-national-anthem-149220970 on September 24, 2024.

Liu, N. (2023, July 3). After winning the Battle of Gettysburg, George Meade fought with—and lost to—the press. *Smithsonian Magazine*. Accessed at www.smithsonianmag.com/history/after-winning-the-battle-of-gettysburg-george-meade-fought-withand-lost-tothe-press-180982454 on September 24, 2024.

Lyons, M. (2024, July 15). In 'Beverly Hills, 90210,' Shannen Doherty redefined teen TV drama. *The New York Times*. Accessed at www.nytimes.com/2024/07/15/arts/television/beverly-hills-90210-shannen-doherty.html on September 24, 2024.

Lyster, R. (2024, March 15). Welcome to the London Book Fair, where everyone knows their place. *The New York Times*. Accessed at www.nytimes.com/2024/03/15/books/london-book-fair.html on September 24, 2024.

MacArthur, C. A., & Graham, S. (2016). Writing research from a cognitive perspective. In C. A. MacArthur, S. Graham, & J. Fitzgerald (Eds.), *Handbook of writing research* (2nd ed., pp. 24–40). Guilford Press.

Madera, J. (2020, May 3). Christine Schutt on writing, reading, teaching, sentences, and more. *Big Other*. Accessed at https://bigother.com/2020/05/03/christine-schutt-on-writing-reading-teaching-sentences-and-more on January 9, 2025.

Madison, J. (1785). *Memorial and remonstrance against religious assessments*. National Archives. Accessed at https://founders.archives.gov/documents/Madison/01-08-02-0163 on February 21, 2025.

Magras, M. (2023, June). *Good Night, Irene* by Luis Alberto Urrea [Review of the book *Good night, Irene*, by L. A. Urrea]. *BookPage*. Accessed at www.bookpage.com/reviews/good-night-irene-luis-alberto-urrea-book-review on September 24, 2024.

Manzulli, M. (2024, June 14). In praise of the domestic sensualist: Laurie Colwin at 80. *Literary Hub*. Accessed at https://lithub.com/in-praise-of-the-domestic-sensualist-laurie-colwin-at-80 on September 24, 2024.

Marche, S. (2011, Winter). Consumer products. *Lapham's Quarterly*, *IV*(1). Accessed at www.laphamsquarterly.org/celebrity/consumer-products on September 24, 2024.

Marchetti, A., & O'Dell, R. (2015). *Writing with mentors: How to reach every writer in the room using current, engaging mentor texts*. Heinemann.

Marchetti, A., & O'Dell, R. (2021). *A teacher's guide to mentor texts, 6–12*. Heinemann.

Marshall, T. (2023, May 30). The future of geography and rise of astropolitics. *Geographical*. Accessed at https://geographical.co.uk/geopolitics/the-future-of-geography-tim-marshall on September 24, 2024.

McAlpin, H. (2024, June 8). 'Forgotten on Sunday' evokes the heartwarming whimsy of the movie 'Amélie' [Review of the book *Forgotten on Sunday*, by V. Perrin]. *NPR*. Accessed at www.npr.org/2024/06/08/nx-s1-4996557/french-novelist-valerie-perrin-new-book-is-forgotten-on-sunday on September 24, 2024.

Meals, R. A. (2020, October 21). A brief history of surgeons. *Lapham's Quarterly*. Accessed at www.laphamsquarterly.org/roundtable/brief-history-surgeons on September 24, 2024.

Miles, T. (2023, April 22). The great American poet who was named after a slave ship. *The Atlantic*. Accessed at www.theatlantic.com/books/archive/2023/04/phillis-wheatley-biography-david-waldstreicher/673824 on September 24, 2024.

Miller, K. (2023, July 31). Titanium clouds engulf this ultrahot Neptune-like planet. *The New York Times*. Accessed at www.nytimes.com/2023/07/27/science/space/titanium-clouds-exoplanet.html on September 24, 2024.

Miller, L. (2020, March 11). The old-fashioned warmth of James McBride [Review of the book *Deacon King Kong*, by J. McBride]. *Slate*. Accessed at https://slate.com/culture/2020/03/deacon-king-kong-james-mcbride-review.html on September 24, 2024.

Miller, L. (2022, February 22). The "African *Game of Thrones*" just keeps getting better [Review of the book series *Dark star*, by M. James]. *Slate*. Accessed at https://slate.com/culture/2022/02/marlon-james-game-thrones-moon-witch-spider-king.html on September 24, 2024.

Miller, L. (2023, July 18). How to short-circuit the outrage machine [Review of the book *Outrage machine*, by T. Rose-Stockwell]. *Slate*. Accessed at https://slate.com/culture/2023/07/outrage-machine-tobias-rose-stockwell-review-social-media.html on September 24, 2024.

Moore, D. (2023, June 21). The long, sad story of the stealing of the Oakland A's. *The Ringer*. Accessed at www.theringer.com/mlb/2023/6/21/23767113/oakland-as-leaving-for-vegas-john-fisher-reverse-boycott on September 24, 2024.

Morrow, B. (2024, June 25). In search of the rarest book in American literature: Edgar Allan Poe's *Tamerlane*. *Literary Hub*. Accessed at https://lithub.com/in-search-of-the-rarest-book-in-american-literature-edgar-allan-poes-tamerlane on September 24, 2024.

Muhammad, G. E. (2015). The role of literary mentors in writing development: How African American women's literature supported the writings of adolescent girls. *The Journal of Education*, *195*(2), 5–14. Accessed at www.jstor.org/stable/44510447 on September 24, 2024.

Murray, D. M. (1985). *A writer teaches writing* (2nd ed.). Boston: Houghton Mifflin.

Nader, R. (2018, Spring). Land of the lawless. *Lapham's Quarterly*, *XI*(2). Accessed at www.laphamsquarterly.org/rule-law/land-lawless on September 24, 2024.

Nadis, S. (2022a, August 4). At long last, mathematical proof that black holes are stable. *Quanta Magazine*. Accessed at www.quantamagazine.org/black-holes-finally-proven-mathematically-stable-20220804 on September 24, 2024.

Nadis, S. (2022b, July 13). Mass and angular momentum, left ambiguous by Einstein, get defined. *Quanta Magazine*. Accessed at www.quantamagazine.org/mass-and-angular-momentum-left-ambiguous-by-einstein-get-defined-20220713 on September 24, 2024.

Nadis, S. (2023, August 16). Math proof draws new boundaries around black hole formation. *Quanta Magazine*. Accessed at www.quantamagazine.org/math-proof-draws-new-boundaries-around-black-hole-formation-20230816 on September 24, 2024.

National Assessment of Educational Progress. (2024a). *Assessment calendar.* Institute of Education Sciences, National Center for Education Statistics. Accessed at https://nces.ed.gov/nationsreportcard/about/calendar.aspx on November 11, 2024.

National Assessment of Educational Progress. (2024b). *Writing.* Institute of Education Sciences, National Center for Education Statistics. Accessed at https://nces.ed.gov/nationsreportcard/writing on September 24, 2024.

National Association of Colleges and Employers. (2024, March). *Career readiness: Competencies for a career-ready workforce.* Accessed at www.naceweb.org/docs/default-source/default-document-library/2024/resources/nace-career-readiness-competencies-revised-apr-2024.pdf?sfvrsn=1e695024_6 on September 24, 2024.

National Center for Education Statistics. (2012). *The Nation's Report Card: Writing 2011—National Assessment of Educational Progress at grades 8 and 12* (NCES 2012-470). Institute of Education Sciences, U.S. Department of Education. Accessed at https://nces.ed.gov/nationsreportcard/pdf/main2011/2012470.pdf on September 24, 2024.

National Council of Teachers of English. (2018, November 14). *Understanding and teaching writing: Guiding principles* [Position statement]. Accessed at https://ncte.org/statement/teachingcomposition on September 24, 2024.

National Governors Association Center for Best Practices & Council of Chief State School Officers. (2010a). *Common Core State Standards for English language arts and literacy in history/social studies, science, and technical subjects.* Authors. Accessed at https://corestandards.org/wp-content/uploads/2023/09/ELA_Standards1.pdf on November 13, 2024.

National Governors Association Center for Best Practices & Council of Chief State School Officers. (2010b). *Common Core State Standards for mathematics.* Authors. Accessed at https://corestandards.org/wp-content/uploads/2023/09/Math_Standards1.pdf on November 13, 2024.

Neikirk, A. (2024a, June 20). Australia's first civilian jury was entirely female. Here's how 'juries of matrons' shaped our legal history. *The Conversation.* Accessed at https://theconversation.com/australias-first-civilian-jury-was-entirely-female-heres-how-juries-of-matrons-shaped-our-legal-history-229283?xid=PS_smithsonian on September 24, 2024.

Neikirk, A. (2024b, July 8). How all-female 'juries of matrons' shaped legal history. *The Conversation.* Accessed at www.smithsonianmag.com/history/how-all-female-juries-of-matrons-shaped-legal-history-180984647 on September 24, 2024.

Nielsen. (2024, June). *The "Cowboy Carter effect"—Increasing young Black listeners' engagement with country music.* Accessed at www.nielsen.com/insights/2024/black-country-music-cowboy-carter-effect on September 24, 2024.

Nuss, E. S., Casper, A., Baker, C. M., Moulton, M., & Torres, W. (2023, July 21). Rip currents are dangerous for swimmers but also ecologically important—Here's how scientists are working to understand these 'rivers of the sea.' *The Conversation.* Accessed at https://theconversation.com/rip-currents-are-dangerous-for-swimmers-but-also-ecologically-important-heres-how-scientists-are-working-to-understand-these-rivers-of-the-sea-208922 on September 24, 2024.

Office of History and Heritage Resources. (n.d.). *The Manhattan Project: An interactive history.* U.S. Department of Energy. Accessed at www.osti.gov/opennet/manhattan-project-history/Science/ParticleAccelerators/computer.html on September 24, 2024.

Office of the Historian. (n.d.). *The Arab-Israeli War of 1948*. U.S. Department of State, Foreign Service Institute. Accessed at https://history.state.gov/milestones/1945-1952/arab-israeli-war on September 24, 2024.

Oksman, T. (2023a, April 9). Mostly through images, a daughter grieves her mother in 'Ephemera' [Review of the book *Ephemera*, by B. Loewinsohn]. *NPR*. Accessed at www.npr.org/2023/04/09/1168334853/briana-loewinsohn-graphic-novel-ephemera-a-love-letter-to-her-mother on September 24, 2024.

Oksman, T. (2023b, June 8). 'The Talk' is an epic portrait of an artist making his way through hardships [Review of the graphic memoir *The talk*, by D. Bell]. *NPR*. Accessed at www.npr.org/2023/06/08/1180103649/the-talk-is-an-epic-portrait-of-an-artist-making-his-way-through-hardships on September 24, 2024.

Orcutt, M. (2023, June 1). How math has changed the shape of gerrymandering. *Quanta Magazine*. Accessed at www.quantamagazine.org/how-math-has-changed-the-shape-of-gerrymandering-20230601/?mc_cid=32f1b382db&mc_eid=ff3c4e7125 on September 24, 2024.

Ornes, S. (2022, September 22). The new math of wrinkling. *Quanta Magazine*. Accessed at www.quantamagazine.org/the-new-math-of-wrinkling-patterns-20220922 on September 24, 2024.

Ornes, S. (2023, July 13). How to build a big prime number. *Quanta Magazine*. Accessed at www.quantamagazine.org/how-to-build-a-big-prime-number-20230713 on September 24, 2024.

Overbye, D. (2022, December 27). The Webb telescope is just getting started. *The New York Times*. Accessed at www.nytimes.com/2022/12/27/science/astronomy-webb-telescope.html on September 24, 2024.

Padmanabhan, J. (2023, April 28). Bilingualism may stave off dementia, study suggests. *The New York Times*. Accessed at www.nytimes.com/2023/04/28/health/bilingualism-memory-dementia.html on September 24, 2024.

Parshall, A. (2022, October 10). Machine learning highlights a hidden order in scents. *Quanta Magazine*. Accessed at www.quantamagazine.org/ai-model-links-smell-molecules-with-metabolic-processes-20221010 on September 24, 2024.

Patterson, G. E., McIntyre, K. M., Clough, H. E., & Rushton, J. (2021). Societal impacts of pandemics: Comparing COVID-19 with history to focus our response. *Frontiers in Public Health*, *9*, Article 630449. Accessed at www.frontiersin.org/journals/public-health/articles/10.3389/fpubh.2021.630449/full on September 24, 2024.

Pazzanese, C. (2023, February 17). One year later: How does Ukraine war end? *The Harvard Gazette*. Accessed at https://news.harvard.edu/gazette/story/2023/02/how-does-ukraine-war-end-experts-say-2023-could-prove-decisive-dangerous on September 24, 2024.

Petrusich, A. (2024, May 17). The anxious love songs of Billie Eilish [Review of the musical album *Hit me hard and soft*, by B. Eilish]. *The New Yorker*. Accessed at www.newyorker.com/magazine/2024/05/27/hit-me-hard-and-soft-billie-eilish-music-review on September 24, 2024.

Phillips, J. (2024, June 28). Julia Phillips on the writing lessons of fairy tales. *Literary Hub*. Accessed at https://lithub.com/julia-phillips-on-the-writing-lessons-of-fairy-tales on September 24, 2024.

Phipps, K. (2023, July 18). Christopher Nolan, Warner Bros., and the struggle for the soul of movies. *The Ringer*. Accessed at www.theringer.com/movies/2023/7/18/23798504/christopher-nolan-oppenheimer-barbie-face-off-david-zaslav on September 24, 2024.

Pina, M. (2024a, June 26). Did the Knicks just get fleeced on the most expensive reunion ever? *The Ringer*. Accessed at www.theringer.com/2024/6/26/24186353/mikal-bridges-trade-new-york-knicks-brooklyn-nets on September 24, 2024.

Pina, M. (2024b, July 29). Team USA looks unstoppable, but it's not a dream team yet. *The Ringer*. Accessed at www.theringer.com/olympics/2024/7/29/24208501/team-usa-jayson-tatum-paris-olympics-2024-mens-basketball on September 24, 2024.

Polgreen, L. (2023, August 8). Why is everyone suddenly listening to a staple of my angsty adolescence? [Editorial]. *The New York Times*. Accessed at www.nytimes.com/2023/08/08/opinion/indigo-girls-barbie-cringe.html on September 24, 2024.

Pomeroy, R. (2024, March 21). The ocean vents where life on Earth likely began. *JSTOR Daily*. Accessed at https://daily.jstor.org/the-ocean-vents-where-life-on-earth-likely-began on September 24, 2024.

Prose, F. (2010, Winter). The original sin. *Lapham's Quarterly*, *III*(1). Accessed at www.laphamsquarterly.org/religion/original-sin on September 24, 2024.

Pryor, L. (2022, March 30). The hidden and eternal spirit of the Great Dismal Swamp. *The Ringer*. Accessed at www.theringer.com/features/2022/3/30/22990907/great-dismal-swamp-resistance-history-feature on September 24, 2024.

Quart, A. (2024, July 18). JD Vance is the toxic byproduct of America's obsession with bootstrap narratives. *Literary Hub*. Accessed at https://lithub.com/jd-vance-is-the-toxic-byproduct-of-americas-obsession-with-bootstrap-narratives on September 24, 2024.

Ray, K. W. (2006). *Study driven: A framework for planning units of study in the writing workshop*. Heinemann.

Richeson, D. S. (2020, September 14). When math gets impossibly hard. *Quanta Magazine*. Accessed at www.quantamagazine.org/when-math-gets-impossibly-hard-20200914 on September 24, 2024.

Richeson, D. S. (2023a, October 30). A brief history of tricky mathematical tiling. *Quanta Magazine*. Accessed at www.quantamagazine.org/a-brief-history-of-tricky-mathematical-tiling-20231030 on September 24, 2024.

Richeson, D. S. (2023b, June 27). How math achieved transcendence. *Quanta Magazine*. Accessed at www.quantamagazine.org/recounting-the-history-of-maths-transcendental-numbers-20230627 on September 24, 2024.

Richeson, D. S. (2024, February 15). Unfolding the mysteries of polygonal billiards. *Quanta Magazine*. Accessed at www.quantamagazine.org/the-mysterious-math-of-billiards-tables-20240215 on September 24, 2024.

Roberts, S. (2024, January 22). A.I.'s latest challenge: The math Olympics. *The New York Times*. Accessed at www.nytimes.com/2024/01/17/science/ai-computers-mathematics-olympiad.html on September 24, 2024.

Rorvig, M. (2021, June 3). Mathematicians identify threshold at which shapes give way. *Quanta Magazine*. Accessed at www.quantamagazine.org/mathematicians-identify-threshold-at-which-shapes-give-way-20210603 on September 24, 2024.

Rountree, H. (2024, August 26). Pocahontas (d. 1617). In *Encyclopedia Virginia*. Accessed at https://encyclopediavirginia.org/entries/pocahontas-d-1617 on September 24, 2024.

Royals, A. (2023, July 2). Hereditary venom: On Nicholas Britell's "Succession: Season 4" soundtrack [Review of the *Succession* fourth season soundtrack, by N. Britell]. *Los Angeles Review of Books*. Accessed at https://lareviewofbooks.org/article/hereditary-venom-on-nicholas-britells-succession-season-4-soundtrack on September 24, 2024.

Salesses, M. (2021). *Craft in the real world: Rethinking fiction writing and workshopping*. Catapult.

Samorodnitsky, D. (2024, June 5). Most life on Earth is dormant, after pulling an 'emergency brake.' *Quanta Magazine*. Accessed at www.quantamagazine.org/most-life-on-earth-is-dormant-after-pulling-an-emergency-brake-20240605 on September 24, 2024.

Saplakoglu, Y. (2023, April 5). Animal mutation rates reveal traits that speed evolution. *Quanta Magazine*. Accessed at www.quantamagazine.org/animal-mutation-rates-reveal-traits-that-speed-evolution-20230405 on September 24, 2024.

Saplakoglu, Y. (2024, June 26). How AI revolutionized protein science, but didn't end it. *Quanta Magazine*. Accessed at www.quantamagazine.org/how-ai-revolutionized-protein-science-but-didnt-end-it-20240626 on September 24, 2024.

Sartini Garner, S. (2023, July 27). A requiem for the Dead. *The Ringer*. Accessed at www.theringer.com/music/2023/7/27/23808537/grateful-dead-and-company-final-tour-john-mayer on September 24, 2024.

Sayles, J. (2022, March 1). No one knows what "Donda 2" means for music, but it's provocative. *The Ringer*. Accessed at www.theringer.com/2022/3/1/22955524/kanye-west-donda-2-review-album-stem-player on November 1, 2024.

Schmemann, S. (2023, January 8). 'She comes back to where she belongs' [Editorial]. *The New York Times*. Accessed at www.nytimes.com/2023/01/08/opinion/benin-bronzes-germany.html on September 24, 2024.

Schneider, N. (2024, June 3). Why the future of democracy could depend on your group chats. *The Conversation*. Accessed at https://theconversation.com/why-the-future-of-democracy-could-depend-on-your-group-chats-229597 on September 24, 2024.

Serwer, A. (2023, July 7). The most baffling argument a Supreme Court justice has ever made. *The Atlantic*. Accessed at www.theatlantic.com/ideas/archive/2023/07/freedmen-race-neutral-supreme-court-affirmative-action-clarence-thomas/674641 on September 24, 2024.

Shaer, M. (2024, August 28). Why is the loneliness epidemic so hard to cure? *The New York Times Magazine*. Accessed at www.nytimes.com/2024/08/27/magazine/loneliness-epidemic-cure.html on September 24, 2024.

Sheffer, A. (2017, August 8). The epilogue of 'The Handmaid's Tale' changes everything you thought you knew about the book. *Electric Literature*. Accessed at https://electricliterature.com/the-epilogue-of-the-handmaids-tale-changes-everything-you-thought-you-knew-about-the-book on September 24, 2024.

Sheffield, R. (2024, April 19). Come for the torture, stay for the poetry: This might be Taylor Swift's most personal album yet [Review of the musical album *The tortured poets department*, by T. Swift]. *Rolling Stone*. Accessed at www.rollingstone.com/music/music-album-reviews/taylor-swift-the-tortured-poets-department-review-1235006977 on September 24, 2024.

Sifton, E. (2010, Winter). Church and state in America. *Lapham's Quarterly*, *III*(1). Accessed at www.laphamsquarterly.org/religion/church-state-america on September 24, 2024.

Singh, R. (2023, June 9). I became a writer when I needed a fresh start. *Electric Literature*. Accessed at https://electricliterature.com/i-became-a-writer-when-i-needed-a-fresh-start on September 24, 2024.

Sinha, C. (2023, April 16). Ana de Armas goes bilingual in *SNL* monologue. *Vulture*. Accessed at www.vulture.com/2023/04/ana-de-armas-goes-bilingual-in-snl-monologue.html on September 24, 2024.

Sloman, L. (2023, January 12). Probability and number theory collide—in a moment. *Quanta Magazine*. Accessed at www.quantamagazine.org/in-a-moment-mathematicians-merge-probability-and-number-theory-20230112 on September 24, 2024.

Smith, C. (2021). *How the word is passed: A reckoning with the history of slavery across America*. Little, Brown and Company.

Smith, T. C. (2023, September 27). How many microbes does it take to make you sick? *Quanta Magazine*. Accessed at www.quantamagazine.org/how-many-microbes-does-it-take-to-make-you-sick-20230927 on September 24, 2024.

Snapes, L. (2023, June 30). Olivia Rodrigo: Vampire review—A brilliant, biting comeback [Review of the song "vampire," by O. Rodrigo]. *The Guardian*. Accessed at www.theguardian.com/music/2023/jun/30/olivia-rodrigo-vampire-review-a-brilliant-bloodletting-comeback on September 24, 2024.

Sokol, J. (2024, April 5). How the ancient art of eclipse prediction became an exact science. *Quanta Magazine*. Accessed at www.quantamagazine.org/how-the-ancient-art-of-eclipse-prediction-became-an-exact-science-20240405 on September 24, 2024.

Songsiridej, A. (2012, Fall). An interview with Christine Schutt. *Tinge Magazine*, *4*. Accessed at www.tingemagazine.org/an-interview-with-christine-schutt on November 13, 2024.

Spiers, E. (2023, April 1). In the Utah ski trial, we are all Gwynnocent [Editorial]. *The New York Times*. Accessed at www.nytimes.com/2023/04/01/opinion/gwyneth-paltrow-ski-trial-what-means.html on September 24, 2024.

Stahl, M. (2023, April 26). The upcoming World Cup could be the most valuable women's tournament in history. *InsideHook*. Accessed at www.insidehook.com/sports/most-valuable-womens-world-cup-ever on September 24, 2024.

Stephens, B. (2024, July 30). Israel's five wars [Editorial]. *The New York Times*. Accessed at www.nytimes.com/2024/07/30/opinion/israel.html on September 24, 2024.

Stern, F. (2008, Winter). Imperial hubris. *Lapham's Quarterly*, *I*(1). Accessed at www.laphamsquarterly.org/states-war/imperial-hubris-german-tale on September 24, 2024.

Stern, J., Ferraro, K., Duncan, K., & Aleo, T. (2021) *Learning that transfers: Designing curriculum for a changing world* [Kindle version]. Corwin.

Stoll, S. (2008, Summer). Pattern recognition. *Lapham's Quarterly*, *I*(3). Accessed at www.laphamsquarterly.org/book-nature/pattern-recognition on September 24, 2024.

Strogatz, S. (2024, February 29). What is the nature of time? *Quanta Magazine*. Accessed at www.quantamagazine.org/what-is-the-nature-of-time-20240229 on February 18, 2025.

Student Nonviolent Coordinating Committee. (n.d.). *Sheriff—Mr Sidney Logan* [Excerpt from the *SNCC Freedom Primer*, explaining the duties of the sheriff of Lowndes County]. Accessed at www.crmvet.org/docs/lcfo_sheriff.pdf on September 23, 2024.

Syme, R. (2019, February 1). An Irving Penn portrait for the coldest days of winter. *The New Yorker*. Accessed at www.newyorker.com/culture/photo-booth/an-irving-penn-portrait-for-the-coldest-days-of-winter on September 24, 2024.

Szalai, J. (2024, March 27). The retired justice who doesn't understand the Supreme Court [Review of the book *Reading the Constitution*, by S. Breyer]. *The New York Times*. Accessed at www.nytimes.com/2024/03/27/books/review/stephen-breyer-reading-the-constitution.html on September 24, 2024.

Tang, B. (2024, July 3). Hurricane Beryl's rapid intensification, Category 5 winds so early in a season were alarming: Here's why more tropical storms are exploding in strength. *The Conversation*. Accessed at https://theconversation.com/hurricane-beryls-rapid-intensification-category-5-winds-so-early-in-a-season-were-alarming-heres-why-more-tropical-storms-are-exploding-in-strength-233780 on September 24, 2024.

Tenorio, P. (2024, July 3). Gregg Berhalter helped rebuild the USMNT. Will he be the one to lead them at the 2026 World Cup? *The Athletic*. Accessed at www.nytimes.com/athletic/5613241/2024/07/03/gregg-berhalter-usmnt-2026-world-cup on September 24, 2024.

Tensley, B. (2023, September/October). Meet Brother Jonathan, the predecessor to Uncle Sam. *Smithsonian Magazine*. Accessed at www.smithsonianmag.com/history/meet-brother-jonathan-the-predecessor-to-uncle-sam-180982818 on September 24, 2024.

Thompson, M., II. (2024, June 20). Willie Mays is a monument to an era of Black baseball gone but never forgotten. *The Athletic*. Accessed at www.nytimes.com/athletic/5577653/2024/06/20/willie-mays-black-baseball-history on September 24, 2024.

Tolentino, J. (2024, June 10). How Cocomelon captures our children's attention. *The New Yorker*. Accessed at www.newyorker.com/magazine/2024/06/17/cocomelon-children-television-youtube-netflix on September 24, 2024.

Treisman, R. (2024, June 20). Centuries-old cherries were found at George Washington's home. What can they tell us? *NPR*. Accessed at www.npr.org/2024/06/20/nx-s1-5009924/mount-vernon-cherries-george-washington on September 24, 2024.

Twenge, J. M. (2023, April 17). The myth of the broke Millennial. *The Atlantic*. Accessed at www.theatlantic.com/magazine/archive/2023/05/millennial-generation-financial-issues-income-homeowners/673485 on September 24, 2024.

Ulin, D. L. (2020, February 28). Review: Once upon a time in . . . South Brooklyn [Review of the book *Deacon King Kong*, by J. McBride]. *Los Angeles Times*. Accessed at www.latimes.com/entertainment-arts/books/story/2020-02-28/deacon-king-kong-by-james-mcbride-review on November 1, 2024.

Vinograd, C., & Nereim, V. (2024, June 24). More than 1,000 Hajj pilgrims died. Here's what to know. *The New York Times*. Accessed at www.nytimes.com/2024/06/24/world/europe/hajj-mecca-explainer.html on September 24, 2024.

Viren, S. (2024, July 10). A painful, urgent reimagining: Emily van Duyne on writing a new history of Sylvia Plath's last years. *Literary Hub*. Accessed at https://lithub.com/a-painful-urgent-reimagining-emily-van-duyne-on-writing-a-new-history-of-sylvia-plaths-last-years on September 24, 2024.

Wallis, P. (2019). Between apprenticeship and skill: Acquiring knowledge outside the academy in early modern England. *Science in Context*, *32*(2), 155–170. https://doi.org/10.1017/S0269889719000164

Walsh, A. (2022, February 22). Of *Terminator* and motherhood: Why my mom's franchise fandom finally makes sense. *Literary Hub*. Accessed at https://lithub.com/of-terminator-and-motherhood-why-my-moms-franchise-fandom-finally-makes-sense on November 1, 2024.

Wegman, J. (2024, February 26). The crisis in teaching constitutional law [Editorial]. *The New York Times*. Accessed at www.nytimes.com/2024/02/26/opinion/constitutional-law-crisis-supreme-court.html on September 24, 2024.

Weldon, G. (2024, June 16). 'House of the Dragon' season premiere: I told you the rats would be a whole thing [Review of the TV series episode "A son for a son," by A. Taylor, Dir.]. *NPR*. Accessed at www.npr.org/2024/06/16/nx-s1-4978889/house-of-the-dragon-recap-season-2-episode-1 on September 24, 2024.

Welty, M. (2024, March 28). Adidas losing Germany to Nike is one of its biggest failures. *Complex*. Accessed at www.complex.com/sneakers/a/matt-welty/nike-signs-german-football-team-adidas-loss on September 24, 2024.

Weiss, J. (2023, April 20). What's a god to a machine? *The Ringer*. Accessed at www.theringer.com/music/2023/4/20/23690896/frank-ocean-coachella-festival-weekend-1-2-cancellation on September 24, 2024.

White, C. [Chris]. (2022, January 13). Why "We Don't Talk About Bruno" is the biggest Disney hit since "Let It Go." *Slate*. Accessed at https://slate.com/culture/2022/01/encanto-soundtrack-we-dont-talk-about-bruno-tiktok.html on September 25, 2024.

White, C. [Curtis]. (2015, Summer). Philanthropy in the end times. *Lapham's Quarterly*, *VIII*(3). Accessed at www.laphamsquarterly.org/philanthropy/philanthropy-end-times on September 25, 2024.

Willcoxon, M. (2024, June 18). Across a continent, trees sync their fruiting to the sun. *Quanta Magazine*. Accessed at www.quantamagazine.org/across-a-continent-trees-sync-their-fruiting-to-the-sun-20240618 on September 25, 2024.

Williams, A. J. (2024, April 4). NASA's search for life on Mars. *JSTOR Daily*. Accessed at https://daily.jstor.org/nasas-search-for-life-on-mars on September 25, 2024.

Wills, M. (2024, March 4). Using false claims to justify war. *JSTOR Daily*. Accessed at https://daily.jstor.org/using-false-claims-to-justify-war on September 25, 2024.

Winchester, S. (2012, Spring). Native tongues. *Lapham's Quarterly*, *V*(2). Accessed at www.laphamsquarterly.org/communication/native-tongues on September 25, 2024.

Wing, L. (1902). *The science of Oriental medicine, diet and hygiene*. Accessed at https://ia803404.us.archive.org/22/items/scienceoforienta00foowrich/scienceoforienta00foowrich.pdf on May 20, 2025.

Wizevich, E. (2024a, June 26). Was this mysterious woman a medieval warrior? *Smithsonian Magazine*. Accessed at www.smithsonianmag.com/smart-news/was-this-mysterious-woman-a-medieval-warrior-180984605 on September 25, 2024.

Wizevich, E. (2024b, June 24). Why the 1924 Democratic National Convention was the longest and most chaotic of its kind in U.S. history. *Smithsonian Magazine*. Accessed at www.smithsonianmag.com/history/why-the-1924-democratic-national-convention-was-the-longest-and-most-chaotic-of-its-kind-in-us-history-180984590 on September 25, 2024.

Wood, C. (2020, February 5). The grand unified theory of rogue waves. *Quanta Magazine*. Accessed at www.quantamagazine.org/the-grand-unified-theory-of-rogue-waves-20200205 on September 25, 2024.

Writing Across the Curriculum Clearinghouse. (n.d.). *Why include writing in my courses?* Accessed at https://wac.colostate.edu/repository/teaching/intro/include on September 25, 2024.

The Writing Center. (n.d.). *Evidence*. University of North Carolina at Chapel Hill. Accessed at https://writingcenter.unc.edu/tips-and-tools/evidence on September 24, 2024.

Writing Tutorial Services. (n.d.). *Using evidence*. Indiana University Bloomington. Accessed at https://wts.indiana.edu/writing-guides/using-evidence.html on September 24, 2024.

Yossman, K. J. (2024, March 13). Where is Kate Middleton? What we know so far. *Variety*. Accessed at https://variety.com/2024/politics/global/where-is-kate-middleton-altered-photo-controversy-1235940634 on September 25, 2024.

Young, M. (2022, September 6). Agatha Christie's latest biographer plumbs a life of mystery [Review of the book *Agatha Christie: An elusive woman*, by L. Worsley]. *The New York Times*. Accessed at www.nytimes.com/2022/09/06/books/review/agatha-christie-elusive-woman-lucy-worsley.html on September 25, 2024.

Zhou, L. (2024, July 3). Simone Biles is so back. *Vox*. Accessed at www.vox.com/culture/358882/simone-biles-olympic-trials-paris-floor-vault on September 25, 2024.

Zoladz, L. (2019, June 28). "A Day in the Life." In Ringer Staff, What is the best Beatles song? *The Ringer*. Accessed at www.theringer.com/movies/2019/6/28/18859229/what-is-best-beatles-song-yesterday on September 25, 2024.

Zoladz, L. (2021, November 17). Taylor Swift's 'All Too Well' and the weaponization of memory. *The New York Times*. Accessed at www.nytimes.com/2021/11/15/arts/music/taylor-swift-all-too-well.html on September 25, 2024.

Index

A

Add Subheadings
   moves that organize, 194, 203–205
   reproducibles for all moves by content area, 233, 243, 253, 263, 273
analysis, 116, 129, 154. *See also* Devil in the Details, the; End with Analysis; Past and Present Connection
Anti-Racist Writing Workshop, The (Chavez), 161
argumentative writing, 28, 49, 50
Ask a Question
   moves that add voice, 160, 164–166
   reproducibles for all moves by content area, 231, 241, 251, 261, 271
authentic voice, 161. *See also* moves that add voice

B

Big Idea, the
   moves that make a claim, 48, 50–52
   reproducibles for all moves by content area, 225, 235, 245, 255, 265
   student samples, 62
Bottom Line, the
   moves that conclude, 176, 186–188
   reproducibles for all moves by content area, 232, 242, 252, 262, 272

C

case for mini moves. *See also* mini moves
   about, 3–5
   mentor texts, benefits of, 7–9
   mentors teaching writing and, 7
   power of intentional writing instruction in every class, 5–6
   what mini moves are, 9–10
   what mini moves bring to your classroom, your department, or your school, 10–12
Cause and Effect Sandwich
   moves that summarize, 122, 132–135
   reproducibles for all moves by content area, 229, 239, 249, 259, 269
Chavez, F., 161
choice board for an "I'm really into…" essay, 20
claims. *See also* Bottom Line, the; Let's Imagine…; Make the Case; moves that make a claim; Say It Again, But Make It Specific
   definition of, 49
   formulas with, 31, 87, 91, 186
Clark, R., 67, 148
classrooms, mini moves in
   about, 13–14
   mini moves in review, 20
   mini-move lesson: step by step, 14–15
   mini-moves videos, tips for making your own, 17
   ways to use mini moves in your classroom, 16–21
communication, impact of, 4
comparisons, 42, 60, 144. *See also* Figurative Language Comparison; Let's Compare; Synthesize It; Then-and-Now
conclusions, writing instruction for. *See* moves that conclude
Connect Personally
   moves that add voice, 160, 169–171

reproducibles for all moves by content area, 231, 241, 251, 261, 271
content-area literacy, 8
contextualizing. *See* moves that contextualize

D

Dash That Describes
    example of, 84
    moves that describe, 82, 89–91
    reproducibles for all moves by content area, 227, 237, 247, 257, 267
data in formulas, 148. *See also* Show Me the Data
dates in formulas, 146. *See also* Double Date
Define and Detail
    moves that summarize, 122, 123–126
    reproducibles for all moves by content area, 229, 239, 249, 259, 269
    student samples, 139
defining. *See also* Define and Detail; moves that define
    formulas with, 68, 70, 72, 74, 76, 124
    importance of, 67
Describing Lists
    moves that describe, 82, 84–86
    reproducibles for all moves by content area, 227, 237, 247, 257, 267
    student samples, 97
descriptions. *See also* Dash That Describes; Describing Lists; Devil in the Details, the; moves that describe; Reference a Visual
    about, 83–84
    formulas with, 84, 87, 89, 106, 129
details in formulas, 124, 146. *See also* Define and Detail; Double Date
Devil in the Details, the
    moves that summarize, 122, 129–132
    reproducibles for all moves by content area, 229, 239, 249, 259, 269
    student samples, 139
Diamond, J., 3
direct instruction. *See also* instruction
    mini moves in your classroom and, 16–17
    reproducibles for mini-move lesson plan template for, 216–217
Double Date
    moves that contextualize, 142, 146–148
    reproducibles for all moves by content area, 230, 240, 250, 260, 270

E

Educated Inference
    moves that contextualize, 142, 151–153
    reproducibles for all moves by content area, 230, 240, 250, 260, 270
End with Analysis
    moves that provide evidence, 100, 116–119
    reproducibles for all moves by content area, 228, 238, 248, 258, 268
    student samples, 120
Engage with Etymology
    circular movement of, 78
    moves that define, 66, 76–79
    reproducibles for all moves by content area, 226, 236, 246, 256, 266
    student samples, 80
English moves
    moves that add voice, 163, 166, 168, 170, 173
    moves that conclude, 180, 182, 185, 187, 190
    moves that contextualize, 145, 147, 150, 153, 156
    moves that define, 69, 71, 73, 75, 78
    moves that describe, 86, 88, 90, 92, 96
    moves that introduce, 30, 32, 35, 40, 43
    moves that make a claim, 52, 54, 56, 59, 61
    moves that organize, 197, 199, 202, 204, 207–208
    moves that provide evidence, 104, 108, 111, 114, 117–118
    moves that summarize, 126, 128, 131, 134, 138
    reproducibles for all moves by content area, 234–243
    reproducibles for the writing application practice for, 276
    standards and mini moves connected, 285–286
evidence, 110, 113, 116, 151. *See also* Educated Inference; Make the Case; moves that provide evidence; Visual Anchoring

F

Figurative Language Comparison
    moves that describe, 82, 93–96
    reproducibles for all moves by content area, 227, 237, 247, 257, 267
    student samples, 97
Fold In, the
    moves that provide evidence, 100, 110–112
    reproducibles for all moves by content area, 228, 238, 248, 258, 268
    student samples, 120

G

Gabriel, R., 4
Gayle Morris Sweetland Center for Writing, 101
Gimme an Example
    moves that define, 66, 74–75
    reproducibles for all moves by content area, 226, 236, 246, 256, 266
gradual release of responsibility, 16
Guide to Using Sources (Harvard College Writing Program), 101
Guns, Germs, and Steel: The Fates of Human Societies (Diamond), 3

H

Harvard College Writing Program, 101
"Hidden and Eternal Spirit of the Great Dismal Swamp, The" (Pryor), 83–84
Hinge Transition
    moves that organize, 194, 198–200
    reproducibles for all moves by content area, 233, 243, 253, 263, 273
Hyperlink Layers
    moves that provide evidence, 100, 102–105
    reproducibles for all moves by content area, 228, 238, 248, 258, 268
    student samples, 119–120

I

imagination. *See* Let's Imagine…
independent writing work
    mini moves in your classroom and, 16, 19, 21
    reproducibles for mini-move lesson plan template for, 221
    spectrum of independent practice, 20
inference. *See* Educated Inference
instruction
    mentor texts, benefits of, 9
    mentors teaching writing and, 7
    power of intentional writing instruction in every class, 5–6
    ways to use mini moves in your classroom and, 16–21
    what mini moves bring to your classroom, your department, or your school, 10–12
introduction, 1–2
introductions, writing instruction for. *See* moves that introduce
It Is What It Is
    moves that define, 66, 68–69
    reproducibles for all moves by content area, 226, 236, 246, 256, 266
    student samples, 80

J

Just-the-Facts
    moves that introduce, 26, 28–30
    reproducibles for all moves by content area, 224, 234, 244, 254, 264
    student samples, 45

K

Keep It Appositive
    moves that define, 66, 72–73
    reproducibles for all moves by content area, 226, 236, 246, 256, 266
    student samples, 80

L

Let's Compare
    moves that contextualize, 142, 143–146
    reproducibles for all moves by content area, 230, 240, 250, 260, 270
    student samples, 157
Let's Imagine…
    moves that describe, 82, 91–93
    reproducibles for all moves by content area, 227, 237, 247, 257, 267
    student samples, 97
List It
    moves that organize, 194, 200–203
    reproducibles for all moves by content area, 233, 243, 253, 263, 273

M

Make It Metaphorical
    moves that add voice, 160, 172–174
    reproducibles for all moves by content area, 231, 241, 251, 261, 271
    student samples, 174
Make the Case
    moves that introduce, 26, 31–33
    reproducibles for all moves by content area, 224, 234, 244, 254, 264
Marchetti, A., 33
mathematics moves
    moves that add voice, 164, 166, 168, 171, 173
    moves that conclude, 180, 182, 185, 188, 190
    moves that contextualize, 145, 147, 150, 153, 156

moves that define, 69, 71, 73, 75, 79
moves that describe, 86, 88, 90, 92, 96
moves that introduce, 30, 32–33, 35, 40, 44
moves that make a claim, 52, 54, 56, 59, 62
moves that organize, 197, 199–200, 202, 205, 208
moves that provide evidence, 104, 108–109, 111, 114–115, 118
moves that summarize, 126, 128, 131, 134–135, 138
reproducibles for all moves by content area, 244–253
reproducibles for the writing application practice for, 277
standards and mini moves connected, 290

mentors/mentor texts
benefits of mentor texts, 7–9
definition of mentor texts, 7
mini moves and, 9–10, 15
reproducibles for student organizer for mini-mentor text stations, 220
teaching writing and, 7

metaphors. See Make It Metaphorical

mini moves. See also case for mini moves; classrooms, mini moves in
about, 9–10
choice board for an "I'm really into…" essay, 20
definition of, 7
mini-move lesson: step by step, 14–15
mini-moves videos, tips for making your own, 17
moves for every writer, 23–25
reproducibles for all moves by content area, 223–273
reproducibles for moves remix, 282
standards and, 283–289
using in your classroom, 16–21
what mini moves bring to your classroom, your department, or your school, 10–12

mini-mentor texts, 7, 220. See also mentors/mentor texts

mini-move lesson plan templates
about, 213–214
reproducibles for mini-move lesson plan template: direct instruction, 216–217
reproducibles for mini-move lesson plan template: independent student work, 221
reproducibles for mini-move lesson plan template: student-driven inquiry, 218–219
reproducibles for student organizer for mini-mentor text stations, 220

reproducibles for the progression of chapters, 215
moves for every writer, 23–25
moves that add voice
about, 161–162
Ask a Question, 164–166
Connect Personally, 169–171
list of moves, 160
Make It Metaphorical, 172–174
Put It in Parentheses, 166–168
reproducibles for all moves by content area, 231, 241, 251, 261, 271
reproducibles for the progression of chapters, 215
reproducibles for the writing application practice, 175, 276, 277, 278, 279
Say It Slang, 162–164
student samples, 174
writing needs and, 162

moves that conclude
about, 177–178
Bottom Line, the, 186–188
list of moves, 176
reproducibles for all moves by content area, 232, 242, 252, 262, 272
reproducibles for the progression of chapters, 215
reproducibles for the writing application practice, 193, 276, 277, 278, 279
Share the Last Word, 183–185
Solve the Problem, 188–191
student samples, 191–192
What We Don't Know and What We Do, 178–180
What's Next?, 181–183
writing needs and, 178

moves that contextualize
about, 143
Double Date, 146–148
Educated Inference, 151–153
Let's Compare, 143–146
list of moves, 142
Past and Present Connection, 154–157
reproducibles for all moves by content area, 230, 240, 250, 260, 270
reproducibles for the progression of chapters, 215
reproducibles for the writing application practice, 158, 276, 277, 278, 279
Show Me the Data, 148–151
student samples, 157
writing needs and, 144

moves that define
about, 67

Engage with Etymology, 76–79
Gimme an Example, 74–75
It Is What It Is, 68–69
Keep It Appositive, 72–73
list of moves, 66
reproducibles for all moves by content area, 226, 236, 246, 256, 266
reproducibles for the progression of chapters, 215
reproducibles for the writing application practice, 81, 276, 277, 278, 279
Say My Name, 70–71
student samples, 80
writing needs and, 68
moves that describe
   about, 83–84
   Dash That Describes, 89–91
   Describing Lists, 84–86
   Figurative Language Comparison, 93–96
   Let's Imagine…, 91–93
   list of moves, 82
   reproducibles for all moves by content area, 227, 237, 247, 257, 267
   reproducibles for the progression of chapters, 215
   reproducibles for the writing application practice, 98, 276, 277, 278, 279
   Say It Again, But Make It Specific, 86–88
   student samples, 97
   writing needs and, 84
moves that introduce
   about, 27
   Just-the-Facts, 28–30
   list of moves, 26
   Make the Case, 31–33
   reproducibles for all moves by content area, 224, 234, 244, 254, 264
   reproducibles for the progression of chapters, 215
   reproducibles for the writing application practice, 46, 276, 277, 278, 279
   Scene-Drop, 36–41
   student samples, 45
   Then-and-Now, 41–45
   What They Said, 33–36
   writing needs and, 28
moves that make a claim
   about, 49
   Big Idea, the, 50–52
   list of moves, 48
   Not-This-But-That, 57–59
   Outline It, 52–54

reproducibles for all moves by content area, 225, 235, 245, 255, 265
reproducibles for the progression of chapters, 215
reproducibles for the writing application practice, 64, 276, 277, 278, 279
student samples, 62–63
Synthesize It, 60–62
This-and-That, 55–57
writing needs and, 50
moves that organize
   about, 195
   Add Subheadings, 203–205
   Hinge Transition, 198–200
   List It, 200–203
   list of moves, 194
   reproducibles for all moves by content area, 233, 243, 253, 263, 273
   reproducibles for the progression of chapters, 215
   reproducibles for the writing application practice, 209, 276, 277, 278, 279
   Topic Sentence Transition, 196–198
   Visual Anchoring, 205–208
   writing needs and, 196
moves that provide evidence
   about, 101–102
   End with Analysis, 116–119
   Fold In, the, 110–112
   Hyperlink Layers, 102–105
   list of moves, 100
   Paraphrase It, 112–116
   Reference a Visual, 105–109
   reproducibles for all moves by content area, 228, 238, 248, 258, 268
   reproducibles for the progression of chapters, 215
   reproducibles for the writing application practice, 121, 276, 277, 278, 279
   student samples, 119–120
   writing needs and, 102
moves that summarize
   about, 123
   Cause and Effect Sandwich, 132–135
   Define and Detail, 123–126
   Devil in the Details, the, 129–132
   list of, 122
   Pivot Synopsis, 127–129
   Quote It to Me, 136–138
   reproducibles for all moves by content area, 229, 239, 249, 259, 269
   reproducibles for the progression of chapters, 215

reproducibles for the writing application practice, 141, 276, 277, 278, 279
student samples, 139–140
writing needs and, 124
Murray, D., 161

N

Not-This-But-That
  moves that make a claim, 48, 57–59
  reproducibles for all moves by content area, 225, 235, 245, 255, 265

O

observations, 28, 129, 133. *See also* Cause and Effect Sandwich; Devil in the Details, the; Just-the-Facts
O'Dell, R., 33
organization, use of term, 195. *See also* moves that organize
Outline It
  moves that make a claim, 48, 52–54
  reproducibles for all moves by content area, 225, 235, 245, 255, 265

P

Paraphrase It
  moves that provide evidence, 100, 112–116
  reproducibles for all moves by content area, 228, 238, 248, 258, 268
parentheses. *See* Put It in Parentheses
Past and Present Connection
  moves that contextualize, 142, 154–157
  reproducibles for all moves by content area, 230, 240, 250, 260, 270
  student samples, 157
Pivot Synopsis
  moves that summarize, 122, 127–129
  reproducibles for all moves by content area, 229, 239, 249, 259, 269
pop culture moves
  moves that add voice, 163, 165, 167–168, 169–170, 172–173
  moves that conclude, 178–179, 181–182, 183–184, 186–187, 189–190
  moves that contextualize, 144–145, 146–147, 148–150, 152, 154–155
  moves that define, 68–69, 70–71, 72–73, 74–75, 76–77
  moves that describe, 85, 87–88, 89–90, 91–92, 94–95

moves that introduce, 28–29, 31–32, 34–35, 38–39, 42–43
moves that make a claim, 50–51, 53–54, 55–56, 57–59, 60–61
moves that organize, 196–197, 198–199, 201, 204, 207
moves that provide evidence, 102–104, 107, 110–111, 113–114, 116–117
moves that summarize, 124–125, 127–128, 130–131, 133–134, 136–137
reproducibles for all moves by content area, 224–233
predictability, impact of, 13
problems, 189. *See also* Solve the Problem
Pryor, L., 83–84
Put It in Parentheses
  moves that add voice, 160, 166–168
  reproducibles for all moves by content area, 231, 241, 251, 261, 271
  student samples, 174

Q

QR codes
  for case for mini moves, 10
  for mini moves in classrooms, 13
questions. *See* Ask a Question
quotations. *See also* Paraphrase It; Quote It to Me; Share the Last Word; What They Said
  formulas with, 34, 113, 136, 183
  use of, 33–35
Quote It to Me
  moves that summarize, 122, 136–138
  reproducibles for all moves by content area, 229, 239, 249, 259, 269
  student samples, 139–140

R

Ray, K., 9
Reference a Visual
  moves that provide evidence, 100, 105–109
  reproducibles for all moves by content area, 228, 238, 248, 258, 268
reporter's questions, 28, 32. *See also* Just-the-Facts
reproducibles for all moves by content area
  English moves, 234–243
  mathematics moves, 244–253
  pop culture moves, 224–233
  science moves, 254–263
  social studies moves, 264–273

reproducibles for mini-move lesson plan template
   direct instruction, 216–217
   independent student work, 221
   student-driven inquiry, 218–219
reproducibles for moves remix, 282
reproducibles for standards and mini moves
   English language arts standards, 285–286
   history/social studies, science, and technical subjects, 287–289
   mathematics standards, 290
reproducibles for student organizer for mini-mentor text stations, 220
reproducibles for the progression of chapters, 215
reproducibles for the writing application practice
   English writing application practice, 276
   mathematics writing application practice, 277
   moves that add voice, 175
   moves that conclude, 193
   moves that define, 81
   moves that describe, 98
   moves that introduce, 46
   moves that make a claim, 64
   moves that organize, 209
   moves that provide evidence, 121
   moves that summarize, 141
   science writing application practice, 278
   social studies writing application practice, 279
restated prompts, 53. *See also* Outline It

S

Salesses, M., 161
Say It Again, But Make It Specific
   moves that describe, 82, 86–88
   reproducibles for all moves by content area, 227, 237, 247, 257, 267
Say It Slang
   moves that add voice, 160, 162–164
   reproducibles for all moves by content area, 231, 241, 251, 261, 271
   student samples, 174
Say My Name
   moves that define, 66, 70–71
   reproducibles for all moves by content area, 226, 236, 246, 256, 266
Scene-Drop
   moves that introduce, 26, 36–41
   reproducibles for all moves by content area, 224, 234, 244, 254, 264
science moves
   moves that add voice, 164, 166, 168, 171, 174
   moves that conclude, 180, 183, 185, 188, 191
   moves that contextualize, 145, 148, 151, 153, 156
   moves that define, 69, 71, 73, 75, 79
   moves that describe, 86, 88, 90, 93, 96
   moves that introduce, 30, 33, 36, 41, 44
   moves that make a claim, 52, 54, 57, 59, 62
   moves that organize, 197, 200, 202, 205, 208
   moves that provide evidence, 105, 109, 112, 115, 118
   moves that summarize, 126, 129, 132, 135, 138
   reproducibles for all moves by content area, 254–263
   reproducibles for the writing application practice for, 278
   standards and mini moves connected, 287–289
sensory imagery formulas, 37. *See also* Scene-Drop
Share the Last Word
   moves that conclude, 176, 183–185
   reproducibles for all moves by content area, 232, 242, 252, 262, 272
   student samples, 191
Show Me the Data
   moves that contextualize, 142, 148–151
   reproducibles for all moves by content area, 230, 240, 250, 260, 270
   student samples, 157
slang. *See* Say It Slang
social studies moves
   moves that add voice, 164, 166, 168, 171, 174
   moves that conclude, 180, 183, 185, 188, 191
   moves that contextualize, 146, 148, 151, 153, 157
   moves that define, 69, 71, 73, 75, 79
   moves that describe, 86, 88, 91, 93, 96
   moves that introduce, 30, 33, 36, 41, 44–45
   moves that make a claim, 52, 54, 57, 59, 62
   moves that organize, 198, 200, 203, 205, 208
   moves that provide evidence, 105, 106–107, 112, 115–116, 118–119
   moves that summarize, 126, 129, 132, 135, 138
   reproducibles for all moves by content area, 264–273
   reproducibles for the writing application practice for, 279
   standards and mini moves connected, 287–289
Solve the Problem
   moves that conclude, 176, 188–191
   reproducibles for all moves by content area, 232, 242, 252, 262, 272

    student samples, 192
sources. *See also* Fold In, the; moves that provide evidence; Quote It to Me; Show Me the Data; What They Said
    formulas with, 34, 110, 136, 148
    hyperlink layers and, 102, 104
standards and mini moves connected, 283–289
structure, use of term, 195. *See also* moves that organize
student inquiry
    mini moves in your classroom and, 16, 17–18
    reproducibles for mini-move lesson plan template for, 218–219
student samples
    moves that add voice, 174
    moves that conclude, 191–192
    moves that contextualize, 157
    moves that define, 80
    moves that describe, 97
    moves that introduce, 45
    moves that make a claim, 62–63
    moves that provide evidence, 119–120
    moves that summarize, 139–140
Study Driven: A Framework for Planning Units of Study in the Writing Workshop (Ray), 9
summarizing. *See* moves that summarize
synopsis. *See* Define and Detail; Pivot Synopsis
Synthesize It
    moves that make a claim, 48, 60–62
    reproducibles for all moves by content area, 225, 235, 245, 255, 265
    student samples, 63

T

Teacher's Guide to Mentor Texts, A (Marchetti and O'Dell), 33
Then-and-Now
    moves that introduce, 26, 41–45
    reproducibles for all moves by content area, 224, 234, 244, 254, 264
    student samples, 45
thesis statements, 49, 52. *See also* claims
This-and-That
    moves that make a claim, 48, 55–57
    reproducibles for all moves by content area, 225, 235, 245, 255, 265
    student samples, 63
Topic Sentence Transition
    moves that organize, 194, 196–198
    reproducibles for all moves by content area, 233, 243, 253, 263, 273
topic-based formulas
    for moves that conclude, 181
    for moves that contextualize, 151, 154
    for moves that describe, 84, 87, 91, 93
    for moves that make a claim, 50, 55, 57, 60
    for moves that provide evidence, 102
    for moves that summarize, 124, 127
transitions. *See* Hinge Transition

V

Visual Anchoring
    moves that organize, 194, 205–208
    reproducibles for all moves by content area, 233, 243, 253, 263, 273
visuals, 106, 205–206. *See also* Reference a Visual; Visual Anchoring
voice and mentor texts, 8. *See also* moves that add voice

W

What They Said
    moves that introduce, 26, 33–36
    reproducibles for all moves by content area, 224, 234, 244, 254, 264
    student samples, 45
What We Don't Know and What We Do
    moves that conclude, 176, 178–180
    reproducibles for all moves by content area, 232, 242, 252, 262, 272
    student samples, 191
What's Next?
    moves that conclude, 176, 181–183
    reproducibles for all moves by content area, 232, 242, 252, 262, 272
writing
    impact of, 3–4
    mentors teaching writing, 7
    power of intentional writing instruction in every class, 5–6
Writing Tutorial Services, 101

Their Stories, Their Voices
Kourtney Hake and Paige Timmerman
Kourtney Hake and Paige Timmerman share a step-by-step, build-your-own framework that helps students excel in writing and life, showing how personal narrative harnesses students' natural urge to tell stories.
BKG173

Every Teacher Is a Literacy Teacher Series

Written by acclaimed experts and practitioners, the Every Teacher Is a Literacy Teacher series details how to promote literacy growth across disciplines and grade bands. Learn how to build a common language, work in collaborative teams, implement literacy-infused instruction, and more.
BKF901, BKF902, BKF903, BKF904, BKF906, BKF907, BKF908, BKF910, BKF915

The Power of Effective Reading Instruction
Karen Gazith
Through research-supported tools and strategies, this book explores how children learn to read and how neuroscience should inform reading practices in schools. K–12 educators will find resources and reproducible tools to effectively implement reading instruction and interventions, no matter the subject taught.
BKG104

The New Art and Science of Teaching Writing
Kathy Tuchman Glass and Robert J. Marzano
Using a clear and well-organized structure, the authors apply the strategies originally laid out in *The New Art and Science of Teaching* to the teaching of writing. In total, the book explores more than 100 strategies for teaching writing across grade levels and subject areas.
BKF796

Authentic Literacy Instruction
Billy Eastman and Amy Rasmussen
Imagine a thriving English classroom—one that's active, experiential, collaborative, and rigorous. *Authentic Literacy Instruction* will help you not just imagine this classroom, but also create it. Use the book's doable action plan to reinvigorate your practices and tap into the passions and strengths of every student.
BKF948

Visit SolutionTree.com or call 800.733.6786 to order.

We don't just help schools make a change, we help them *be* the change

REAL IMPACT. RELEVANT SOLUTIONS. RESULTS-DRIVEN APPROACH.

From funding to faculty retention, the evolving demands schools face can be overwhelming. That's where we come in. With professional development rooted in decades of research and delivered by many of the educators who literally wrote the book on it, we empower schools to achieve meaningful change with real, sustainable results.

The change starts here. We can make it happen together.

See how we can get real results for your school or district.

Scan the code or visit:

SolutionTree.com/Results-Driven

 Solution Tree

LET'S SEE WHAT **WE CAN** DO TOGETHER